# TEXTBOOK ON
# HOUSING LAW

# TEXTBOOK ON

# HOUSING LAW

## Jill Morgan, LLB, M.Phil,
### Solicitor

OXFORD
UNIVERSITY PRESS

# OXFORD
UNIVERSITY PRESS

Great Clarendon Street, Oxford OX2 6DP

Oxford University Press is a department of the University of Oxford.
It furthers the University's objective of excellence in research, scholarship,
and education by publishing worldwide in

Oxford  New York

Auckland  Bangkok  Buenos Aires  Cape Town  Chennai
Dar es Salaam  Delhi  Hong Kong  Istanbul  Karachi  Kolkata
Kuala Lumpur  Madrid  Melbourne  Mexico City  Mumbai  Nairobi
São Paulo  Shanghai  Taipei  Tokyo  Toronto

Published in the United States
by Oxford University Press Inc., New York

A Blackstone Press Book

British Library Cataloguing in Publications Data

Data available

Library of Congress Cataloguing in Publications Data

Data available

ISBN 1-85431-730-X

3 5 7 9 10 8 6 4 2

Typset by Montage Studios Limited, Horsmonden, Kent
Printed in Great Britain
on acid-free paper by
Biddles Limited, Guildford  and King's Lynn

# Contents

**Preface**                                                    xiii

**Table of Cases**                                               xv

**Table of Statutes**                                         xxvii

**Table of Secondary Legislation**                          xxxvii

### 1    An Introduction to Housing Law                          1

1.1 What is a home?   1.2 The functions of housing policy   1.3 The
determinants of housing policy   1.4 Housing tenure in England and
Wales   1.5 Social trends   1.6 The historical context of housing
law   References

### 2    The Private Rented Sector: Legislative History, Decline and Characteristics                                               8

2.1 Legislative history of the private rented sector   2.1.1 Private
letting before 1915   2.1.2 The Increase of Rent and Mortgage
Interest (War Restrictions) Act 1915   2.1.3 1919–1954: the pendulum of control and decontrol   2.1.4 The Rent Act 1957   2.1.5 The
Rent Act 1965   2.1.6 The phasing out of controlled tenancies   2.1.7
Furnished lettings and resident landlords   2.1.8 The Rent Act
1977   2.1.9 The 1980s to the present: attempts to revive the private
rented sector   2.2 The decline of the private rented sector   2.3
Characteristics of the private rented sector   2.3.1 Landlords   2.3.2
Tenants   2.4 Type and standard of housing in the private rented
sector   References

3  **Requirements of Protection under the Rent Act 1977 and Housing Act 1988**                                              24

3.1 The Rent Acts   3.1.1 Requirements of Rent Act protections   3.2
The Housing Act 1988   3.2.1 Requirements of Housing Act 1988
protection   3.3 Concepts common to tenancies under the Rent Act
1977 and Housing Act 1988   3.3.1 There must be a 'tenancy'   3.3.2
There must be a 'dwelling-house'   3.3.3 The dwelling-house must be
'let as a separate dwelling'   3.3.4 The dwelling-house must be let as
'a' separate dwelling   3.3.5 The dwelling-house must be let as a
'separate' dwelling   References

4  **Differences in the Requirements of Protection under the Rent Act 1977 and the Housing Act 1988**                        35

4.1 Introduction   4.2 The statutory tenancy under the Rent Act
1977   4.2.1 Introduction   4.2.2 Requirements of a statutory tenancy   4.2.3 The nature and value of the statutory tenancy   4.2.4 The
requirement of continued residence for a statutory tenancy   4.3
Occupation as the tenant's 'only or principal home'   4.4 The tenant
must be an individual (s. 1, Housing Act 1988)   4.5 Assured
shorthold tenancies   4.5.1 Introduction   4.5.2 Creation of an assured shorthold tenancy   4.5.3 Exceptions   4.5.4 Written statement
of terms   References

5  **Exclusions from Full Protection under the Rent Act 1977 and Housing Act 1988**                                          46

5.1 Introduction   5.2 Exclusions from the status of protected tenancy   5.3 Exclusions from the status of assured tenancy   5.4 Exclusions applicable to both the Rent Act 1977 and the Housing Act
1988   5.4.1 Tenancy of a dwelling-house outside rateable value limits
(s. 4, Rent Act 1977; sch. 1, para. 2 Housing Act 1988)   5.4.2
Tenancy at no/low rent (s. 5(1), Rent Act 1977; sch. 1, para. 3,
Housing Act 1988)   5.4.3 Tenancy of dwelling-house let with other
land (s. 26, Rent Act 1977; sch. 1, para. 6, Housing Act 1988)   5.4.4
Lettings to students (s. 8, Rent Act 1977; sch. 1, para. 8, Housing Act
1988)   5.4.5 Holiday lettings (s. 9, Rent Act 1977; sch. 1, para. 9,
Housing Act 1988)   5.4.6 Tenancies of agricultural holdings (s. 10,
Rent Act 1977; sch. 1, para. 7, Housing Act 1988)   5.4.7 Licensed
premises (s. 11, Rent Act 1977; sch. 1, para. 5, Housing Act
1988)   5.4.8 Lettings by resident landlords (s. 12, Rent Act 1977;
sch. 1, para. 10, Housing Act 1988)   5.4.9 Crown lettings (s. 13, Rent
Act 1977, as amended by s. 73, Housing Act 1980; sch. 1, para. 11,
Housing Act 1988)   5.4.10 Lettings by (quasi-) public bodies (ss. 14,

15 and 16, Rent Act 1977; sch. 1, para. 12, Housing Act 1988) 5.4.11 Business Tenancies (s. 24(3), Rent Act 1977; Housing Act 1988, sch. 1, para. 4 5.5 Miscellaneous exceptions 5.5.1 Tenancies of overcrowded dwellings 5.5.2 Parsonge houses 5.5.3 Tenancies granted by mortgagor without consent of mortgagee References

## 6 Repossession under the Rent Act 1977 and Housing Act 1988     58

6.1 Introduction 6.2 Rent Act 1977: basic principles 6.2.1 Contracting out 6.2.2 Termination by the tenant 6.3 Housing Act 1988: basic principles 6.3.1 Contracting out 6.3.2 Termination by the tenant 6.4 Termination by the landlord 6.4.1 Rent Act 1977 6.4.2 Housing Act 1988 6.5 Reasonableness 6.6 Suspension, adjournment and postponement 6.7 Suitable alternative accommodation 6.7.1 'Alternative' accommodation 6.7.2 Security of tenure 6.7.3 Place of work 6.7.4 Extent and character 6.7.5 Removal expenses 6.8 Grounds for possession 6.8.1 Introduction 6.8.2 Overlapping grounds in the Rent Act 1977 and Housing Act 1988 6.8.3 Grounds for possession under the Rent Act 1977 6.8.4 Grounds for possession under the Housing Act 1988 6.9 Termination of assured shorthold tenancies 6.9.1 By the tenant 6.9.2 By the landlord

## 7 Harassment, Unlawful Eviction and the Protection from Eviction Act 1977     81

7.1 Legislative history 7.2 Criminal liability 7.2.1 Unlawful eviction 7.2.2 Harassment 7.2.3 Enforcement 7.2.4 Using violence to secure entry to premises 7.3 Civil liability 7.3.1 Contract 7.3.2 Tort 7.4 Forfeiture 7.5 Eviction without due process of law 7.5.1 Excluded tenancies and licences 7.6 Notice to quit References Further reading

## 8 The History of Social Housing     100

8.1 Introduction 8.2 From the nineteenth century to the First World War 8.3 The inter-war years 8.3.1 The Housing and Planning Act 1919 8.3.2 The Housing Act 1923 8.3.3 The Housing (Financial Provisions) Act 1924 8.3.4 The Housing Act 1930 8.4 1945–1964 8.5 1964–1979 8.6 From 1979 to the present 8.7 Housing associations 8.7.1 What are housing associations? 8.7.2 The funding of housing associations 8.7.3 The nature and accountability of housing associations 8.7.4 Registered social landlords 8.7.5 Registered social landlords and the right to acquire References

**9   The Allocation of Housing by Local Authorities**          118

9.1 The legal framework for the provision of council housing   9.2 The tension between allocations and homelessness   9.3 The housing register   9.3.1 Information on the register   9.3.2 Qualifying persons   9.3.3 Refusal of application or removal of name from register   9.4 Allocations under Part VI, Housing Act 1996   9.4.1 General principles   9.4.2 The allocation scheme   9.4.3 Types of allocation scheme   9.4.4 Reasonable preference   9.4.5 Additional preference   9.4.6 Challenging the authority's decision   References

**10   Secure and Introductory Tenancies under the Housing Act 1985**          130

10.1 Introduction   10.2 Introductory tenancies   10.3 Secure tenancies   10.3.1 Definition   10.3.2 The landlord condition   10.3.3 The tenant condition   10.3.4 Exclusions from secure status under the Housing Act 1985   10.3.5 Termination of the secure tenancy by the tenant   10.3.6 Termination of the secure tenancy by the landlord   References

**11   Rights and Duties of Secure Tenants**          152

11.1 Assignment   11.1.1 Exchange   11.1.2 Relationship breakdown   11.1.3 Assignment to a successor   11.2 Taking in lodgers and subletting   11.3 Improvements   11.4 Variation   11.5 Information   11.6 Consultation   11.7 Management   11.8 The right to buy   11.8.1 Introduction   11.8.2 Council house sales before 1980   11.8.3 Council house sales since 1980   11.8.4 The subject-matter of the right to buy   11.8.5 The 'qualifying tenant' and the 'qualifying period'   11.8.6 Properties excluded from the right to buy   11.8.7 The purchase price   11.8.8 The discount   11.8.9 Discount repayment on premature, non-exempt disposal   11.8.10 Right to acquire on rent to mortgage terms   11.8.11 The right to buy procedure   11.8.12 Enforcing the right to buy   References   Further reading

**12   The Privatisation of Council Housing**          174

12.1 Introduction   12.2 Legal routes to the privatisation of council housing   12.3 Large scale voluntary stock transfers   12.3.1 Consultation   12.3.2 Restrictions on large scale voluntary transfers   12.4 Housing action trusts   12.4.1 Composition and functions of a housing action trust   12.4.2 Disposal of housing by housing action trusts   12.5 Compulsory competitive tendering and best value   References

## 13   The Regulation of Rents     188

13.1 The private rented sector: legislative background   13.2 Fair rents under the Rent Act 1977   13.2.1 Introduction   13.2.2 Determination of a fair rent   13.3 Rents under the Housing Act 1988   13.3.1 Assured tenancies   13.3.2 Assured shorthold tenancies   13.4 Housing association rents   13.4.1 Tenancies granted before 15 January 1989   13.4.2 Tenancies granted on or after 15 January 1989   13.5 The significance of housing benefit   13.6 Local authority rents   References   Further reading

## 14   Succession     205

14.1 Introduction   14.2 Succession under the Rent Act 1977   14.2.1 Death of the original tenant before 15 January 1989   4.2.2 Death of the original tenant on or after 15 January 1989   14.2.3 Same-sex partners   14.2.4 Death of the first successor before 15 January 1989   14.2.5 Death of the first successor on or after 15 January 1989   14.3 Succession under the Housing Act 1988   14.3.1 Introduction   14.3.2 Fixed-term assured tenancies   14.3.3 Periodic assured tenancies (contractual or statutory)   14.4 Succession to secure tenancies   14.4.1 General principles   14.4.2 Who is entitled to succeed?   14.4.3 Periodic tenancies   14.4.4 Fixed-term tenancies   14.5 Succession to introductory tenancies   14.6 Residence with the tenant   References

## 15   The Responsibility for Repairs     217

15.1 Introduction   15.2 Express obligations   15.3 The meaning of 'repair'   15.3.1 The distinction between repair, renewal and improvement   15.3.2 The relative costs   15.3.3 Inherent defects   15.4 The standard of repair   15.5 Landlords' contractual obligations imposed by common law   15.5.1 Letting of furnished accommodation   15.5.2 Obligation to repair common or essential parts   15.5.3 Correlative obligations   15.5.4 Houses in the course of construction   15.6 Landlords' contractual obligations imposed by statute   15.6.1 Premises let at a low rent   15.6.2 Sections 11–16, Landlord and Tenant Act 1985   15.7 Obligations arising in tort   15.7.1 Nuisance   15.7.2 Negligence   15.7.3 Occupiers Liability Act 1957   15.7.4 Section 4, Defective Premises Act 1972   15.7 Tenants' obligations   15.7.1 Tenant-like user   15.7.2 Doctrine of waste   References   Further reading

## 16   Remedies for Disrepair, Overcrowding and Houses in Multiple Occupation     230

16.1 Introduction   16.2 Tenant's remedies   16.2.1 Damages   16.2.2 Self-help/set-off against rent   16.2.3 Specific performance   16.2.4 Appointment of a receiver   16.2.5 Repudiatory

breach   16.2.6 The right to repair scheme for secure and introductory
tenants   16.3   Landlords'   remedies   16.3.1   Damages   16.3.2
Foreiture   16.3.3   Self-help   16.4 Public law remedies: Environ-
mental Protection Act 1990   16.4.1 General principles   16.4.2
Statutory nuisances   16.4.3 Enforcement   16.5 Public remedies;
Part VI, Housing Act 1985   16.5.1 The fitness standard   16.5.2
Action under s. 189   16.5.3 Action under s. 190   16.6 Part X,
Housing Act 1985: overcrowding   16.7 Houses in multiple occupation   16.7.1 What is a 'house in multiple occupation'?   16.7.2
Registration   16.7.3 General works notices   16.7.4 Duty to keep
premises fit for the number of occupants   16.7.5 Manage-
ment   16.7.6 Execution of works by local authority   16.7.7 Overcrowding   References

17   **Homelessness: Definitions, Causes and Historical Context**          243

17.1 Definitions of homelessness   17.1.1 Rooflessness   17.1.2
Houselessness   17.1.3 Insecure accommodation   17.1.4 Intolerable
housing conditions   17.2 Causes of homelessness   17.3 Who are the
homeless?   17.4 How many people are homeless?   17.5 The historical context   17.5.1 The Poor Law   17.5.2 The National Assistance
Act 1948   17.5.3 Housing (Homeless Persons) Act 1977   17.5.4
The Housing Act 1996   17.6 Other homelessness legislation   17.6.1
Section 21(1)(a), National Assistance Act 1948   17.6.2 Section
67(2), National Health Service and Community Care Act
1990   17.6.3 Children Act 1989   References

18   **The Implementation of the Homelessness Legislation
     I: Eligibility, Homelessness, Priority need and
                        Intentionality**                                       263

18.1 Introduction   18.2 Initial inquiries   18.3 Eligibility   18.4
Homeless   18.4.1 General principles   18.4.2 Reasonableness   18.4.3
General housing conditions   18.4.4 Availability   18.5 Threatened
with homelessness   18.6 Priority need   18.6.1 General principles   18.6.2 Pregnancy   18.6.3 Dependent children   18.6.4 Vulnerability   18.6.5 Emergency   18.7 Intentionality   18.7.1 General
principles   18.7.2 Deliberate act or failures to act   18.7.3 Whose act
or omission results in intentional homelessness?   18.7.4 What is a
'deliberate' act or omission   18.7.5 Was an act or omission in good
faith?   18.7.6 Causation and the chain of intentionality   18.7.7
Availability   18.7.8 Was it reasonable to continue to occupy the
accommodation?   18.7.9 Collusion   18.7.10 Failure to secure accommodation   References

**19   The Implementation of the Homelessness Legislation
II: Duties of Local Authorities, Local Connection and the Right
to a Review**                                                                                287

19.1 Introduction   19.2 Duties under the Housing Act 1996   19.2.1
Duty of local housing authority to provide advisory services   19.2.2
Interim duty to accommodate   19.2.3 Duties to specific categories of
applicant   19.2.4 Suitable alternative accommodation in the district
19.2.5 Local connection   19.2.6 Cessation of the duty under s. 193
19.2.7 Power to continue providing accommodation   19.2.8 Sources
of accommodation   19.2.9 Availability   19.2.10 Suitability   19.3
Challenging the decision of a local authority   19.3.1 Internal review   19.3.2 Local Government Ombudsman   References

**Index**                                                                                                      303

# Preface

Preparing lectures for a new course in Housing Law at the University of East Anglia sparked off an interest in the stories behind the law which, in turn, prompted me to delve into books on housing policy and practice. Law students can easily be misled into thinking that the law operates in a vacuum and that it reigns supreme in dictating the course of people's lives. This book is an attempt, therefore, not only to present housing law in a way which, hopefully, is accessible to students but also to give a flavour of the context in which the law operates, and to indicate that the possession of rights is often far removed from their effective enforcement. I hope too that it will convey some of the enthusiasm which I have for this exciting and dynamic branch of English law.

This book deals with the 30% or so of households in England and Wales who are not owner-occupiers. Purists could argue that a full picture should include home ownership. The main drawback is, of course, that such coverage would increase the size of the book considerably. It is also the case that the law which impinges on home ownership from a housing perspective (notably mortgages) is dealt with in textbooks on Land Law. Another topic which is not dealt with here is long residential leases. Again, the technicalities are admirably dealt with in texts on Landlord and Tenant Law (such as *A Practical Approach to Landlord and Tenant* by Simon Garner).

Finally, there are a number of people whom I should like to thank for helping me to put this book together. Without the assistance of Nick Wikely, I should have found it immeasurably more difficult to embark on the teaching of Housing Law. The help he gave me mapped out the path which my Housing Law course was to take, and has similarly influenced the shape of this book. Thanks are due too to Mike Biles, Martin Davey and Michael Haley for their comments and suggestions on various chapters, and to Blackstone Press, especially Heather Saward for having faith in this project. Most of all, I am grateful to Stephen, Lucy and Ellie for their encouragement and forebearance.

*Jill Morgan*
*1998*

# Table of Cases

A.G. Securities v Vaughan [1988] 3 WLR 1205 28, 132
Abbeyfield (Harpenden) Society Ltd v Woods [1968] 1 WLR 374 27
Abingdon RDC v O'Gorman [1968] 2 QB 811 141
Abrahams v Wilson [1971] 2 QB 88 72
Aldrington Garages v Fielder (1979) 39 P & CR 461 26
Anglo-Italian Properties Ltd v London Rent Assessment Panel [1969]
 1 WLR 730 196
Anstruther-Gough-Calthorpe v McOscar [1924] 1 KB 716 218, 220
Antoniades v Villiers [1988] 3 WLR 1205; [1988] 3 All ER 1058 27, 28, 33
Appleton v Aspin (1988) 20 HLR 182; (1988) 04 EG 123 59
Ashburn Anstalt v Arnold (W. J.) & Co. [1988] 2 All ER 147 26
Ashgar v Ahmed (1984) 17 HLR 25 92
Aslan v Murphy (No. 1) [1989] 3 All ER 130 27, 29
Associated Provincial Picture Houses Ltd v Wednesbury Corporation
 [1947] 2 All ER 680 128
Attley v Cherwell District Council (1989) 21 HLR 613 136
Atyeo v Fardoe (1978) 27 P & CR 494 39
Ayari v Jetha (1991) 24 HLR 639 92

Baker v MacIver (1990) 22 HLR 328 73
Bardrick v Haycock (1976) 31 P & CR 420 53, 54
Barnes v Barratt [1970] 2 QB 657 31
Barnes v Gorsuch (1982) 43 P & CR 294 54
Barnes v Sheffield CC (1995) 27 HLR 719 240
Barnett v O'Sullivan [1995] 04 EG 141 53
Baron v Phillips (1978) 38 P & CR 91 38
Barrett v Lounova (1982) Ltd [1989] 1 All ER 351 222
Barton v Fincham [1921] 2 KB 291 59, 77
Basingstoke & Dean Borough Council v Paice [1995] 2 EGLR 9 134
Battlespring v Gates [1983] 268 EG 355 64
Beck v Scholz [1953] 1 All ER 814 40
Bedding v McCarthy (1993) 27 HLR 103 43

Belcher v M'Intosh (1839) 2 Mood & R 186                                    220
Belcher v Reading Corporation (1950) 1 Ch 380                              203
Berkeley v Papadoyannis [1954] 2 QB 149                                      37
Betty's Cafes v Phillips Furnishing Stores [1959] AC 20                      78
Bevington v Crawford (1974) 232 EG 191                                       40
Bird v Hildage [1948] 1 KB 91                                                69
Birmingham City DC v Kelly [1986] 2 EGLR 239; (1985) 17 HLR 572       234, 235
Bishop of Gloucester v Cunnington [1943] 1 All ER 101                        56
Black v Oliver [1978] QB 870                                                191
Booker v Palmer [1942] 2 All ER 674                                          27
Bostock v Bryant (1990) 22 HLR 449                                           31
Boyle v Verrall (1997) 04 EG 145                                             62
Boynton-Wood v Trueman (1961) 177 EG 191                                     60
Bradley v Chorley BC (1985) 17 HLR 305                                      224
Bradshaw v Baldwin-Wiseman (1985) 17 HLR 260                                 62
Branchett v Beaney, Coster and Swale Borough [1992] 3 All ER 910             91
Brewer v Jacobs [1923] 1 KB 528                                              36
Brickfield Properties Ltd v Hughes (1988) 20 HLR 108                     39, 41
Briddon v George [1946] 1 All ER 609                                         64
Bristol City Council v Lovell [1996] NPC 1930                               166
Brock v Wollams [1949] 2 KB 388                                             208
Brown v Bestwick [1950] 2 All ER 338                                         37
Brown v Brash and Ambrose [1948] 2 KB 247                            38, 39, 41
Brown v Draper [1944] KB 309                                                 38
Brown v Liverpool Corporation [1969] 3 All ER 1345                         225
BTE Ltd v Merseyside and Cheshire RAC [1992] 16 EG 111                     195
Buchman v May [1978] 2 All ER 993                                        26, 52
Burrows v Brent LBC [1996] 4 All ER 577                                     140
Bushford v Falco [1954] 1 All ER 957                                         39
Buswell v Goodwin [1971] 1 All ER 418                                       223

Calabar Properties v Stitcher (1983) 268 EG 697                            231
Camden LBC v Hawkins [1988] March Legal Action 18                          143
Camden LBC v Oppong (1996) 28 HLR 701                                       140
Cameron v Young [1908] AC 176                                               218
Campden Hill Towers v Gardner [1977] 1 All ER 739                          225
Carega Properties SA v Sharratt [1979] 1 WLR 928                       208, 209
Carter v SU Carburetter Co. Ltd [1942] 2 All ER 228                         42
Caruso v Owen (1983) LAG Bulletin 106                                        91
Cassell & Co. v Broome [1972] AC 1027                                        92
Cavalier v Pope [1906] AC 428                                               227
Central YMCA Housing Association Ltd v Goodman (1992) 24 HLR 109           134
Central YMCA Housing Association Ltd v Saunders (1991) 23 HLR 212          134
Chamberlain v Farr [1942] 2 All ER 567                                       25
Chandler v Strevett [1947] 1 All ER 164                                      73
Chapman v Hughes (1923) 129 LT 223                                           71
Charles v Charles [1984] LAG Bull 81                                        282
Cheryl Investments Ltd v Saldhana, Royal Life Saving Society v Page
    [1978] 1 WLR 1329                                                        32
Chios Property Investment Co. Ltd v Lopez (1988) 20 HLR 120                208
City of Westminster v Peart (1991) 24 HLR 389                              154

Cobb v Lane (1952) 1 TLR 1037                                                        27
Cobstone Investments Ltd v Maxim [1984] 2 All ER 635                                71
Cockburn v Smith [1924] 2 KB 119                                                   221
Cole v Harris [1945] 1 KB 474                                                       33
Collier v Stoneman [1957] 1 WLR 1108                                          209, 215
Collins v Hopkins [1923] 2 KB 617                                                  221
Commercial General Administration v Thomsett (1979) 250 EG 547                      70
Conron v LCC [1922] 2 Ch 283                                                       119
Coombs v Parry (1987) 19 HLR 384                                                    73
Cooper v Tait (1984) 48 P & CR 460                                                  53
Costelloe v London Borough of Camden [1986] Crim LR 249                             83
Court v Robinson [1951] 2 KB 60                                                     31
Coventry City Council v Doyle [1981] 2 All ER 184                                  236
Crago v Julian (1991) 24 HLR 306                                                   154
Crawley BC v Sawyer (1988) 20 HLR 98                                                41
Cresswell v Hodgson [1951] 1 All ER 710                                             64
Cumming v Danson [1942] 2 All ER 653                                                64
Cunliffe v Goodman [1950] 2 KB 237                                                  78
Curl v Angelo [1948] 2 All ER 189                                                   30
Curtis and Others v London RAC [1997] 4 All ER 842                                 195

Dakyns v Price [1948] 1 KB 22                                                       67
Dallhold Estates (UK) Pty Ltd v Lindsey Trading Properties Inc [1994] 1 EGLR 93 69
Dame Margaret Hungerford Charity Trustees v Beazeley [1993] 2 EGLR 143              65
Dance v Welwyn Hatfield DC [1990] 1 WLR 1097                                       165
Davies v Bristow [1920] 2 KB 428                                                    36
Davis v Johnson [1979] AC 317                                                        3
Dawncar Investments Ltd v Plews (1993) 25 HLR 639                                   68
De Falco v Crawley BC [1980] QB 460                                           259, 284
De Markozoff v Craig (1949) 93 Sol Jo 693                                           67
De Vries v Sparks (1927) 137 LT 441                                                 77
Dealex Properties Ltd v Brooks [1966] 1 QB 542                                     211
Dellenty v Pellow [1951] 2 All ER 716                                               69
Demetriou v Robert Andrews (Estate Agencies) Ltd (1990) 62 P & CR 536              217
Demuren v Seal Estates Ltd (1978) 249 EG 440                                        26
Devonport v Salford City Council (1983) 8 HLR 54                                   280
Din v Wandsworth LBC [1981] 3 All ER 881                                  283, 284, 288
Dixon v Tommis [1952] 1 All ER 725                                                  38
Douglas-Scott v Scorgie [1984] 1 WLR 716                                           225
Drane v Evangelou [1978] 1 WLR 455                                                  92
Dudley and District Benefit Building Society v Emerson [1949] Ch 707;
    [1949] 2 All ER 252                                                          56, 75
Dudley Metropolitan Borough Council v Bailey (1990) 22 HLR 424                     139
Duke of Westminster v Guild [1985] QB 688; [1984] 3 All ER 144                     222
Dyson Holdings v Fox [1976] QB 503                                            207, 284
Dyson v Kerrier District Council [1980] 1 WLR 1205                            284, 288

Ealing Family Housing Association v Taylor [1987] December Legal Action 15         143
Edmunds v Jones [1957] 1 WLR 1118                                                  215
Elmcroft Developments Ltd v Tankersley-Sawyer (1984) 15 HLR 63               219, 220
Elvidge v Coventry City Council [1993] 4 All ER 903                           134, 135

Enfield LBC v French (1985) 17 HLR 211                                            149
Enfield London Borough Council v McKeon [1986] 1 WLR 1007                   165, 166
Ephraim v London Borough of Newham, ex parte Mirza (1993) 25 HLR 207        291
Evans v Collins [1965] 1 QB 580                                                   203

Facchini v Bryson [1952] 1 TLR 1386                                                26
Family Housing Association v Jones [1990] 1 All ER 385                       132, 133
Family Housing Association v Miah (1982) 5 HLR 94                            132, 136
Ferguson v Butler 1918 SLT 228                                                     71
Fernandes v Pavardin (1982) 5 HLR 33                                               62
Feyereisel v Parry [1952] 2 QB 29                                                  51
Firstcross Ltd v East West (Export/Import) Ltd (1980) 41 P & CR 145                38
Fisher v Taylors Furnishing Stores Ltd [1956] 2 All ER 78                          78
Fitzpatrick v Sterling Housing Association Ltd [1997] 4 All ER 991                210
Foreman v Beagley [1969] 1 WLR 1387                                          215, 216
Francke v Hakmi [1984] CLY 1906                                                    52
Freeman v Wansbeck [1984] 2 All ER 746                                       150, 167
Furnival v Grove (1860) 8 CB(NS) 496                                               60

Gammans v Ekins [1950] 2 All ER 140                                          207, 209
Gardner v Ingram (1890) 61 LT 729                                                  97
Gidden v Mills [1925] 2 KB 713                                                     32
Gilmour Caterers Ltd v St. Bartholomews Hospital Governers [1956] 1 QB 387         79
GLC v London Borough of Tower Hamlets (1983)15 HLR 54                             235
Gofor Investments v Roberts (1975) P & CR 366                                  38, 39
Goodrich v Paisner [1957] AC 65                                                    33
Gray v Brown (1993) 25 HLR 144                                                     30
Green v Eales (1841) 2 QB 225                                                     225
Greene v Chelsea BC [1954] 2 QB 127                                               228
Greenfield v Berkshire County Council (1996) 28 HLR 691                           136
Griffiths v English (1981) 2 HLR 126                                               54
Groveside Properties Ltd v Westminster Medical School (1984) 47 P & CR 507         51
Guppys (Bridport) Ltd v Brookling (1984) 14 HLR 1; (1984) 269 EG 846          92, 94
Guppys (Bridport) Ltd v Carpenter (1973) 228 EG 1919                              192

Habinteg Housing Association v James (1994) 27 HLR 299                            227
Hammersmith and Fulham LBC v Monk [1992] 1 AC 47                                   98
Hampstead Way Investments Ltd v Lewis-Weare [1985] 1 WLR 164;
    [1985] 1 All ER 564                                                            40
Haniff v Robinson [1992] 3 WLR 875                                             36, 95
Haringey London Borough Council v Stewart [1991] 2 EGLR 252                       141
Harrison v Hammersmith & Fulham London Borough Council [1981] 1 WLR 650 130
Harrogate BC v Simpson (1984) 17 HLR 205                                     210, 213
Hart v Emelkirk (1983) 267 EG 946                                                 231
Harte v Frampton [1948] 1 KB 73                                                    73
Haskins v Lewis [1931] 2 KB 1                                                      37
Havant and Waterloo UDC, CPO (No.4), Re [1951] 2 KB 779                           118
Hawes v Evendon [1953] 2 All ER 737                                               207
Hawkins v Coulsdon & Purley UDC [1954] 1 QB 319                                   228
Heath v Drown [1973] AC 497                                                        79
Hedgedale Ltd v Hands (1991) 23 HLR 158                                           216

Heglibiston Establishment v Heyman (1977) 76 P & CR 351                    72
Helby v Rafferty [19791 1 WLR 13                                          207
Hereford City Council v O'Callaghan [1996] CLY 3831                       213
Herne v Bembow (1813) 4 Taunt 463                                         229
Highway Properties v Kelly (1971) 17 DLR 3d 710                           233
Hildebrand v Moon (1989) 37 EG 123                                        216
Hill v Barclay (1810) 16 Ves 402                                          231
Hill v Rochard [1983] 1 WLR 478                                            67
Hillbank Properties Ltd v Hackney LBC [1978] QB 998                       238
Hiller v United Dairies (London) Ltd [1934] 1 KB 57                        37
Hilton v Plustitle [1988] 1 WLR 149                                        42
Holloway v Povey (1984) 271 EG 195                                         72
Hopcutt v Carver (1969) 209 EG 1069                                        70
Hopwood v Cannock Chase DC [1975] 1 All ER 796                            225
Horford Investments Ltd v Lambert [1976] Ch 39               13, 31, 32, 33
Hounslow LBC v Pilling (1993) 25 HLR 305                                   98
Hughes v Greenwich London Borough Council [1993] 4 All ER 577             135
Hussain v Singh [1993] 2 ECLR 70                                           69
Hussein v Mehlman [1992] 2 EGLR 87                                        232
Hussey v Camden London Borough Council (1995) 27 HLR 5                    134
Hyde Housing Association v Harrison (1990) 23 HLR 57                      136
Hyde v Pimley [1952] 2 QB 506                                              77

Irvine v Moran [1991] 1 EGLR 262                                          225
Islam, Re [1983] 1 AC 688                                                 273

Jackson v Harbour [1924] EGD 99                                            73
Jeune v Queens Cross Properties Ltd [1974] Ch 97                          231
John Lovibond & Sons v Vincent [1929] 1 KB 687                             37
Jones and Massey v Cook and Cook (1990) 22 HLR 319                         65
Jones v Jones [1997] 2 WLR 373                                            153
Jones v Whitehill [1950] 2 KB 204                                         209

Keeves v Dean [1924] 1 KB 685                                          36, 37
Kelley v Goodwin [1947] 1 All ER 810                                       73
Kelly v Monklands DC 1986 SLT 165                                        276
Kennealy v Dunne [1977] QB 837                                         68, 73
Kenny v Preen [1963] 1 QB 499                                              91
Kensington & Chelsea RBC v Simmonds (1996) 29 HLR 507                     143
Kidder v Birch (1983) 265 EG 773                                           73
Kissias v Lehany [1979] CLY 1625                                           73

Lace v Chantler [1944] KB 368                                              26
Lally v Royal Borough of Kensington & Chelsea (1980) The Times, 27 March  279
Lambert v Ealing LBC [1982] 2 All ER 394                                  284
Lambeth LBC v Stubbs (1980) LGR 650                                       236
Landford Property Co. v Athanassoglou [1948] 2 All ER 722                 40
Lane v Cox [1897] 1 QB 415                                           217, 227
Langdon v Horton [1951] 1 All ER 60                                       209
Langford Property Co. v Goldrich [1949] 1 KB 511                           32
Lavender v Betts [1942] 2 All ER 723                                       91

Lee Parker v Izzet [1971] 1 WLR 1688                                           231
Leith Properties Ltd v Springer [1982] 3 All ER 731                            77
Lewis-Graham and Lewis-Graham v Canachar (1992) 24 HLR 132                     54
Lillieshall Road Housing Co-operative Ltd v Brennan & Brennan (1992) 24 HLR 195
                                                                              136
Liverpool City Council v Irwin [1976] 2 All ER 39                             221
London Borough of Camden v Alexandrou (1997) 74 P & CR D33                    155
London Borough of Southwark v Williams [1971] 2 All ER 175                    253
London RAC v St George's Court Ltd (1984) 48 P & CR 230                       194
Lowe v Lendrum (1950) 159 EG 423                                              72
Lower Street Properties v Jones (1996) 28 HLR 877                             43
Luby v Newcastle-under- Lyme Corporation [1965] 1 QB 214                      203
Luganda v Service Hotels Ltd [1969] 2 Ch 209                                  30
Lurcott v Wakely & Wheeler [1911] 1 KB 905                                    219
Luxmore v Robson (1818) 1 B & Ald 584                                         224
Lyon v Read (1844) 13 M & W 285                                               60

Mafo v Adams [1970] 1 QB 548                                                  37
Malton Urban Sanitary Authority v Malton Farmers Manure Co.
   (1879) 4 Ex D 302                                                         235
Manaton v Edwards [1985] 2 EGLR 159                                           73
Mancetter Developments Ltd v Garmanson Ltd and Givertz
   [1986] 1 All ER 449                                                       229
Manchester Bonded Warehouse Co. v Carr (1880) 5 CPD 507                       229
Marsh v Cooper [1969] 1 WLR 803                                               33
Mason v Skilling [1974] 1 WLR 1437                                192, 194, 195
McCall v Abelesz [1976] 2 WLR 151; [1976] 1 All ER 727                  87, 90, 93
McCormack v Namjou [1990] CLY 1725                                            93
McDonnell v Daly [1969] 3 All ER 851                                          67
McDougall v Easington DC (1989) 58 P & CR 193                                 218
McGhee v London Rent Assessment Panel (1969) 113 SJ 384                       193
McGreal v Wake (1984) 269 EG 1254                                            231
McHale v Daneham (1979) 249 EG 969                                            52
McIntyre v Merthyr Tydfil District Council (1989) 21 HLR 320                  168
McMillan v Singh (1984) 17 HLR 120                                            92
Melville v Bruton [1996] EGCS 57                                              94
Metropolitan Holdings v Laufer (1974) 233 EG 1011                             194
Metropolitan Properties Co. (FGC) Ltd v Lannon [1968] 1 WLR 815              192
Metropolitan Properties Co. Ltd v Wooldridge (1969) 20 P & CR 64             193
Metropolitan Property Holdings v Finegold [1975] 1 WLR 349              191, 193
Mikeover Ltd v Brady [1989] 3 All ER 618                                      29
Millington v Duffy (1985) 17 HLR 232                                          92
Mistry v Isidore [1990] 2 EGLR 97                                             74
Montagu v Browning [1954] 1 WLR 1039                                          31
Moodie v Hosegood [1952] AC 61                                                206
Morgan v Liverpool Corporation [1927] 2 KB 131                                223
Morgan v Murch [1970] 1 WLR 778                                               216
Morrison v Jacobs [1945] KB 577                                               36
Mountain v Hastings (1993) 25 HLR 427                                         63
Murray v Lloyd [1989] 1 WLR 1060                                              37
Mykolyshyn v Noah [1970] 1 WLR 1271                                           66

N & D (London) Ltd v Gadsden [1992] 1 EGLR 112                                    199
Naish v Curzon (1986) 51 P & CR 229                                                74
National Carriers v Panalpina [1981] 1 WLR 728                                     232
National Coal Board v Thorne [1976] 1 WLR 543                                      235
Neale v del Soto [1945] 1 KB 144                                                    33
Nevile v Hardy [1921] 1 Ch 404                                                      65
Newham LB v Patel [1978] 13 HLR 77                                                 226
Norris v Checksfield [1991] 4 All ER 327; [1991] 23 HLR 425                      27, 97
Norwich City Council v Secretary of State for the Environment [1982] 1 All ER 737 172
Notting Hill Housing Trust v Etoria [1989] CLY 1912                                 41
Nottingham Corporation v Newton [1974] 2 All ER 760                                236
Nwokorie v Mason (1993) 26 HLR 60; McMillan v Singh (1984) 17 HLR 120               92

O'Brien v Robinson [1973] 1 All ER 583                                             226
O'Leary v Islington LBC (1983) 9 HLR 81                                            142
O'Malley v Seymour (1978) 250 EG 1083                                               26
Ortiz v City of Westminster (1995) 27 HLR 364                                      277
Otter v Norman [1989] AC 129; [1988] 3 WLR 321                                   47, 48

Palmer v McNamara (1991) 23 HLR 168                                                 30
Panayi and Pyrkos v Roberts (1993) 25 HLR 421                                       43
Parker v Camden LBC [1985] 2 All ER 141                                            231
Parsons v Nasar (1991) 23 HLR 1                                                     84
Peabody Donation Fund v Higgins [1983] 1 WLR 1091                                  154
Peabody Housing Association Ltd v Green (1978) 38 P & CR 644                       115
Peachy Property Corporation Ltd v Robinson [1967] 2 QB 543                          64
Pembery v Lamdin [1940] 2 All ER 434                                               220
Percy E Cadle & Co. Ltd v Jacmarch Properties [1957] 1 QB 323                       78
Perera v Vandiyar [1953] 1 WLR 672                                                  91
Perry v Sharon Development Co. Ltd [1937] 4 All ER 390                             222
Phene v Popplewell (1862) 12 CB(NS) 334                                             60
Ponder v Hillman [1969] 3 All ER 694; [1969] 1 WLR 1261                             31
Preston BC v Fairclough (1983) 8 HLR 70                                         60, 138
Price v Gould (1930) 143 LT 333                                                    209
Progressive Mailing House Pty v Tabah Pty (1985) 157 CLR 17                        233
Proudfoot v Hart (1890) 25 QBD 42                                             220, 226
Prudential Assurance v London Residuary Body [1992] 3 All ER 504                    26
Pulleng v Curran (1982) 44 P & CR 58                                                31

Quennell v Maltby [1979] 1 WLR 318                                                  75
Quick v Taff-Ely BC [1985] 3 All ER 321                                   220, 223, 235

R v Abrol [1972] Crim LR 318                                                        87
R v Bath City Council, ex parte Sangermano (1984) 17 HLR 94                        277
R v Battersea, Wandsworth, Mitcham and Wimbledon Rent Tribunal,
    ex parte Parikh [1957] 1 WLR 410                                                47
R v Bexley LBC, ex parte Bentum, R v Tower Hamlets LBC, ex parte Begum
    (Ferdous) [1993] 2 WLR 609                                                276, 280
R v Bloomsbury & Marylebone County Court, ex parte Blackburne
    (1984) 14 HLR 56; (1985) 275 EG 1273                                            59
R v Bokhari [1974] Crim LR 559                                                      87

R v Brennan and Brennan [1979] Crim LR 603                                      90
R v Brent LBC, ex parte Awua [1995] 2 WLR 315                                  271
R v Brent LBC, ex parte Baruwa (1997) 29 HLR 915                               282
R v Brent LBC, ex parte Macwan (1994) 26 HLR 528                               300
R v Bristol CC, ex parte Johns (1993) 25 HLR 249                               128
R v Bristol City Council, ex parte Bradic (1995) 27 HLR 398              259, 278
R v Bristol City Council, ex parte Browne [1979] 3 All ER 344                 295
R v Burke [1991] 1 AC 135                                                       86
R v Canterbry City Council, ex parte Gillespie (1987) 19 HLR 7                128
R v Cardiff CC, ex parte Cross (1982) 6 HLR 1                                  238
R v Cardiff City Council, ex parte John (1982) 9 HLR 56                       280
R v Chiltern DC ex parte Roberts et al (1990) 23 HLR 387                      267
R v Croydon LBC ex parte Toth (1988) 20 HLR 576                                42
R v Ealing LBC, ex parte Sidhu (1983) 2 HLR 45                       270, 271, 276
R v East Northamptonshire DC, ex parte Spruce (1988) 20 HLR 508               280
R v Evangelo Polycarpou (1978) 9 HLR 129                                       87
R v Exeter City Council, ex parte Tranckle (1994) 26 HLR 244                  283
R v Hammersmith & Fulham LBC, ex parte Advic (1996) 28 HLR 897                294
R v Hammersmith & Fulham LBC, ex parte M and Others
    (1997) The Times, 19 February                                            259
R v Hammersmith & Fulham LBC, ex parte P (1989) 22 HLR 21                     283
R v Hammersmith and Fulham London Borough, ex parte Duro-Rama
    (1983) 9 HLR 71                                                           272
R v Hillingdon LBC, ex parte Streeting [1980] 1 WLR 1425; R v Secretary of
    State for the Environment, ex parte Tower Hamlets LBC [1993] QB 632        264
R v Hillingdon London Borough Council, ex parte Pulhofer
    [1986] AC 484                                                    244, 268, 271
R v Kensington & Chelsea RLBC, ex parte Hammell [1989] QB 518                 269
R v Kensington & Chelsea RLBC, ex parte Kihara, (1996) 29 HLR 147             278
R v Kensington & Chelsea Royal London Borough Council, ex parte
    Ben-el-Mabrouk (1995) 27 HLR 564                                         272
R v Lambeth LBC, ex parte Carroll (1988) 20 HLR 142                           277
R v Leeds CC, ex parte Adamiec (1991) 24 HLR 138                              282
R v London Borough of Barnet, ex parte O'Connor (1990) 22 HLR 486            280
R v London Borough of Barnet, ex parte Rughooputh (1993) 25 HLR 607          283
R v London Borough of Brent, ex parte Awua [1995] 3 WLR 215          259, 284, 288
R v London Borough of Brent, ex parte Macwan (1994) 26 HLR 528               289
R v London Borough of Camden, ex parte Wait (1986) 18 HLR 434                288
R v London Borough of Croydon, ex parte Jarvis (1993) 26 HLR 194             272
R v London Borough of Croydon, ex parte Toth (1988) 20 HLR 576               138
R v London Borough of Ealing, ex parte Sukhija (1994) 26 HLR 726             281
R v London Borough of Hammersmith & Fulham ex parte Beddowes
    [1987] 1 All ER 369                                                      157
R v London Borough of Hillingdon, ex parte Tinn (1988) 20 HLR 305            282
R v London Borough of Newham, ex parte Dada [1995] 1 FLR 842                 259
R v London Borough of Newham, ex parte Dawson (1994) 26 HLR 747              129
R v London Borough of Newham, ex parte Ugbo (1993) 26 HLR 263                272
R v London Borough of Tower Hamlets, ex parte Monaf (1988) 20 HLR 329        272
R v Manchester City Council, ex parte Baragrove Properties Ltd
    (1991) 23 HLR 337                                                        202
R v Medina BC, ex parte Dee (1992) 24 HLR 562                                268

R v Newcastle upon Tyne County Court, ex parte Thompson (1988)
20 HLR 430; (1988) 26 EG 112 — 59
R v Newham London Borough Council, ex parte Miah (1995) 28 HLR 279 — 123, 127
R v North Devon District Council, ex parte Lewis [1981] 1 WLR 328 — 280
R v Northavon DC, ex parte Smith (1994) 26 HLR 659 — 260
R v Oldham Metropolitan Borough Council, ex parte Garlick
[1993] 2 WLR 609 — 259, 276, 280
R v Panel on Take-overs and Mergers, ex parte Datafin plc [1987] QB 815 — 115
R v Peterborough City Council, ex parte Carr (1990) 22 HLR 206 — 273
R v Phekoo [1981] 1 WLR 1117 — 87
R v Port Talbot BC, ex parte Jones [1988] 2 All ER 207 — 125
R v Port Talbot Borough Council, ex parte McCarthy (1991) 23 HLR 207 — 276
R v Portsmouth CC, ex parte Knight (1983) 10 HLR 115 — 267
R v Preseli DC, ex parte Fisher (1984) 17 HLR 147 — 268
R v Reigate and Banstead BC, ex parte Di Domenico (1987) 20 HLR 153 — 277
R v Rent Officer for London Borough of Camden, ex parte Plant
(1981) 257 EG 713 — 26, 52
R v Rent Officer of the Nottingham Registration Area ex parte Allen
(1986) P & CR 41; (1985) 17 HLR 481 — 30
R v Rochester upon Medway CC, ex parte Williams [1994] EGCS 35 — 280
R v Royal Borough of Kensington & Chelsea, ex parte Bayani
(1990) 22 HLR 406 — 279
R v Rushcliffe Borough Council ex parte Summerson (1992) 25 HLR 577 — 288
R v Rushmoor BC, ex parte Barrett (1988) 20 HLR 366 — 169
R v Secretary of State for the Environment, ex parte Royal Borough of
Kensington & Chelsea (1987) 19 HLR 161 — 90
R v Sheffield City Council, ex parte Leek (1994) 26 HLR 669 — 277
R v Slough Borough Council, ex parte Ealing London Borough Council
[1981] QB 801 — 288, 293
R v South Herefordshire DC, ex parte Miles (1983) 17 HLR 82 — 268
R v Southwark, ex parte Cordwell (1994) 26 HLR 107 — 237
R v Spratt, Wood & Smylie [1978] Crim LR 102 — 87
R v Thanet District Council, ex parte Reeve (1981) The Times,
25 November — 282
R v Vale of White Horse DC, ex parte South and Hay (1984) 17 HLR 160 — 294
R v Wandsworth LBC, ex parte Banbury (1986) 19 HLR 76 — 277
R v Wandsworth LBC, ex parte Hawthorne [1994] 1 WLR 1442 — 282
R v Wandsworth LBC, ex parte Onwudiwe (1993) 26 HLR 302 — 281
R v Wandsworth LBC ex parte Nimako-Boateng (1984) 11 HLR 95 — 282
R v Wandsworth London Borough Council ex parte Crooks (1995)
The Independent, 30 March) — 288, 289
R v Waveney DC, ex parte Bowers [1983] QB 238 — 270, 271, 277
R v West Dorset DC, ex parte Phillips (1984) 17 HLR 336 — 280
R v West Kent Housing Association, ex parte Sevenoaks DC (1994)
Inside Housing, 28 October 1994 — 115
R v Westminster CC, ex parte Ali (1983) 11 HLR 83 — 268, 272
R v Westminster City Council, ex parte Castelli and Tristan-Garcia
(1996) 28 HLR 616 — 265
R v Wolverhampton Metropolitan Borough Council, ex parte Watters
(1997) 29 HLR 931 — 123, 127
R v Woodspring, ex parte Walters (1984) 16 HLR 73 — 279

R v Wycombe DC, ex parte Holmes (1990) 22 HLR 150                          269
R v Wyre BC, ex parte Joyce (1983) 11 HLR 73                                281
R v Yuthiwattana (1984) 128 SJ 661                                           83
R v Zafar Ahmad (1986) 18 HLR 416                                            87
Ramdath v Daley (1993) 25 HLR 273                                            92
Ravenseft Properties Ltd v Davstone (Holdings) Ltd [1980] QB 12            219
Reading BC v Isley [1981] CLY 1323                                          213
Redspring v Francis [1973] 1 All ER 640                                      67
Reeves v Davies (1921) 2 KB 486                                              35
Reohorn v Barry Corporation [1956] 2 All ER 742                             78
Richards v Green (1984) 11 HLR 1                                             39
Rimmer v Liverpool City Council [1984] 1 All ER 930                        227
Ritcher v Wilson [1963] 2 QB 426                                            73
Robbins v Jones (1863) 15 CB(NS) 221                                        218
Roland House Gardens v Gravitz (1975) 29 P & CR 43                          38
Rookes v Barnard [1964] AC 1129                                             92
Ross v Collins [1964] 1 WLR 425                                            209
Rowe v Truelove (1976) 241 EG 533                                           73
Royal Borough of Kensington & Chelsea v Hayden (1985) 17 HLR 114           132
Rushcliffe BC v Watson (1991) 24 HLR 124                                    146
Russell v Booker (1982) 263 EG 513                                          32

S.L. Dando Ltd v Hitchcock [1954] 2 QB 317                                  38
Salford City Council v McNally [1976] AC 379                               235
Salter v Lask [1925] 1 KB 584                                         205, 208
Sampson v Wilson [1995] 3 WLR 455; (1994) 26 HLR 486                     92, 94
Samrose Properties Ltd v Gibbard [1958] 1 WLR 235                        49, 50
Sandra Kay McNerny v Lambeth London Borough Council (1988) 21 HLR 188   228
Sarson v Roberts [1895] 2 QB 395                                           221
Schneiders & Sons v Abrahams [1925] 1 KB 301                               72
Schon v Camden London Borough Council (1987) P & CR 361                     86
Sefton Holdings Ltd v Cairns [1988] 14 EG 58                               209
Shafr v Yagambrun (1994) CLY 1450                                           92
Sharpe v City of Manchester (1977) 5 HLR 712                               227
Sheffield City Council v Jepson (1993) 25 HLR 299                          142
Short v London Borough of Tower Hamlets (1986) 18 HLR 171                  157
Shrewsbury & Atcham BC v Evans (1997) 30 HLR 123                           146
Siddiqui v Rashid [1980] 1 WLR 1018                                      64, 68
Skinner v Geary [1931] 2 KB 546                                          39, 40
Smith v Bradford Metropolitan Council (1982) 44 P & CR 171                 228
Smith v Bristol CC [1981] LAG Bull 287                                     280
Smith v Marrable (1843) 11 N & W 5                                         221
Smith v Nottingham County Council (1981) The Times, 13 November             91
Smith v Penny [1947] KB 230                                                 73
Smith v Scott [1972] 3 All ER 645                                          144
Solle v Butcher [1950] 1 KB 671                                            190
Somma v Hazelhurst and Savelli [1978] 1 WLR 1014                            26
South Glamorgan County Council v Griffiths (1992) 24 HLR 334               135
Spath Holme Ltd v Greater Manchester and Lancashire Rent Assessment
    Committee (1995) 28 HLR 107                                       192, 195
Spraggs v Prentice (1950) 100 LJ 451; 156 EG 346                            30

Springett v Harold [1954] 1 All ER 568                                                        235
St Catherine's College v Dorling [1979] 3 All ER 250                              32, 33, 51
Standingford v Bruce [1926] 1 KB 466                                                          77
Stanton v Southwick [1920] 2 KB 642                                                          223
Stent v Monmouth DC (1987) 19 HLR 269                                                  218
Stratford v Syrett [1958] 1 QB 107                                                              25
Street v Mountford [1985] 1 AC 809; [1985] 2 All ER 289          26, 27, 48, 52, 132
Summers v Salford Corporation [1943] AC 283                                            223
Swanbrae v Elliott (1987) 19 HLR 87                                                          216

Tagro v Carfane [1991] 2 All ER 235; (1991) HLR 250                              93, 94
Taylor v Newham LBC [1993] 2 All ER 649                                                  166
Thomes v Fryer [1970] 1 WLR 845                                                                73
Thompson v Elmbridge Borough Council (1987) 19 HLR 526                  139, 141
Thurrock UDC v Shina (1972) 23 P & CR 205                                              84
Tickner v Hearn [1960] 1 WLR 1406                                                          38, 39
Televantos v McCulloch (1991) 23 HLR 412                                                  69
Tilling v Whiteman [1980] AC 1                                                                    74
Todd-Heatley v Benham (1888) 40 Ch D 80; [1886–90] All ER Rep Ext 1537    71
Torridge DC v Jones (1987) 19 HLR 526                                                      139
Total Oil Great Britain Ltd v Thompson Garages (Biggin Hill) Ltd
    [1972] 1 QB 318                                                                                    232
Tower Hamlets London Borough Council v Miah (1992) 24 HLR 199          137
Tredway v Machin (1904) 91 LT 310                                                            227
Turner v Wandsworth London Borough Council [1994] 1 EGLR 134            79

Uckuzular v Sandford-Hill [1994] CLY 1770                                                83

Wainwright v Leeds City Council (1984) 270 EG 1289                                219
Wallis v Hands [1893] 2 Ch 75                                                                      60
Walsh v Griffiths- Jones and Durant [1978] 2 All ER 1002                            26
Walter v Selfe (1851) WDe G & Smj 315                                                        71
Waltham Forest LBC v Thomas [1992] 2 AC 198                                          216
Wandsworth LBC v Fadayomi [1987] 3 All ER 474                                      148
Wandsworth London Borough Council v Hargraves [1994] EGCS 115          142
Ward v Warnke (1990) 22 HLR 496                                                                27
Wareing v White (1984) 270 EG 851                                                            192
Warren v Austen [1947] 2 All ER 185                                                            67
Warren v Keen [1953] 2 All ER 1118                                                            228
Warriner v Wood (1944) 144 EG 81                                                                38
Watson v Lucas [1980] 1 WLR 1493                                                        207, 208
Wedd v Porter [1916] 2 KB 41                                                                      229
Western Heritable Investment Co. v Husband [1983] 2 AC 849;
    [1983] 3 WLR 429                                                                            194, 195
Westminster City Council v Clarke [1992] 2 AC 288                                  30, 133
Wheat v Lacon [1966] 1 All ER 582                                                              227
Whitbread v Ward (1952) 159 EG 494                                                            71
Whitham v Kershaw (1886) 16 QBD 613                                                      229
Whitty v Scott-Russell [1950] 2 KB 32                                                            32
Wigley v Leigh [1950] 1 All ER 73                                                              38, 39
Wilkes v Goodwin [1923] 2 KB 86                                                                  47

Williams v Khan (1982) 43 P & CR 1                                      191
Williams v Perry [1924] 1 KB 936                                        31
Williamson v Pallant [1924] 2 KB 173                                    64
Woking BC v Bistram (1995) 27 HLR 1                                     143
Wolf v Waddington (1989) 22 HLR 72                                      54
Wolfe v Hogan [1949] 2 KB 194                                           32
Wood Factory Pty v Kiritos Pty (1985) 2 NSWLR 105                       233
Wood v Cooper [1894] 3 Ch 671                                           71
Woodspring v Taylor (1982) 4 HLR 95                                     142
Woodward v Docherty [1974] 2 All ER 844                                 47
Woolwich v Dickman [1996] 3 All ER 204                                  59
Wright v Howell (1948) 92 Sol Jo 26                                     30
Wycombe Health Authority v Barnett (1982) 264 EG 619                225, 229

Yates v Morris [1951] 1 KB 77                                           71
Yelland v Taylor [1957] 1 WLR 459                                      64
Yewbright Properties v Stone (1980) 40 P & CR 402                       67
Yoland Ltd v Reddington (1982) 5 HLR 41                                 66

# Table of Statutes

Access to Neighbouring Land Act
  1992   226
Addison Act *see* Housing and Planning
  Act 1919
Agricultural Holdings Act 1986   53
Agricultural Tenancies Act 1995   53
Artisans and Labourers' Dwellings Act
  1868   101, 102
Artisans and Labourers' Dwellings
  Improvement Act 1875   101, 102,
  159
Asylum and Immigration Act 1996
  122, 264
  s. 11   259
  Sch. 1   259

Building Act 1984
  s. 76(1)   236

Caravan Sites Act 1968
  Part II   267
Chamberlain Act *see* Housing
  Act 1923
Child Support Act 1991
  300, 301
Children Act 1989   260
  s. 20   278
  s. 20(1)   260
  s. 20(3)   260
  s. 27   260, 278, 279
  Sch. 1   124
    para. 1   132, 153, 169, 212, 214

Chronically Sick and Disabled Persons
  Act 1970   167
  s. 3   118
Companies Act 1985
  115
Criminal Justice and Public Order Act
  1994
  s. 80(1)   267
Criminal Law Act 1977   83
  s. 6   90
Cross Act *see* Artisans and Labourers'
  Dwellings Improvement Act 1875

Defective Premises Act 1972
  227
  s. 4   228
  s. 4(1)–(2)   228
  s. 4(4)   228

Environmental Protection Act 1990
  234–6, 238
  Part III   234
  s. 79   234, 236
  s. 79(1)(a)   235
  s. 79(7)   235
  s. 80   227, 234, 236
  s. 80(1)–(2)   235
  s. 80(3)–(4)   236
  s. 81   234
  s. 82   234, 236
  s. 82(7)   236
  s. 82(12)   236

Family Law Act 1996   154
  s. 30(3)   40
  s. 30(4)(a)   40
  s. 30(4)(b)   41
  s. 36   40
  s. 36(10)   40
  Sch. 7   37
    para. 5   154
    para. 10   154
Finance Act 1988   19
Finance Act 1996
  Sch. 30   15
Finance (No. 2) Act 1992
  s. 38   20
  s. 59   53
  Sch. 10   53
Furnished Housing (Rent Control) Act
  1946   12

Greenwood Act *see* Housing Act 1930

Housing Act 1923   104–5
Housing Act 1924   17
Housing Act 1930   105–7
Housing Act 1935   106
Housing Act 1949   17, 107
Housing Act 1952   159
Housing Act 1957   196
Housing Act 1961   17, 109
Housing Act 1964   17, 113
Housing Act 1969   12, 17, 109, 237
Housing Act 1974   113
Housing Act 1980   14, 77, 110, 115,
  130, 158, 162, 172
  s. 17   116
  s. 48   132, 133
  s. 65   54
  s. 66   74
  s. 73   55
Housing Act 1985   37, 48, 55, 56, 97,
  110, 114, 130–51, 154, 203, 224,
  258
  Part I   140
  Part II   140, 148–51
  Part III   140, 258, 259
  Part IV   60, 95, 130, 157
  Part V   116, 132, 157, 168, 182
  Part VI   118, 236–8
  Part VII   136
  Part VIII   118
  Part IX   118, 300

Housing Act 1985 — *continued*
  Part X   155, 238, 269, 300
  Part XI   118, 238–40, 300
  s. 8   118
  s. 9(1)–(2)   119
  s. 9(5)   119
  s. 10   119
  s. 11   119
  s. 11(1A)   221
  s. 11A   119
  s. 12   119
  s. 21(1)   119
  s. 22   120
  s. 24   181, 202, 203
  s. 24(2)   202
  s. 24(3)–(4)   203
  s. 27   158, 170
  s. 27AB   158, 185
  s. 27BA   158, 185
  s. 32   176
  s. 33   176
  s. 33(2)   177
  s. 34   176
  s. 34(4A)   177
  s. 43   176
  s. 65   119
  s. 65(2)   287, 289, 292
  s. 79   130, 132
  s. 79(1)   132, 134
  s. 79(3)   132, 133, 164
  s. 79(4)   132
  s. 80   130, 132, 135, 178
  s. 80(1)   134
  s. 81   41, 130, 132, 135
  s. 82   130, 165
  s. 82(3)   138
  s. 83   130, 138, 139, 140, 151, 153
  s. 83(1)(b)   139
  s. 83(2)   139
  s. 83(3)   139, 144
  s. 83(4)   139
  s. 83A(1)   139
  s. 84   130
  s. 84(2)   143
  s. 84(2)(b)   148
  s. 84(3)–(4)   140
  s. 85   130, 140
  s. 86   130, 212
  s. 86(1)   138
  s. 87   130, 213
  s. 88   130, 212

Housing Act 1985 — *continued*
  s. 89   124, 130, 150, 212, 214
  s. 89(2)(b)   214
  s. 90   130
  s. 90(3)   214
  s. 91   130, 152
  s. 91(3)(c)   152, 154
  s. 92   124, 130, 146, 147, 152, 168, 170, 212
  s. 92(3)–(6)   153
  s. 93   130
  s. 93(1)–(2)   155
  s. 94   130
  s. 94(2)   155
  s. 94(3)(a)–(b)   155
  s. 94(4)   155
  s. 94(6)   155
  ss. 95–117   130
  s. 96   233, 238
  s. 97(1)–(3)   155
  s. 98(1)   155
  s. 98(2)   156
  s. 99(1)–(2)   156
  s. 99(4)   156
  ss. 99A–99B   156
  s. 100   156
  s. 102(1)(a)–(b)   156
  s. 103   156
  s. 103(2)   156
  s. 103(3)(a)   156
  s. 104   157, 224
  s. 104(1)   157
  s. 104(1)(b)–(c)   157
  s. 104(2)(b)   157
  s. 104(3)   157
  s. 105   157, 178
  s. 106   157
  s. 106A   158, 178
  s. 106A(3)   178
  s. 113   213
  s. 113(1)–(2)   213
  s. 118(1)   164
  s. 118(2)   165
  s. 119   164
  s. 119(2)   165
  s. 120   166
  s. 121   165, 166, 170
  s. 122   167, 170
  s. 122(3)   171
  s. 123   165
  s. 124   170

Housing Act 1985 — *continued*
  s. 125   168, 170, 171
  s. 125(1)   171
  s. 125D   171
  s. 126   167
  s. 127   167
  s. 127(1)(b)–(c)   168
  s. 127(2)–(3)   168
  s. 128   167
  s. 129(2)–(3)   168
  s. 130   168
  s. 136   168
  s. 138(1)   165, 166, 171
  s. 138(3)   165, 166, 171
  ss. 140–141   171
  s. 143   5
  s. 143A   170
  s. 143B   170
  s. 143B(3)–(4)   170
  s. 144   5, 171
  ss. 145–146   5
  s. 147   5, 170
  ss. 148–149   5
  s. 150   5, 170, 171
  s. 150(3)   171
  s. 151   5
  s. 151(2)   170
  ss. 151A–151B   170
  s. 152   5
  s. 153   5
  ss. 153A–153B   171
  s. 155   169
  s. 155(2)   169
  s. 159(1)   169
  s. 164   171
  ss. 165–166   172
  s. 170   172
  s. 171   165
  s. 171A-H   176
  s. 181   170
  s. 189   237, 238
  s. 189(1)   237
  s. 190   237–8
  s. 191(1)   237
  s. 191A   238
  s. 193   238
  s. 264(1)   237
  s. 265(1)   237
  s. 289   237
  s. 324   238
  s. 325   239

Housing Act 1985 — *continued*
  s. 326(2)–(3)  239
  ss. 328–331  239
  s. 335  239
  ss. 337–338  239
  s. 345(1)  240
  s. 346  240
  s. 346A  240
  s. 352  273
  s. 352(1A)  240
  s. 353(A)  241
  ss. 358–359  242
  s. 362  242
  ss. 372–373  241
  ss. 375–376  241
  s. 379  90, 241
  s. 381  241
  s. 604  237
  s. 605  118, 236
  Sch. 1  135
    para. 1  135
    para. 1A  135
    para. 2  135
    para. 2(4)  136
    paras 3–5  136
    paras 6–10  137
    paras 11–12  138
  Sch. 2  69, 78, 140, 148, 165
    Part I  140
    Part II  140, 177
    Part III  140
    Part IV
      para. 1  148
    Part V  149, 178
    Part X  149
  Sch. 3  152, 153
  Sch. 3A  178
    para. 3(1)–(2)  178
    para. 5  178
  Sch. 4  164
    para. 1  164
    para. 2(a)  164
  Sch. 5  166
    paras 1–3  166
    para. 7  167
    para. 9  167
    para. 10(1)–(2)  167
    para. 11  167
  Sch. 6A  170
    para. 2  170
    paras 6–7  170

Housing Act 1985 — *continued*
  Sch. 10
    para. 2  241
Housing Act 1988  14, 15, 18, 19, 22,
    24–34, 35–45, 46–57, 58–80, 82, 83,
    84, 85, 86, 95, 96, 97, 110, 111, 113,
    114, 130, 134, 140, 154, 163, 176,
    189, 194, 196–200, 203, 206, 207,
    208, 211–12, 214, 216, 225
  Part I  48, 82, 148, 190
  Part III  49
  Part IV  49, 175
  s. 1  25, 31, 42, 78
  s. 1(1)  25
  s. 3  132, 134
  s. 3(3)  34
  s. 5  43, 60, 62, 80
  s. 5(1)  60, 62
  s. 5(2)  60, 197
  s. 5(3)  197
  s. 5(4)  62
  s. 5(5)  60
  s. 6  62
  s. 7  60
  s. 7(1)  60
  s. 7(3)–(4)  63
  s. 7(6)  61
  s. 8  62, 63, 70
  s. 8(1)(a)–(b)  62
  s. 8(3)(b)–(c)  63
  s. 8(4)  63
  s. 9(1)–(3)  64
  s. 9(4)  65
  s. 10  34, 134
  s. 11  68
  s. 13  196, 197, 198, 199
  s. 13(1)(b)  197
  s. 13(2)  197, 200
  s. 13(2)(b)–(c)  197
  s. 13(3)  197
  s. 13(4)  197, 198
  s. 13(5)  197
  s. 14  197, 198
  s. 14(1)  198
  s. 14(2)  198
  s. 14(2)(c)  199
  s. 14(3)  199
  s. 14(4)  198
  s. 14(7)–(8)  198
  s. 15  62
  s. 16  234

Housing Act 1988 — *continued*
s. 17   79, 212
s. 17(1)   212
s. 17(2)   212
s. 17(2)(c)   208
s. 17(4)   212
s. 19A   43, 62, 80
s. 20   42, 43, 62
s. 20A   44
s. 20A(2)   44
s. 20A(4)   44
s. 21   42, 58, 62, 65, 80
s. 21(1)(a)–(b)   80
s. 21(4)   80
s. 21(4)(a)   80
s. 21(5)–(7)   80
s. 22   200
s. 22(2)(a)   200
s. 22(2)(aa)   200
s. 22(3)   200
s. 22(4)(a)   200
s. 22(4)(c)   200
s. 27   93, 94
s. 27(6)(a)–(b)   93
s. 27(7)–(8)   93
s. 28   93, 94, 95
s. 29   88
s. 34(1)(c)(iii)   66
s. 34(3)   77
s. 38   49, 176
s. 39   44, 199
s. 39(6)(f)   197
ss. 41–42   198
s. 45(1)   25
s. 60   180
s. 60(4)–(5)   180
s. 61   180, 182
s. 61(4)   181
s. 62   181
s. 63(1)   181
s. 63(1)(c)   183
s. 63(2)–(3)   182
s. 64   181
s. 65   182
ss. 67–68   182
s. 74   182
s. 79   182
s. 81   182
s. 84   183
s. 84A(4)–(5)   183
s. 85   181

Housing Act 1988 — *continued*
s. 88   181
s. 115   50
s. 116   225
s. 116(1)   221
ss. 117A–117H   183
s. 124   171
Sch. 1   46, 48
   para. 1   48
   para. 2   25, 49
   para. 3   25, 50
   para. 4   25, 56
   para. 5   25, 53
   para. 6   25, 50
   para. 7   25, 53
   para. 8   25, 51
   para. 9   25, 51–2, 75
   para. 10   25, 53
   para. 10(1)(b)–(c)   55
   paras 11–12   25, 55
   para. 13   25, 48
   Part 3   55
Sch. 2   53, 58, 60, 62, 198
   Parts I–II   68
   Part III
      para. 1   65
      para. 2(a)   66
      para. 3(1)(b)   66
Sch. 2A   43, 62
   paras 1–2   43
   paras 3–9   44
Sch. 4   216
   para. 2   208
Schs 7–8   181
Housing Act 1996   15, 22, 43, 49, 69,
   70, 113, 115, 119, 120, 130, 143,
   146, 175, 213, 240, 244, 245, 249,
   258–9, 264, 266, 270, 271, 276, 278,
   289–301
Part V   131
Part VI   120, 121, 122, 124–9, 136,
   289, 296, 298
Part VII   145, 259, 263, 264, 285,
   289, 290, 292, 295, 297, 300
s. 2   114, 115
ss. 16–17   164
s. 22   123
s. 58(2A)–(2B)   271
s. 60   271
s. 73   241
s. 96   43, 245

Housing Act 1996 — *continued*
s. 97   44
s. 100(1)   200
ss. 105–119   46
s. 124   131
s. 125(2)   131
s. 125(5)   131, 135
s. 127(1)   131
s. 128(3)–(4)   131
s. 129   131
ss. 131–132   131, 214
s. 132   214
s. 133   131, 214
s. 133(3)   135
s. 134   124, 131
s. 135   131
s. 147(1)   144
s. 147(2)   140
s. 148   72
s. 152   144
s. 152(2)–(3)   145
s. 152(6)–(7)   145
s. 153(1)   145
s. 153(6)   146
s. 157(1)   146
s. 158(1)   145
s. 159   124
s. 159(2)   124
s. 160   124
s. 161   122
s. 161(2)   122
s. 162   121
s. 162(3)   121
s. 163   122
s. 163(2)   122
s. 164   123, 124
s. 166   122
s. 167   120, 124, 128, 245
s. 167(1)   124
s. 167(2)   126, 127
s. 167(2)(a)–(b)   245
s. 167(4)   127
s. 167(6)   127
s. 167(8)   125
s. 168(1)   126
s. 168(3)   126
ss. 175–218   259
s. 175   243, 271
s. 175(1)   266, 270
s. 175(1)(a)   266, 267
s. 175(1)(b)   266, 270

Housing Act 1996 — *continued*
s. 175(1)(c)   266
s. 175(2)   299
s. 175(2)(a)–(b)   267
s. 175(3)   245, 267
s. 175(4)   274
s. 176   273
s. 176(a)–(b)   273
s. 177(1)   269
s. 177(2)   272
s. 178(1)   269
s. 179   290, 291
s. 182   259
s. 184   263, 264, 265, 290, 294
s. 184(3)   264
s. 185   265, 295, 301
s. 185(1)   264
s. 186   265, 295, 301
s. 188   49, 259, 264, 265, 290, 298
s. 189   259
s. 189(1)   274
s. 189(1)(b)   276
s. 189(1)(c)   275, 277
s. 190   49, 298, 301
s. 190(2)(a)–(b)   291
s. 190(3)   291
s. 191   301
s. 191(1)   274, 279, 280, 285, 294
s. 191(2)   282
s. 191(3)   279, 285
s. 191(4)   279, 285, 292
s. 192   301
s. 192(2)   291
s. 193   122, 127, 263, 274,
         289, 291, 292, 293, 294,
         295–6, 301
s. 193(2)   294
s. 193(3)   291
s. 193(5)   295
s. 193(6)   296
s. 193(6)(a)   295
s. 193(6)(b)   296
s. 193(6)(d)   296
s. 193(7)   296
s. 193(9)   296
s. 194   127, 291
s. 194(2)   296
s. 194(5)–(6)   297
s. 195   122, 301
s. 195(2)   127, 274, 291, 292
s. 195(4)   294

Housing Act 1996 — *continued*
s. 195(5)   274, 291
s. 196   301
s. 196(3)(c)   296
s. 196(4)   292
s. 196(7)   296
s. 197   126, 263, 285, 291, 292, 293, 301
s. 197(1)   301
s. 197(2)   274, 292
s. 197(3)–(4)   292
s. 198   259, 264, 292, 293, 295
s. 198(1)   301
s. 198(5)   293, 301
s. 199   259, 294
s. 200   49, 298
s. 200(3)–(4)   302
s. 202   264
s. 202(4)   302
s. 204(1)   302
s. 204(4)   49, 298, 302
s. 206   297
s. 206(2)   297
s. 207   136, 297
s. 207(1)(a)–(b)   298
s. 208(1)–(4)   297
s. 209   44
s. 209(2)   49
s. 209(3)   298
s. 210   300
ss. 211–212   259
s. 213   294, 298, 299
s. 352   241
Sch. 7   43
Schs 9–11   46
Housing and Building Control Act 1984   162, 169, 233
Housing Finance Act 1972   12, 110
Housing (Financial Provisions) Act 1924   105, 107
Housing (Financial Provisions) Act 1933   106
Housing Grants, Construction and Regeneration Act 1996
Part I   118
Housing (Homeless Persons) Act 1977   119, 249, 257–8, 264, 287, 293
Housing and Planning Act 1919   103–4, 106

Housing and Planning Act 1986   130, 176
s. 9   149
s. 14(1)   268
s. 18   48
Sch. 4
para. 1   48
Housing Rents and Subsidies Act 1975   110
Housing Repairs and Rents Act 1954   11
Housing Subsidies Act 1956   108
Housing and Town Planning Act 1909   102, 159
Housing and Town Planning Act 1919   17
Housing of the Working Classes Act 1885   223
Housing of the Working Classes Act 1890   102, 159
Part I   102
Part III   102

Increase of Rent and Mortgage Interest (Restrictions) Act 1920   10
s. 12(1)(g)   205
Increase of Rent and Mortgage Interest (War Restrictions) Act 1915   8, 9, 10, 188
Increase of Rent and Mortgage Interest (War Restrictions) Act 1919   10
Industrial and Provident Societies Act 1965   115

Landlord and Tenant Act 1927
s. 18(1)   233
Landlord and Tenant Act 1954   51
Part I   44, 46, 95
Part II   14, 32, 51, 53, 56, 138
s. 2(4)   50
s. 23(1)   32
s. 30   14
s. 30(1)(b)   70
s. 30(1)(f)   78
Landlord and Tenant Act 1985
s. 8   222, 223
s. 8(2)   223
s. 8(6)   223
s. 10   223
s. 11   157, 220, 223–6, 228, 232
s. 11(1)   224, 226
s. 11(1A)   225

Landlord and Tenant Act 1985
— *continued*
  s. 11(1B)   226
  s. 11(2)   224
  s. 11(3)   226
  s. 11(3A)   226
  s. 11(4)   226
  s. 11(6)   226
  s. 12   157, 223–6
  ss. 13–15   157, 223–6
  s. 16   157, 223–6
  s. 16(b)   224
  s. 17   231
Landlord and Tenant Act 1987
  ss. 21–24   232
  s. 48   69
Landlord and Tenant (Licensed
    Premises) Act 1990   53
Law of Property Act 1925
  s. 52   59, 154
  s. 53(1)   59
  s. 101   75
  s. 146   234
  s. 146(1)   36
Leasehold Property (Repairs) Act
    1938   234
Leasehold Reform Act 1967   46, 160
Leasehold Reform, Housing and Urban
    Development Act 1993   46, 171,
    176, 183, 233
  s. 106   167
  s. 107   170
  s. 115   171
  s. 121   233, 238
  s. 122   156
  s. 132(1)   158
  ss. 135–136   179
Limitation Acts   83
Local Government Act 1888   102
Local Government Act 1972
  s. 111   144
  s. 195   256
  s. 222   144
Local Government Act 1988   184
Local Government Act 1989   163
Local Government Act 1992   184
  s. 9   184
Local Government and Housing Act
    1989   111, 177, 179, 202, 237, 240
  Part VII   118, 238
  ss. 79–80   203

Local Government and Housing Act
  — *continued*
  s. 149   49
  s. 161(1)   119
  s. 186   46
  Sch. 10   44
Local Government, Planning and Land
    Act 1980   184

Matrimonial Causes Act 1973   153
  s. 23   169
  s. 23A   132, 153, 212
  s. 24   124, 132, 153, 169, 212, 214
  s. 24A   169
Matrimonial and Family Proceedings Act
    1984   124
  s. 17(1)   132, 153, 169, 212, 214
Mental Health Act 1959   294
Mobile Homes Act 1983   30

National Assistance Act 1948
    252–7, 278
  s. 21(1)(a)   252, 259
  s. 21(1)(b)   252, 253, 254, 255, 287
  s. 36(1)   253
National Health Service and Community
    Care Act 1990   244
  s. 67(2)   259
Noise and Statutory Nuisance Act
    1993   234

Occupiers' Liability Act 1957 227
  s. 2   227
  s. 4   227

Pluralities Act 1838   56
Police and Criminal Evidence Act 1984
  s. 24   144
Poor Law   251, 252, 253
Poor Law Amendment Act 1834   251
Protection from Eviction Act 1964   82
Protection from Eviction Act 1977   50,
    60, 81–99, 267
  s. 1   89, 93
  s. 1(1)   83, 88
  s. 1(2)   83, 94
  s. 1(3)   86, 87, 88, 90, 94
  s. 1(3)(a)–(b)   86
  s. 1(3A)   88, 94
  s. 1(3B)–(3C)   88
  s. 1(4)   88

Protection from Eviction Act 1977
— *continued*
s. 1(6)   89
s. 2   82, 94
s. 3   34, 52, 55, 82, 83, 95, 96
s. 3(1)   95
s. 3A   95, 96, 97
s. 3A(2)–(3)   96
s. 3A(5)(a)   96
s. 3A(6)   96
s. 3A(7)(a)   97
s. 3A(8)   97
s. 5   34, 35, 52, 55, 82, 83, 97
s. 5(1)   97
s. 5(1A)   97
s. 13(a)–(b)   83
Public Health Act 1872   101
Public Health Act 1875   8, 101
Public Health Act 1936
ss. 91–100   234

Race Relations Act 1976   144
Rent Act   10, 15, 38, 66
Rent Act 1957   81, 82, 109, 254, 255
Rent Act 1965   11–12, 84, 110, 188, 206
Part III   82
Rent Act 1968   12, 13
Rent Act 1974   13, 33, 47, 48, 53
Rent Act 1977   13–14, 15, 18, 24–34,
46–57, 58–80, 82, 83, 86, 94, 95, 96,
97, 113, 132, 140, 141, 146, 148,
154, 189, 190–6, 203, 205–11, 216,
234, 266
Part II   68
Part IV   48
Part VI   200
s. 1   24, 34, 41
s. 1(1)   24
s. 1(6)   25
s. 2   31, 37, 61
s. 2(1)(a)   35, 38, 211
s. 2(1)(b)   211
s. 3(2)   234
s. 3(2B)   95
s. 3(3)   35
s. 3(4)   36
s. 4   24, 46, 49
s. 5   24, 46
s. 5(1)   50
s. 5A   48
s. 6   24, 46

Rent Act 1977 — *continued*
s. 7   24, 46, 47
s. 8   24, 46, 51, 95
s. 9   24, 46, 51–2
ss. 10–11   24, 46, 53, 137
s. 12   24, 46, 53
s. 13   24, 46, 55
ss. 14–15   24, 46, 48, 55
s. 16   24, 46, 55
s. 18   24
s. 19   25
s. 19(7)   52
s. 22   132, 134
s. 22(3)   34
s. 22(5)   34
s. 24(3)   32, 56
s. 26   50
s. 44   190
s. 44(1)   190
s. 66   190
s. 67(3)   191
s. 70(1)   191, 192, 193
s. 70(2)   192
s. 70(3)   192, 193
s. 70(4)   193
s. 72(1)   191
s. 73   191
s. 98   59, 60
s. 98(1)   58, 59, 65
s. 98(2)   58, 68
s. 100(1)–(3)   64
s. 101   56
ss. 119–120   13, 50
s. 121   13
ss. 123–126   13
s. 127   13, 50
s. 128   13
s. 152(1)   25
Sch. 1
para. 2(2)   208
para. 12   36
para. 13   37
Part I
paras 2–3   211
Sch. 2
para. 1(a)–(b)   55
para. 2A   55
para. 4   54
Sch. 15   36, 58, 65, 70
Part I   58, 61, 68
Part II   53, 58, 61, 148

Rent Act 1977 — *continued*
  Part III
    para. 1    73
    para. 2    68
  Part IV
    para. (a)    74
    para. (c)–(f)    74
    para. 3    65
    paras 4–5    66
  Part V
    para. (b)–(e)    74
Rent Acts    3, 12, 13, 14, 24, 25, 26, 31,
  32, 36, 37, 40, 42, 46, 47, 49, 50, 59,
  130, 189, 206, 207, 216
Rent (Agriculture) Act 1976
  49
Rent and Mortgage Interest Restrictions
  Act 1923    10
Rent and Mortgage Interest Restrictions
  Act 1939    10, 11
Rent and Mortgage Interest Restrictions
  (Amendment) Act 1933    10

Sexual Offences Act 1956
  s. 6    275
Small Tenements Recovery Act 1838    9
Social Security Administration Act
  1992    201
Social Security Contributions and
  Benefits Act 1992    201
Supreme Court Act 1981
  s. 37    231

Torrens Act *see* Artisans and Labourers'
  Dwellings Act 1868
Tribunals and Inquiries Act 1992    190

Unfair Contract Terms Act 1977    228
  s. 1    228
  s. 2(1)–(2)    228

Vagrancy Acts    250

Wheatley Act *see* Housing (Financial
  Provisions) Act 1924

# Table of Secondary Legislation

Allocation of Housing and Homelessness
(Amendment) Regulations 1997
(SI 1997/631)   122
Allocation of Housing and Homelessness
(Review Procedures and
Amendment) Regulations 1996
(SI 1996/3133)   123
Allocation of Housing (Procedure)
Regulations 1997
(SI 1997/483)   125
Allocation of Housing (Reasonable
Preference) Regulations 1997
(SI 1997/1902)   121
Allocation of Housing Regulations 1996
(SI 1996/2753)   122
Assured and Protected Tenancies
(Lettings to Students) Regulations
1988 (SI 1988/1683)   51
Assured Tenancies and Agricultural
Occupancies (Forms) Regulations
1988 (SI 1988/2203)   43, 63

County Court Rules
Ord. 49
r. 6A   42

Homelessness (Persons Subject to
Immigration Control) (Amendment)
Order 1997 (SI 1997/628)   265
Homelessness (Suitability of
Accommodation) Order 1996
(SI 1996/3204)   300

Homelessness (Suitability of
Accommodation) (Amendment)
Order 1997 (SI 1997/1741)   301
Housing Accommodation and
Homelessness (Persons subject to
Immigration Control) Order 1996
(SI 1996/1982)   265
Housing Benefit (General) Amendment
Regulations 1996
(SI 1996/965)   202
Housing Benefit (General) Regulations
1987   201
Housing (Management of Houses in
Multiple Occupation) Regulations
1990 (SI 1990/830)   241
Housing (Reasonable and Additional
Preference) Regulations 1997
(SI 1997/1902)   289
Housing (Right to Buy) (Maximum
Discount) Order 1989
(SI 1989/513)   168
Housing (Right to Buy) (Prescribed
Forms) Regulations 1986
(SI 1986/2194)   170

Introductory Tenants (Review)
Regulations 1997 (SI 1997/22)   131

Local Government Act 1988
(Competition) (Defined Activities)
(Housing Management) Order 1994
(SI 1994/1671)   184

Notices to Quit (Prescribed Information)
    Regulations 1988
    (SI 1988/2201)   97

Public Services Contract Regulations
    1993 (SI 1993/3228)
    184

Rent Officers (Additional Functions)
    Order 1995   201

Secure Tenancies (Notices) Regulations
    1987 (SI 1987/755)   139
    para. 2(1)   139
Secure Tenants of Local Housing
    Authorities (Right to Repair)
    Regulations 1994   233

**European regulations**
Regulation 1612/68   264
    art. 9(1)   264

# ONE

## An introduction to housing law

### 1.1   WHAT IS A HOME?

House and home stand at the centre of people's lives. A house provides shelter, and is a place in which people can store and display most of their possessions, but it is more than 'bricks and mortar' and 'a roof over one's head'. Decent housing is 'a place that is dry and warm and in reasonable repair. It also means security, privacy, sufficient space; a place where people can grow, make choices, become more whole people' (Archbishop of Canterbury's Commission, 1985: 230). Ideally, it promotes 'emotional and social health' by providing 'psychological security, physical ties with one's community and cultures and a means to express one's individuality' (Schaefer, 1987) and it is well known that good housing promotes good physical health. The needs served by housing are complex and constantly changing as cultural and living standards evolve and households grow and disperse (Donnison et al, 1982: 11).

### 1.2   THE FUNCTIONS OF HOUSING POLICY

Housing policy consists of 'measures designed to modify the quality, quantity, price and ownership and control of housing' (Malpass et al, 1994: 9). The political aspect emerges from the way in which policy is put into practice. The main objective of housing policy is generally considered to be the provision of

> sufficient affordable housing so that every household enjoys real choice between housing options, each of which offers good physical standards, security of possession, an attractive neighbourhood, convenient location and all at a price or rent that the household can afford (Merrett, 1992: 48).

It is clear, however, that housing policy need not be designed to *improve* housing conditions and that governments sometimes deliberately withhold investment in housing for the benefit of other services such as health and education (Donnison et al, 1982: 13).

Central government formulates policy and, through legislation, can provide the powers and the financial means for its implementation. However, the major responsibility for translating policy into action is borne by local authorities, housing associations, building societies, builders, landlords and others which, as policy-making bodies in their own right, are likely to modify central government policy at local level, a point which goes some way to explaining why 'the impact of new policies is rarely as dramatic as either their advocates hope for or their critics fear' (Donnison et al, 1982: 161). In addition, the legislation passed to give effect to housing policy will be interpreted and further refined by the courts. Over the years, therefore, by a process akin to 'Chinese Whispers', an effect quite different from that anticipated by the promoters of the legislation may be produced. The courts may also point the way for the reform of housing law and a consequent rethinking of housing policy. Finally, it is important to recognise that housing does not exist in a vacuum but is affected by, for example, economic policy and personal taxation policy.

## 1.3   THE DETERMINANTS OF HOUSING POLICY

Housing policy (and, therefore, housing law) depends on how housing itself is viewed. At one extreme it can be regarded as a commodity (like a car or video) subject to the laws of the market-place, i.e. supplied if and when entrepreneurs see the opportunity of a reasonable return and bought by those able and willing to pay the price which will yield that return. Accordingly, it is given no special treatment to distinguish it from any other commodity and no provision is made to give landlords and tenants any rights or obligations over and above those which are contractually agreed (Doling et al, 1984: 1). Such a state of affairs has not existed in England and Wales since the middle of the nineteenth century.

Housing is a vehicle whereby wealth can be stored and accumulated. However, it has a number of features which distinguish it from other commodities. The housing market differs from other markets in that houses and households can move between the ownership market (in which the houses themselves are bought and sold) and the rental market (where only the use of house-room is bought and sold). The multiplicity of interests which can exist in land are unmatched with regard to other commodities and, because a house is fixed in one place, a person who buys or rents housing is also buying or renting accessibility to employment opportunities, city centre services, the countryside, and so on (Holman, 1987: 5, 6). Houses take a comparatively long time to build and are expensive to produce and, unlike other commodities, they cannot be imported from abroad, even if they can be produced more cheaply in, for example, South Korea (Ivatts, 1988: 198). Above all, the fact that housing serves one of the most basic human needs means that it warrants special treatment.

The modified market model has underpinned social policy in Great Britain for most of the twentieth century under both Labour and Conservative governments but it has been particularly marked since 1979. Market competition rather than state action has been promoted as the most effective mechanism by which resources can be most efficiently distributed. Adherents of the market model expect people to be self-reliant or, if necessary, to rely on the market, their families, and the generosity and support of other members of their communities, rather than the state. The message has been that the state should confine itself to protecting private property and wealth (which itself enables people to be self-reliant) and creating conditions which help the market to run smoothly. Direct state support is acknowledged as necessary for the elderly, disabled or very poor, who lack the capacity to compete effectively in a market system but, even then, the feeling is that support should be kept to a minimum. The market philosophy is based on the theory that a degree of inequality stimulates initiative and effort. The overriding aim is to minimise public spending in favour of low rates of taxation which stimulate economic enterprise and initiative.

State intervention in housing has been seen as creating problems, rather than solving them. The Rent Acts which were in operation from 1915 until 1988, gave tenants long-term security of tenure at a 'fair rent', thereby restricting freedom of contract in the private rented sector and 'inhibiting the exercise by private owners of formerly sacrosanct rights of property' (see *Davis* v *Johnson* [1979] AC 317 at pp. 348E–G per Lord Scarman). Over the past 10 years, therefore, rent control in the private rented sector has all but been removed and security of tenure much diminished. In the public sector, council housing has been criticised for its inefficiency, its erosion of people's freedom and motivation to compete in the market, and the way in which it has allowed social inequality to become politicised and exploited for electoral gain. Steps have been taken, therefore, to reduce the role played by local authorities, and to increase the role of housing associations, in the provision and management of social housing — the attraction of housing associations being 'their independence from local political control and dependence on direct central government support — a more aceptable form of public landlordism' (Cole et al, 1994: 210).

Now, because council housing is seen as a last resort, it is considered inferior to housing provided by the market. This contrasts with the National Health Service and state education, for example, which are used by the bulk of the population — even those who can afford to pay for private medical provision and to send their children to fee-paying schools. As a result, the National Health Service and state schools gain a level of political support which ensures that the services they provide are of a higher quality than would be the case if they were used only by the poor. Secondly, there is an increase in the polarisation of society between those who can provide for themselves through the market system and those who have to rely on provision by the state or the voluntary sector. Council housing is increasingly populated by the elderly, the unemployed and benefit-dependent. The 'privatisation' of council housing has not, however, meant a withdrawal of the state. Indeed, the whole process has only been made possible by extensive legislative intervention.

Left wing commentators, who subscribe to the social democratic model (see Clapham, 1990: 28–31), take the view that homelessness, overcrowding, disrepair and so on stem from the fundamental inability of the market to produce enough satisfactory housing, especially for the poorer sections of society. They argue that 'in all countries of advanced capitalism ... state housing has been introduced after conditions in the private sector have reached the level of human degradation' (Karnavou, 1981: 52). Because of the inequalities inherent in, and engendered by, market society, state intervention is regarded as necessary to ensure that there is 'an adequate supply of suitable accommodation at a price which the poorest can afford' (Malpass et al, 1994: 5). The provision of housing is thus regarded as a social service, the state deciding how much to supply and how it is allocated. Moreover, the choice offered by the market is illusory. It may work 'rather more satisfactorily for the better off' but 'tends to establish a close link between poverty and poor housing' (ibid.).

## 1.4   HOUSING TENURE IN ENGLAND AND WALES

**Table 1.a   Housing tenure in England and Wales**

|        | Owner-occupied | Rented from local authorities and new towns | Rented from private landlords | Rented from housing associations |
|--------|:----:|:----:|:----:|:----:|
|        | % | % | % | % |
| 1914   | 10 | negligible | 90 | |
| 1951   | 31 | 17 | 52 | |
| 1971   | 52 | 29 | 19 | |
| 1989   | 67.5 | 22 | 7.7 | 2.8 |
| 1998   | 68 | 16 | 9 | 4 |

There are four main types of tenure in Great Britain: owner-occupation, council renting, housing association renting and private renting, and the above table shows how their fortunes have waxed and waned during the twentieth century. It will be observed that the most dramatic change has occurred in the decline of the private rented sector and the growth of owner-occupation. It has been argued that private renting was a mode of provision which was appropriate in the nineteenth century when the new urban working class earned low wages and had little opportuity to save. Renting thus enabled them to obtain access to an essential commodity which they could not afford to buy outright. The decline of the private rented sector is said to reflect its economic obsolescence in the twentieth century and home ownership is a more appropriate form of housing provision in the context of twentieth century capitalism, given the substantial and sustained growth in the real income of the working population (Malpass et al, 1994: 14, 15). It is quite true that the expansion of home ownership has been possible only because of an increase in real incomes. But that is only part of the story. The move to home ownership could not have occurred without the ready availability of mortgage finance, the capacity to sustain a mortgage depending on greater stability in employment than that enjoyed by a large part of the working population in the nineteenth century. Furthermore, the growth in owner-occupation as an alternative to private renting was politically determined and, to a large extent, made possible by financial incentives such as favourable tax treatment.

Tenure gives an indication of the terms on which households occupy their homes but each one is far more complex than its label implies. Owner-occupation will be a very different experience for someone who has recently taken out a large mortgage to buy a converted flat in a run-down inner city area, than for another person who has paid off his or her mortgage on an executive detached residence in the provinces. The boundaries between the tenures are sometimes blurred as, for example, in the rent to mortgage scheme contained in ss. 143 to 153, Housing Act 1985.

Moreover, a major misconception about housing in Great Britain is that the private sector depends wholly on the market, while the public sector depends wholly on state intervention. In fact, both private and public sectors receive state support and use private institutions to meet their needs. Public housing is really only publicly managed — not financed out of taxation but from 'loans raised directly or indirectly from the money market' (Bright et al, 1995: 21). Local authorities have acted as developers to produce public housing, but most dwellings were 'built by private contractors, with privately produced materials on land bought from private owners with capital borrowed from private financial institutions' (Malpass et al, 1994: 8). Both local authorities and housing associations are also increasingly involved in building for sale. In the private sector, rents are effectively underwritten by housing benefit in many cases and support is given to owner-occupation by the tax system. Tax relief on mortgage interest has been available since 1929. Schedule A income tax for owner occupiers was ended in 1963 (by a Conservative government) and sole or main residences were totally excluded from liability to capital gains tax in 1965 (by a Labour government).

Indeed, since 1945, there have been substantial areas of broad inter-party consensus. Between the 1950s and the early 1970s, both Conservative and Labour governments extended owner-occupation and council housing. In the early 1950s, the Conservatives even facilitated the construction of more council dwellings than owner-occupied houses, whilst under Labour in the mid-1960s and late 1970s more private sector houses were started than council properties. Until 1979, both parties agreed that council housing should be a 'general needs' tenure.

Legislators have treated each tenure separately 'as if each was an independent entity unaffected by and unaffecting events and processes in other tenures' (Doling et al, 1984: 7) and, for the sake of clarity and convenience, this book is to some extent guilty of the same offence. However, it is important to recognise that changes in one part of the housing system can affect the others. The plea has also been made that government should make a break with the 'tenure fetishism' of the past and that all tenures should be regarded as 'legitimate vehicles in eradicating housing poverty' (Merrett, 1992: 48).

## 1.5  SOCIAL TRENDS

The expansion of owner-occupation and a related decline in opportunities to rent over the past 20 years have taken place in the context of important social trends. First, significant changes have taken place in employment. There has been a redistribution of work opportunities from men to women, but more particularly from the unskilled and less educated to those possessing educational and professional qualifications. Britain's long-term economic decline, together with the impact of industrial obsolescence and new technology, have combined to produce a larger pool of people who are permanently or semi-permanently unemployed. These 'marginalised poor' can be found in all tenures but tend to be concentrated in social housing (Malpass et al, 1994: 17). Not only has unemployment risen but significant changes have occurred in patterns of employment. Historically, flexible or 'atypical' employment (temporary, casual and part-time work) has been concentrated on the weakest groups in the labour market but recent years have witnessed the spread of temporary employment into white-collar jobs which previously enjoyed long-term security. The most noteworthy change in the labour market has occurred in the number of people in self-employment, an increase from 1,825,000 in 1977 to 3,230,000 in 1997. While the majority of people employed have enjoyed a continuing increase in real incomes, there has been a massive rise in income inequality and a commensurate spread in poverty and welfare dependance. Almost 20% of the population live in households which rely on the safety net of income support for a subsistence income. In 1991, two-thirds of local authority and housing association tenanted households recorded no earning member.

Another important factor which impinges upon the demand for housing is the increase in the number of households which has taken place in Great Britain since the Second World War, partly because households now contain fewer people:

**Table 1.b    Households: by type of household and family**

|                                                      | 1961 | 1971 | 1981 | 1991 | 1996/7 |
|------------------------------------------------------|------|------|------|------|--------|
|                                                      | %    | %    | %    | %    | %      |
| Living alone — under pensionable age                 | 4    | 6    | 8    | 11   | 12     |
| — above pensionable age                              | 7    | 12   | 14   | 16   | 15     |
| 2 or more unrelated adults                           | 5    | 4    | 5    | 3    | 2      |
| Couple, no children                                  | 26   | 27   | 26   | 28   | 28     |
| Couple with dependent children                       | 38   | 35   | 31   | 25   | 26     |
| Married couple with non-dependent children only      | 10   | 8    | 8    | 8    | 6      |
| Lone parent with dependent children                  | 2    | 3    | 5    | 6    | 7      |
| Lone parent with non-dependent children              | 4    | 4    | 4    | 4    | 3      |
| Two or more families                                 | 3    | 1    | 1    | 1    | 1      |

Source: Office for National Statistics, 1998: Table 2.3.

In 1996/7 there were 23.5 million households in Great Britain, over 40% more than in 1961. The average household size fell from 3.1 in 1961 to 2.4 in 1996/7 and there has been a particularly large increase in the number of people living alone (27% in 1996/7, compared with 14% in 1961) (Office for National Statistics, 1998; 42). A growing proportion of single person households consists of elderly people. Less than 40% of households fit the model of the conventional nuclear family but 'housing policy has not even begun to come to terms with the shift in the foundations of British family life that these social statistics represent' (Newton, 1994: 78)

## 1.6 THE HISTORICAL CONTEXT OF HOUSING LAW

Housing is a subject in which history plays an important part. Houses themselves are 'like old clothes, handed down from earlier generations and remodelled with varying success' (Donnison et al, 1982: 16–17), a fact which has significant implications for the question of who is to bear the responsibility for their maintenance and repair. More importantly, perhaps, contemporary housing policy is shaped by 'policy mechanisms and institutional traditions which have been inherited from the past' and is 'the outcome of a process of accretion over a long period' (Malpass et al, 1994: 24). It is for this reason that so much attention is paid here to the historical background of current housing law, the shape and structure of which has been moulded by past failures and successes.

**References**

Archbishop of Canterbury's Commission on Urban Priority Areas, *Faith in the City: A Call for Action by Church and Nation*, London: Church House Publishing, 1985.

Bright, S. and Gilbert, G., *Landlord and Tenant: The Nature of Tenancies*, Oxford: Clarendon Press, 1995.

Clapham, D., Kemp, P. and Smith, S., *Housing and Social Policy*, Basingstoke: Macmillan, 1990.

Cole, I. and Furbey, R., *The Eclipse of Council Housing*, London: Routledge, 1994.

Doling, J. and Davies, M., *Public Control of Privately Rented Housing*, Aldershot: Gower, 1984.

Donnison, D. and Ungerson, C., *Housing Policy*, Harmondsworth: Penguin, 1982.

Holman, A., *Housing Policy in Britain*, London: Croom Helm, 1987.

Ivatts, J., 'Rented Housing and Market Rents: a Social Policy Critique', *Social Policy and Administration*, 1988, vol. 22, pp. 197–209.

Karnavou, E., 'Defending the Council Housing System or Opposing the Sales?', *Crticial Social Policy*, 1981, vol. 1, Issue 2, pp. 50–53.

Malpass, P. and Murie, A., *Housing Policy and Practice*, Basingstoke: Macmillan, 1994.

Merrett, S., 'Housing Legislation and the Future of the Private Rental Sectors', in Best, R. (ed.), *The Future of Private Renting*, York: Joseph Rowntree Foundation, 1992.

Newton, J., *All in One Place: The British Housing Story 1973–1993*, London: CHAS, 1994.

Office for National Statistics, *Social Trends 28*, London: The Stationery Office, 1998.

Schaefer, M., 'Health Principles and Housing', *World Health Journal*, July 1987.

# TWO

## The private rented sector: legislative history, decline and characteristics

### 2.1 LEGISLATIVE HISTORY OF THE PRIVAE RENTED SECTOR

#### 2.1.1 Private letting before 1915

By the time the first statutory rent controls directed specifically at the private sector were introduced by the Increase of Rent and Mortgage Interest (War Restrictions) Act 1915, the housing market had already been subject to legal regulation for some years. As the nineteenth century progressed, more and more local councils introduced by-laws designed to stamp out the consequences of poor quality and insanitary construction, and in 1875 the Public Health Act was passed, giving general powers to sanitary authorities to make by-laws which provided detailed control over building standards and layout.

In the nineteenth and early twentieth centuries, working-class housing in England was let by landlords on a weekly basis. Short lets allowed labour mobility because they enabled tenants to leave their accommodation at short notice. They were regarded, therefore, as particularly suitable in an industrial society in which much work was carried out on a casual basis. Long lets had been common in the eighteenth century but by the later nineteenth century were confined to middle-class households (which did not need to move around frequently to be close to work) and agricultural tenancies (Daunton, 1987: 20, 21).

Rents of residential properties rose continuously until 1914, accounting for an ever increasing share of earnings. The lower the income the higher the proportion devoted to rent. 'Flitting' was the most common form of rent evasion and in London, where furnished accommodation was fairly common among the poorer classes, absconding tenants had a habit of pawning the furniture. The high rate of residential mobility was not confined to casual labourers, but extended to the skilled working-class in search of better accommodation (Englander, 1983: ch.1). Some tenants took advantage of the cumbersome procedures which existed for recovery of possession (a trial by jury at which the plaintiff was required to prove his or her title to the property in dispute) and as a result the Small Tenements Recovery Act 1838 was passed. The Act provided that where a tenant of a small tenement (defined as premises rented for not more than £20 per annum) refused to give up possession on expiry of notice to quit, the landlord should serve notice indicating an intention to apply to the justices to recover possession. If the tenant did not appear at the hearing or failed to show why possession was not being given, the justices could issue a warrant putting the matter in the hands of the constabulary. The grounds for termination of the tenancy by the landlord were deemed irrelevant. Even so, a tenant who was in arrears would receive a week's notice, followed by a warrant of ejectment ordering departure within 21 days and would enjoy four weeks' rent-free occupation, therefore, before the landlord secured possession (Daunton, 1987: 23).

The pre-war housing market faced serious problems. The rate of population growth had fallen, wages stagnated, and interest rates rose. Councils, faced with having to pay for improved sanitation, water supply, schools, etc., sought to defray the cost through the rating system which in turn became an increasing burden on landlords. While a building boom at the turn of the century had created a surplus of houses, the years immediately up to 1914 witnessed the construction of fewer houses than usual and 'the War created conditions which made rent control possible', turning a cyclical downturn into a permanent structural change (Englander, 1983: 193). Men volunteered for, or were drafted into, the armed forces, families moved to join relatives in other parts of the country and others went in search of well-paid work in munitions factories, thus aggravating already difficult housing conditions in many towns. In Barrow, for example, where Vickers had an engineering factory, the working population went up from 16,000 to 35,000 during the first three years of the war and overcrowding reached the level of nine or ten people to a room (Orbach, 1977: 11). Demand for houses exceeded supply, especially in industrial towns and cities, and rents rose accordingly. Rent strikes began within weeks of the declaration of war and there was particular concern over the unrest among munitions workers, especially in Glasgow (Dickens, 1977: 341–351).

### 2.1.2   The Increase of Rent and Mortgage Interest (War Restrictions) Act 1915

Rent control was introduced by the Increase of Rent and Mortgage Interest (War Restrictions) Act 1915. Some commentators have viewed the Act as a 'working class victory' over a 'bourgeois state' representing the interests of a 'capitalist class' (Damer, 1980). Others have seen it as 'a sop to industrial militants', designed to interfere as little as possible with the interests of banking and industrial capital (Dickens, 1977: 350). On a more practical level perhaps, it was 'a short-term response to the exigencies of running a semi-controlled war economy', the government being compelled to try to regulate the economy and, where necessary, 'to subordinate market forces to the efficient prosecution of the war' (Englander, 1983: 193; Saunders, 1990: 22; Holmans, 1987: 387–8).

The 1915 Act provided that the rents of all houses below a certain rateable value should be set at the amount which had existed on 3 August 1914. It also provided security of tenure, thereby setting out a basic framework for the regulation of the private rented sector — rent control and security of tenure — which continued until 1988. Britain was not alone in introducing rent control at this time. Most of the protagonists involved in the First World War did so as they too were faced with housing shortages arising out of a virtual halt to building and large-scale movements of population. In other countries, however, rent controls were either removed after the 'post-war readjustments' (as in the USA) or landlords were offered some compensation for loss of rental (as in France and Germany). Britain was unusual in that decontrol was slow and only partial, and no compensation was provided (Daunton, 1987: 28).

### 2.1.3    1919–1954: the pendulum of control and decontrol

As its name suggests, the 1915 Act was seen as a temporary measure, designed to deal with war-time difficulties, and its operation was restricted to the duration of the war and six months after. However, it was inevitable that with a post-war shortage of some 600,000 houses, decontrol would result in immediate rent increases. The Increase of Rent and Mortgage Interest (War Restrictions) Act 1919 permitted rent increases of 10% (which did not come close to covering the wartime inflation) and doubled the rateable value limits of the houses brought under control, thus extending controls to 98% of all residential tenancies. The rateable value limits were increased still further in 1920 so that all but largest houses subject to control. The Increase of Rent and Mortgage Interest (Restrictions) Act 1920 also provided for succession to the tenancy by the widow of a tenant who had died intestate or by a member of the tenant's family if the tenant was a woman, or was unmarried and intestate, thus adding a third element to the Rent Act regime: statutory succession. A fall in prices and interest rates led to the Rent and Mortgage Interest Restrictions Act 1923 under which sitting tenants remained subject to control but all new lettings were excluded.

Over the next 10 years there was a massive investment in public housing for general needs (see **Chapter 8**) and it could be argued that, except for the bottom end of the market, the housing shortage had been ended. The response of the Conservative government was the Rent and Mortgage Interest Restrictions (Amendment) Act 1933, the purpose of which was to remove rent controls by stages on all but the lowest-value properties. Confidence was restored in the future of housing investment and once more landlords began to borrow against the security of future rental income. In 1934, 39,000 dwellings for rent were built for private landlords. This had risen to over 74,000 in 1938 by which time an estimated 2.75 million dwellings were let on controlled tenancies out of a total of 6.5 million privately rented dwellings (Holmans, 1987: 400).

The Rent and Mortgage Interest Restrictions Act 1939 — one of a number of Acts hurried through Parliament in preparation for the outbreak of war —

brought the great majority of residential properties under control again. Rents were held at the level at which they had stood when the Act became law (1 September 1939). For about 60% of the stock, that was the rent agreed between landlord and tenant; for the other 40% it was the controlled rent. The security of tenure for controlled tenants was in substance the same as provided for by earlier legislation. Repossession was possible only by order of the court and then only within narrowly defined parameters (e.g. non-payment of rent, wilful damage, allowing the property to be used for immoral purposes, or, for a dwelling occupied by virtue of employment, that the accommodation was needed for a new employee).

The Housing Repairs and Rents Act 1954 was the first major effort after the Second World War to encourage private enterprise to provide accommodation for letting. It entailed that all new housing built for letting, and those properties which had been converted in order to be let as housing, should fall outside Rent Act control. Limited increases in controlled rents were permitted on proof of recent repairs by the landlord. Otherwise they remained until 1957 at the levels set by the 1939 Act (by which time the value of money had fallen by one-half.)

### 2.1.4   The Rent Act 1957

A much more significant statute than its immediate predecessors was the Rent Act 1957 which, put simply, raised controlled rents to twice the gross rateable value as it stood in 1956. All houses with a rateable value of more than £40 in London and £30 elsewhere (approximately the top 10% of the market) were subject to almost immediate decontrol. Tenants whose dwellings were decontrolled could not be evicted immediately, but were to be given at least six months' notice which could not expire within 15 months of the Act's commencement. A power to extend block decontrol to lower tranches of rateable values by statutory instrument was never used. Control also ceased to apply to lettings where there was a change of tenant.

It is important to realise that decontrol affected not only rents but also security of tenure. Under the law as it stood in 1957, and indeed had done since 1915, tenants' rights were all or nothing. Controlled tenants had full security, including a right of succession for a widow or other member of the family living with the tenant. Tenants of lettings not subject to control had no statutory protection against eviction other than the right (introduced by the 1957 Act) to a minimum of four weeks' written notice. Previously they had been entitled to only one week's notice. In Inner London especially, where there was a shortage of accommodation, rents rose dramatically and some landlords, of whom Rachman was the most notorious, used heavy-handed tactics to 'persuade' controlled tenants to leave (see **Chapter** 7).

### 2.1.5   The Rent Act 1965

Most of the properties decontrolled by the 1957 Act were brought back into protection on a change of government by the Rent Act 1965. The 1965 Act overhauled the system, introducing 'regulated tenancies' and a new system of rent control involving the registration of fair rents via rent officers and Rent Assessment Committees. This was a means of imposing individual rather than national restrictions. The onus was on the landlord or (more commonly) the tenant or both of them to apply to the rent officer for registration of a fair rent which then became the maximum rent which the landlord could charge. For the first time, security of tenure existed independently of a controlled rent. The Act also extended the provisions for succession, establishing a right to a second transmission for the first successor's widow or a member of his or her family. The Rent Act 1968 consolidated all former Rent Acts.

It has been said that, with the benefit of hindsight, the security provided by the Rent Act 1965 was 20 years too late. Social policies, developed during World War II to reduce insecurity in health provision, education and welfare, had been put into legal effect between 1945 and 1950. The National Insurance scheme, for example, was revised and extended to ameliorate the financial consequences of wages lost through sickness, injury or unemployment. The creation of the National Health Service in 1948 reduced the risk posed to a household's finances by the cost of lengthy or complex medical and hospital treatment. The security afforded by the Rent Act 1965 can be seen therefore as bringing private rented housing into line with health provision and the general availability of welfare benefits (Holmans, 1987: 444, 445).

### 2.1.6  The phasing out of controlled tenancies

The Housing Act 1969 provided for the transfer from controlled to regulated tenancies of dwellings in satisfactory repair and with all the basic amenities. Because controlled rents were fixed, they were falling further and further out of line with current values. It was in the landlord's interests, therefore, to let property under regulated rather than controlled tenancies. The 1969 Act gave landlords an incentive to improve their properties, while the Housing Finance Act 1972 provided for the staged transfer of the remainder, unless formally declared to be unfit for human habitation. Both the 1969 and 1972 Acts required a fair rent to be registered in order to transfer the tenancy to regulation and provided for the resulting increase in rent to be phased over different periods depending on the circumstances. Since transfer from control to deregulation was likely to result in a steep increase in rents, private tenants were to be protected against financial hardship by the introduction of a mandatory scheme of means-tested rent allowances, equivalent to the rent rebates of local authority tenants.

### 2.1.7  Furnished lettings and resident landlords

None of the legislation so far mentioned gave protection to furnished lettings. A separate code of protection was introduced for them by the Furnished Houses (Rent Control) Act 1946. The Act provided lesser protection for furnished premises, on the assumption that a tenant taking this type of accommodation did not intend to stay there permanently. Application could be made to a Rent Tribunal for a reasonable rent to be fixed and for the operation of a notice to quit to be deferred for up to six months. By the mid 1970s it was apparent that landlords were choosing to let property furnished, often poorly, so as to avoid regulation (see **Chapter 5**). The Rent Act 1974 ended the distinction between furnished and unfurnished lettings and also introduced a 'resident landlord' exemption designed to encourage owner-occupiers to let part of their homes without the tenant gaining full protection — a policy which persists in the current legislation. Tenants of resident landlords had 'restricted contracts' with broadly the same rights as previously enjoyed by tenants of furnished accommodation.

### 2.1.8  The Rent Act 1977

Referring to the origins of the Rent Act 1977 in the 1915 Act, Lord Hailsham likened it to 'the squalid buildings in the courtyards of the Royal Courts of Justice, Strand [which] form a melancholy commentary on the French adage, "Il n'y a rien ainsi permanent que le provisoire"' (*Hansard*, HL Debs, vol. 382, col. 694). The Rent Act 1977, a consolidating Act which brought together the 1968 and 1974 Acts, seeks to protects tenants by:

(a)   limiting the maximum amount of rent a landlord can charge (achieved by the machinery of the fair rent scheme);
(b)   conferring security of tenure on tenants by:

(i)   requiring the landlord to obtain a court order before actually regaining possession, and then
(ii)   limiting the grounds on which the landlord may obtain an order for possession;

(c)   prohibiting/controlling the payment of 'premiums' (i.e. capital sums in addition to rent, popularly referred to as 'key money', see ss. 119–121, 123–128) as a condition of the grant of a tenancy to which the Acts apply; and
(d)   conferring succession rights.

As demand for rented housing generally outstrips supply, the landlord is usually in the stronger bargaining position and it is this inequality which has led to government intervention in the relationship, in particular to protect the tenant from rising rents and eviction. As Scarman LJ said in *Horford Investments Ltd* v *Lambert* [1976] Ch 39 at 52:

The policy of the Rent Acts was and is to protect the tenant in his home, whether the threat be to exhort a premium for the grant or renewal of his tenancy, to increase his rent, or to evict him ... The Rent Acts have throughout their history constituted an interference with contract and property rights for a specific purpose — the redress of the balance of advantage enjoyed in a world of housing shortage by the landlord over those who have to rent their homes.

The Rent Act 1977, which is still in force, is examined more fully in **Chapters 3 to 6**.

### 2.1.9   The 1980s to the present: attempts to revive the private rented sector

The Housing Act 1980 abolished the remaining controlled tenancies (about 0.2 million) and introduced two new forms of letting: protected shorthold tenancies and assured tenancies. Protected shorthold tenancies were granted for a fixed term of between one and five years. During the fixed term, the tenant enjoyed the same security of tenure as a regulated tenant, but when the term expired, the landlord was under no obligation to renew the tenancy and the court was obliged to grant possession should the landlord apply for it. The fair rent concept was retained. Assured tenancies were designed to encourage new accommodation to be built by 'approved landlords' (such as pension funds, housing associations and building societies). Rents were free from Rent Act control, but lettings were subject to the business tenancy code of control contained in the Landlord and Tenant Act 1954, Part II. This meant that the tenant had security for the contractual term and at end of term had a right to a new lease at a market rent. The landlord could oppose the application for a new tenancy on a number of grounds set out in s. 30 of the 1954 Act: disrepair attributable to the tenant's default, persistent delay in paying rent, other substantial breaches of obligation under the tenancy, the provision of suitable alternative accommodation, and the landlord's intention to demolish or substantially to reconstruct the premises. The scheme brought little new property into the private rented sector and only a small minority of those who had applied for and received approval were financial insitutions of the type which the scheme had been intended to attract (Kemp, 1993: 65). As regards holders of new restricted contracts, the Housing Act 1980 transferred security of tenure from Rent Tribunals to courts which were obliged to grant possession on application by a resident landlord, with a delay not to exceed three months.

After 1979 in particular, the government's housing policy focused on the encouragement of owner-occupation. The Conservative Party's election manifesto of 1987 continued to give pride of place to home ownership, but also promised a new package related to rented provision. A 'right to rent' would involve a fuller deregulation of private renting and a more substantial role for housing associations. In its 1987 White Paper, the government expressed the view that the decline of the private rented sector was attributable to the twin evils of rent control and security of tenure. It recognised, however, that the abolition of all controls, leaving determination of rent levels and the extent of security of tenure to be settled contractually beween landlord and tenant with no statutory constraint, would not give sufficient protection to tenants' interests (Department of the Environment, 1987: para. 3.9).

The aims of the Housing Act 1988, as regards the private rented sector, are quite different from those of the Rent Acts. While the former concentrated on tenant protection, the 1988 Act was intended to regenerate a freer market in housing and to reverse the decline in the private rented sector. This was to be achieved by:

(a)   removing rent restrictions and permitting lettings to be made at market rents;

(b)   changing the security of tenure system, by extending the shorthold tenancy concept and introducing new mandatory grounds for possession; and

(c)   changing the law on succession to statutory tenancies.

Fears were expressed that the move to market rents would lead to a new wave of Rachmanism and that landlords would force out existing Rent Act tenants (paying a fair rent) in order to replace them with new market rent tenants. To meet these concerns the 1988 Act also strengthened the pre-existing laws on harassment and unlawful eviction. Rent Act 1977 regulated tenancies in existence at 15 January 1989 (the date on which the Housing Act 1988 came into force) continue but, subject to a few exceptions, no new regulated tenancies can be created.

During the 1990s, the expansion of home ownership remained one of the Conservative government's key policy objectives but the importance of the private rented sector was also recognised in providing a home for the 'substantial minority of households — in particular the young, the mobile and those with low incomes — who need or prefer to rent' (The Government's Expenditure Plans 1990–91 to 1992–93, Cmnd. 1008, London: HMSO, 1990). In its 1995 White Paper, the government stated its determination 'to sustain the revival in the private rented sector that deregulation has achieved' (Department of the Environment, 1995: 20). To this end, the Housing Act 1996 makes it easier to create assured shorthold tenancies (see **4.5.2**) and has also made changes to the grounds on which possession can be recovered when property is let on an assured tenancy (see **Chapter 6**).

In an attempt to attract institutional investment in the sector, the Housing Act 1996 provides for the creation of Housing Investment Trusts. In the early part of the twentieth century when private renting formed the principal source of housing, institutions such as insurance companies were major landlords. Between 1960 and 1980, spurred on by the shift towards owner-occupation and the emergence of other types of investment which could be used as a hedge against inflation, most corporate and institutional investors broke up and disposed of their rental portfolios, selling either to private landlords or into owner-occupation. In the 1995 White Paper, the government observed that the lack of a suitable investment vehicle acted as an obstacle to more institutional investment in residential property. Most financial institutions, it was said, do not wish to take on the management obligations which direct ownership involves (Department of the Environment, 1995: 22). It proposed, therefore, that institutions should be given the opportunity to invest in Housing Investment Trusts (HITs) set up to own and manage residential property. This was effected by sch. 30, Finance Act 1996. HITs enjoy the same exemption from capital gains tax as traditional investment trusts and are subject to a reduced rate of corporation tax (24% instead of 33%) on income derived from residential lettings. They seem to have been greeted with cautious enthusiasm, account having been taken of the fact that the private rented sector has a capital value of over £150 billion and an estimated gross annual income of £13.5

billion. Reasons given for the private rented sector offering an attractive investment opportunity include:

(a)    a favourable political climate under which the Labour government is expected to continue the support for the expansion of the private rented sector which it showed in opposition;

(b)    landlord and tenant legislation 'which balances the interests of both parties';

(c)    a rising level of demand for properties let at market rents owing to changes in the structure of society (the increase in the number of single and small households, including the growth in the student population) and increased flexibility in the labour market;

(d)    low inflation;

(e)    total returns forecasted as averaging 12% per annum over the next three years (Collet and Phillips, 1997).

HITs are quoted on the stock exchange with a minimum size of £30 million. The same limits on purchase price apply as applied to the Business Expansion Scheme (see **2.3.1**), and the property must be unlet or subject to a shorthold tenancy when it is acquired. As HIT property, it must be let under an assured tenancy. If HITs do take off, it is anticipated that change will be gradual and may take up to 20 years (Birch, 1996).

## 2.2   THE DECLINE OF THE PRIVATE RENTED SECTOR

The supply of private rented accommodation in Great Britain has declined from about 90% of the total housing stock in 1900 to about 10% today. The British private rented sector is the smallest in the Western world. In Switzerland 56% of all housing is privately rented, 42% in Germany , and 30% in Canada, the US and France (*The Times*, 5 January 1997).

The long decline of private renting has been the outcome of a complex set of factors, the relative importance of which has varied over time. One of these factors has been the appeal of rented property as an investment. In the nineteenth century, prospective landlords could obtain a mortgage to cover about two-thirds of a property's purchase price. If interest rates increased, they passed on as much of the cost as possible by raising rents. Most landlords were small capitalists, content with a secure return on their investment, who could achieve an 8% gross return from letting, a sum which compared favourably with other forms of investment (Balchin, 1989: 92). In the 1880s, 'rising local property taxes (following the extension of the franchise) and static wage levels (which limited the rents which tenants could afford to pay) combined to squeeze landlords' profits' (Saunders, 1990: 21). With the extension of limited liability in the late nineteenth century, investment in joint stock companies became a possibility for people of modest means, and the development of the Stock Exchange and building societies, the expansion of government and municipal stock, and increased investment opportunities overseas meant that investment in private rented property became a much less attractive proposition.

Rising standards in housing also played a part in the decline of the sector. Together with higher construction costs and rent control, they put a brake on the production of houses to rent after the First World War. The price of new houses quadrupled between 1914 and 1920, putting economic rents beyond the means of most potential tenants. The Housing and Town Planning Act 1919 enabled local authorities partly to make good the deficiency of supply by giving them powers to provide subsidised housing for the needs of the working class. The subsequent growth of local authority rental housing 'attracted many of the more affluent and reliable households among the pool of potential tenants' (Saunders, 1990: 25).

For a decade after the end of the First World War virtually no slum clearance took place. Until the housing shortage was reduced there was little sense in demolishing existing houses even though they were unsatisfactory. In 1930, however, local authorities were required to draw up plans for slum clearance, and displaced households were rehoused in accommodation built by local authorities. Again, after the Second World War slum clearance was held in abeyance, the main objective being the supply of dwellings. Between 1953, when the government announced its intention to recommence slum clearance, and 1981, over a million dwellings (one-fifth of the private rented housing stock) were simply demolished (Holmans, 1987: 432).

Slum clearance went hand in hand with housing rehabilitation. The Housing Act 1949 made discretionary improvement grants available. The amount payable was increased significantly by the Housing Act 1969 which also withdrew most of the restrictive conditions previously attached to the payment of grants (in particular a minimum length of time for which the owner must live in the house where grant aided work has been done or let it to a tenant). The housing price boom of 1971–3 provided an additional incentive to landlords, who were unable to charge sufficiently high post-improvement rents to recoup their share of the cost of improvements, to sell their properties into owner-occupation. The Housing Acts of 1961, 1964 and 1969 increased controls over houses in multiple occupation. Again, landlords sold vacated properties into owner-occupation and tenants turned to the public sector.

An important factor in the failure of the private rented sector has been the lack of political support given to private landlords. Since the nineteenth century, most private landlords have been small, lower middle class investors. A consequence of their association with the Dickensian slums and, more recently, Rachman, is that they have often been regarded as a 'morally repugnant form of capitalist' and have failed to find 'a sympathetic ear in Westminster, Whitehall or Fleet Street.' Unlike other countries such as Sweden and the US, there has never been any political support in Great Britain for publicly subsidising the private landlord. (Saunders, 1990: 22; Ginsburg, 1989: 58; Daunton, 1987: 30–39). Apart from improvement grants, the only subsidies provided to private landlords have been Exchequer grants payable on new housing built for letting under the Housing Act 1924 (Kemp 1992: 61). Subsidies and preferential tax treatment have put local authority tenants and owner-occupiers in a far better position than private landlords and tenants.

Recent Conservative governments have blamed statutory rent control and security of tenure for the decline of the private rented sector. Because of rent controls, the return to private sector landlords has been inadequate to persuade them to stay in the market or to keep property in repair. People who might have been prepared to grant a temporary letting have also been deterred by laws on security of tenure which make it impossible to regain their property when necessary (Department of the Environment, 1987: paras. 1.3, 1.8). It should be borne in mind, however, that decontrol in the past has not spurred on an upturn in the number of houses made available for private renting. The responses of landlords to decontrol in 1933 and 1957 were many and varied: some did not raise rents at all; some did raise rents but only a little; and some raised them to such an extent that tenants fell into arrears, were evicted and the properties sold into owner-occupation. Any additional income was not necessarily spent on repair and maintenance. Above all, the private rented sector continued to decline (Doling and Davies, 1984). Since the Housing Act 1988 came into force, the number of households renting from private landlords in England has increased — by 17% from 1.7 million in 1988 to 2 million in 1994 (Department of the Environment, 1995: 21). Interestingly, the figure was 1.92 million in 1984 when the Rent Act 1977 was providing extensive security of tenure (including generous succession rights) and a fair rent regime for most new tenants in the private rented sector. The increase since 1988 probably owes less to initiatives contained in the Housing Act 1988 (assured shorthold tenancies, market rents, etc.) than to the slump in the property market (Newton, 1994: 108–109). The one in ten landlords who are currently letting their properties specifically because they cannot sell them, may well sell them back into owner-occupation as the housing market continues to recover.

Between 1914 and 1939 over 1 million privately rented houses (14% of the total housing stock in 1914) were sold into owner-occupation, mostly to sitting tenants at substantial discounts. Running parallel to this, however, an annual average of over 66,000 dwellings were sold to private landlords. In the 1930s home ownership became a reality for an increasing proportion of the population: interest rates were low, land, materials and labour were cheap and building societies (which had expanded rapidly in the 1920s) went out to attract borrowers. Planning legislation exerted little control over residential development. To have made a profit, landlords would have had to have charged rents which were uncompetitive with mortgage repayments (Saunders, 1990: 23–25). For most of the period since the Second World War, very few houses have been built for private renting.

## 2.3  CHARACTERISTICS OF THE PRIVATE RENTED SECTOR

### 2.3.1  Landlords

Private letting is a small-scale industry which is dominated by private individuals rather than companies. In this respect, therefore, it has changed very little and has not been subject to the trends towards concentration and centralisation witnessesed in other areas of the economy (Kemp, 1992: 17). Individual landlords own just over half of privately rented properties. Sixty four per cent own fewer than five lettings and 82% own fewer than 10. Forty nine per cent acquired the property as an investment, 38% bought the property to live in at some time, and 17% inherited. (Some respondents gave more than one answer.) Forty four per cent of partnership and company landlords own fewer than 24 properties but 33% own more than 250. Sixty per cent acquired the property for investment reasons; 30% to house an employee (Department of the Environment, 1995: 21).

Thus, while a minority of private landlords are property companies (which may also have interests in business and office accommodation and in property dealing and development), the majority are small and own only one or two tenanted properties. Many of the latter may see letting as a way of reducing their own housing costs such as mortgage payments or council tax. They may have become landlords on a short-term basis while they are abroad or because they need to move but are experiencing difficulty in selling their houses. A survey carried out in 1993/4 showed that about one in ten private lettings were owned by landlords who were only in the sector because of the property slump (Crook et al, 1995: 45). The difficulty and/or expense of removing a tenant may be nuisance for commercial landlords but usually they can either afford to put up with a tenant or remove him or her via the legal process or by offering him or her a financial inducement. Small landlords (especially resident landlords) generally have relatively little money, patience or legal awareness to deal with tenants who cannot or will not move. Their limited resources and expertise also have repercussions as regards repairs and maintenance.

There is a perennial complaint that people will not invest in rented housing because other forms of investment are more lucrative, and that subsidies or tax concessions are needed, therefore, to make them change their minds. In recent years tax incentives have been introduced to try to overcome this 'yield gap. ' The Business Expansion Scheme (BES) was launched in 1983 to encourage small private investors to provide venture capital to unquoted companies. Tax relief on whole of the initial investment (up to £40,000) could be claimed at the investor's top rate of tax. Thus, for a higher rate tax payer, an investment of £40,000 would actually cost £24,000 after BES relief at the 40% tax rate was taken into account. After 1986, there was no liability to capital gains tax on the disposal of qualifying shares provided that the investor kept them for five years. The Finance Act 1988 extended the scheme to include companies which carried on the business of providing and maintaining properties to let by way of assured (not assured shorthold) tenancies under the Housing Act 1988. The companies could either build new properties or acquire existing ones which were not already let. Upper limits were placed on the value of each property (£125,000 in Greater London and £85,000 elsewhere). The initial response to the scheme was encouraging, £320 million being invested in 1988/9. Even local authorities became involved in the scheme, the Conservative-controlled Royal London Borough of Kensington and Chelsea initiating two BES share issues: one to promote housing for employees to encourage teaching staff to move into the area and the other to address the borough's broader housing needs (*Independent*, 28 May 1992). As house prices fell in the late 1980s and early 1990s, investors' expectations of capital growth diminished and they became concerned about their ability to exit after five years. One way in which companies responded was by the introduction of 'contracted-exit' schemes, typically requiring the vendor (such as a university or housing association) to buy back the properties at the end of the qualifying period at an agreed price above that at which they had originally sold, thus provided shareholders with a profit. Another response was to exploit the slump in the property market by buying up unsold or repossessed houses. A report by the Joseph Rowntree Foundation in 1992 described as 'predators' the 8 out of 72 new housing companies launched under the BES in 1990/1 tax year which had bought repossessed houses at auction or in bulk from builders who could not sell (*Independent*, 10 August 1992).

During its lifetime, the BES raised about £2 billion for about 1,750 companies, 250 involving investment in residential property (*Independent*, 12 March 1992). Over 80,000 flats and houses were bought by BES companies. Almost 40% were university, 10% housing association and around 25% entrepreneurial company dwellings. Building societies and insurance companies also became involved in the scheme (see *Estates Gazette*, 1992, vol. 12, pp. 114–115). Repossessed housing accounted for over 20,000 units and it is estimated that the BES financed only 12,000 new units, the remainder simply being transferred into private renting from other tenures or from one segment of the private rented sector to another, as in the case of university accommodation (Crook et al, 1995: 18–20). The scheme proved to be extremely costly to the Treasury (it worked out at about £20,000 per unit) and was described by the editor of *BESt Investment*, the industry newsletter, as 'a lousy use of taxpayer's money' (*Independent*, 11 March 1992). The BES was ended on 31 December 1993 by Finance (No. 2) Act 1992, s. 38, the reason given by the then Chancellor, Norman Lamont, being that it was too complex.

### 2.3.2 Tenants

The private rented sector no longer caters for general housing needs in the way it once did. It contains a small sub-sector of luxury properties situated mainly in London but otherwise it has four main roles (Kemp, 1992: 10), providing accommodation for:

(a)    young, newly formed households and the mobile, including job movers;
(b)    a number of elderly people;
(c)    households on low incomes who are unable to gain access to owner-occupation and social housing or who have left these tenures because of rent/mortgage arrears, relationship breakdown; etc; and
(d)    employees in housing provided by their employers, such as farm workers, people working in the armed forces, and caretakers.

Over a third of private tenants are under 30 and more than a third are single, compared with one in seven households generally. Many private tenants frequently move home: in 1993/4, 40% had been at their present address for less than a year. Half of private tenants have a full-time paid job, about the average for all tenures, but twice the proportion for social sector tenants. Such figures would seem to bear out the picture which is often painted of the private rented sector: that it serves as 'an essential first stage for young people leaving home, including students and those saving a deposit to buy their own home [and] contributes to a healthy economy by assisting labour mobility' (Department of the Environment, 1995: 20) and it is true that it provides initial housing for a high proportion of white collar workers, most of whom become home owners after a few years (Harloe, 1990: 93).

It should not be forgotten, however, that the sector also houses a substantial group of older tenants. About 20% of private sector tenants are aged 65 or older and 8% have lived in the same house for 40 years or more, dating back to the time when private renting was much more common (Department of the Environment, 1995: 20). The young and the elderly live in different types of housing. Young households mainly live in furnished, low-quality, poor-value for-the-money, but reasonably accessible furnished accommodation, often small converted flats or rooms with shared facilities in urban areas. These days they are likely to be assured shorthold tenants. The elderly, on the other hand, live mainly in unfurnished properties, in houses rather than flats, with more space but few amenities. More of this type of accommodation is still subject to a form of rent control and legally guaranteed security of tenure (Harloe, 1990: 91).

The private rented sector is also home to people who are unable to gain access to other tenures, i.e., who cannot afford owner-occupation and are not in priority categories for public housing. The Major government saw private renting in terms of 'a complement to the social rented sector for people on low incomes, 'so that those who found themselves temporarily on a low income could be supported through housing benefit. It was felt that short-term help to enable them to rent in the private rented sector could be a 'better and more cost-effective solution than providing a home in the social rented sector.' For those in longer term need of help, private rented housing with housing benefit could provide a home until a social rented tenancy became available. In some cases, it could provide a long-term solution to their housing needs (Department of the Environment, 1995: 20).

Thus, although it is assumed that for many people the private rented sector represents a 'temporary solution on the route to home ownership, marriage and traditional family life', the truth is that 'many of the lowest income non-family households are trapped for years in insecure, low standard privately rented accommodation paying high housing costs' (albeit with the assistance of housing benefit). The situation is not likely to improve in the near foreseeable future owing to the low number of properties available to rent, especially in the major towns and cities and 'an increasing demand for housing by a range of low-income households in accordance with demographic trends indicating a growing number of non-nuclear family households' (Watson, 1986: 8).

## 2.4  TYPE AND STANDARD OF HOUSING IN THE PRIVATE RENTED SECTOR

Converted flats figure significantly in the private rented sector (26% compared with only 6% of housing as a whole). Terraced houses and purpose-built flats are found in this sector in about the same proportions as for all housing, while detached and semi-detached houses are less common (Leather et al, 1997). The English House Condition Survey 1991 found that 20% of all properties in the private rented sector are unfit for human habitation. Five hundred and thirty six thousand private tenants (almost one-third of all private tenants) live in the worst housing, which is dominated by pre-1919 housing and converted flats. Nearly three-quarters of those in the worst privately rented housing have below average incomes (compared with 60% of all private tenants) (Department of the Environment, 1993: 111, 112).

In conclusion, the private rented sector can be seen to have enjoyed something of a chequered history. Whether the Housing Acts of 1988 and 1996 have ended its seemingly inexorable decline is questionable. Certainly a healthy private rented sector is important, not least because of the current job climate in which both main political parties are supportive of a flexible workforce (characterised by short-term contracts and part-time working), the members of which may find it difficult to sustain the traditional 25-year mortgage. One way in which the private rented sector may be regenerated is by a new type of landlord, exemplified by Quality Street which operates mainly in the private sector but also provides social housing. Set up by the Nationwide Building Society in 1988, Quality Street owns or manages 6,000 properties. Unusually for the private sector, most of its properties are let under assured, rather than assured shorthold, tenancies. It also builds homes for letting (*Observer*, 25 February 1996, p. 18).

**References**

Balchin, P.N., *Housing Policy: an Introduction*, London: Routledge, 1989.
Birch, J., 'Hitting the Target', *Roof*, May/April 1996, pp. 30–31.
Collet, A., and Phillips, C., 'Landlords go househunting', *Estates Gazette*, 1997, vol. 20, pp. 144–146.
Crook, A., Hughes, J. and Kemp, P., *The Supply of Privately Rented Homes Today and Tomorrow*, York: Joseph Rowntree Foundation, 1995.
Crook, T., and Kemp, P., *Private Landlords in England*, London: HMSO, 1996.
Damer, S., *State, Class and Housing: Glasgow 1885–1919* in J. Melling (ed.) *Housing, Social Policy and the State*, London: Croom Helm, 1980.
Daunton, M., *House and Home in the Victorian City: Working Class Housing 1850–1914*, 1983.
Daunton, M., *A Property Owning Democracy?*, London: Faber, 1987.
Department of the Environment, Housing: The Government's Proposals, Cm. 214, London: HMSO, 1987.
Department of the Environment, *The English House Condition Survey: 1991*, London: HMSO, 1993.
Department of the Environment, *Our Future Homes: Opportunity, Choice Responsibility*, Cmnd. 2901, London: HMSO, 1995.
Dickens, P., *Social Change, Housing and the State — Some Aspects of Class Fragmentation and Incorporation: 1915–1946* in Harloe, M. (ed.) *Urban Change and Conflict*, London: Centre for Environmental Studies, 1977, pp. 341–351.

Doling, J. and Davies, M., *Public Control of Privately Rented Housing*, Aldershot: Gower, 1984.

Englander, D., *Landlord and Tenant in Urban Britain 1838–1918*, Oxford: Clarendon Press, 1983.

Ginsburg, N., 'The Housing Act 1988 and its Policy Context: A Critical Commentary', *Critical Social Policy*, 1989, Vol. 9, Issue 1, pp. 56–81.

Harloe, M., *Great Britain* in Van Vliet, W. (ed.), *International Handbook of Housing Policies and Practices*, New York, Westport and London: Greenwood Press, 1990.

Holmans, A., *Housing Policy in Britain*, London: Croom Helm, 1987.

Kemp, P., Best, R. et al, 'Beyond the BES: An Overview of Trends, Problems and Prospects' in *The Future of Private Renting: Consensus and Action*, York: Joseph Rowntree Foundation, 1992.

Kemp, P., *Rebuilding the Private Rented Sector?* in Malpass, P. and Means, R. (eds), *Implementing Housing Policy*, Buckingham: Open University Press, 1993.

Leather, P. and Morrison, T., *The State of UK Housing: a Factfile on Dwelling Conditions*, Bristol: The Policy Press, 1997.

Malpass, P., and Murie, A., *Housing Policy and Practice*, 3rd edn, Basingstoke: Macmillan, 1990.

Newton, J., *All in One Place: The British Housing Story 1973–1993*, London: CHAS, 1994.

Orbach, L.F., *Homes for Heroes: a Study of the Evolution of British Public Housing*, London: Seeley, 1977.

Saunders, P., *A Nation of Home Owners*, London: Unwin Hyman, 1990.

The Government's Expenditure Plans 1990–91 to 1992–93, Cmnd. 1008, London: HMSO 1990.

Watson, S., 'Women and Housing or Feminist Housing Analysis?', *Housing Studies*, 1986, vol. 1, p. 1.

# THREE

# Requirements of protection under the Rent Act 1977 and Housing Act 1988

## 3.1 THE RENT ACTS

The Rent Acts have become less significant with the decline of the private rented sector. By the early 1980s, Rent Act evasion and avoidance had become so common-place that there was conjecture as to whether the Acts had any practical relevance at all (Doling, 1984). The Housing Act 1988 hammered the final nail into their coffin by providing that (subject to a few exceptions) no new Rent Act tenancies could be granted on or after 15 January 1989. While the number of regulated tenancies still in existence is now relatively low (in 1994, they accounted for 14% (310,000) of all private tenancies: Green at al, 1996: 55), the Rent Act 1977 is considered in some detail in this and the next four chapters, not only because many of its provisions are identical to those of the Housing Act 1988, but also because it represents perhaps the apogee of tenant protection and will be with us for some time.

### 3.1.1 Requirements of Rent Act protection

A tenancy falling within the Rent Act 1977 is known as a 'protected tenancy' during the contractual term (s. 1). At the end of the contractual term, a 'statutory tenancy' comes into existence and the tenant will still enjoy the protection afforded by the 1977 Act so long as he or she continues to occupy the demised premises as his or her residence (see **4.2**). Protected and statutory tenancies are collectively known as 'regulated tenancies' (s. 18).

There are three requirements of a protected tenancy:

   (a)   there must be 'a tenancy under which a dwelling-house (which may be a house or part of a house) is let as a separate dwelling' (s. 1(1));

   (b)   the tenancy must comply with the rateable value and rental limits (ss. 4 and 5);

   (c)   the tenancy must not be excluded under ss. 6–16.

Rateable value, rental limits and exclusions are described in detail in **Chapter 5**.

## 3.2    THE HOUSING ACT 1988

### 3.2.1    Requirements of Housing Act 1988 protection

The requirements of the Housing Act 1988 are that:

(a)    'a tenancy under which a dwelling-house is let as a separate dwelling is ... an assured tenancy if and so long as:

(i)    the tenant or, as the case may be, each of the joint tenants is an individual; and
(ii)    the tenant or, as the case may be, at least one of the joint tenants occupies the dwelling-house as his only or principal home; and
(iii)    the tenancy is not one which, by virtue of subsection (2) or subsection (6) below, cannot be an assured tenancy' (s. 1);

(b)    the rental and rateable value limits must not be exceeded (sch. 1, paras. 2 and 3);
(c)    the tenancy must not be exempted (sch. 1, paras. 4–13).

Rateable value, rental limits and exclusions are described in detail in **Chapter 5**.

## 3.3    CONCEPTS COMMON TO TENANCIES UNDER THE RENT ACT 1977 AND HOUSING ACT 1988

### 3.3.1    There must be a 'tenancy'

The term 'tenancy' includes periodic and fixed-term tenancies of any length, equitable tenancies, express tenancies at will in respect of which rent is being paid (*Chamberlain* v *Farr* [1942] 2 All ER 567), tenancies at sufference, tenancies by estoppel (*Stratford* v *Syrett* [1958] 1 QB 107) and sub-tenancies (s. 152(1), Rent Act 1977; s. 45(1), Housing Act 1988). A genuine licence falls outside the protection of both Acts but certain types of contractual licence created before 15 January 1989 may be protected as restricted contracts under the Rent Act 1977 (s. 19, Rent Act 1977).

The extensive protection given to tenants by the Rent Acts made many landlords anxious to avoid creating leases which might not be terminable for many years to come. Since protection hinged on the existence of a tenancy, landlords often granted what appeared to be licences instead of tenancies. For many years the courts generally adhered to the principle that the relationship between the parties was determined by the law, rather than the label attached to it. To depart from this approach would, said Lord Denning, 'make a hole in the Rent Acts through which could be driven — I will not say in these days a coach and four — but an articulated vehicle' (*Facchini* v *Bryson* [1952] 1 TLR 1386 at 1389–1390).

In the 1970s and early 1980s, however, 'the courts allowed the boundary between legitimate avoidance and illicit evasion of the Rent Act to shift in response to some perceived need to stimulate rather than fetter the supply of rented accommodation in large urban centres' (Gray, 1993: 725 n. 1). Perhaps they saw themselves as adopting a pragmatic and fundamentally humane approach, the problem of homelessness, and the housing shortage generally, having been the subject of considerable publicity for some time. More probably, they wanted to put a stop to what they considered to be an unreasonable interference by the Rent Acts with the property rights of landlords and thus took a somewhat blinkered view of the housing situation, ignoring the fact that people would agree to and sign anything in order to get a roof over their heads. In a string of cases (e.g. *Somma* v *Hazelhurst and Savelli* [1978] 1 WLR 1014; *Buchman* v *May* [1978] 2 All ER 993 and *Aldrington Garages* v *Fielder* (1979) 39 P & CR 461) the Court of Appeal held (despite the transparent intention to avoid Rent Act protection) that the intentions of the parties — as manifested in the tenancy agreement — were paramount in determining whether an agreement was a lease or a licence. In only a few cases were the labels attached to evasive devices overturned. (See *Walsh* v *Griffiths-Jones and Durant* [1978] 2 All ER 1002; *Demuren* v *Seal Estates Ltd* (1978) 249 EG 440; *O'Malley* v *Seymour* (1978) 250 EG 1083; *R* v *Rent Officer for LB of Camden, ex parte Plant* (1981) 257 EG 713). The turning point was *Street* v *Mountford* [1985] 1 AC 809 in which the House of Lords made it clear that what the parties call their agreement is by no means conclusive and that the intention of the parties will be deduced from the realities of the arrangement in practice, rather than that which is expressed in the agreement. As Lord Templeman said: 'The manufacture of a 5 pronged implement for manual digging results in a fork, even if the manufacturer . . . insists that he intended to make and has made a spade' (at p. 819).

**3.3.1.1  The hallmarks of a tenancy**  The 'hallmarks' of a tenancy have been identified as exclusive possession for a period of time which is certain or capable of being rendered certain (*Street* v *Mountford*). While rent is usually payable, it is not an essential ingredient of a tenancy (*Ashburn Anstalt* v *Arnold (W. J.) & Co.* [1988] 2 All ER 147), although it is an essential ingredient of Rent Act 1977 and Housing Act 1988 protection. As regards certainty, a finite point must either be expressed or implied from the outset or be capable of being rendered certain. Thus in *Lace* v *Chantler* [1944] KB 368, an agreement that a house should be let 'furnished for the duration' (meaning the duration of the war) was void for uncertainty because, at the time when the lease took effect, no-one knew how long the war would last. See too *Prudential Assurance* v *London Residuary Body* [1992] 3 All ER 504.

In *Street* v *Mountford*, the House of Lords stated that, in order to determine an occupier's status, the courts need only enquire 'whether as a result of an agreement relating to residential accommodation, the occupier is a lodger or a tenant.' A person will be a lodger only where 'the landlord provides attendance or services (such as cleaning the room or changing the linen) which require the landlord or his servants to exercise unrestricted access to and use of the premises.' The decision in *Abbeyfield (Harpenden) Society Ltd v Woods* [1968] 1 WLR 374 (in which the occupier of a room in an old peoples' home was held to be a licensee even though he had exclusive possession of his room) was approved. A broader approach is appropriate, however, and a combination of factors should be taken into account, when the fact of exclusive occupation is in issue. Where this is the case, the court must ask itself:

(a)   Is there a grant of exclusive possession to the occupier? Exclusive possession is the right to exclude everyone from the premises, including the landlord. In the words of Lord Donaldson MR it is 'the touchstone by which the "spade" of tenancy falls to be distinguished from the "fork" of lodging' (*Aslan v Murphy* [1989] 3 All ER 130 at p. 133). The fact that the landlord has reserved a right to enter any part of the accommodation to inspect or repair it does not destroy the occupier's exclusive possession.

(b)   If there is exclusive possession, is it referable to some relationship other than a tenancy? There may be occasions when an occupier has exclusive possession but none the less is merely a licensee, e.g., a service occupier (i.e., an employee who occupies the employer's premises in order better to perform the duties as an employee: *Norris v Checksfield* [1991] 23 HLR 425), or there has been something in the circumstances, e.g., a family arrangement, or act of friendship or generosity, which negatives any intention to enter into legal relations (as in *Cobb v Lane* (1952) 1 TLR 1037 where the owner of house allowed her brother to live in it rent-free, and *Booker v Palmer* [1942] 2 All ER 674, where evacuees were allowed to stay in a cottage rent-free for the duration of the war; cf. *Ward v Warnke* (1990) 22 HLR 496).

**3.3.1.2   Non-exclusive possession agreements**   One way in which landlords have purported to disguise the grant of a tenancy has been by way of 'non-exclusive possession agreements' under which rights of shared occupation only are granted to two or more people, reserving to the landlord the right to select another occupier if one should vacate the premises, or to introduce another occupier at any time, or to use the whole or part of the accommodation himself or herself. The House of Lords' decision in *Street v Mountford* concerned a single occupier and the owner had conceded that there was exclusive possession. The judgment, therefore, was not directly concerned to analyse purported non-exclusive occupation licences. None the less, Lord Templeman exhorted the courts to be astute in detecting and frustrating 'sham devices and artificial transactions whose only objective is to disguise the grant of a tenancy and to avoid the Rent Acts.'

The leading authority on non-exclusive occupation agreements is the decision of the House of Lords in *Antoniades v Villiers* [1988] 3 WLR 1205 in which an unmarried couple occupied an attic flat, comprising a bedroom, a bedsitting room, a kitchen and a bathroom. The furniture in the bedsitting room consisted of a bed settee, a table-bed, a sideboard and a chair. When the owner showed the flat to the couple, he agreed to put a double bed in the bedroom. Each of the proposed occupants concurrently signed identical agreements described as licences which reserved a right to the owner to occupy the flat himself or permit others to do so. The House of Lords held that the two agreements were interdependent. The couple had acquired, and enjoyed, exclusive occupation of the whole of the flat in consideration for periodical payments. They had a tenancy. The clause giving the landlord power to share occupation with them was only designed to disguise the grant of a tenancy. It was a sham or pretence. The flat was situated in an attic with a sloping roof and was too small for sharing between strangers and was not suitable for multiple occupation.

In *A.G. Securities* v *Vaughan* [1988] 3 WLR 1205 (consolidated with *Antoniades* v *Villiers* for the purposes of the House of Lords hearing), the flat in question consisted of four bedrooms, a kitchen and a bathroom. The company customarily granted short-term licence agreements to individual occupiers. At different times between 1982 and 1985, it entered into four separate agreements with four different people. The agreements, each for six months, were in the same form — except for the amount payable — and gave each occupant the right to use the flat in common with up to three others. They did not reserve a right for the company to share the flat but they did provide that further licences could be granted, up to four in total. When one occupant left, the company could nominate a replacement and had the final say on who should fill each vacancy even though, in practice, it was willing to accept someone put forward by the remaining occupiers. The company never specified that any occupant should have a particular bedroom and from time to time people changed rooms. In the House of Lords Lord Templeman said that if the four occupants had been jointly entitled to exclusive possession then, on the death of one of them, the right of survivorship would have come into play and the remaining three would have been entitled to joint and exclusive occupation. In fact, however, they could not exclude a fourth person nominated by the company. The four agreements were independent of one another. The four unities necessary to create a joint tenancy — possession, interest, time and title — were not present, nor was there any suggestion of sham or pretence in respect of the individual agreements.

The effect of *A. G. Securities* v *Vaughan* is that where individuals join the sharing arrangement at different times so that there is a genuine turnover in the occupation of the premises and the separate agreements can in reality be seen as a series of individual rights of occupation, there will be no joint tenancy unless at some subsequent time it is expressly granted. If each of the occupiers has exclusive possession of a particular room, it might be possible to argue that he or she is a tenant of that room. The fact that there is shared use of, for example, a sitting room or bathroom does not of itself prevent a protected or an assured tenancy from arising. This argument was not made in *A. G. Securities* v *Vaughan* but Lord Oliver in any event felt that individual tenancies would arise only 'if the facts support the marking out with the landlord's concurrence of a particular room as the exclusive domain of a particular individual' (at p. 1223).

'A joint tenancy is one where the tenancy commences on the same day for all, where the rent should not be altered without due notice to all and possibly where all are jointly liable for the rent' (per Sir George Waller [1988] 2 All ER 193). This last point formed the central issue in *Mikeover Ltd* v *Brady* [1989] 3 All ER 618 where cohabitees were each required to sign separate but identical agreements which required them to make separate payments to the owners as consideration for the right to occupy. When one of them later moved out of the flat, the remaining occupant offered to pay her share of the monthly payment. This offer was rejected by the owners. The Court of Appeal held that the effect of the two agreements was to confer on the couple together a right of joint exclusive occupation. There was no unity of interest, however, because the provisions for the payment of rent created separate obligations, rather than a joint obligation to pay the whole rent.

In *Aslan* v *Murphy (No. 1)* [1989] 3 All ER 130 the credibility of a non-exclusive occupation agreement was stretched to the limit. Whether the provisions as to non-exclusive occupation were pretences was not considered, however, the Court of Appeal's decision focusing on the retention of keys by the owner. Mr Murphy occupied a basement room measuring 4' 3" x 12' 6" under an agreement which stated that the 'licensor' was not willing to grant the 'licensee' exclusive possession of any part of the room. The use of the room given to Mr Murphy was, according to the document, in common with the licensor and/or such other licensees or invitees as the licensor might permit from time to time to use it (presumably, given the size of the room, only if they arranged themselves into a human pyramid!). The agreement limited Mr Murphy's use of the room to the hours between midnight and 10.30 a.m. and between noon and midnight and it provided for various services, including house-keeping, the cleaning of rooms and windows, the collection of rubbish, the provision of household supplies, and the provision and laundering of bed-linen. It was stipulated that the 'licensor' would retain the keys to the room and had an absolute right of entry at all times. Lord Donaldson, delivering the judgment of the Court of Appeal, stated that provisions as to keys 'do not have any magic in themselves.' What matters is why a provision for keys appears in the bargain. If it appears that the owner is retaining keys in case of emergency, or to read the meters or to carry out repairs 'none of these underlying reasons would of themselves indicate ... that the occupier was in law a lodger.' If, on the other hand, the true bargain is that the owner will provide genuine services (such as frequent cleaning, daily bed-making and the regular provision of clean bed-linen) for which the retention of keys is necessary, it would be possible to infer that the occupier is a lodger rather than a tenant. Since in *Aslan* virtually no services were provided during the currency of the agreement, there were no underlying reasons for access from which it was possible to infer that Mr Murphy was a lodger.

Simply because there are a number of cases in which non-exclusive possession agreements have been overturned, does not mean that such agreements are always held to be ineffective. A non-resident landlord can validly reserve the right to share, even if he or she does not actually exercise that right, nor have a clear intention of doing so, so long as the possibility of moving into the premises is genuinely within his or her contemplation at the time of the tenancy. The question which must be addressed is whether or not there is a real prospect of the landlord's doing so at some future time (*Gray* v *Brown* (1993) 25 HLR 144). It is important to remember, however, that the need for landlords to use such evasive measures has all but disappeared since the advent of assured shorthold tenancies under the Housing Act 1988.

### 3.3.2    There must be a 'dwelling-house'

There is no statutory definition of 'dwelling-house' but the term covers anywhere immobile which is designed or adapted for living in. It must be a place where the tenant can carry on all the 'ordinary activities of daily existence' — especially sleeping, cooking and eating. Thus, a bedsitting room with cooking facilities can be a 'dwelling-house' even though the occupier shares bathroom facilities elsewhere in the building (*Westminster City Council* v *Clarke* [1992] 2 AC 288). A dwelling-house can include even a shed, a converted coach, a permanently moored boat, or a well-equipped beach hut (*Spraggs* v *Prentice* (1950) 100 LJ 451; 156 EG 346). Whether a caravan is a dwelling-house depends on the circumstances of the letting, especially whether it is sometimes moved and services (e.g. water, sewage, electricity) disconnected (*R* v *Rent Officer of the Nottingham Registration Area ex parte Allen* (1986) P & CR 41; (1985) 17 HLR 481). Even if they are not protected under the Rent Act 1977 or Housing Act 1988, caravans may still qualify for security under the Mobile Homes Act 1983.

If one or more of the major activities of life cannot take place on the premises, the tenancy is not protected or assured (*Curl* v *Angelo* [1948] 2 All ER 189 — a room in a hotel annexe used solely as a bedroom; *Wright* v *Howell* (1948) 92 Sol Jo 26 — an unfurnished room, with no water supply or cooking facilities, in which the tenant no longer slept). In *Palmer* v *McNamara* (1991) 23 HLR 168 (a case concerning the resident landlord exemption), the room in question contained a folding-bed, sink, fridge and kettle but no cooker (because the landlord could not cook and was happy to live off cold meals and take-aways). The court held that the room was not prevented from being a dwelling merely because the landlord did not want a cooker. To hold otherwise would have meant that an unfurnished flat would not qualify as a dwelling.

Under the Rent Act 1977, protection attaches to 'a dwelling-house (which may be a house or part of a house)'. Of course, it is common for more than one dwelling-house to exist within the walls of a single building. In *Luganda* v *Service Hotels Ltd* [1969] 2 Ch 209 (a case on restricted contracts) a single furnished room equipped with a gas ring was held to be 'part of a house'. The 'house' in question had formerly consisted of four houses but was now a hotel with 88 rooms.

### 3.3.3    The dwelling-house must be 'let as a separate dwelling'

**3.3.3.1    Rent**    Fundamental to the Rent Act 1977 (and to a lesser extent, the Housing Act 1988) is the provision of machinery for the regulation and control of the rent. This could not operate if the rent payable were not quantifiable in money terms. Rent could not, therefore, include the value of services rendered by the tenant for the benefit of the landlord such as the cleaning of rooms, and the payment of gas and electricity bills (*Barnes* v *Barratt* [1970] 2 QB 657). However, in *Montagu* v *Browning* [1954] 1 WLR 1039 Lord Denning stated that:

> ... in cases where rent is not payable in money but in kind, as in goods or services, then, so long as the parties have by agreement quantified the value in terms of money, the sum so quantified is the rent of the house within the meaning of the [Rent Acts]; and if it exceeds two-thirds of the rateable value, the house is within the Acts.

Thus where the tenant, who was employed by his landlord, occupied rent-free accommodation provided by his employer and received a smaller wage as a result, it was proper to quantify the rent by reference to the reduction in wages. In *Bostock* v *Bryant* (1990) 22 HLR 449 where the accommodation was provided on the basis that the occupier paid the gas and electricity bills, it was said that:

> it would be a most unsatisfactory arrangement if a tenancy could be a protected tenancy one moment and an unprotected tenancy the next, depending the fluctuating fuel bills of summer and depending on when notice terminating the tenancy was served (per Stuart Smith LJ at p. 455).

**3.3.3.2 The purpose of the letting**   For the purposes of a Rent Act *protected* tenancy, it is irrelevant that the tenant never lives there (*Horford Investments* v *Lambert* [1976] 1 Ch 39). A *statutory* tenant under the Rent Act must, however, continue to occupy the property 'as his residence' if he or she is to enjoy protection (s. 2, Rent Act 1977). A person can be an assured tenant only if he or she occupies the premises in question as his or her only or principal home (s. 1, Housing Act 1988; see (a)(ii) at **3.2.1**).

Premises are let as a dwelling if the lease provides that they will be occupied for residential purposes. Where the use of a building changes during the course of the lease, the general rule is that the original terms of the tenancy, and not subsequent actual user, determine the purpose of the letting. Conversely, if the lease describes the premises as let for business purposes (*Ponder* v *Hillman* [1969] 3 All ER 694; [1969] 1 WLR 1261 — 'all that shop and premises'), or contains user covenants expressly prohibiting residential user, or clearly contemplates a particular purpose (*Court* v *Robinson* [1951] 2 KB 60 — user only as a working men's social club) or there is a verbal agreement that they will not be used as a dwelling (*Williams* v *Perry* [1924] 1 KB 936), neither the Rent Acts nor the Housing Act 1988 can apply to the tenancy at any time unless the landlord consents to, or accepts, a change from business to residential user. Similarly, where a business tenant unilaterally changes the use of the premises from busines to residential, the tenancy will be neither protected nor assured (*Pulleng* v *Curran* (1982) 44 P & CR 58) unless the landlord by an express or implied consent (such as a prolonged acceptance of the rent with knowledge of the change) or waiver, agrees to the change and varies the terms of the lease.

Where the purpose of the letting is not discernible from the tenancy agreement, the courts will look at the surrounding circumstances and whether the property is constructed as a dwelling-house or as business premises, e.g., a lock-up shop. If the construction of the property does not indicate one way or another the intended use of the property then the actual user of the premises must be considered (see *Wolfe* v *Hogan* [1949] 2 KB 194; *Russell* v *Booker* (1982) 263 EG 513; *Gidden* v *Mills* [1925] 2 KB 713 — warehouse converted into a garage with living rooms above held to fall within the Rent Acts).

If the tenancy agreement permits both business and residential user, the letting will be subject to the Landlord and Tenant Act 1954, Part II unless the business user is merely incidental to the residential user (*Cheryl Investments Ltd* v *Saldhana, Royal Life Saving Society* v *Page* [1978] 1 WLR 1329 — business letting held not to exist where a doctor who was the tenant of a residential property had, on one or two occasions, seen a patient in the lounge in an emergency). Section 24(3), Rent Act 1977 states that a tenancy cannot be a regulated tenancy if it is one to which the Landlord and Tenant Act 1954, Part II applies, i.e., if the property comprised in the tenancy is or includes premises which are occupied by the tenant for the purpose of a business carried on by him or her, or for those and other purposes (s. 23(1), Landlord and Tenant Act 1954). A letting of a dwelling-house to a tenant for the purpose of the tenant making a profit from sub-letting is not a letting for business purposes as no business is carried on there (*Horford Investments* v *Lambert* [1976] 1 Ch 39).

### 3.3.4   The dwelling-house must be let as 'a' separate dwelling

Both Acts can apply only to lettings of one unit. However, two or more physically separate units, demised together, may together constitute a single dwelling as in *Langford Property Co.* v *Goldrich* [1949] 1 KB 511 in which two self-contained but not adjoining properties (which had previously been separately let) were let together for the first time under one tenancy and occupied by the tenant as a home for himself and his family. The properties were held to constitute one dwelling-house for the purpose of the Rent Acts. This decision was followed in *Whitty* v *Scott-Russell* [1950] 2 KB 32 where a house, cottage and land attached thereto were demised in one lease, the tenant covenanting to use the whole premises as 'a private dwelling-house only'.

In *Horford Investments* v *Lambert* [1976] 1 Ch 39 two houses (which had already been converted into a number of units of accommodation) were leased separately by the landlords to the same tenant who covenanted not to use them other than as residential premises in multiple occupation. The court held that the term 'dwelling' should be given a singular construction and that neither tenancy fell within the definition of a protected tenancy as both houses had been let as a number of separate dwellings. This principle was followed in *St Catherine's College* v *Dorling* [1979] 3 All ER 250 in which the college rented a large house for sub-letting to persons 'pursuing or intending to pursue a course of study.' The house contained rooms suitable for use as study/bedsitting rooms by five students who would share the kitchen and bathroom. It was held that the Rent Act did not apply, the property having been let not let as 'a' dwelling but as several dwellings.

In cases such as *Horford Investments* v *Lambert* and *St Catherine's College* v *Dorling*, where the head tenancy fails to fulfil all the criteria for statutory protection, the sub-tenancies may (unless they are excluded) be protected as against the tenant.

### 3.3.5    The dwelling-house must be let as a 'separate' dwelling

Most tenants will have exclusive possession of all the accommodation they use, being totally separate from other occupiers. Further, as indicated at **3.3.1.2**, joint tenants are not regarded as sharers but are deemed to occupy their accommodation as a single entity (*Antoniades* v *Villiers* [1988] 3 All ER 1058). It is often the case, however, that the demised premises are not self-contained and the tenant is given the right to share certain rooms (such as a kitchen or bathroom), either with the landlord or with other tenants.

**3.3.5.1    Accommodation shared with the landlord**    Before 1974, a tenant who shared 'living' accommodation with his or her landlord was not fully protected under the Rent Acts but had the benefit of what is now a restricted contract. A tenant who shared accommodation other than living accommodation with the landlord was fully protected.

In *Goodrich* v *Paisner* [1957] AC 65, Viscount Simonds said (at p. 76) that 'a sharing involves the right of simultaneous use of a living room in such a manner that the privacy of the landlord or the tenant, as the case may be, is invaded.' In *Neale* v *del Soto* [1945] 1 KB 144 the Court of Appeal held that there was sharing of the house where the landlord and tenant each had exclusive use of some rooms in a house but the use in common of the garage, kitchen, bathroom, lavatory, coal house and conservatory. A bathroom may be accommodation of a kind 'essential to modern standards,' but it is not a 'living' room since the tenant's use and enjoyment of it will not (presumably) coincide with the landlord's exercise of his or her right to its exclusive use. A tenant who shared just the bathroom with his landlord did not, therefore, share 'living' accommodation (*Cole* v *Harris* [1945] 1 KB 474). In *Goodrich* v *Paisner* the right given to the tenant of four unfurnished rooms in the landlord's house 'together with the use in common with the landlord of the back bedroom on the first floor' was held not to confer upon the tenant a right to use the bedroom whenever he wanted. It was presupposed that the parties would arrange between themselves not to use the room at the same time so that use by one would not amount to an invasion of the other's privacy. Whether user in common amounts to sharing is a question of fact and degree. In *Marsh* v *Cooper* [1969] 1 WLR 803 it was held (applying *Goodrich* v *Paisner*) that there could not be a sharing because the kitchen was too small (8' x 6') to be a living room and its use by the landlord's employee only minimal.

The Rent Act 1974 introduced the resident landlord rules, which do not require any element of sharing of living or other accommodation, but merely that the landlord should be resident in the same building. These rules, which are more fully explained in **Chapter 5**, operate to give the tenant a restricted contract instead of a protected tenancy where the arrangement was entered into before 15 January 1989. Under the Housing Act 1988, no new restricted contracts can be created and a tenancy granted by a resident landlord cannot be an assured tenancy. It will, however, be subject to ss. 3 and 5, Protection from Eviction Act 1977 unless the landlord or any member of his or her family share accommodation with the tenant, in which case the tenancy will be excluded and the provisions of ss. 3 and 5 will not apply (see **Chapter 7**).

**3.3.5.2 Accommodation shared with other tenants** Where a non-resident landlord grants a tenant exclusive occupation of, say, a bedroom but the tenant shares the remainder (kitchen, bathroom, sitting-room) with someone else, the separate accommodation cannot be regarded as a dwelling-house since the 'ordinary activities of daily existence' will be carried on in the house as a whole rather than in the room by itself (see **3.3.2**). No distinction is drawn between 'living' and other accommodation.

However, the tenant will have a protected or assured tenancy of the separate accommodation despite the sharing element if s/he meets the basic requirements set out in s. 1, Rent Act 1977 or the Housing Act 1988 as appropriate. Protection is secured in two ways. First, whilst the tenant is in possession of the separate accommodation, any term or condition purportedly modifying his or her right to use the shared living accommodation is ineffective (s. 22(3), Rent Act 1977; s. 3(3), Housing Act 1988). That is to say that the landlord cannot exclude the tenant from the shared areas without lawfully evicting him or her from the whole. Secondly, a possession order cannot be made in respect of the shared accommodation unless an order is also made in respect of the separate accommodation (s. 22(5), Rent Act 1977; s. 10, Housing Act 1988).

**References**
Doling, J., 'Have the Rent Acts become Irrelevant?', *Estates Gazette*, 1984, vol. 270, p. 1148.
Gray, K., *Elements of Land Law*, London: Butterworths, 1993.
Green, H., Thomas, M., Iles, N. and Down, D., *Housing in England 1994/95*, London: HMSO, 1996.

# FOUR

# Differences in the requirements of protection under the Rent Act 1977 and the Housing Act 1988

## 4.1 INTRODUCTION

Four main differences exist between the Rent Act 1977 and the Housing Act 1988:

(a) the statutory tenancy under the Rent Act 1977 (see **4.2**);
(b) the requirement that an assured tenant under the Housing Act 1988 must occupy the dwelling-house as his or her 'only or principal home' (see **4.3**);
(c) the requirement that an assured tenant under the Housing Act 1988 must be an individual (see **4.4**); and
(d) the assured shorthold tenancy under the Housing Act 1988 (see **4.5**)

## 4.2 THE STATUTORY TENANCY UNDER THE RENT ACT 1977

### 4.2.1 Introduction

The statutory tenancy is a concept unique to the Rent Act 1977. At common law, the expiry or termination of a contractual tenancy ends the tenant's rights of occupation. The Rent Act 1977, however, confers a statutory tenancy on the former protected tenant if and so long as he occupies the dwelling-house as his or her residence (s. 2(1)(a), Rent Act 1977).

A statutory tenant may surrender his or her tenancy or, subject to s. 5, Protection from Eviction Act 1977, bring it to an end by giving the notice to quit specified in the original lease (s. 3(3)). If no notice is specified, not less than three months' notice must be given. Disclaimer by the tenant's trustee in bankruptcy brings the statutory tenancy to an end and the whole of the bankrupt's former interest is then reinvested in the landlord (*Reeves* v *Davies*

(1921) 2 KB 486). Otherwise, a statutory tenancy can be terminated only by court order which will be granted only if the landlord can provide suitable alternative accommodation for the tenant or establish one of the grounds for possession contained in sch.15, Rent Act 1977 (see **Chapter 6**).

The landlord need not serve a notice to quit before seeking possession (s. 3(4)) nor a notice under s. 146(1), Law of Property Act 1925 where the tenant is in breach of covenant (*Brewer* v *Jacobs* [1923] 1 KB 528, in which it was said that the statutory tenant 'must find his protection, if any, within the [Rent Acts] and other Acts do not apply at all'.). A landlord cannot lawfully evict a statutory tenant against whom he or she has a possession order, except by execution of a warrant of possession (*Haniff* v *Robinson* [1992] 3 WLR 875, see **7.5**).

### 4.2.2   Requirements of a statutory tenancy

For a statutory tenancy to exist the following requirements must be met:

(a)   the tenant must hold over from a contractual tenancy which has terminated by expiry of a fixed term, notice to quit, or forfeiture;

(b)   the tenancy must have been a protected tenancy at the date of its termination;

(c)   the tenant must have been occupying the premises as a residence at the date of termination (regardless of whether or not he or she was living in the premises throughout the contractual period of the tenancy); and

(d)   he or she must continue to occupy the dwelling-house as his or her residence.

A landlord's acceptance of rent from a statutory tenant who holds over after the tenancy has ended, does not create a new or renewed contractual tenancy because the landlord has no choice but to accept it (*Davies* v *Bristow* [1920] 2 KB 428; *Morrison* v *Jacobs* [1945] KB 577). The tenant cannot contract out of his or her statutory entitlement but he or she may ask for, or receive, payment from the landlord as a condition of giving up possession. A request to, or payment from, anyone other than the landlord constitutes an offence (sch. 1, para. 12, Rent Act 1977).

### 4.2.3   The nature and value of the statutory tenancy

Statutory tenants are not true tenants since they have no estate or interest in the premises, no existing contract of tenancy and no right at common law to retain possession. What they do possess is a statutorily protected 'status of irremoveability' (per Lush J in *Keeves* v *Dean* [1924] 1 KB 685 at p. 686), i.e., a right as against all the world to remain in possession until they are turned out by an order of the court. They can also bring an action in trespass against anyone who enters the premises without their permission. The statutory tenant's right is 'a purely personal one, and as such ... must cease the moment (the tenant) parts with the possession or dies' (per Bankes LJ in *Keeves* v *Dean* at p. 690).

Generally speaking, a statutory tenancy is not assignable (*Keeves* v *Dean*) and cannot be transmitted by will (*John Lovibond & Sons* v *Vincent* [1929] 1 KB 687). However, up to two statutory transmissions may take place in favour of the spouse and or members of the family of the deceased tenant (see **Chapter 14**). Furthermore, the landlord may agree to a transfer of a statutory tenancy to a third party (sch. 1, para. 13, Rent Act 1977) and sch. 7, Family Law Act 1996 enables the court, during divorce proceedings and until remarriage, to vest protected or statutory tenancies in the non-tenant spouse. Similar provisions apply to cohabiting heterosexual couples. A statutory tenant may sublet part of the premises and remain a statutory tenant of the part he or she retains (*Berkeley* v *Papadoyannis* [1954] 2 QB 149) but if the whole is sublet, the statutory tenancy will cease, as the residence requirement of s. 2 will no longer be satisfied (*Haskins* v *Lewis* [1931] 2 KB 1; *Brown* v *Bestwick* [1950] 2 All ER 338).

A statutory tenancy is a valuable asset despite the fact that it 'cannot be bought and sold on the open market' and, because of the residence requirements, 'cannot be seen as an income-producing asset'. (Hand, 1980: 355, 356). In *Murray* v *Lloyd* [1989] 1 WLR 1060 the plaintiff recovered damages of £115,000 from the solicitors who had given negligent advice which led to her losing the opportunity of becoming a statutory tenant. Most regulated tenants are people of much more modest means so that 'in the circles in which these parties move possession of [a flat subject to a satutory tenancy] is one of the most significant rights of property that any of them ever see in their lives' (per Widgery LJ in *Mafo* v *Adams* [1970] 1 QB 548 at p. 557).

### 4.2.4 The requirement of continued residence for a statutory tenancy

Until 1968 the Rent Acts did not themselves require that the tenant should occupy the dwelling-house in question as his or her home. The courts, however, soon recognised the intention of the new legislation and insisted on such a condition being met.

The residence rules which apply to statutory tenancies apply also to the resident landlord exception, and have some bearing too on the requirement for assured status under the Housing Act 1988 and for a secure tenancy under the Housing Act 1985, that the tenant occupies the dwelling-house as his or her only or principal home.

The only person who can become a statutory tenant is the person who was the protected tenant on termination of the tenancy and it is his or her residence which must continue in order to keep the statutory tenancy alive. If a statutory tenant ceases to reside, the protection of the Rent Act 1977 is lost completely and a landlord bringing possession proceedings need only prove ownership of the premises, the termination of the contractual tenancy and the fact that the tenant no longer resides there.

#### 4.2.4.1 Company lets  A limited liability company can be a protected tenant within the Rent Act 1977, but it cannot 'reside' in a dwelling-house personally and is incapable, therefore, of becoming a statutory tenant (*Hiller* v

*United Dairies (London) Ltd* [1934] 1 KB 57). Even if the tenancy was granted to a company on the basis that someone else was to reside in the property, no statutory tenancy exists in favour of that other person (*S.L. Dando Ltd* v *Hitchcock* [1954] 2 QB 317; *Firstcross Ltd* v *East West (Export/Import) Ltd* (1980) 41 P & CR 145).

**4.2.4.2 Absentee tenants** To retain possession or occupation for the purpose of retaining protection the tenant cannot be compelled to spend twenty four hours in all weathers under his own roof for three hundred and sixty-five days in the year' (per Asquith LJ in *Brown* v *Brash and Ambrose* [1948] 2 KB 247 at p. 254). Thus, the tenant of a house in London who spends his week-ends in the country or his or her summer holiday in Scotland does not necessarily cease to be in occupation. Nevertheless, absence may be continuous and sufficiently long to raise an inference that possession or occupation has come to an end. The question is one of fact and degree. A tenant may be absent from his or her dwelling for several years (see, e.g., *Wigley* v *Leigh* [1950] 1 All ER 73; *Gofor Investments* v *Roberts* (1975) P & CR 366) but still regarded as occupying the premises as a residence within the meaning of s. 2(1)(a) provided that, in accordance with the principles laid down in *Brown* v *Brash and Ambrose*, he or she can show both (a) a continuing physical presence and (b) an intention to return.

(a)   *A physical presence (corpus possessionis)*   There must be some outward and visible evidence of the tenant's intention to return, e.g. furniture (*Gofor Investments Ltd* v *Roberts*, ibid.; *Brown* v *Draper* [1944] KB 309; *Dixon* v *Tommis* [1952] 1 All ER 725); a caretaker to look after the premises (*Wigley* v *Leigh*, ibid.); or relatives (*Dixon* v *Tommis*, ibid.; *Roland House Gardens* v *Gravitz* (1975) 29 P & CR 43; *Warriner* v *Wood* (1944) 144 EG 81). In *Brown* v *Brash and Ambrose* (ibid.) the tenant was sentenced to two years' imprisonment, leaving his partner and children in occupation. Soon afterwards she moved out, taking the children and all but three items of furniture. Thereafter, the tenant's relatives came in for a few hours each week to clean. Ten months after his partner had left, the tenant was released from prison. The Court of Appeal held that the tenant had stopped residing at the premises when his partner and children left. Although he possessed the *animus possidendi*, he lacked any *corpus possessionis*, because there was no intention that the three items of furniture should constitute symbols of possession. The fact that his absence was involuntary did not assist him. Once lost, his Rent Act protection could not be revived. In practice, tenants who intend to be absent for any length of time should leave personal belongings such as books, clothes, crockery and cutlery and furniture.

(b)   *An intention to return (animus revertendi)*   This must be more than a vague wish or 'pipe-dream' (per Geoffrey Lane LJ in *Baron* v *Phillips* (1978) 38 P & CR 91 at p. 103). It must be 'a real hope, coupled with the practical possibility of its fulfilment within a reasonable time' (per Ormerod LJ in *Tickner* v *Hearn* [1960] 1 WLR 1406 at p. 1410). What is a reasonable time depends on the circumstances. If the tenant is forced to leave by 'some sudden calamity', such as hospitalisation, a sentence of imprisonment or a flood, it will be regarded as a temporary expedient (*Bushford* v *Falco* [1954] 1 All ER 957). In *Tickner* v *Hearn* the tenant, a schizophrenic, was absent for five and a half years which she spent in a mental hospital. That she was 'mentally unsound' did not mean, on the facts, that she was incapable of forming an intention to return to the premises. In *Wigley* v *Leigh* (ibid.) the tenant sublet her house and lived with relatives in Northern Ireland for five years while her husband was away on war service. She intended to return to the house in 1945, when her husband was demobilised, but ill-health kept her in Northern Ireland until 1949. During her absence, the tenant employed a servant to stay at the house, to look after it and keep it ready for occupation and she spent a considerable amount on its upkeep and improvements. At the time of the hearing in *Gofor Investments* v *Roberts* (ibid.) (a case described as 'the salvation of many an absent tenant': Bridge, 1988: 302) the tenants had been living in Morocco and Malta for five years and were intending to return within three to five years. They had left their furniture and two sons in the premises (see too *Richards* v *Green* (1984) 11 HLR 1; *Atyeo* v *Fardoe* (1978) 27 P & CR 494).

### 4.2.4.3 Occupation through other people

It was emphasised in *Skinner* v *Geary* [1931] 2 KB 546 that personal occupation by the tenant is an essential prerequisite of a statutory tenancy. Even if the statutory tenant is away for a long time, however, the statutory tenancy may continue if he or she:

> couples and clothes his inward intention with some formal, outward, and visible sign of it; that is, instals in the premises some caretaker or representative, be it a relative or not, with the status of a licensee and with the function of preserving the premises for his own ultimate home-coming (per Asquith LJ in *Brown* v *Brash* [1948] 2 KB 247 at p. 254).

In the absence of *animus possidendi* on the part of an absent tenant, occupation by someone on his or her behalf will not preserve a statutory tenancy.

In *Brickfield Properties Ltd* v *Hughes* (1988) 20 HLR 108, a statutory tenant of a flat in London (in which he kept books and furniture) lived most of the time with his wife in a cottage in Lancashire. Between 1978 and 1987 he did not visit the flat at all. His wife visited it three times. During this period the flat was occupied by his three adult children and a son-in-law. The tenant's wife was in poor health and the tenant intended to return to London if her health became worse or she died. It has been said that:

> it demands an inordinately metaphysical construction of the role of the furniture to describe it, after nearly ten years, as the deliberate symbol of the father's continuing occupation, and a supremely unrealistic view of the children's residence as being primarily for the benefit of safeguarding the flat for his eventual return (Bridge, 1988).

However, the court had to contend with the 'insurmountable obstacle' of *Gofor Investments* (**4.2.4.2**) and, because there was a real possibility of the tenant's return to the flat within a reasonable time, the landlord's application for possession was dismissed.

Where the statutory tenant leaves the matrimonial home, security of tenure is not lost so long as his or her spouse continues to occupy the property as a residence (s. 30(4)(a), Family Law Act 1996). The tenant remains liable under the tenancy but, by s. 30(3), the landlord is obliged to accept payments from the occupier as if they were from the tenant. Unlike married couples, non-tenant cohabitants have no automatic right to pay rent and the landlord can therefore refuse payment but heterosexual non-tenant cohabitants can apply for occupation orders and acquire the right to pay rent/remain in occupation (s. 36). Orders are for up to six months, and may be extended for a further period not exceeding six months (s. 36(10)).

**4.2.4.4  Residence in two homes**    A tenant may occupy two properties at the same time, maintaining Rent Act 1977 protection in either or both. Comparatively short periods of occupation in one home may suffice as in *Landford Property Co.* v *Athanassoglou* [1948] 2 All ER 722 in which the claimant had a cottage in the country but was also the tenant of a flat in London where he slept (but rarely took a meal) on an average of twice a week, and *Bevington* v *Crawford* (1974) 232 EG 191 where the tenants lived mainly in Cannes and spent approximately two to three months each year in their rented accommodation in Harrow. However, 'occupation merely as a convenience for ... occasional visits' is not sufficient (*Beck* v *Scholz* [1953] 1 All ER 814 at p. 816). In *Hampstead Way Investments Ltd* v *Lewis-Weare* [1985] 1 WLR 164; [1985] 1 All ER 564 the statutory tenant's new wife and stepchildren joined him in his flat. Some years later they bought and moved into a house situated half a mile away. The flat was then occupied by the tenant's stepson, but the tenant carried on sleeping there five times a week so that he did not disturb his wife when he returned home early in the morning from his job at a night club. He kept his work clothes at the flat, his mail was delivered there and he paid the rent and all other outgoings except the gas bill which was paid by his stepson. He did not eat there, however, nor entertain his friends there. The House of Lords held that the house and flat could not together constitute a single unit of living accommodation since they were half a mile apart. The tenant's limited use of the the flat, and the fact that one essential activity of daily life, i.e. eating, was not carried out there, meant that his occupation was insufficient to make it his second home. There was not therefore the required residence and thus no security of tenure.

One object of the Rent Acts was 'to provide as many houses as possible at a moderate rent.' It follows therefore that:

a man who does not live in a house and never intends to do so is ... withdrawing from circulation that house which was intended for occupation by other people. To treat [such a man] ... as a person entitled to be protected, is completely to misunderstand and misapply the policy of the Acts (per Scrutton LJ in *Skinner* v *Geary* [1931] 2 KB 546 at p. 564).

The problem does not arise in relation to public sector secure tenants and assured tenants who can only obtain protection as to their only or principal homes (s. 81, Housing Act 1985 and s. 1, Housing Act 1988).

## 4.3   OCCUPATION AS THE TENANT'S 'ONLY OR PRINCIPAL HOME'

This requirement contrasts with the conditions of protection under the Rent Act 1977 in two respects:

(a)   there is no need for the tenant to occupy the premises during the contractual tenancy; and
(b)   occupation for the purposes of a statutory tenancy is as 'a' residence, rather than as the only or principal home.

Many of the cases under the 1977 Act in which tenants have retained their statutory tenancies in spite of lengthy absences would be decided differently under the 1988 Act. However, the *Brown* v *Brash* test (intention to return coupled with some physical sign of that intention on the premises, see **4.2.4.2**) still applies and where the tenant's absence is caused by residence somewhere other than in a different 'home', s. 1 may still be satisfied. In *Notting Hill Housing Trust* v *Etoria* [1989] CLY 1912 (in which *Brickfield Properties* v *Hughes* was applied, see **4.2.4.3**), the tenant was serving a life sentence for murder but there was a real possibility that he would be released on licence in 1995. It was held that he had retained his secure status. His intention to return was obvious from the presence of his furniture and the continued occupation of his brother.

As in the case of statutory tenancies under the Rent Act 1977, occupation by the tenant's spouse as his or her only or principal home is treated as occupation by the tenant as his or her only or principal home (s. 30(4)(b), Family Law Act 1996).

The requirement of occupation by the tenant as his or her only or principal home is the same as one of the requirements for a secure tenancy under s. 81, Housing Act 1985. However, 'the decided cases indicate that the requirement is not greatly different from the "occupation as a residence test"'. In *Crawley BC* v *Sawyer* (1988) 20 HLR 98 a weekly tenant left his council flat sometime in 1995 to live with his girlfriend in a property he was helping her to buy. The gas and electricity supplies to the flat were cut off but the tenant carried on paying the rent and rates, visited the flat about once a month, and once spent a week there. The council served a notice to quit. By the time of its expiry, the relationship between the tenant and his girlfriend had ended. He returned to the flat soon afterwards. The council brought possession proceedings. The Court of Appeal upheld the decision of the county court judge that the flat had always remained the tenant's principal home, even while he was living with his girlfriend. The tenant asserted throughout that he had every intention of returning to the flat and did not intend to give it up. It should be noted that a secure tenancy is conferred *at any time* 'the tenancy condition' is satisfied so that the tenant can move in and out of protection. Surely, however, to suggest that the flat remained the tenant's only or principal home while he was living with his girlfriend means that there is little meaningful difference between occupation as a residence and occupation as the tenant's principal home (Bridge, 1988; see too *R* v *Croydon LBC ex parte Toth* (1988) 20 HLR 576).

## 4.4   THE TENANT MUST BE AN INDIVIDUAL (s. 1, HOUSING ACT 1988)

In an attempt to avoid the Rent Acts, landlords sometimes required prospective tenants to buy 'off-the-shelf' limited companies (which licenced or authorised an individual to occupy a house or flat) to which the lease was then granted. The advantage of the arrangment from the landlord's point of view was that the company's inability to occupy the premises personally meant that it could not claim a statutory tenancy and had no security of tenure, therefore, after the contractual tenancy had expired. In *Hilton* v *Plustitle* [1988] 1 WLR 149, the fact that the company had no assets of its own and was incapable of performing the covenants other than through the occupier (who paid the rent and other outgoings) was regarded as irrelevant. The court was not entitled to hold that the whole arrangement was a 'sham' merely because the letting was to a company so as to avoid the Rent Act 1977 (see Rodgers, 1989). While the company tenant is entitled to the benefit of the fair rent provisions (*Carter* v *SU Carburetter Co. Ltd* [1942] 2 All ER 228), an application to the rent officer to fix a fair rent may, of course, result in a notice to quit.

Under the Housing Act 1988, a letting to a company cannot be an assured tenancy, nor can a letting to a company and an individual as joint tenants.

## 4.5   ASSURED SHORTHOLD TENANCIES

### 4.5.1   Introduction

An assured shorthold tenancy (AST) is a species of assured tenancy and must comply, therefore, with all the requirements for an assured tenancy set out in s. 1, Housing Act 1988. The main difference between the two types of tenancy lies in the security of tenure which tenants obtain. A landlord who seeks possession of premises let under an assured tenancy must serve a notice of seeking possession and obtain a court order on one of a number of mandatory or discretionary grounds for possession. In the case of an AST, however, provided that the landlord has served the requisite notice under s. 21, Housing Act 1988 (see **6.9.2**), possession is automatic and may be obtained through an accelerated paper procedure in the county court (see CCR Ord. 49, r. 6A).

As originally enacted, an AST was an assured tenancy which was granted for an initial fixed period of not less than six months and contained no power for the landlord to determine the tenancy within that period, other than by way of forfeiture. There was no upper limit as to its duration. By s. 20, Housing Act 1988, notice in the prescribed form (or one which was 'substantially to the like effect') that there was an AST had to be given to the tenant before entering into the agreement. Failure to serve a s. 20 notice resulted in the creation of an assured tenancy.

The 1995 White Paper described the 'procedures' which have to be gone through to create a valid AST (service by the landlord of the s. 20 notice on the tenant) as 'a trap for inexperienced landlords' which 'may deter owners of empty properties from putting them to use' (Department of the Environment, 1995: 22). It might have been thought that service of a single notice on the prospective tenant (albeit one which had to comply with the Assured Tenancies and Agricultural Occupancies (Forms) Regulations 1988, SI 1988/2203) would not be imposing too onerous a burden upon landlords, let alone deterring them from letting their empty properties. That ASTs constituted 8% of tenancies in the private rented sector in 1990, 40% in 1994/5, and some 70% in 1996 (Department of the Environment, 1995; HL Debs on Housing Bill 1996, *Hansard*, vol. 572, col.1854) suggests that most private sector landlords grasped the basic principles of AST creation without too much difficulty, but there have been a number of reported cases which demonstrate that some landlords did indeed manage to fall foul of s. 20. In *Panayi and Pyrkos* v *Roberts* (1993) 25 HLR 421 the landlords granted a tenancy of a flat for a term of 12 months from 7 November. Prior to the grant they served the tenant with a s. 20 notice in a non-prescribed form, which gave 6 May as the termination date. The Court of Appeal held that a notice with an incorrect date is not 'substantially to the like effect' as a notice with a correct date. The notice was therefore invalid and the consequence was that the tenant had been granted an assured, rather than an assured shorthold, tenancy (see Smith, 1993; *Bedding* v *McCarthy* (1993) 27 HLR 103; *Lower Street Properties* v *Jones* (1996) 28 HLR 877).

### 4.5.2 Creation of an assured shorthold tenancy

The Housing Act 1996 removes the requirement to serve prior notice so that it has become easier to let property on assured shorthold terms. Section 19A, Housing Act 1988 (inserted by s. 96, Housing Act 1996) provides that an assured tenancy which is entered into on or after the 20 April 1997 is an AST. No longer is there any requirement that the tenancy is for a fixed term. Further, an assured shorthold tenancy will arise when a fixed-term assured tenancy comes to an end in accordance with s. 5 of the 1988 Act after that date.

### 4.5.3 Exceptions

All new assured tenancies are assured shorthold tenancies unless they are made pursuant to a contract entered into before 20 April 1997 or fall within the list of exceptions contained sch. 2A to the 1988 Act (inserted by sch. 7, Housing Act 1996):

(a)  *Tenancies excluded by notice*  The landlord can still grant a fully assured tenancy but must serve prior notice on the tenant, stating that the assured tenancy is not an assured shorthold (sch. 2A, para. 1). The landlord can also choose to grant the greater security after the tenancy has been entered into (sch. 2A, para. 2). Assured tenancies are most likely to be used by registered social landlords, who are also subject to the security regime of the 1988 Act. However, when housing the homeless they will have to use assured shorthold tenancies (s. 209, Housing Act 1996).

(b) *Tenancies containing a provision*   Tenancies containing a provision to the effect that the tenancy is not an assured shorthold tenancy (sch. 2A, para. 3).

(c) *Tenancies under s. 39* (sch. 2A, para. 4)   This concerns the succession provisions under the Rent Act 1977. The first succession to a member of the deceased tenant's family and all second successions will continue to take effect as fully assured rather than assured shorthold tenancies (see **Chapter 14**).

(d) *Former secure tenancies* (sch. 2A, para. 5)   Where property is transferred from local authorities to housing associations (e.g. under large-scale voluntary transfers) or to the private sector (e.g. on the termination of a Housing Action Trust), tenants will move from being secure to assured but not assured shorthold tenants (see **Chapter 12**).

(e) *Tenancies under sch. 10 to the Local Government and Housing Act 1989* (sch. 2A, para. 6)   Where a long tenancy at a low rent expires, security of tenure is governed either by the Landlord and Tenant Act 1954, Part I, in which case the tenancy becomes a statutory tenancy under the Rent Act 1977, or by sch. 10 to the 1989 Act, in which case it becomes assured. In the latter case, such tenancies will not become ASTs.

(f) *Tenancies replacing non-shortholds* (sch. 2A, paras. 7, 8)   Where an assured tenant is offered a replacement tenancy by the landlord, the tenant may serve a prescribed form notice on the landlord that it is to be an assured shorthold tenancy.

(g) *Assured agricultural occupancies* (sch. 2A, para. 9)

### 4.5.4   Written statement of terms

Because all ASTs were formerly for a fixed term, and notice had to be served before the tenancy was entered into, nearly all assured shorthold tenancy agreements were in writing. Now that no notice need be served and no fixed term is required, an AST can be created orally. The government resisted attempts by the Opposition to require landlords to provide a written tenancy agreement for all shortholds but did concede that tenants should have the right to a written statement of certain terms of the tenancy when demanded by the tenant. Section 20A, Housing Act 1988 (inserted by s. 97, Housing Act 1996) imposes a duty on landlords to provide statements of the terms of ASTs, i.e.,

(a)   the date the tenancy began or came into being;
(b)   the rent payable and the dates on which it is payable;
(c)   any term providing for an express rent review;
(d)   if the tenancy is fixed term, its length. (s. 20A(2)).

It is a criminal offence for a landlord to fail without reasonable excuse to comply with the tenant's request within 28 days as from receipt of the notice (s. 20A(4)).

## References

Bridge, S., 'The Security of Tenure of Absent Tenants', *The Conveyancer*, vol. 52, 1988, pp. 300–305.

Department of the Environment, *Our Future Homes: Opportunity, Choice Responsibility*, Cmnd. 2901, London: HMSO, 1995.

Hand, C., 'The Statutory Tenancy: an Unrecognised Proprietory Interest', *The Conveyancer*, 1980, vol. 44, pp. 351–360.

Rodgers, C., 'Shams, Subtenancies and Evasion of Protective Legislation', *The Conveyancer*, 1989, vol. 53, pp. 196–204.

Smith, P. F., 'Not Much Deviation Allowed', *The Conveyancer*, 1993, vol. 57, pp. 301–307.

# FIVE

# Exclusions from full protection under the Rent Act 1977 and Housing Act 1988

## 5.1 INTRODUCTION

Even if a tenancy fulfils all the requirements of a protected or assured tenancy, it may nevertheless be excluded from protection by the express exceptions contained in ss. 4–16, Rent Act 1977 or sch. 1, Housing Act 1988, or one of the miscellanous exceptions set out elsewhere. This does not necessarily mean, however, that the tenant is completely unprotected. For example, lettings made before 15 January 1989 by a resident landlord or where the rent includes payments for board and attendance may be restricted contracts under the Rent Act 1977, while tenants of properties outside the rateable value limits may have rights to stay in occupation at the end of the contractual term of the lease, or to extend the lease, or even to buy the freehold (see the Landlord and Tenant Act 1954, Part I; Leasehold Reform Act 1967; s. 186, Local Government and Housing Act 1989; the Leasehold Reform, Housing and Urban Development Act 1993; and ss. 105–119 and schs. 9–11, Housing Act 1996).

## 5.2 EXCLUSIONS FROM THE STATUS OF PROTECTED TENANCY

Such is the extent of the protection afforded by the Rent Acts to regulated tenants that landlords and their advisers have displayed considerable ingenuity in using some of the exceptions in order to circumvent their provisions. 'Every time Parliament acts to protects tenants from excessive rents or eviction at the whim of a landlord, the more cunning and unscrupulous landlords embark on the search for loopholes in the law' (*Hansard*, 1974, vol. 896, col. 297).

From 1920 until 1974, full Rent Act protection was reserved for unfurnished tenancies. If rent for a dwelling included payment for the use of furniture, then the tenancy would be a furnished letting within the jurisdiction of the rent tribunal which merely had the powers to set a reasonable rent and to postpone a notice to quit. Many landlords sought to exploit this exception by supplying linoleum (*Wilkes* v *Goodwin* [1923] 2 KB 86) or a few sticks of second-hand furniture. In *Woodward* v *Docherty* [1974] 2 All ER 844, Scarman LJ observed (at p. 846) that the housing shortage, which had existed since 1914, could force a tenant 'to accept furniture he does not want in order to obtain accommodation he desperately needs, even though by accepting it he loses security of tenure which he would dearly love to have.' He also remarked on the ready availability of 'furniture of a sort, capable in a way of furnishing flats and rooms . . . available at junk shops and other emporia at no very great price.'

The Rent Act 1974 brought furnished tenancies into the full protection of the Rent Acts, thereby blocking off a convenient escape route for landlords. It also introduced the exceptions in respect of:

(a)  student lettings by educational institutions;
(b)  holiday lettings; and
(c)  resident landlords.

A few years later it was observed that 'the exceptions granted in the 1974 Act towards certain kinds of tenancies and services have now become the new loopholes of today' (Stafford, 1978: 103). A particularly popular ploy was the so-called 'holiday let' (the locations of the properties concerned being places such as Brixton, Lambeth and East Ham) for which landlords required references from employers, parents and banks (Weir, 1975).

Some landlords utilised the exclusion which applied where the dwelling-house was let in good faith at a rent which included payments in respect of board and attendance (s. 7, Rent Act 1977). Usually such tenancies constituted restricted contracts. If, however, the payments for board formed a substantial proportion of the rent, the tenancy was outside the Act altogether. The Acts contain no definition of 'board' and in *Wilkes* v *Goodwin* [1923] 2 KB 86 at p. 110 Younger LJ used the dictionary defintion of 'daily meals provided in a lodging or boarding house according to stipulation; the supply of daily provisions. ' In his opinion, it suggested sufficiency: 'a provision by the landlord of such food as in the case of a particular tenancy would ordinarily be consumed at daily meals and would be obtained and prepared by the tenant himself, if it were not provided for by somebody else.' However, the majority in that case (Banks and Scrutton LJ) considered that, subject to the *de minimis* rule, any amount of board would do. In *R* v *Battersea, Wandsworth, Mitcham and Wimbledon Rent Tribunal, ex parte Parikh* [1957] 1 WLR 410 Lord Goddard even went so far as to suggest (obiter) that a sandwich would count as 'board.' Megarry, cited with approval by the House of Lords in *Otter* v *Norman* [1989] AC 129; [1988] 3 WLR 321, stated that 'in practice the dividing line appears to fall between the early morning cup of tea on the one hand and "bed and breakfast" on the other.' Many landlords took the view that raw provisions were sufficient to constitute 'board' and contracted, therefore, to provide their tenants 'with a weekly box of groceries containing such items as milk, cornflakes, bread and eggs' (Waite, 1981: 460).

In *Otter* v *Norman* the House of Lords held that a breakfast of two bread rolls with butter, jam and marmalade, unlimited tea or coffee with milk and sugar, additional milk for cornflakes (which the tenant provided himself), and a glass of milk which the tenant drank in his own room amounted to 'board' since anything more than *de minimis* excluded the tenancy from protection. Even though the meal was a modest one, its regularity of serving prevented any finding of bad faith. Given the uncertainty over the status of residential licences raised by *Street* v *Mountford* [1985] 2 All ER 289, it was suggested that the decision in *Otter* v *Norman* would lead to board and attendance achieving new significance as a means of avoiding the 1977 Act (Rodgers, 1988: 642). On the other hand, as Lord Bridge commented (at p. 901), serving even such a modest daily meal as the continental breakfast was hardly likely to appeal to the unscrupulous landlord as a soft option. It would involve not only the cost of the food and drink provided but also shopping for provisions, preparation and service of meals on the premises and cleaning and washing up afterwards.

It is difficult to ascertain the extent to which agreements were manipulated so as to give the appearance of coming within one of the statutory exclusions, but a survey in 1976 found that the landlords of 48% of the sampled lettings had altered their lettings policies as a result of the Rent Act 1974. Of these, 15% would only be relet on licence agreements or 'rent-free', 14% would only be let on holiday agreements and a further 16% no longer provided furniture (Paley, 1978).

## 5.3   EXCLUSIONS FROM THE STATUS OF ASSURED TENANCY

The exclusions contained in the Housing Act 1988 bear a close resemblance to those of the Rent Act 1977, but they are not identical. In particular, a letting which includes payments in respect of board or attendance can be an assured tenancy so long as all the other conditions are satisfied. Nor does the list of exclusions contained in sch. 1 to the Housing Act 1988 mention 'shared ownership leases' which were expressly excluded from Rent Act protection (s. 5A, Rent Act 1977, added by s. 18, sch. 4, para. 1, Housing and Planning Act 1986). The shared ownership lease was a method by which sitting tenants could buy council houses on an instalment basis under the 'right to buy' legislation (see **Chapter 11**). The object of excluding such leases from the Rent Act 1977 was to ensure that the tenant could not rely on the Act instead of the terms of the lease if, for example, the tenant were to default. Such tenancies could not in any event be protected tenancies by reasons of ss. 14 and 15, Rent Act 1977 (see **5.4.10**) as they were restricted to tenants of local authorities and other bodies whose tenants were secure tenants under the Housing Act 1985.

The general rule is that tenancies entered into before 15 January 1989, the date on which Part I, Housing Act 1988 came into force, or pursuant to a contract made before that date, cannot be assured (sch. 1, para. 1). This point is emphasised by sch. 1, para. 13 which provides that tenancies granted before the commencement of the Housing Act 1988 which qualify as protected tenancies under the Rent Act 1977, housing association tenancies under Part IV of the 1977 Act, or secure tenancies under the Housing Act 1985, or where a person is a protected occupier under the Rent (Agriculture) Act 1976, are not assured tenancies. Such tenancies continue to be governed by their old regimes. However, s. 38 of the 1988 Act provides that tenants who move from the public to the private sector, under Part III or IV of the Housing Act 1988 or by large-scale voluntary transfers, become assured tenants on transfer regardless of the dates their tenancies were entered into.

If a local authority enters into an arrangement with a private landlord or housing association to discharge its interim duties to homeless households under s. 188, 190, 200, or 204(4), Housing Act 1996, the tenancy cannot be an assured tenancy for 12 months unless the landlord notifies the tenant that the tenancy is to be regarded as an assured or an assured shorthold tenancy (s. 209(2), Housing Act 1996).

Provided that it does not amount to a sham, an exclusion can legitimately be employed as an avoidance device. In *Samrose Properties* v *Gibbard* [1958] 1 WLR 235, Lord Evershed accepted that 'a landlord is entitled to arrange his affairs (so) that the legal result will bring him outside the statutory provisions.... If they fail, that does not, therefore, reflect on the ethics of their business methods' (at p. 504). However, there is little point in landlords and their advisers trying to avoid the Housing Act 1988. Assured shorthold tenancies (which have become even easier to create since the Housing Act 1996 came into effect) give tenants virtually no security of tenure. The exceptions to the 1988 Act are, therefore, much more likely to cover genuine situations, rather than those which have been manipulated to fit them, as was often the case under the Rent Acts.

## 5.4   EXCLUSIONS APPLICABLE TO BOTH THE RENT ACT 1977 AND THE HOUSING ACT 1988

### 5.4.1   Tenancy of a dwelling-house outside rateable value limits (s. 4, Rent Act 1977; sch. 1, para. 2, Housing Act 1988)

Although some Rent Acts brought virtually all tenancies under control (see **Chapter 2**), statutory protection has not generally applied to the most expensive housing. Tenants who can afford to rent more expensive housing are usually in a better position to negotiate their own terms. The Rent Acts function, therefore, as 'Parliament's recognition of tenants' weaknesses as negotiators and their inability to buy a fair bargain' (Nicol, 1981: 37).

To enjoy statutory protection, a tenancy granted prior to 1 April 1990 must fall within certain rateable value limits. Domestic rating was abolished on 1 April 1990 and replaced by the community charge, itself since replaced by council tax. A tenancy granted after that date will be protected or assured if the rent payable for the time being does not exceed £25,000 per annum (s. 4, Rent Act 1977 as amended by SI 1990/434, pursuant to s. 149, Local Government and Housing Act 1989). Since, with very few exceptions, no new protected tenancies can be created after 15 January 1989, the rental value limits will rarely be applicable to tenancies created under the Rent Act 1977.

### 5.4.2 Tenancy at no/low rent (s. 5(1), Rent Act 1977; sch. 1, para. 3, Housing Act 1988)

Again a distinction must be made between tenancies granted before 1 April 1990 and those granted afterwards. As regards the former, a tenancy will not be protected or assured if either no rent is payable or the rent payable is less than two-thirds of the rateable value on the appropriate day. In respect of post-1990 protected tenancies, the minimum annual rent payable is at least £1,000 in Greater London or £250 elsewhere.

Two types of situation are covered by this exclusion. The first is where the tenant is being allowed to occupy the property rent-free or for a nominal payment. No doubt this has something to do with the fact that the Rent Acts have always dealt first and foremost with rent control, and only secondarily with security of tenure. As to what consitutes rent for the purpose of the 1977 and 1988 Acts, see **3.3.3.1**. A rent-free tenancy granted after the commencement of the Housing Act 1988 is an 'excluded tenancy' for the purposes of the Protection from Eviction Act 1977, see **7.5.1**.

The second type of situation in which the exclusion operates is where the tenant has bought a long lease of the property for a lump sum or premium and pays only a small, annual ground rent. The payment of premiums or the making of loans as a condition of the grant, renewal, continuance or assignment of a Rent Act protected tenancy is unlawful, and anyone who requires or receives such a premium or a loan commits a criminal offence (ss. 119, 120, Rent Act 1977). An established exception to this general rule applies to long tenancies (defined in s. 2(4), Landlord and Tenant Act 1954, as terms certain exceeding 21 years). Most long tenancies will be excluded from Rent Act protection by virtue of being at a low rent but where the rent is sufficiently high, so that the tenancy is protected, premiums and loans will be lawful as long as the conditions listed in s. 127 of the Rent Act 1977 (as amended by s. 115, Housing Act 1988) are satisfied.

The Housing Act 1988 contains no prohibition on the demand of a premium prior to entry into an assured tenancy and it is left to the market to dictate whether premiums an be charged as part of the consideration for the tenancy being granted. However, an attempt to avoid regulation by charging the tenant a large sum on entering into the tenancy while reserving only a low rent might be viewed as a pretence and ineffective to exclude protection. In *Samrose Properties Ltd* v *Gibbard* [1958] 1 WLR 235, the tenant paid a large premium for the grant of a fixed term of one year's duration, and then a quarterly rent which was less than two-thirds of the rateable value of the dwelling-house. In the written agreement the landlord stated that it did not wish to grant a lease to which the Rent Acts would apply. The Court of Appeal held that the premium should be added to the annual total of the quarterly rent to calculate the annual rent. On this basis, the tenant was entitled to the protection of the Rent Acts.

### 5.4.3 Tenancy of dwelling-house let with other land (s. 26, Rent Act 1977; sch. 1, para. 6, Housing Act 1988)

Under both the Rent Act 1977 and the Housing Act 1988 special provision is made where the dwelling-house is let together with land other than the site of the dwelling-house. If the main purpose of the letting is to provide a home for the tenant or, where there is a joint tenancy, at least one of the joint tenants, then the other land will be treated as part of the dwelling-house. It will not be protected or assured, however, if it consists of agricultural land exceeding two acres in extent. Most of the case law has dealt with mixed lettings of business and residential property. In *Feyereisel* v *Parry* [1952] 2 QB 29, the Rent Act was held not to apply to the letting of a campsite which included a bungalow, because the bungalow was an adjunct to the campsite.

### 5.4.4 Lettings to students (s. 8, Rent Act 1977; sch. 1, para. 8, Housing Act 1988)

If students had protected or assured tenancies they would be able to stay in halls of residence even after their courses had come to an end, leaving little or no accommodation available for new students. The 1977 and 1988 Acts provide therefore that a tenancy granted to a person who is pursuing (or who intends to pursue) a course of study at a specified educational institution is not protected or assured if it is granted either by the institution itself or by another specified institution or body of persons. Specified educational institutions include all universities and publicly funded establishments of further education and certain other associated bodies (Assured and Protected Tenancies (Lettings to Students) Regulations 1988, SI 1988/1683). It has been pointed out that the phrase 'person who is pursuing or intends to purse a course of study' is not necessarily an apt description for all students so that an objective test should be applied, rather than one 'which might be an incentive for constructive laziness' (Farrand, 1974).

Private landlords may also utilise the exclusion by letting premises to a university or college which in turn sub-lets to its students. Under the Rent Act 1977 the head tenancy might be protected (enabling use to be made of the fair rent provisions), but no statutory tenancy could arise on the termination of the contractual tenancy because the institution would be incapable of residing on the premises. As far as the Housing Act 1988 is concerned, a letting to an educational institution for sub-letting to students cannot be an assured tenancy because the tenant is not an individual. It may also be that the letting is subject to the rules on business tenancies contained in the Landlord and Tenant Act 1954, Part II. In *Groveside Properties Ltd* v *Westminster Medical School* (1984) 47 P & CR 507 the landlord let a furnished flat to the school to be occupied by its students. The school paid the outgoings, kept the keys and its secretary frequently visited the premises. It was held that the school had the necessary degree of occupation and was running a business for the purpose of the 1954 Act. It is possible too that there is no letting as a 'separate' dwelling (*St Catherine's College* v *Dowling* [1979] 3 All ER 250, see **3.3.4**).

Mandatory grounds for possession apply under both Acts to the letting of the premises during vacations (see **Chapter 6**).

### 5.4.5 Holiday lettings (s. 9, Rent Act 1977; sch. 1, para. 9, Housing Act 1988)

Lettings for the purpose of conferring on the tenant the right to occupy the dwelling-house for a holiday were first excluded in 1974. The object of this exclusion is to enable landlords to let out premises for a holiday and to recover possession of them when it is over. Such lettings fell outside full Rent Act protection and the provisions regarding restricted contracts (s. 19(7)). As a result, landlords who could show that their tenants were 'holiday-makers' were given the opportunity 'to operate in the uncontrolled free market' (Lyons, 1984: 286). Not surprisingly, this led to 'a remarkable boom in holday lets in places not noted for the quality of their waters or the mildness of their sea breeze' (Widdison, 1982: 29).

The leading case on the effectiveness of 'artificial' holiday lets is *Buchmann* v *May* [1978] 2 All ER 993. Mrs May, a New Zealand national, had a residence permit to live in Great Britain until December 1974. In October 1974 she agreed with Mr Buchmann to take a further three-month letting of premises in Norbury which she and her husband and child had occupied for about two years under a series of short lets. The tenancy agreement stated that the letting was 'solely for the purpose of the tenant's holiday in the London area'. At the end of the tenancy she refused to vacate, claiming that she had a protected tenancy. In reasoning typical of pre-*Street* v *Mountford* cases, the Court of Appeal felt that it could not look beyond the actual agreement; the statement it contained as to the purpose of the letting prevailed. While the court should be on its guard to detect a sham, the onus was on the tenant to establish that a provision had been inserted so as to deprive him or her of Rent Act protection; it was not for the landlord to establish that the purpose expressed in the agreement was the true purpose. Whether or not the letting in *Buchmann* was in fact a sham is unclear: Mrs May was in the country on a series of temporary resident permits, she had been abroad for several months before signing the disputed agreement and had told the landlord that she wished to stay in England for only two months more.

As there is no statutory definition of 'holiday', the Court of Appeal in *Buchmann* v *May* resorted to the definition given in the *Shorter Oxford English Dictionary* of 'a period of cessation from work or a period of recreation.' It has been held in the county court that a working holiday can come within the definition of a holiday (*McHale* v *Daneham* (1979) 249 EG 969). However, in *R* v *Rent Officer for London Borough of Camden, ex parte Plant* (1981) 257 EG 713, it was held that the landlord could not have intended a genuine six month holiday letting because he knew that the prospective occupiers were student nurses. In *Francke* v *Hakmi* [1984] CLY 1906 it was said that:

> a holiday is a temporary suspension of one's normal activity not necessarily implying a period of recreation. A temporary suspension involves such a period of time as would indicate that one intends to resume one's normal activity at its conclusion and that period is not so long as to imply that another activity had taken its place (see Lyons, 1984).

A holday letting granted after 15 January 1989 is an excluded tenancy so that the court order and four-week notice-to-quit rules contained in ss. 3 and 5 of the Protection from Eviction Act 1977 do not apply. It is lawful, therefore, for the landlord to recover possession, once the tenancy has expired, without an order of the court.

Off-season lets of holiday accommodation may be protected or assured but are subject to mandatory grounds for possession (Rent Act 1977, sch. 15, Part II, Case 13; Housing Act 1988, sch. 2, Ground 3) provided the landlord complies with a notice requirement and the letting is for a term not exceeding eight months (see **6.8.2.8**).

### 5.4.6 Tenancies of agricultural holdings (s. 10, Rent Act 1977; sch. 1, para. 7, Housing Act 1988)

A tenancy is not protected or assured if the dwelling-house is comprised in an agricultural holding (within the meaning of the Agricultural Holdings Act 1986) or in a farm business tenancy (within the meaning of the Agricultural Tenancies Act 1995) and is occupied by the person responsible for the control of the farming or management of the holding, whether as a tenant or the tenant's employee or agent.

### 5.4.7 Licensed premises (s. 11, Rent Act 1977; sch. 1, para. 5, Housing Act 1988)

A tenancy of a dwelling-house which consists of or comprises premises licensed for the sale of intoxicating liquors for consumption on the premises (e.g. a public house) cannot be a regulated or assured tenancy. However, since the introduction of the Landlord and Tenant (Licensed Premises Act) 1990, a tenancy of licensed premises will probably be a business tenancy under the Landlord and Tenant Act 1954, Part II.

### 5.4.8 Lettings by resident landlords (s. 12, Rent Act 1977; sch. 1, Para.10, Housing Act 1988)

The resident landlord exemption was introduced by the Rent Act 1974 to encourage owners to let any spare rooms in their homes safe in the knowledge that 'they will be able to recover possession at the end of the contractual tenancy (as they may very understandably wish to do so should the tenant prove incompatible) and to enable them to sell what is probably their major asset with vacant possession' (*Barnett* v *O'Sullivan* [1995] 04 EG 141, per Hirst LJ at p. 143). It was also intended to avoid 'that sort of social embarrassment arising out of close proximity which the landlord had accepted in the belief that he could bring it to an end at any time allowed by the contract of the tenancy' (*Bardrick* v *Haycock* (1976) 31 P & CR 420, per Scarman LJ. See too *Cooper* v *Tait* (1984) 48 P & CR 460 at p. 462 per Eveleigh LJ). Further impetus has been given to the letting of spare rooms by home owners by 'rent a room relief' (introduced by the Finance (No. 2) Act 1992, s. 59 and sch. 10) which permits rent to be received from the lettings of furnished accommodation in the landlord's only or main residence free from income tax up to a limit of £3,250. About one household in every hundred has lodgers (Department of the Environment, 1995: 204).

Tenancies granted on or after 14 August 1974 (but before 15 January 1989) are not protected under the Rent Act 1977 if the following conditions are all satisfied:

(a)   the dwelling-house forms part only of a building and, *except in a case where the dwelling-house also forms part of a flat,* the building is not a purpose-built block of flats; and
(b)   at the grant of the tenancy the landlord occupied as his or her residence another dwelling forming part of the building; and
(c)   at all times since the grant of the tenancy the landlord (or successor) has occupied as his or her residence another dwelling forming part of the building.

The words in italics were added by s. 65, Housing Act 1980 so that the resident landlord exception also applies (as to tenancies granted on or after 28 November 1980) where the landlord lives in an individual flat in a purpose-built block and has let off part of that flat to a tenant. If, however, a landlord owns all or several flats in a purpose-built block, occupying one and letting the others, the resident landlord exception does not apply.

Purpose-built blocks are excluded because, in accordance with *Bardrick v Haycock*, they are likely to be places where the occupiers lead separate lives. A purpose-built block of flats is one which as originally constructed contained, and now contains, two or more flats (Rent Act 1977, sch. 2, para. 4). Thus, in *Barnes v Gorsuch* (1982) 43 P & CR 294 a house which had been converted into flats did not satisfy the definition. However, it might be possible to argue that the identity of the building has changed where, for example, it was completely gutted and rebuilt inside.

There is no statutory definition of the term 'building'. In *Bardrick v Haycock* the landlord lived in an extension which had its own entrance and no means of internal communication with the main house which had been converted into flats. The Court of Appeal upheld the county court decision that the extension and house did not comprise one building and the resident landlord exemption did not, therefore, apply. In *Griffiths v English* (1981) 2 HLR 126, an extension had been built on either side of the main house which was divided into flats. The landlord lived in one extension and the tenant lived in the other. The Court of Appeal held that, despite the absence of any internal communication, there was the necessary element of close proximity which the exclusion was designed to avoid. That the appearance was that of one building and had once been in single occupation, and the absence of separate gardens for the main house and the extensions were all material facts which the trial judge was entitled to take into account. In *Wolf v Waddington* (1989) 22 HLR 72 the Court of Appeal declined to interfere with the judge's finding that an extension on the first floor of a property which was partly above a garage and partly above the ground floor of the house was part of the same building even though the extension was self-contained and had its own entrance and an alleyway ran at ground level between the two parts of the house. See too *Lewis-Graham and Lewis-Graham v Canachar* (1992) 24 HLR 132.

As regards occupation by the landlord as a residence, reference should be made to the case law on residence for the purpose of a statutory tenancy under the Rent Acts. As a result, liberal interpretations of the residence requirement which operate in the tenant's favour, namely the 'two homes' cases, can be used in this context by the landlord.

The requirement of continuous residential occupation by the landlord is relaxed where the building is sold or transferred to trustees, or vested in the landlord's personal representatives after his or her death. The relevant provisions are contained in paras. 1(a) and (b) and para. 2A of sch. 2 to the 1977 Act and Part 3 of sch. 1 to the 1988 Act.

The conditions of the resident landlord exemption under the Housing Act 1988 are very similar to the resident landlord provisions of the Rent Act 1977. However, they differ in three significant respects:

(a)   The landlord can only satisfy the residence requirements (at the grant and subsequently) if he or she occupies a dwelling in the same building as 'his only or principal home' (sch. 1, para. 10(1)(b), (c), Housing Act 1988). Thus, in contrast to the position under the Rent Act 1977, a landlord cannot establish resident landlord status in respect of more than one home.

(b)   The tenant of a resident landlord under the 1977 Act enjoyed the protection of a restricted contract. Restricted contracts cannot be created after the commencement of the 1988 Act, and a tenancy granted by a resident landlord after that date cannot be assured. The court order and notice to quit requirements of ss. 3 and 5 of the Protection from Eviction Act 1977 will nevertheless apply.

(c)   A tenancy granted after the commencement of the 1988 Act will be an excluded tenancy if the tenant shares accommodation with the landlord or a member of his or her family. Sections 3 and 5 of the Protection from Eviction Act 1977 will not apply. This means that once the tenancy has expired, the landlord may lawfully recover possession without having to take court proceedings.

### 5.4.9   Crown lettings (s. 13, Rent Act 1977, as amended by s. 73, Housing Act 1980; sch. 1, para. 11, Housing Act 1988)

Where the property is owned by the Crown or by a government department, a residential letting cannot be protected or assured. However, this does not apply to lettings by the Crown Estate Commissioners.

### 5.4.10   Lettings by (quasi-) public bodies (ss. 14, 15 and 16, Rent Act 1977; sch. 1, para. 12, Housing Act 1988)

Lettings by local authorities, housing associations and housing cooperatives cannot be protected tenancies under the Rent Act 1977. Before the Housing Act 1988 came into force most such lettings were secure tenancies governed by the Housing Act 1985. It should be noted, however, that as from 15 January 1989, new lettings by housing associations are generally assured tenancies governed by the Housing Act 1988.

**5.4.11   Business tenancies (s. 24(3), Rent Act 1977; Housing Act 1988, sch. 1, para. 4)**

As stated in **3.3.3.2**, s. 24(3), Rent Act 1977 provides that a tenancy cannot be regulated if it is a tenancy to which Part II of the Landlord and Tenant Act 1954 applies. However, the fair rent provisions contained in the Rent Act 1977 meant that it would be to the tenant's advantage to establish that he or she was a protected tenant, even though he or she used the premises for the purposes of a business. The exclusion loses its significance under the Housing Act 1988 as landlords are able to charge a market rent under both regimes. The procedure for obtaining possession of premises let on a business tenancy is highly technical and fraught with pitfalls: it may be that a tenant may on advice see himself or herself in a stronger bargaining position as a business tenant than as an assured tenant.

## 5.5   MISCELLANEOUS EXCEPTIONS

### 5.5.1   Tenancies of overcrowded dwellings

Section 101, Rent Act 1977 provides that at any time when a dwelling-house is overcrowded within the meaning of the Housing Act 1985 (see **16.6**), in such circumstances as to render the occupier guilty of an offence, nothing in the Act shall prevent the immediate landlord from obtaining possession. The tenant is deprived of his or her security while overcrowding lasts, but rent control still applies until such time as a possession order is made.

Overcrowding is not dealt with in the Housing Act 1988 in relation to assured tenancies.

### 5.5.2   Parsonage houses

Church of England parsonage houses are excluded from the Rent Act 1977 and presumably from the Housing Act 1988 by virtue of the Pluralities Act 1838 (*Bishop of Gloucester* v *Cunnington* [1943] 1 All ER 101). There is no such exception in respect of other denominations, although both the 1977 and 1988 Acts provide mandatory grounds for possession where the dwelling is held for the purpose of being available for occupation by a minister of religion, and is required for such occupation.

### 5.5.3   Tenancies granted by mortgagor without consent of mortgagee

A lease which is granted by a mortgagor whose statutory power of leasing is excluded or curtailed, binds the landlord and tenant. However, the tenant will not be protected as against a prior legal mortgagee by the Rent Act 1977 and the Housing Act 1988 (*Dudley and District Benefit Building Society* v *Emerson* [1949] 2 All ER 252).

## References

Department of the Environment, *Our Future Homes: Opportunity, Choice, Responsibility*, Cmnd 2901, London: HMSO, 1995.

Farrand, J.T., *The Rent Act 1997 [and] The Protection from Eviction Act 1997*, London: Sweet & Maxwell, 1978.

Lyons, T.J., 'The Meaning of Holiday under the Rent Acts', *The Conveyancer*, 1984, pp. 286–295.

Nicol, A., 'Outflanking Protective Legislation — Shams and Beyond', *Modern Law Review*, 1981, vol. 44, pp. 21–39.

Paley, B., *Attitudes to Letting in 1976*, London: HMSO, 1978.

Rodgers, C.P., 'Making a Meal out of the Rent Acts: Board, Attendance and the Protected Tenancy', *Modern Law Review*, 1988, vol. 51, pp. 642–651.

Stafford, D.C., *The Economics of Housing Policy*, London: Croom Helm, 1978.

Waite, A., 'Dodging the Rent Acts', *New Law Journal*, 1981, vol. 131, pp. 460–462.

Weir, A., 'Landlords Exploit Rent Act Loopholes', *Roof*, October 1975, pp. 11–14.

Widdison, R., 'Plugging Loopholes in the Rent Act', *Roof*, March/April 1982, pp. 29–31.

# SIX

# Repossession under the Rent Act 1977 and Housing Act 1988

### 6.1  INTRODUCTION

Both the Rent Act 1977 and the Housing Act 1988 give the tenant security of tenure by preventing the landlord from exercising his or her common law right to end the tenancy. Under both regimes, the landlord can only regain possession of the premises with a court order. This will be granted if the landlord:

(a)  in the case of a Rent Act regulated tenant, provides suitable alternative accommodation, or establishes one or more of the grounds for possession contained in sch. 15 to the 1977 Act;

(b)  in the case of an assured tenant, establishes one or more of the grounds for possession listed in sch. 2 to the 1988 Act;

(c)  in the case of an assured shorthold tenant, establishes one or more of the grounds for possession in sch. 2 to the 1988 Act or serves notice under s. 21.

### 6.2  RENT ACT 1977: BASIC PRINCIPLES

A court cannot make an order for possession of a dwelling-house which is let on a protected tenancy or subject to a statutory tenancy unless it considers it reasonable to make such an order and either:

(a)  it is satisfied that suitable alternative accommodation is available for the tenant or will be when the order in question takes effect; or

(b)  the circumstances are as specified in any of the Cases in Part I of sch. 15 to the Rent Act 1977 (s. 98(1)).

The court must make an order for possession if the circumstances of the case are as specified in any of the Cases in Part II of sch. 15 (s. 98(2)).

### 6.2.1 Contracting out

It is well established that the parties cannot contract out of the Rent Acts; to do so would mean ousting the jurisdiction of the court under s. 98. Thus, in *Barton v Fincham* [1921] 2 KB 291 it was held that an order for possession could not be made against the tenant, even though he had freely agreed in writing to give up possession on a certain day and had received payment in return. It was emphasised that the statutory fetter had been placed not upon the landlord's action but upon the court's:

> Parties cannot by agreement give the Courts jurisdiction which the Legislature has enacted they are not to have (per Atkin LJ at p. 299).

In *R v Bloomsbury & Marylebone County Court, ex parte Blackburne* (1984) 14 HLR 56; (1985) 275 EG 1273, it was held that the court could not make a consent order for possession of a dwelling-house subject to a statutory tenancy unless the judge had obtained from the tenant or his legal representative the concession that the tenant was not entitled to the protection of the Rent Acts (see too *R v Newcastle upon Tyne County Court, ex parte Thompson* (1988) 20 HLR 430; (1988) 26 EG 112). In *Appleton v Aspin* (1988) 20 HLR 182; (1988) 04 EG 123, an agreement by the protected tenant to give up possession to an intending purchaser was held to be rendered inoperative by s. 98(1). In *Woolwich v Dickman* [1996] 3 All ER 204, consent forms signed by protected tenants agreeing that a subsequent mortgage should take priority over their tenancy were held to be ineffective for the same reason.

### 6.2.2 Termination by the tenant

If the protected tenancy is brought to an end by notice to quit served by the tenant upon the landlord or by surrender, and the tenant vacates the property with the intention of ceasing to reside there, there is no need for the landlord to bring possession proceedings. If, however, the tenant continues to occupy the dwelling-house as a residence, a statutory tenancy comes into being. If, in the latter scenario, the landlord has contracted to sell or to lease the property in reliance on the tenant's notice to quit, Case 5 gives him or her — on satisfying certain conditions — the opportunity to apply to the court for an order for possession.

A tenancy may be surrendered by express agreement or by operation of law (implied surrender). If the term is for more than three years, an express surrender must be by deed (s. 52, Law of Property Act 1925); otherwise it must be in writing (s. 53(1), Law of Property Act 1925). It must operate immediately and and cannot be expressed to take effect on a future date. A surrender by operation of law arises where there is unequivocal conduct of the parties which is inconsistent with the continuation of an existing tenancy and their behaviour makes it inequitable for one of the parties to claim that a tenancy still exists. Examples of surrender by operation of law occur where the tenant agrees to give up the tenancy, in consequence of which the landlord resumes possession of the premises (*Phene* v *Popplewell* (1862) 12 CB(NS) 334) the tenant is absent from the premises for a lengthy period and owes a substantial amount of rent (*Preston BC* v *Fairclough* (1983) 8 HLR 70) the tenant returns the keys to the the landlord who, a few days later, demolishes the building (*Furnival* v *Grove* (1860) 8 CB(NS) 496, cf. *Boynton-Wood* v *Trueman* (1961) 177 EG 191 in which the landlord took the keys to carry out repairs), a new lease is created between landlord and tenant or between the landlord and a third party with the tenant's agreement (*Lyon* v *Read* (1844) 13 M & W 285; *Wallis* v *Hands* [1893] 2 Ch 75).

## 6.3  HOUSING ACT 1988: BASIC PRINCIPLES

Security of tenure is provided for assured tenants by ss. 5 and 7, Housing Act 1988 which are modelled on the method of conferring security under the Housing Act 1985, Part IV (see **Chapter 10**).

An assured tenancy cannot be brought to an end by the landlord except by an order of the court (s. 5(1)). If an assured tenancy which is a fixed-term tenancy comes to an end otherwise than by virtue of:

(a)    an order of the court; or
(b)    a surrender or other action on the part of the tenant;

then a statutory periodic tenancy comes into being (s. 5(2)). The court cannot make an order for possession of a dwelling-house let on an assured tenancy except on one or more of the grounds set out in sch. 2 to the Act (s. 7(1)).

### 6.3.1  Contracting out

Any surrender, notice to quit or other document executed, signed or given by the tenant, before or at the time the tenancy is entered into, to bring the tenancy to an end in the future, will be of no effect (s. 5(5)). Any attempt to contract out after the date of the tenancy will probably be unenforceable by the landlord, the same rules applying to attempts by the parties to oust the jurisdiction of the court under s. 7(1) as those which apply in relation to s. 98, Rent Act 1977. If, however, the tenancy cases to be assured (for example where the tenant ceases to occupy the property as his or her only or principal home), the landlord may terminate it under the general law by notice to quit.

### 6.3.2  Termination by the tenant

Section 5(2) of the Act specifically allows for the termination of a fixed-term tenancy by 'surrender or other action on the part of the tenant.' A periodic assured tenancy can be terminated by a tenant's notice to quit given at any time, provided that the tenant complies with the Protection from Eviction Act 1977.

## 6.4    TERMINATION BY THE LANDLORD

### 6.4.1    Rent Act 1977

First, any contractual tenancy must be brought to an end at common law, by notice to quit (in the case of a periodic tenancy) or effluxion of time or forfeiture (in the case of a fixed-term tenancy). In proceedings to forfeit a Rent Act protected tenancy, the judge has to decide whether the lease should be forfeited and, if appropriate, whether relief should be given. If the lease is forfeited, a statutory tenancy is created. The judge should then consider whether a Rent Act ground for possession has been proved.

Once the contractual tenancy has been terminated, a statutory tenancy arises (s. 2). Where the landlord is seeking to recover possession from a person who is already a statutory tenant, a notice to quit is not necessary but a failure to warn the tenant, by, e.g. a letter before action, may affect the issue of reasonableness if possession is sought on a discretionary ground.

A landlord will be able to obtain an order for possession only if:

(a)    he or she can satisfy the court that suitable alternative accommodation is available for the tenant and the court considers it reasonable to make an order for possession; or

(b)    he or she can establish one or more of the discretionary cases listed in sch. 15, Part I and the court considers it reasonable to make an order for possession; or

(c)    he or she can establish one or more of the mandatory cases listed in sch. 15, Part II.

### 6.4.2    Housing Act 1988

**6.4.2.1    Fixed-term tenancies**    Possession during the currency of the fixed term can only be sought if the terms of the tenancy make provision for it to be brought to an end prematurely by a right of re-entry by way of forfeiture, determination by notice or otherwise and even then only on certain grounds, i.e., Ground 2, 8 or 10–15 (s. 7(6), Housing Act 1988). A landlord will nearly always reserve a right of re-entry for the tenant's breach of covenant.

The other principal mechanism for bringing a fixed-term tenancy to an end before its expiry date is a break clause. Break clauses entitle the landlord (or the tenant) to terminate the tenancy by notice at specific intervals during the term. Operation of the break clause by the tenant will be effective to terminate the tenancy. Operation by the landlord, however, results in the fixed-term tenancy ending on the date specified in the landlord's notice and a statutory periodic tenancy arising. This statutory periodic tenancy can be terminated only by an order of the court, the landlord having proved to the court's satisfaction one or more of the specified grounds for possession.

**6.4.2.2    Statutory periodic tenancies**    When a fixed-term assured tenancy comes to an end other than by order of the court or by action by the tenant, a statutory periodic assured tenancy automatically arises. The terms of the statutory periodic tenancy are the same as those of the tenancy which immediately preceded it (s. 5) but the landlord may vary them within the first complete year of the statutory periodic tenancy coming into being (s. 6). A qualified covenant against sub-letting or assignment is implied into every periodic assured tenancy, whether statutory or not (s. 15). The statutory periodic tenancy will continue until the landlord obtains an order for possession under s. 21, or a new assured or assured shorthold tenancy is granted to the tenant of the same or substantially the same dwelling-house (s. 5(4)). Where the fixed term is granted after 28 February 1997, the statutory periodic tenancy which arises on its termination under s. 5 will be an assured shorthold, provided that it does not fall within any of the exceptions contained in sch. 2A to the 1988 Act (s. 19A, Housing Act 1988).

**6.4.2.3  Periodic tenancies**   A landlord cannot terminate a periodic assured tenancy by serving a notice to quit. A periodic assured tenancy (whether contractual or statutory) can only be brought to an end by the landlord obtaining an order of the court (s. 5(1)). First, however, a s. 8 notice must be served.

**6.4.2.4  Notice of proceedings**   A landlord who wishes to start possession proceedings must first serve a notice of seeking possession on the tenant (s. 8, Housing Act 1988). If there are two or more joint landlords, the notice may validly be served by one of them (s. 8(1)(a)). The court may dispense with the notice requirement if it considers it just and equitable to do so (s. 8(1)(b)). This power to dispense does not apply where possession is sought on the basis of Ground 8 (two months' rent arrears). In *Fernandes* v *Pavardin* (1982) 5 HLR 33, it was held on the facts that oral notice was enough to justify waiver of the requirement for written notice, there being no suggestion of misunderstanding by the tenants and no injustice or inequality resulting from failure to serve written notice. Stephenson LJ, in the minority, considered that the approach need not be restricted to to considerations of injustice or inequality. In *Bradshaw* v *Baldwin-Wiseman* (1985) 17 HLR 260 the court expressed the view that the minority approach in *Fernandes* was to be preferred, and the court should look at all the circumstances of the case affecting both landlord and tenant, and those in which the failure to give written notice arose. In *Boyle* v *Verrall* (1997) 04 EG 145, the landlord had intended to create an assured shorthold tenancy but the county court judge was not satisfied that the requisite s. 20 notice had been served. The result was the creation of an assured tenancy which was terminable only on one of the grounds specified in sch. 2 to the 1988 Act. Recovery of possession on Ground 1 depended on its being 'just and equitable' to dispense with the service of written notice on the tenant, at the time the tenancy was created, that the landlord might require the property back for her own or her husband's use. The Court of Appeal held that all the circumstances of the case should be considered. The giving of oral notice might be an important factor favouring dispensation but was not necessarily a pre-requisite of dispensation. Nor, if oral notice was absent, was dispensation restricted to 'exceptional cases'. Had the judge applied the correct test, he could only have concluded that it was just and equitable to dispense with the requirement of notice.

A notice of seeking possession must comply with certain requirements:

(a)   It must be in the prescribed form, or a form substantially to the same effect (Assured Tenancies and Agricultural Occupancies (Forms) Regulations 1988).

(b)   It must inform the tenant that the landlord intends to bring possession proceedings.

(c)   It must state on which ground or grounds the landlord intends to rely and also give particulars of them. The grounds specified in the notice may be altered or added to with the leave of the court.

(d)   It must inform the tenant that proceedings will not be begun earlier than a date specified in the notice (s. 8(3)(b)) which in most cases should be not earlier than two weeks from the date of the service of the notice. If the landlord specifies that he or she wishes to rely upon Ground 1 (owner-occupier), Ground 2 (mortgagee's power of sale), Ground 5 (occupation required for minister of religion), Ground 6 (intention to demolish or reconstruct), Ground 7 (death of tenant), Ground 9 (suitable alternative accommodation) or Ground 16 (employee), the date specified in the notice should be not less than two months from the date of service of the notice and, in the case of a periodic tenancy, the earliest date on which the tenancy could be brought to an end by notice to quit given by the landlord on the same date as service of the notice (s. 8(4)).

(e)   It must inform the tenant that those proceedings will not begin later than 12 months from the date of service of the notice (s. 8(3)(c)).

In *Mountain* v *Hastings* (1993) 25 HLR 427, the landlord was seeking possession of an assured tenancy on a number of grounds, one of which was Ground 8. The s. 8 notice summarised the text of each ground instead of giving the full text as was required by the prescribed form of notice. The notice would be valid if it set out fully the the substance of the ground so that it gave the tenant such information as would enable her to do what she could to protect herself against the loss of her home. The notice in question was defective, however, because it did not convey the substance of Ground 8. It simply stated that 'at least three months rent is unpaid', omitting to mention that the rent must be unpaid for three months' at the date of service of the notice *and* at the date of the hearing.

Once a s. 8 notice of intention to bring possession proceedings has been served (or the court has used its discretion to dispense with the requirement of notice), the landlord will be able to obtain an order for possession if he or she can establish:

(a)   one or more of the mandatory Grounds 1 to 8, in which case the court must grant a possession order (s. 7(3)); or

(b)   one or more of the discretionary Grounds 9 to 16 and the court considers it reasonable to grant a possession order (s. 7(4)).

## 6.5  REASONABLENESS

Reasonableness is not an issue if a landlord is seeking an order of possession by establishing a mandatory ground for possession but it must always be considered if the landlord is pleading one of the discretionary grounds for possession or, alternatively, seeking to establish, in the case of a Rent Act regulated tenant, that suitable alternative accommodation is available. Even where a ground or case itself in terms involves a requirement of reasonableness, the general issue of reasonableness must itself be separately considered. Failure by the court to consider reasonableness means that the order can be set aside and in *Peachy Property Corporation Ltd* v *Robinson* [1967] 2 QB 543, where the tenant did not enter an appearance or serve any defence, a judgment entered in default was held by the Court of Appeal to be ineffective.

The onus is upon the landlord to convince the court that it is reasonable to order possession. In *Cumming* v *Danson* [1942] 2 All ER 653 at p. 655, Lord Greene MR explained that:

> ... the judge is to take into account all relevant circumstances as they exist at the date of the hearing ... in ... a broad commonsense way as a man of the world, ... giving such weight as he thinks right to the various factors. Some factors may have little or no weight, others may be decisive, but it is quite wrong for him to exclude from his consideration matters which he ought to take into account.

There appears to be virtually no limit to the factors which the court can taken into account. They include such matters as the health of the parties (*Briddon* v *George* [1946] 1 All ER 609), their ages (*Battlespring* v *Gates* [1983] 268 EG 355), the financial consequences if an order for possession is made (*Williamson* v *Pallant* [1924] 2 KB 173), the public interest (*Cresswell* v *Hodgson* [1951] 1 All ER 710), loss of amenities (*Siddiqui* v *Rashid* [1980] 1 WLR 1018), and the conduct of the parties (*Yelland* v *Taylor* [1957] 1 WLR 459). The judge must look at the effect on each party of the court making or withholding the order (*Cresswell* v *Hodgson*).

## 6.6  SUSPENSION, ADJOURNMENT AND POSTPONEMENT

Where possession is sought on discretionary grounds, the court may adjourn proceedings for possession for such period as it thinks fit, or, on the making of a possession order or, at any time before its execution, stay or suspend execution of the order or postpone the date of possession for such period as it thinks fit (just) (s. 100(1), (2), Rent Act 1977; s. 9(1), (2), Housing Act 1988). On any such adjournment, stay, suspension or postponement, the court must impose conditions as to the payment of any rent arrears or mesne profits, or such other conditions as it thinks fit, unless it considers that this would cause exceptional hardship to the tenant or would otherwise be unreasonable (s. 100(3), Rent Act 1977; s. 9(3), Housing Act 1988). Where the tenant complies with conditions which have been imposed, the court may, if it thinks fit, discharge or rescind the possession order (s. 9(4)). If the tenant fails to comply, the landlord may apply for a possession order.

The court commonly exercises its discretion to suspend the operation of a possession order, especially where possession is sought on the basis of rent arrears. 20,771 actions for possession were brought by private landlords in 1995 and suspended orders were made in 9,325 of them (Lord Chancellor's Department, 1996: 39, Table 4.5). However, these powers do not apply to the mandatory grounds, nor to recovery of possession against assured shorthold tenants under s. 21, Housing Act 1988.

## 6.7  SUITABLE ALTERNATIVE ACCOMMODATION

Strictly speaking, this is a ground for possession but it is dealt with separately here because it does not appear in the list of grounds contained in sch. 15 to the Rent Act 1977. In the Housing Act 1988 it is dealt with under Ground 9.

Subject to the requirement of reasonableness, the court may make an order for possession if the landlord can show that suitable alternative accommodation is available for the tenant or will be so when the possession order takes effect. Although s. 98(1) makes it clear that the issues of reasonableness and alternative accommodation should be established independently of each other, the courts have inclined to the view that it is easier to show reasonableness where alternative accommodation is offered. As Scott LJ stated in *Cumming* v *Danson* [1942] 2 All ER 653:

> There is a fundamental difference ... between an application for possession where no alternative accommodation is offered and an application where it is offered. In my view, the measure of reasonableness to be established by the landlord is much smaller in regard to the burden of proof in the case where alternative accommodation is offered ...

A certificate from the local housing authority stating that it will provide suitable alternative accommodation for the tenant by a specified date is conclusive evidence that such accommodation will be available (Rent Act 1977, sch. 15, Part IV, para. 3; Housing Act 1988, sch. 2, Part III, para. 1) but 'suitability' remains a question within the discretion of the judge (*Jones and Massey* v *Cook and Cook* (1990) 22 HLR 319) and the question of whether it is reasonable to make the order must still be addressed (*Dame Margaret Hungerford Charity Trustees* v *Beazeley* [1993] 2 EGLR 143). Because demand for local authority housing outstrips supply, such certificates are rarely issued. Thus, the landlord must either provide the accommodation himself or herself or arrange for it to be made available from another private landlord. Either way, it will be up to the landlord to establish its suitability (*Nevile* v *Hardy* [1921] 1 Ch 404).

To be suitable, the accommodation offered must consist of premises which are.

(a)   to be let on a protected tenancy or an assured tenancy (as appropriate) or, in the court's opinion, provide equivalent security of tenure; and

(b)   reasonably suitable to the needs of the tenant and his or her family as regards proximity to place of work, and either:

(i)    similar as regards rental and extent to the accommodation afforded by dwelling-houses provided in the neighbourhood by any housing authority for persons with like needs to the tenant and his or her family, or

(ii)   reasonably suitable to the means of the tenant and to his or her and his or her family's needs as regards extent and character; and

(c)   provided with similar or reasonably suitable furniture, where furniture was provided under the regulated or assured tenancy, as the case may be (sch. 15, Part IV, paras. 4, 5, Rent Act 1977; sch. 2, Part III, para. 3(1)(b), Housing Act 1988).

The word 'family' bears the same meaning as it does in the context of succession to a Rent Act statutory tenancy (see **Chapter 14**).

### 6.7.1   'Alternative' accommodation

Although the Acts refer to 'alternative' accommodation, part of the existing premises can suffice, as in *Mykolyshyn* v *Noah* [1970] 1 WLR 1271 in which the landlord offered the same flat minus the sitting-room which the tenant had used merely for storing furniture. In *Yoland Ltd* v *Reddington* (1982) 5 HLR 41 the court held that the part currently occupied by the tenants, less the part which they had (lawfully) sub-let, was suitable but it was not reasonable to make the order. The lavatory and bathroom were shared with the sub-tenants who were friends of the family. If the order was made, the tenants might find themselves left in part of a house, the rest of which remained empty and uncared for or, if the landlords relet the part currently occupied by the sub-tenants, having to share the bathroom and lavatory with strangers.

### 6.7.2   Security of tenure

Whether the security of tenure offered is 'reasonably equivalent' will depend upon the facts of the case. Where the tenant is currently a protected or statutory tenant, the court may direct that the alternative accommodation should be held on a protected tenancy if 'in the circumstances, the grant of an assured tenancy would not afford the required security' (s. 34(1)(c)(iii), Housing Act 1988). This is one of the few ways in which a protected tenancy can be created after 15 January 1989.

Where the tenant is an assured tenant, the alternative accommodation must be let on an assured tenancy (but not an assured shorthold tenancy or subject to one of the mandatory grounds dependent upon service of a notice, i.e., Grounds 1 to 5) or, alternatively, on terms which give the tenant reasonably equivalent security (sch. 2, Part III, para. 2(a), Housing Act 1988).

### 6.7.3  Place of work

'Place of work' refers to the place where the work is largely carried out (*Dakyns v Price* [1948] 1 KB 22). It need not be a single place of work such as an office or factory, but may be an area in which the tenant travels to carry out his or her work. The distance, the means of transport available, the amount of time and degree of inconvenience in making the journey between home and the place of work may all be considered (*Yewbright Properties v Stone* (1980) 40 P & CR 402).

### 6.7.4  Extent and character

Suitability as regards extent and character is decided by reference to objective criteria and the court will consider the particular tenant's housing needs, rather than any incidental advantages enjoyed with the present accommodation, or the tenant's own peculiar wishes and desires. In *Hill v Rochard* [1983] 1 WLR 478, the tenants had spent 16 years in a 'handsome period country house' with one and a half acres of land, including a paddock and outbuildings, which enabled them to keep a pony and a number of cats and dogs. The alternative accommodation offered was a modern, detached, four-bedroomed house on a housing estate on the outskirts of a nearby village. It was the 'character' of this accommodation which was challenged, rather than its 'extent'. The Court of Appeal held that the alternative accommodation was 'suitable.' In considering the tenants' housing needs, the court may look at the environment to which the tenants have become accustomed in their present accommodation, and to see how far the new environment differs. Here, however, the court was being asked to say that the character was unsuitable, not from the point of view of the tenants' needs, but in relation to 'their own particular taste for amenities, which go ... beyond their needs even for a person who is entitled to sustain a high standard of living' (per Eveleigh LJ at p. 486).

Account should be taken, however, of the tenant's professional needs as in, for example, *De Markozoff v Craig* (1949) 93 Sol Jo 693 (accommodation offered unsuitable for tenant to entertain business acquaintances and had no garden for the tenant's child), *McDonnell v Daly* [1969] 3 All ER 851 (proposed accommodation would not enable the tenant to carry out his profession as an artist because it lacked a studio), and *Warren v Austen* [1947] 2 All ER 185 (the alternative accommodation lacked the amenities to enable the tenant to continue to take in paying guests in order to supplement his low income).

Environmental factors, such as noise and smells, are also relevant to whether or not the accommodation is suitable as regards character. In *Redspring v Francis* [1973] 1 All ER 640, it was held that an order of possession would not be reasonable where an elderly lady, who had occupied a flat in a quiet residential street for 30 years, was offered a flat in a very noisy street next door to a fried fish shop, and near to a hospital, cinema and public house, a yard at the back being scheduled for use as a transport depot. However, environmental factors can only be taken into account if they relate to to the character of the property itself, as opposed to personal factors. *Redspring v Francis* was distinguished in *Siddiqui* v *Rashid* [1980] 1 WLR 1018, in which the alternative accommodation (situated in Luton) was held to be suitable despite the objections of the tenant (who lived in London but worked in Luton) that it would take him away from his friends, mosque and cultural interests. In *Dawncar Investments Ltd* v *Plews* (1993) 25 HLR 639, the tenant, who had a young child, occupied a flat in a quiet road in a pleasant part of Hampstead. She was offered a flat in Kilburn which was internally superior to her present accommodation but it was in a busy road used by heavy lorries and near to a timber yard, railway and two public houses. The trial judge expressed his concern over 'a woman like Miss Plews' having to live in the alternative accommodation 'because of the noise, traffic, heavy lorries, proximity of railway lines, general roughness of the area and of the inhabitants', and the Court of Appeal accepted his decision that for environmental reasons it was not suitable.

### 6.7.5   Removal expenses

Where the landlord obtains an order for possession on Ground 9 of the Housing Act 1988, the tenant is entitled to reasonable removal expenses from the landlord, and can sue the landlord if he or she fails to pay them (s. 11). There is no equivalent provision under the Rent Act 1977.

## 6.8   GROUNDS FOR POSSESSION

### 6.8.1   Introduction

The Rent Act 1977 contains 20 grounds for possession and the Housing Act 1988 contains 16. If the landlord proves one of the discretionary grounds (Rent Act 1977, sch. 15, Part I, Cases 1–10; Housing Act 1988, sch. 2, Part II, Grounds 9–16), the court will grant possession only if it considers that it is reasonable to make the order.

The mandatory grounds were introduced in an attempt to encourage lettings, the 'owner-occupier' ground of Case 11 having made its first appearance in 1965. If the landlord proves the requirements of one of the mandatory grounds (Rent Act 1977, sch. 15, Part II, Cases 11–20; Housing Act 1988, Part I, Grounds 1–8), the court must grant possession (s. 98(2)) and the question of whether it is reasonable to grant an order for possession is irrelevant (*Kennealy* v *Dunne* [1977] QB 837).

All the mandatory cases under the Rent Act 1977 require the landlord to serve written notice upon the tenant not later than 'the relevant date' stating that possession may be recovered under the case in question. The relevant date is defined by sch. 15, Part III, para. 2 and in most cases it will be the start of the tenancy. Under Cases 11, 12, 19 and 20, the court may dispense with the requirement of notice if it is of the opinion that it is just and equitable to do so. Obviously it is in the landlord's interest to make out a case for one of the mandatory grounds.

The Housing Act 1988 places greater emphasis on the mandatory grounds which include some grounds which are only discretionary under the Rent Act 1977. A number of grounds contained in the 1988 Act resemble the cases operating under the Rent Act 1977, but several are new or revised, notably Ground 1 (a revised owner-occupier ground); Ground 6 (a new ground, enabling the landlord to obtain possession for redevelopment); Ground 8 (a new ground based on proof of serious rent arrears); Ground 11 (a new ground which permits recovery of possession for persistent rent arrears); Ground 14 (a ground, revised and extended by the Housing Act 1996, which enables the landlord to obtain possession where the tenant is guilty of nuisance, annoyance or illegality) and Ground 14A (a new domestic violence ground, introduced by the Housing Act 1996 for assured tenancies where the landlord is a Registered Social Landlord or charitable housing trust. It is virtually identical to Ground 2A of sch. 2 to the Housing Act 1985 which applies to secure tenancies (see **10.3.6.5**).

An accelerated possession procedure, which came into force on 1 November 1993, abolishes court hearings in many cases relating to assured shorthold tenancies (both fixed term and periodic) and to certain mandatory grounds for possession (i.e. Grounds 1, 3, 4, 5). A court order is still required. It may be utilised only if there is no other claim for relief (such as rent arrears) besides possession and costs.

### 6.8.2   Overlapping grounds in the Rent Act 1977 and Housing Act 1988

#### 6.8.2.1   Non-payment of rent or breach of any other obligation   Case 1

of the Rent Act 1977 allows the landlord to recover possession where 'any rent lawfully due from the tenant has not been paid.' Before commencing possession proceedings, the landlord should send the tenant a 'letter before action' demanding payment and threatening legal action if the arrears are not paid by a certain date. The court is unlikely to consider it reasonable to make a possession order if the landlord has failed to warn the tenant and to give him or her an opportunity to pay what is owing. However, no order can be made if the rent is then paid because the rent is no longer 'lawfully due'; the commencement of proceedings is the date at which the breach must exist (*Bird* v *Hildage* [1948] 1 KB 91). If payment is made after the start of proceedings, the court can order possession but is unlikely to do so unless there is a long history of non and late payment of rent (*Dellenty* v *Pellow* [1951] 2 All ER 716). If arrears are still unpaid at the time of the hearing, the court will take into account all the surrounding circumstances and will probably not order possession in the case of an isolated breach or if only a small sum is owing. It may not be reasonable to order possession against a tenant who is withholding rent because the landlord has breached a repairing covenant (*Televantos* v *McCulloch* (1991) 23 HLR 412), or if the landlord has failed to comply with his or her obligation under s. 48, Landlord and Tenant Act 1987 to furnish the tenant with an address in England and Wales at which notices (including notices in proceedings) may be served on him or her by the tenant (*Hussain* v *Singh* [1993] 2 ECLR 70; *Dallhold Estates (UK) Pty Ltd* v *Lindsey Trading Properties Inc* [1994] 1 EGLR 93).

The Housing Act 1988 Act takes a much tougher stand on rent arrears, and contains no less than three separate grounds for possession: one mandatory and two discretionary. The discretionary Ground 10 corresponds in material aspects to Case 1 of sch. 15 to the Rent Act 1977. It requires that 'some rent lawfully due' from the tenant:

(a)   is unpaid on the date on which the proceedings for possession are begun; and

(b)   was in arrears at the date when the s. 8 notice was served.

Ground 11 (which is based on s. 30(1)(b), Landlord and Tenant Act 1954) applies even if no rent is outstanding on the date on which proceedings for possession are begun but the tenant has persistently delayed paying rent (e.g. *Hopcutt* v *Carver* (1969) 209 EG 1069, where the court refused to grant a new business tenancy, the tenant of some 20 years' standing having been persistently late in paying his rent over the last two years, at one time delaying for five months).

Mandatory Ground 8 is one of the most contentious grounds for possession contained in the 1988 Act. It applies where both at the date when the s. 8 notice is served *and* at the date of the hearing, at least two months' rent (eight weeks' where rent is payable weekly or fortnightly) is unpaid. The former period of three months (13 weeks) was reduced to two by the Housing Act 1996. Tenants who fall foul of Ground 8 may well be in receipt of housing benefit. Housing benefit is paid four weeks in arrears and, although most claims are settled within 14 days of the housing authority receiving all the necessary documentation, about one-third of all authorities fail to pay on time (*Hansard*, HL Debates, 1996, vol. 572, col. 613). Of course, the court order will take another three months or so for the landlord to obtain, by which time the housing benefit claim should have been settled so that the mandatory ground will no longer be available. Further, local authorities may make a payment on account of housing benefit until any claim is finally determined. None the less, the Housing Corporation Guidance to Housing Associations is that they should refrain from using Ground 8.

If, by the date of the hearing, the tenant has paid the arrears or at least enough to reduce the amount outstanding to below the level necessary for possession to be granted under Ground 8, the landlord will no longer be able to rely on the mandatory ground. It is in the landlord's interest, therefore, to include Grounds 10 and 11 as alternatives in the s. 8 notice.

**6.8.2.2   Breach of a tenancy obligation**   Case 1 of the Rent Act 1977 and Ground 12 of the Housing Act 1988 apply where 'any obligation of the ... tenancy ... has been broken or not performed.' This includes a breach of any of the obligations of the tenancy, except those of a personal nature, e.g. to remain in the landlord's employment. It applies to breach of implied as well as express obligations, and whether or not the breach still exists at the date of the hearing. If the breach as been remedied, however, this will be significant to the issue of reasonableness. In *Commercial General Administration* v *Thomsett*

(1979) 250 EG 547, a term of the tenancy required the tenant 'not to do or permit to be done anything which may be or become a nuisance or annoyance or be injurious or detrimental to the reputation of the premises. ' An over-persistent admirer of the tenant, who was an actress, had annoyed adjoining occupiers by telephoning, ringing the entry phone and shouting. The tenant held rowdy parties and gave newspaper interviews which, it was said, 'lowered the tone.' The court refused to order possession. 'Permit' means to give leave for an act which could not otherwise legally be done, or to abstain from taking reasonable steps to prevent the act where it is within a person's power to prevent it. The tenant had installed an Ansaphone, disconnected the entry phone, called the police to eject partygoers and conducted interviews off the premises.

**6.8.2.3  Nuisance, immoral or illegal user**    A court may order possession under Case 2 of the Rent Act 1977:

> where the tenant or any person residing or lodging with him or any sub-tenant has been guilty of conduct which is a nuisance or annoyance to adjoining occupiers, or has been convicted of using the dwelling-house or allowing it to be used for immoral or illegal purposes.

'Nuisance' was defined in *Walter v Selfe* (1851) WDe G & Smj 315 at p. 322 per Knight-Bruce VC, as being 'an inconvenience materially interfering with the ordinary comfort physically of human existence, not merely according to elegant or dainty modes and habits of living, but according to plain and sober and simple notions among the English people.' 'Annoyance' is a wider term than nuisance and has been described as something which 'reasonably troubles the mind and pleasure ... of the ordinary English inhabitants of a house even though it may not appear to amount to physical detriment to comfort' (*Todd-Heatley v Benham* (1888) 40 Ch D 80; [1886–90] All ER Rep Ext 1537, per Bowen LJ; see also *Wood v Cooper* [1894] 3 Ch 671). It may consist of a physical interference, e.g. making excessive noise, producing a lot of dust, allowing water to overflow onto someone else's premises (*Ferguson v Butler* 1918 SLT 228; *Chapman v Hughes* (1923) 129 LT 223) or it may be the result of conduct (allowing the premises to be used for prostitution: *Yates v Morris* [1951] 1 KB 77) or verbal abuse and obscene language (*Cobstone Investments Ltd v Maxim* [1984] 2 All ER 635). The nuisance or annoyance does not have to take place on the demised premises (e.g. *Whitbread v Ward* (1952) 159 EG 494, in which the tenant's 'undue familiarity' with the landlord's 16-year-old daughter in an alley some 200 yards away from the premises was held to be an annoyance). Nuisance and annoyance includes anything which disturbs adjoining occupiers, i.e., those who live sufficiently close to be affected by the tenant's conduct on the demised premises and not necessarily, therefore, in a property which physically touches the tenant's premises (*Cobstone Investments Ltd v Maxim*, ibid.).

As regards immoral or illegal purposes, the landlord must show that the premises themselves were connected with the crime; it is 'not enough that the tenant has been convicted of a crime with which the premises have nothing to do beyond merely being the scene of its commission' (*Schneiders & Sons* v *Abrahams* [1925] 1 KB 301 per Scrutton LJ at p. 311). If the tenant has been convicted of the possession of drugs but the drugs were merely found in the tenant's pocket or handbag, this would not amount to using the premises. It would be different if the premises were used as storage or as a hiding-place (*Abrahams* v *Wilson* [1971] 2 QB 88).

In *Heglibiston Establishment* v *Heyman* (1977) 76 P & CR 351 it was held that a term in the tenancy agreement not to use the premises for immoral purposes was intended to prevent the flat in question from being used as a brothel or for prostitution. The tenant was not in breach, therefore, by permitting his son to live with him, together with a woman to whom he was not married.

As originally drafted, Ground 14 of the Housing Act 1988 was basically the same as Case 2 of the Rent Act 1977. However, it has been revised by s. 148, Housing Act 1996:

The tenant or a person residing in *or visiting* the dwelling-house—

    (a)   has been guilty of conduct *causing or likely to cause* a nuisance or annoyance to a person residing, *visiting or otherwise engaging in a lawful activity* in the locality, or

    (b)   has been convicted of—

        (i)   using the dwelling-house or allowing it to be used for immoral or illegal purposes, *or*

        (ii)   *an arrestable offence committed in, or in the locality of, the dwelling-house.*

The revisions are shown in italics. This ground is considered in more detail in **Chapter 10**, an identical revision having been made to the 'nuisance and annoyance ground' in relation to secure tenancies.

### 6.8.2.4 Deterioration of the dwelling-house as the result of the tenant's neglect

Possession may be recovered under Case 3 of the Rent Act 1977 where the condition of the dwelling-house has, in the opinion of the court, deteriorated owing to acts of waste by, or the neglect of default of, the tenant or any person residing or lodging with him or her or any sub-tenant of his or hers, where the court is satisfied that the tenant has not, before the making of the order in question, taken such steps as he or she ought reasonably to have taken for the removal of the lodger or sub-tenant as the case may be.

Case 3 can apply even if there is no breach of any term of the tenancy or of any common law duty (*Lowe* v *Lendrum* (1950) 159 EG 423) but the tenant cannot be held responsible for any neglect prior to his or her tenancy (*Holloway* v *Povey* (1984) 271 EG 195, in which the garden had been seriously neglected).

Ground 13 of the Housing Act 1988 goes beyond Case 3 in that it extends also to a deterioration in the condition of any of the common parts serving the dwelling-house. This will include staircases, corridors, lifts, etc.

**6.8.2.5 Deterioration of the furniture** The wording of Case 4 is similar to that of Case 3 but applies to 'any furniture provided for use under the tenancy'. It is identical to Ground 15 of the Housing Act 1988.

**6.8.2.6 Dwelling previously occupied, or required for future occupation, by the landlord or the landlord's family**

*(a) Rent Act 1977* Case 9 (a discretionary ground) permits recovery of possession where the the dwelling-house is reasonably required for occupation as a residence for the landlord (which includes his or her spouse and any children who are minors: *Ritcher* v *Wilson* [1963] 2 QB 426; *Smith* v *Penny* [1947] KB 230), or by one of the landlord's adult children, his or her father or mother, or a parent-in-law. This case cannot be utitlised by a person who became the landlord by purchase when the tenant was already in occupation. The landlord must need the premises 'with a view to living there for some reasonable period, definite or indefinite, and not so that the property can be sold' (*Rowe* v *Truelove* (1976) 241 EG 533).

The landlord will have to show that one of the specified categories of relative has a genuine need for the dwelling-house in order to satisfy a court that it is 'reasonably required' for their occupation. Factors to be taken into account include the size and health of the landlord's family, their present housing needs (*Kennealy* v *Dunne* [1977] QB 837), their current residence (or lack thereof), a probable change of circumstances (*Kidder* v *Birch* (1983) 265 EG 773), and the proximity of the property to the landlord's place of work (*Jackson* v *Harbour* [1924] EGD 99). The requirement for accommodation need not be immediate but in *Kissias* v *Lehany* [1979] CLY 1625, possession was refused where the landlord stated that he required a basement for his daughter to live in on her marriage which might take place in two years time.

The court must not make an order for possession under Case 9 if it is satisfied that, having regard to all the circumstances of the case, including the question whether other accommodation is available for the landlord or the tenant, greater hardship would be caused by granting the order than by refusing to grant it (sch. 15, Part III, para. 1, Rent Act 1977). The burden of proof is on the tenant. The court should consider all who may be affected — 'relatives, dependants, lodgers, guests, and the stranger within the gates — but should weigh such hardship with due regard to the status of the persons affected, and their 'proximity' to the tenant or landlord, and the extent to which, consequently, hardship to them would be hardship to him' (*Harte* v *Frampton* [1948] 1 KB 73 at p. 79).

The question is: 'Who will suffer the greater hardship?' The court should must take into account all the relevant circumstances of the case, e.g. the financial means of both parties (*Kelley* v *Goodwin* [1947] 1 All ER 810), their mental and physical health (*Thomes* v *Fryer* [1970] 1 WLR 845), and the availability of other accommodation (*Coombs* v *Parry* (1987) 19 HLR 384; *Chandler* v *Strevett* [1947] 1 All ER 164; *Manaton* v *Edwards* [1985] 2 EGLR 159; *Baker* v *MacIver* (1990) 22 HLR 328).

Mandatory Case II comes into play where the landlord occupied the dwelling-house as his or her residence at some time before the letting and it was then let to the tenant on a regulated tenancy. It can apply where joint owner-occupiers are reclaiming possession of premises as a residence for only one of them (*Tilling* v *Whiteman* [1980] AC 1). Not later than the relevant date the landlord must have served notice on the tenant that possession might be required on this ground. The notice requirement may be dispensed with by the court if it considers it just and equitable to do so. The court must grant possession if one of the conditions (a), or (c)–(f) outlined in Part IV of sch. 15 (added by s. 66, Housing Act 1980) are satisfied, namely:

(a)   the dwelling-house is required as a residence for the owner or any member of his or her family who resided with the owner when he or she last occupied the dwelling-house as a residence;

(b)   the owner has retired from regular employment and requires the dwelling-house as a residence;

(c)   the owner has died and the dwelling-house is required as a residence for a member of his or her family who was residing with him or her at the time of his or her death;

(d)   the owner has died and the dwelling-house is required by a successor in title as his or her residence or for the purpose of its sale;

(e)   see **6.8.2.7**   (repossession by a mortgagee) below;

(f)   the dwelling-house is not reasonably suited to the needs of the owner, having regard to his or her place of work, and he or she requires it for the purpose of disposing of it with vacant possession and of using the proceeds of sale in acquiring, as his or her residence, a dwelling-house which is more suitable to those needs.

There has been sufficient occupation as a residence where, before the letting, the landlord lived mainly in South Africa but occupied the property when visiting the UK on business and for holidays (*Naish* v *Curzon* (1986) 51 P & CR 229) and used the property on weekdays for a period of eight or nine weeks before the letting, during which he had no home elsewhere (*Mistry* v *Isidore* [1990] 2 EGLR 97).

Mandatory Case 12 applies where the dwelling-house was let by an owner who intended to occupy it on his or her retirement from regular employment and possession is now required. Unlike Case 11, there is no requirement that the owner previously occupied the premises as his or her residence. The tenant must have been given notice not later than the relevant date that possession might be required under this case and one of the conditions in paras. (b) to (e) of Part V of sch. 15 must be satisfied (see above).

*(b)   Housing Act 1988*   Ground 1 can be used if:

not later than the beginning of the tenancy the landlord gave notice in writing to the tenant that possession might be recovered on this ground or the court is of the opinion that it is just and equitable to dispense with the requirement of notice and (in either case):

(a)   at some time before the beginning of the tenancy, the landlord who is seeking possession or, in the case of joint landlords seeking possession, at least one of them occupied the dwelling-house as his only or principal home; or

(b)   the landlord who is seeking possesison or, in the case of joint landlords seeking possession, at least one of them requires the dwelling-house as his or his spouse's only or principal home and neither the landlord (or in the case of joint landlords, any one of them) nor any other person who, as landlord, derived title under the landlord who gave the notice mentioned above acquired the reversion for money or money's worth.

Although this ground bears a passing resemblance to the discretionary Case 9 and the mandatory Case 11 under the Rent Act 1977, it differs from both in significant respects. To succeed in recovering possession under this ground, the landlord may rely on either:

(a)   past occupation of the dwelling-house as his or her only or principal home (which need not have immediately preceded the grant of the tenancy). No intention to occupy in the future need be proved: the landlord may simply want to sell with vacant possession; or

(b)   a need for the dwelling-house presently as his or his spouse's only or principal home. No past use of it as such need be shown, unless he or she is a landlord by purchase (for money or money's worth).

**6.8.2.7   Repossession by a mortgagee**   Condition (e) of Case 11 of the 1977 Act and Mandatory Ground 2 of the Housing Act 1988 are very similar. They apply where the mortgage was granted before the beginning of the tenancy and the mortgagee requires vacant possession for the purpose of exercising the power of sale conferred by the mortgage or by s. 101 of the Law of Property Act 1925. Notice must have been given that possession might be required on this ground or the court must be satisfied that it is just and equitable to dispense with such notice.

Most mortgages expressly prohibit letting by the mortgagor without the mortgagee's prior consent. If such consent is not obtained, the mortgagee will not normally be bound by the lease, even where the tenant is protected as against the mortgagor by the 1977 and 1988 Acts (*Dudley and District Building Society* v *Emerson* [1949] Ch 707; *Quennell* v *Maltby* [1979] 1 WLR 318).

**6.8.2.8   Out of season holiday lettings**   A holiday letting is excluded from being an assured tenancy by sch. 1, para. 9, Housing Act 1988 (see **5.4.5**). A letting of holiday accommodation out of season may be outside the definition of a holiday letting and capable, therefore, of qualifying for protection under the 1988 Act. Ground 3 of the 1988 Act applies where the dwelling-house is let under a tenancy for less than eight months and the dwelling-house was, at some time within the period of 12 months immediately preceding the tenancy, occupied under a right to occupy it for a holiday. Not later than the beginning of the tenancy, the landlord must have served written notice on the tenant that possession might be claimed under this ground. A similar ground for possession is contained in Case 13 of the 1977 Act but since 15 January 1989, no lettings can be granted which would enable this case to be utilised.

**6.8.2.9   Student accommodation**   Possession may be claimed on Ground 4 of the Housing Act 1988 where the dwelling-house is let under a tenancy for a term of years certain not exceeding 12 months and at some time within the period of 12 months ending on the relevant date the dwelling-house was let by a specified educational institution as student accommodation. The tenant must have been informed in writing not later than the relevant date that possession might be required on this ground. It enables colleges and universities to let its residential accommodation during vacations. This ground is the same as Case 14 of the Rent Act 1977.

**6.8.2.10   Ministers of religion**   Lettings of Church of England parsonages are excluded from the Rent Act 1977 and the Housing Act 1988. There is no such exclusion for other religions but Case 15 and Ground 5 provide mandatory grounds for possession where the dwelling-house is held for the purpose of being available for occupation by a minister of religion as a residence from which to perform the duties of his or her office. The tenant must have been given written notice that possession might be required on this ground and the court must be satisfied that the dwelling-house is required for occupation by a minister of religion as such a residence.

**6.8.2.11   Dwelling required for the landlord's employee**   Under Case 8 of the Rent Act 1977, the landlord must satisfy the court that:

(a)   he or she employed the present tenant to whom the dwelling-house was let in consequence of that employment; and
(b)   the tenant has ceased to be in that employment, and
(c)   the dwelling-house is reasonably required for someone engaged in full-time employment by the landlord or by one of his or her tenants, and that the contract of employment was made conditional on the provision of housing.

Ground 16 of the Housing Act 1988 is more favourable to the landlord than Case 8 in that the landlord does not have to show that the premises are required for residence by a new employee. However, as it is a discretionary ground, the landlord is more likely to obtain possession if the premises are needed for a new employee.

**6.8.3   Grounds for possession under the Rent Act 1977**

**6.8.3.1   Notice to quit by the tenant (Case 5)**   Possession may be recovered under this case:

where, in consequence of a notice to quit given by the tenant, the landlord has contracted to sell or let the dwelling-house or has taken any other steps as the result of which he would, in the opinion of the court, be seriously prejudiced if he could not obtain possession.

The purpose of this case is to protect a landlord who might otherwise be liable to a third party for breach of a contract of sale or an agreement for a lease. Thus, it could not be relied upon by a landlord who intended to sell but had not contracted to do so (*Barton* v *Fincham* [1921] 2 KB 291). Notice to quit here means the service of a valid notice; it does not apply where the tenant disappears and returns the keys (*Standingford* v *Bruce* [1926] 1 KB 466), or where the tenant informally agrees to leave (*De Vries* v *Sparks* (1927) 137 LT 441).

**6.8.3.2  Assigning or subletting without the landlord's consent (Case 6)**  The purpose of this case is 'to give some protection to a landlord against the risk of finding some person wholly unknown to him irrevocably installed in his property' (*Hyde* v *Pimley* [1952] 2 QB 506 at p. 512). It can be relied upon against both the tenant and a sub-tenant (*Leith Properties Ltd* v *Springer* [1982] 3 All ER 731) and applies even where the tenancy agreement does not prohibit assignment or sub-letting. From a practical point of view, Case 6 applies only to contractual tenants; a statutory tenant cannot assign a tenancy and a statutory tenant who sub-lets the whole of the premsies will cease to occupy the premises as his or her residence.

**6.8.3.3  Subletting of part at an excessive rent (Case 10)**  The landlord can claim possession where the tenant is charging his or her sub-tenant more than the maximum recoverable rent for the premises sub-let by virtue of the fair rent provisions (see **Chapter 13**).

**6.8.3.4  Agricultural property**  Cases 16, 17 and 18 contain complex provisions which apply to property occupied by agricultural employees and tenants who occupy premises of former agricultural employees. They are outside the scope of this book.

**6.8.3.5  Protected shorthold tenancies (Case 19)**  As stated in **2.1.9**, the protected shorthold tenancy was a creation of the Housing Act 1980. Such tenancies had to be for a fixed term of between one and five years and, at the end of the term, Case 19 provided landlords with a mandatory ground for possession in addition to all the other cases. Since no new protected shorthold tenancy have been created since 15 January 1989, all protected shorthold tenancy existing at that date will by now have run their course. If, however, on or after that date, a landlord grants a tenancy to a tenant who, before the grant, held a protected shorthold tenancy, the new tenancy will be an assured shorthold tenancy (s. 34(3), Housing Act 1988).

**6.8.3.6  Landlord is a 'Member of the Regular Armed Forces of the Crown' (Case 20)**  The landlord must have been a member of the armed forces when he or she (a) acquired and (b) let the dwelling-house. Written notice (which the court may dispense with if it considers it just and equitable to do so) must have been served on the tenant prior to the grant of the tenancy that possession might be required under this case. The court must be satisfied that the property is now required as a residence for the owner.

### 6.8.4  Grounds for possession under the Housing Act 1988

Some of the Rent Act 1977 discretionary grounds have no equivalent in the 1988 Act. Case 5 (tenant's notice to quit) has disappeared because an assured tenancy is brought to an end by the tenant's notice to quit, even if the tenant remains in possession. Case 6 (assignment or sub-letting of the whole without consent) does not apply, although Ground 12 (breach of obligation) would cover the case of an assignment or sub-letting in breach of covenant and a tenant who sub-lets the whole will cease to satisfy the residence requirement of s. 1. Case 10 (overcharging of sub-tenant) is inapplicable.

**6.8.4.1  Demolition or reconstruction (Ground 6)**  This ground is modelled on s. 30(1)(f), Landlord and Tenant Act 1954, and sch. 2, Ground 10, Housing Act 1985. The landlord must prove an intention to demolish or reconstruct (i.e. rebuild, involving substantial interference: *Percy E Cadle & Co. Ltd* v *Jacmarch Properties* [1957] 1 QB 323) the whole or a substantial part of the dwelling-house or to carry out substantial works to it. The intention is to be established at the date of the hearing (*Betty's Cafes* v *Phillips Furnishing Stores* [1959] AC 20). The existence of the landlord's intention is a question of fact and degree and must be assessed objectively. It must have 'moved out of the zone of contemplation — the sphere of the tentative, the provisional and the exploratory — and moved into the valley of decision' (*Cunliffe* v *Goodman* [1950] 2 KB 237 at p. 254).

It will be easier for the landlord to establish the requisite intention where the premises are 'old and worn out or are ripe for development, the proposed work is obviously desirable, plans and arrangements are well in hand, and the landlord has the means and ability to carry out the work.' The court will not be so readily satisfied, however, where 'the premises are comparatively new or the desirability of the project is open to doubt, when there are many difficulties still to be surmounted, such as the preparation and approval of plans or the obtaining of finance, or when the landlord has in the past fluctuated in his mind as to what to do with the premises' (per Denning LJ in *Reohorn* v *Barry Corporation* [1956] 2 All ER 742 at p. 744). It will assist the landlord if any necessary planning permission or building regulation consent has been obtained by the time of the hearing.

An intention to carry out the demolition and reconstruction need not be the primary purpose and in *Fisher* v *Taylors Furnishing Stores Ltd* [1956] 2 All ER 78, the fact that the landlords intended to occupy the rebuilt premises themselves was held not to deprive them of their right to possession. The tenant has no recourse against a landlord who recovers possession and then changes his or her mind (*Reohorn* v *Barry Corporation*, ibid.).

It must be the landlord who intends to demolish or reconstruct but the work need not be done by the landlord personally; it may be done by the landlord's employees or agents or by building contractors, or even under a building lease by which the lessee is to do the rebuilding (*Gilmour Caterers Ltd* v *St. Bartholomews Hospital Governers* [1956] 1 QB 387; *Turner* v *Wandsworth London Borough Council* [1994] 1 EGLR 134).

The landlord must show that the intended work cannot reasonably be carried out without the tenant giving up possession of the dwelling-house, because:

(a)   the tenant is not willing to allow access or other facilities as would permit the intended work to be carried out (but see *Heath* v *Drown* [1973] AC 497); or

(b)   the nature of the intended work is such that it could not be carried out even if the landlord had such access; or

(c)   the tenant is not willing to accept an assured tenancy of part of the dwelling-house as would enable the intended work to be carried out; or

(d)   the nature of the intended work is such that a tenancy of part is not practicable.

**6.8.4.2   Death of tenant (Ground 7)**   Possession may be recovered under this ground where 'the tenancy is a periodic tenancy (including a statutory periodic tenancy) which has devolved under the will or intestacy of the former tenant and the proceedings for the recovery of possession are begun not later than 12 months after the death of the former tenant or, if the court so directs, after the date on which, in the opinion of the court, the landlord or, in the case of joint landlords, any one of them became aware of the former tenant's death.

Provided that there has been no statutory succession by the tenant's spouse or cohabitant (see **Chapter 14**), the tenancy can devolve under the tenant's will or intestacy. Ground 7 may be used to recover possession where a person has thus inherited a periodic tenancy. Where there has been a statutory succession under s. 17, Ground 7 will become available on the death of the successor.

If the landlord accepts rent from the new tenant, a new periodic tenancy is not created unless the landlord agrees in writing to a change in the terms of the tenancy (e.g. as to the rent payable, the period of the tenancy, the premises which are let).

There is no equivalent ground for possession in the Rent Act 1977.

**6.8.4.3   Domestic violence (Ground 14A)**   This ground is available only where the landlord is a Registered Social Landlord or charitable housing trust. It may be used where the dwelling-house was occupied by a married couple or a couple living together as husband and wife and (a) one or both partners is a tenant of the dwelling-house, and (b) one of them has left the dwelling-house because of violence or threats of violence by the other towards the departing partner or a member of his or her family who was residing with him or her immediately before the departure. The court must also be satisfied that the partner who has left is unlikely to return.

**6.8.4.4   Grant induced by false statement (Ground 17)**   Possession may be recovered under this ground where the landlord was induced to grant the tenancy by a false statement made knowingly or recklessly by (a) the tenant, or (b) a person acting at the tenant's instigation.

## 6.9   TERMINATION OF ASSURED SHORTHOLD TENANCIES

### 6.9.1   By the tenant

Unlike an assured tenant, an assured shorthold tenant has no statutory right to terminate a fixed-term tenancy early by notice, nor is this permitted by the vast majority of fixed-term tenancy agreements. The Conservative government resisted an Opposition amendment to include such a right on the basis that it would deprive the landlord of the expectation of a rent during an initial fixed term (*Hansard*, HC Standing Committee G, 7 March 1996, col. 256).

### 6.9.2   By the landlord

Assured shorthold tenancies created before 28 February 1997 (the date on which s. 19A, Housing Act 1988 came into force) must be for a minimum term of six months and there must be no power for the landlord to bring the tenancy to an end any earlier than six months, other than by forfeiture or a power of re-entry. The court cannot make an order for possession of such an assured shorthold tenancy unless the fixed term has come to an end (s. 21(1)(a), (4), Housing Act 1988). This confers upon the tenant a minimum period of security of tenure (unless there is provision for forfeiture or re-entry, and one of the grounds for possession for an assured tenancy can be relied upon). As there is no requirement of a fixed term of six months for assured shorthold tenancies created since 28 February 1997, s. 21 has been amended to prevent possession being ordered until at least six months has elapsed from the grant of the tenancy (s. 21(5)–(7)). The six months runs from the grant of the original tenancy, and not the start of any replacement tenancy whether this arises by virtue of an agreement with the landlord or as a statutory periodic tenancy under s. 5, Housing Act 1988.

An assured shorthold tenancy may be terminated in the same ways (i.e. using the same grounds for possession) as any assured tenancy but s. 21 contains what is, in effect, an additional mandatory ground for possession enabling the landlord (or at least one of them, in the case of a joint tenancy) to recover possession by giving the tenant not less than two months' written notice stating that he or she requires possession of the dwelling-house (s. 21(1)(b), (4)(a), Housing Act 1988). The court cannot use its discretion to consider the issue of reasonableness, nor to suspend the making of the order.

# SEVEN

# Harassment, unlawful eviction and the Protection from Eviction Act 1977

## 7.1 LEGISLATIVE HISTORY

As stated in **Chapter 2**, the history of rent regulation since 1915 consists of a series of measures moving from control to decontrol and back again, reflecting responses by various governments to perceived housing shortage or sufficiency in the private rented sector. Throughout this entire period, however, the private rented sector was in decline and the Rent Act 1957 — one of the most controversial measures passed by the Macmillan government — was a last ditch attempt to revive private investment in rented housing. The Rent Act 1957 immediately decontrolled rents of more expensive houses (i.e. those with a rateable value of over £40 in London and £30 elsewhere) while the rents of the rest became decontrolled when the sitting tenant left — a process known as 'creeping decontrol'. This gave landlords an incentive to dispose of sitting tenants and to replace them with tenants paying higher rents.

The 1957 Act is associated with 'Rachmanism', a term which has become virtually synonymous with harassment and unlawful eviction. Perec Rachman started to build up his property empire in 1954 by buying up long leases which had only a short time left to run. The houses he bought, which were often in a poor state of repair, were divided up into flats of three or four rooms and let to controlled tenants at low rents. Rachman paid these tenants large sums of money to leave (a practice sometimes referred to as 'winkling') and then converted the flats into furnished single room dwellings. Even though furnished tenants possessed lesser rights than controlled tenants as regards security of tenure and rent control, the housing shortage in Inner London made it easy for Rachman to let his properties at high rents, often to immigrants who found it difficult to obtain accommodation elsewhere. In due course, he realised that there was no point in paying controlled tenants if they could be persuaded to go by some other means. Rachman and his hirelings certainly used harassment but it 'belonged to a brief episode in his career and constituted no more than a small and unrepresentative aspect of his normal commercial operations' (Nelken, 1983: 4). Thus, while the Rent Act 1957 gave Rachman's activities some further impetus, it should be remembered that he had been carrying out his dubious business practices some time before the Act was passed, most of his profits deriving from his policy of charging high rents but carrying out few repairs. An interesting question is why certain of his activities were made illegal while others — such as winkling — were not, even though they ultimately achieved the same end.

Rachman was only one of many similar landlords but he came to public attention because of his connection with the 'Profumo affair' which involved Christine Keeler, a call girl who had formerly been Rachman's mistress, John Profumo, one of her clients and the then Secretary of State for War, and Eugene Ivanov, an assistant Russian Naval Attaché at the Russian Embassy in London. The matter led to questions in the House of Commons and the so-called Rachman debate on 22 July 1963 on the 'Rent Act 1957 and Property Profiteering'.

Harold Wilson, then leader of the Opposition, pointed out that Rachman's was 'a lurid version of a story which goes on in more sombre, sepia tones in other slum empires and in other cities as well as London'. The photophobic world of slimy creatures revealed when a stone is turned over had nothing, he said, to compare with 'the revolting creatures of London's underworld, living there, shunning the light, growing fat by battening on human misery'. He explained how, so as to avoid 'the palsied hand of official control', loopholes in the Companies Act were used — with the assistance of lawyers and accountants — to create 'a proliferation of interlocking companies' so that any official action which may be taken — sanitary notices, certificates of disrepair, or compulsory acquisition — could be frustrated by a total inability to identify the property's owner (*Hansard*, HC Debs, vol. 681, cols. 1058–9).

A Labour government — which had pledged to give urgent assistance to tenants — was returned to power in October 1964. Soon afterwards, the Protection from Eviction Act 1964 was passed, the first piece of legislation to make it an offence to evict a tenant without first obtaining a court order. This temporary measure was replaced by Part III of the Rent Act 1965 which created the criminal offences of unlawful eviction and harassment. The relevant provisions were consolidated in the Protection from Eviction Act 1977 which remains the principal statutory provision in this area, although Part I of the Housing Act 1988 made a number of important changes. As well as dealing with unlawful eviction and harassment, the 1977 Act restricts the ways in which landlords can terminate leases or licences of residential property: it prohibits them from forfeiture by peaceable re-entry (s. 2), it prevents recovery of possession other than by court order even where the lease or licence has been effectively terminated (s. 3), and it requires that a minimum written notice of four weeks is given (s. 5).

The fair rent provisions of the Rent Act 1977 meant that a landlord stood to make significant financial gain if he or she could persuade a protected or statutory tenant to leave the dwelling and then relet it under the Housing Act 1988 at a market rent. Accordingly the 1988 Act created a new offence of harassment, amended the existing one, and strengthened the civil law to enable residential occupiers who have been evicted illegally or forced out by harassment to claim greater compensation. At the same time, however, the 1988 Act excludes certain categories of occupant from the protection afforded by ss. 3 and 5, thus sanctioning the use of peaceful self-help. Determining the occupier's status is crucial, therefore, as it dictates whether or not he or she is entitled to any protection and, if so, the course of action which is most appropriate. It also has a bearing on the amount of damages which the occupier is likely to recover.

## 7.2  CRIMINAL LIABILITY

### 7.2.1  Unlawful eviction

By s. 1(2), Protection from Eviction Act 1977:

> if any person unlawfully deprives the residential occupier of any premises of his occupation of the premises or any part thereof, or attempts to do so, he shall be guilty of an offence unless he proves that he believed, and had reasonable cause to believe, that the residential occupier had ceased to reside in the premises.

A 'residential occupier' means 'a person occupying premises as a residence, whether under a contract or by virtue of any enactment or rule of law giving him the right to remain in occupation or restricting the right of any person to recover possession of the premises' (s. 1(1)). Thus, it includes not only tenants covered by the Rent Act 1977 and Housing Act 1988 but also those whose dwelling-houses have a rateable value outside the limits of those Acts, licensees, tenants of local authorities and squatters who have achieved 12 years' adverse possession under the Limitation Acts. Trespassers receive no protection because they have no right to be in occupation, but they may none the less seek recourse to the Criminal Law Act 1977.

In *R* v *Yuthiwattana* (1984) 128 SJ 661, it was held that the offence under s. 1(2) must have the 'character of eviction' which need not be permanent, but could be for months or weeks during which the evicted occupier had to find other accommodation. Locking the tenant out for a day and a night would not suffice but could well be harassment within the scope of s. 13(a) or (b). In *Costelloe* v *London Borough of Camden* [1986] Crim LR 249, it was held that exclusion of the occupier for an hour could be within s. 1(2) if the landlord intended it to be permanent but for some reason (e.g. after intervention by the police) the occupier was readmitted. In *Uckuzular* v *Sandford-Hill* [1994] CLY 1770, an unlawful eviction was held to have taken place where the tenant returned home at 12.30 a.m. to discover her landlord and an unknown companion inside it. The locks had been changed. The police declined to intervene. The plaintiff spent the night with friends, returning to the house at 4.30 a.m. in an unsuccessful attempt to retrieve some of her valuables. She eventually gained entry, via the intervention of her solicitors, at 5 p.m.

Re-instatement may be ordered by mandatory interlocutory injunction (*Parsons* v *Nasar* (1991) 23 HLR 1).

Section 1(2) applies to 'any premises' (which may consist of one room only: *Thurrock UDC* v *Shina* (1972) 23 P & CR 205) or 'any part thereof', so that the offence will have been committed if the landlord bars the occupier's access merely to, e.g. the bathroom or kitchen. Since the premises need not have been let as a dwelling, it appears that 'a boat, cave, pigsty, cart shed, greenhouse or cow house' could all constitute 'premises' so long as they are occupied as a residence (Farrand, 1978: 431). It should also be noted that the offence can be committed by people other than landlords, e.g., managing agents, and perhaps even solicitors who serve invalid notices to quit. The offence of unlawful eviction was not amended by the Housing Act 1988.

### 7.2.2  Harassment

**7.2.2.1  What is harassment?**    Harassment takes many forms and includes such acts as refusing to allow occupiers access to parts of the premises or only allowing access at particular times, preventing occupiers from having guests or visitors, frequent visits by the landlord or the landlord's agent without warning and at unsociable hours, threatening the tenant, entering the tenant's home without permission, allowing the property to fall into such disrepair that it is uncomfortable or dangerous to live in, starting building works and leaving them unfinished or sending in builders without notice or at unreasonable times, removing or restricting services such as hot water or heating, or failing to pay bills so that services are cut off, opening occupiers' mail and removing their belongings. Actual physical violence appears to be rare but threats of violence and verbal abuse are frequent (Jew, 1994: 15). What in isolation may be comparatively minor actions can accumulate and cause the occupier considerable anxiety and distress.

**7.2.2.2  The causes of harassment**    Harassment (and unlawful eviction) are persistent problems within the private rented sector. When the 1965 Act was passed, profiteering commercial landlords were thought to be the main culprits. However, the Milner Holland Committee on Housing in Greater London which reported in 1965 concluded that the type of landlord guilty of such conduct 'bears little resemblance to the big business stereotype' and that 'relatively few abuses can be attributed to companies' (Holland, 1965: 256, 260). As such, the law on harassment and unlawful eviction rarely affects the ways in which commercial landlords operate because harassment is not, and never has been, a common business practice (Nelken, 1983: 8). The legislation, therefore, is most relevant to small landlords who are often ignorant of their own obligations and of tenants' rights. Unless they employ the service of managing agents, small landlords are less likely to vet tenants before they accept them and are more likely to conduct their arrangements on an informal basis. Even where private landlords seek legal advice, the understanding of housing law possessed by many solicitors in private practice ranges from 'inadequate to non-existent' (Burrows, 1990: 17). Both landlords and tenants are often under the impression that landlords have complete control over the property they let and can evict a tenant at any time, using force if necessary. It is commonly thought that little can be done if the landlord 'threatens, intimidates, abuses or even steals from the tenant' (Jew, 1994: 21).

In some areas, 50% of cases of harassment and unlawful eviction are attributable to restrictions on housing benefit and delays in its payment which cause tenants to fall into rent arrears. An upturn in the property market may encourage landlords who want to sell the property to use harassment or unlawful eviction to obtain vacant possession. Landlords who have had action taken against them by local authorities to force compliance with repairing obligations, amenity standards, fire safety or planning notices, or whose rents have been lowered by rent officers may also try to get rid of occupiers, without going through the appropriate legal channels (Jew, 1994: 9).

It must not be thought, however, that landlords have a monopoly on unacceptable behaviour. Sometimes their actions are a desperate response to their tenants' failure to pay the rent or to treat the property in the way in which they expect it to be treated. Sometimes occupiers will refuse to move after their tenancy or licence has ended, even if they have no statutory security of tenure, deliberately consuming as much gas and electricity as possible.

### 7.2.2.3  Who is affected?

A survey carried out on behalf of Shelter in 1989 found, not surprisingly, that tenancies created before the implementation of the Housing Act 1988 figured more prominently in the statisitics than those tenancies created after 15 January 1989 (Burrows, 1990). Research carried out for the Campaign for Bedsit Rights in 1993 revealed that assured and assured shorthold tenants were the most likely to be harassed. Households who would be in priority need under the homeless persons legislation accounted for around half of all harassment and unlawful eviction complaints made to local authorities. People from racial minorities were disproportionately affected as were single parents and households with low incomes in receipt of housing benefit (Jew, 1994: 9).

A survey carried out in 1993/4 found that 7% of privately renting households in England had experienced some attempt by their landlord to get them to leave or to make them feel uncomfortable. This figure includes legitimate action taken by the landlord to recover possession from tenants who had mistreated the property or failed to pay the rent for more than three months. It was highest among regulated tenancies and lowest where there was a resident landlord and no security. Only 3% reported that the landlord had entered the accommodation without permission or used threats or intimidating behaviour (Carey, 1995).

While one of the aims of the Housing Act 1988 was to strengthen the law on harassment, it has been asserted that assured shorthold tenancies serve merely to exacerbate the reluctance of tenants to pursue their legal rights:

If it is only a short time anyway before the tenancy ends, many tenants will silently endure their landlord's criminal actions in the hope that the tenancy will be renewed. As a result and, not least, because harassment often results in the tenant being in a constant state of fear, the majority of incidents and offences remain hidden, unreported to statutory authorities' (Jew, 1994: 21–2).

**7.2.2.4   Harassment: the offences**   By s. 1(3), Protection from Eviction Act 1977:

if any person with intent to cause the residential occupier of any premises

(a)   to give up occupation of the premises or any part thereof; or
(b)   to refrain from exercising any right or pursuing any remedy in respect of the premises or part thereof;

does acts likely to interfere with the peace or comfort of the residential occupier or members of his household, or persistently withdraws or withholds services reasonably required for the occupation of the premises as a residence, he shall be guilty of an offence.

The word 'likely' was substituted for the word 'calculated' by the Housing Act 1988. The offence is now easier to establish, but still requires an intent to cause the occupier to give up his or her occupation or to refrain from exercising his or her rights. As regards the former, one issue is whether or not the tenant has to give up occupation permanently or whether an offence will have been committed if he or she gives it up only temporarily. In *Schon* v *Camden London Borough Council* (1987) P & CR 361, the installation of a bathroom immediately above the tenant's room involved strengthening the floor underneath. Access could be gained from above by pulling up the floor boards or from below via the tenant's room. The landlord and tenant failed to agree on alternative accommodation for the two weeks during which the work was to be carried out so that the tenant remained *in situ*. The building works brought the ceiling down and the tenant's room was rendered uninhabitable. It was held that no offence under s. 1(3)(a) had been committed. The landlord had no intention that the tenant should give up her room permanently, nor had the ceiling been brought down with the intent of causing her to go. There was said to be strong argument that 'occupation' had the same meaning as for the purposes of a statutory tenancy under the Rent Act 1977, so that the tenant was still in occupation during her absence if her possessions remained on the demised premises and she intended to return. The landlord's acts could have connoted an intent to cause the tenant 'to refrain from exercising any right' (i.e. her right to occupy in person for the two-week period), thus falling within s. 1(3)(b) but this was not pleaded.

It has been established that the 'rights' referred to in s. 1(3)(b) are not confined to those arising out of the contractual relationship between the plaintiff and defendant. In *R* v *Burke* [1991] 1 AC 135, the landlord prevented the tenant from using a bathroom and lavatory situated outside his room in the basement by storing furniture in the bathroom and corridor. He padlocked the door to another lavatory and deliberately disconnected the front door bell which connected with the basement floor. The judge found that the tenant had no contractual right to use a particular lavatory or bathroom, nor that the landlord should maintain a system of front door bells. Thus, the landlord's actions were not in breach of the tenancy agreement but the House of Lords none the less upheld his conviction.

For the offence to be committed, either:

(a)   acts likely to interfere with the residential occupier's peace and comfort must have been committed; or

(b)   services persistently withdrawn or withheld.

Although the plural 'acts' is used, a single act suffices (*R* v *Evangelo Polycarpou* (1978) 9 HLR 129). In *R* v *Bokhari* [1974] Crim LR 559, the acts (ostensibly 'repairs') consisted of knocking holes in walls and ceilings, disconnecting mains services, blocking sinks and drains, removing fittings and leaving rubble. In *R* v *Spratt, Wood & Smylie* [1978] Crim LR 102, rent was owing and the house was in an insanitary and dirty state. Accompanied by two friends (one of whom was armed with a monkey wrench and a cleaver), the landlord went to the house where the tenant's brother was made to strip off (to prevent him from escaping) and to reveal what he believed to be the tenant's whereabouts. In due course, he was also made to clean and tidy the house. The three men, all without previous convictions, were each given six months' imprisonment for harassment.

In *R* v *Zafar Ahmad* (1986) 18 HLR 416, the landlord asked the tenant to vacate her flat for three months while improvements were being carried out. The tenant had agreed in principle to the the landlord's plans, but no agreement had been reached over whether the rent would continue to be payable while the work was taking place. She came home one day to find that all her bathroom fittings had been removed. Over the next year the landlord did no further work and the bathroom remained out of use. It was held that the landlord's failure to complete the building works, although a breach of the tenancy agreement, did not fall within s. 1(3). There was evidence that once the landlord had removed the bathroom fittings he formed the intention of evicting the tenant. Afterwards, however, he did not 'do acts' but merely failed to rectify damage already caused.

It was emphasised by Ormrod J in *McCall* v *Abelesz* [1976] 2 WLR 151 at pp. 159–160 that, where 'services' are concerned, something more than a 'hopeful inactivity' has to be shown and in *R* v *Abrol* [1972] Crim LR 318, the Court of Appeal said there must be 'an element of deliberate continuity in withholding [them]'.

It is a defence for the accused to prove that he or she honestly believed that the victim was not a residential occupier but the court may direct the jury that there has to be a reasonable basis for the belief. In *R* v *Phekoo* [1981] 1 WLR 1117 the owner had threatened two men found on the property that he would 'bring his mates round' and 'carve up' one of them. He believed, honestly but mistakenly, that the two men had no right to be there. The Court of Appeal held that the prosecution must prove specific intent to harass someone who the defendant knew or believed to be a residential occupier and not merely a squatter.

Often the prosecution has been unable to prove that the defendant landlord specifically intended to cause the occupier to leave, rather than just make life unpleasant in the hope that he or she might decide to go. To counter these problems s. 1(3A) (introduced by s. 29, Housing Act 1988) provides that:

the landlord of a residential occupier or an agent of the landlord shall be guilty of an offence if—

(a)  he does acts likely to interfere with the peace or comfort of the residential occupier or members of his household; or
(b)  he persistently withdraws or withholds services reasonably required for the occupation of the premises in question as a residence;

and (in either case) he knows, or has reasonably cause to believe, that the conduct is likely to cause the residential occupier to give up the occupation of the whole or part of the premises or to refrain from exercising any right or pursuing any remedy in respect of the whole or part of the premises.

Thus, s. 1(3A) creates an offence which can be committed only by certain individuals, i.e., the landlord of the residential occupier concerned ('landlord' being defined as including any superior landlord (s. 1(3C))), or an agent of the landlord. The *actus reus* is identical to s. 1(3); the only difference is the *mens rea*. Whether or not the landlord intended the occupier to leave is not relevant; what matters is whether a reasonable man (having at his disposal the facts known to the landlord) would believe the occupier to be likely to give up possession as the result of the landlord's behaviour.

Section 1(3B) provides that a person shall not be guilty of an offence under s. 1(3A) if he or she proves that he or she had reasonable grounds for doing the acts or withdrawing or withholding the services in question.

It should be noted that the offence is not limited to the occupier and members of his or her family but extends to members of his or her 'household'.

A person found guilty of an offence under s. 1(1) or s. 1(3), as amended, is subject to a maximum penalty of six months' imprisonment or a £2,000 fine or both. If convicted on indictment, imprisonment may be for up to two years and/or an unlimited fine my be imposed (s. 1(4)).

## 7.2.3  Enforcement

The law on harassment and unlawful eviction has been criticised for being ineffective. The number of prosecutions and the consequent convictions has always been low:

| 1985 | 62  |
|------|-----|
| 1986 | 64  |
| 1987 | 83  |
| 1988 | 73  |
| 1989 | 101 |
| 1990 | 106 |
| 1991 | 98  |
| 1992 | 114 |
| 1993 | 85  |
| 1994 | 108 |
| 1995 | 77  |

Home Office, 1995: 120, Table 5.20.

The police can prosecute s. 1 offences but take the view that the responsibility for bringing prosecutions lies with local authorities. They do not normally intervene unless physical violence is involved and, if they do intervene, they prefer to charge landlords/licensors with 'ordinary' criminal offences such as assault, obstructing a police officer, conduct likely to provoke a breach of the peace or criminal damage. The response of the police seems to depend on the station and/or officer concerned. It has been maintained, however, that a lack of awareness of anti-harassment and illegal eviction laws often leads to police officers declining to intervene in landlord and tenant disputes and sometimes actually assisting landlords in evicting tenants illegally (Jew, 1994: 11).

Section 6 also gives local authorities the power to bring prosecutions. Many authorities have tenancy relations officers whose jobs include dealing with harassment and illegal eviction complaints. Very often the task is given to other officers — including environmental health officers, homeless persons officers and members of the legal department — who have other complex and demanding tasks to perform (Jew, 1994: 10). Although most cases of harassment and unlawful eviction take place outside normal office hours, over a third of authorities have no 24-hour emergency service to deal with them.

Local authorities generally prosecute wherever there is any real chance of success. Unlawful eviction is relatively easy to prove but harassment is more problematic, especially in the absence of corroborative evidence which will be particularly difficult to obtain where there is a long delay between the commission of the alleged offence and the court hearing (Burrows, 1990: 59). In a minority of authorities the decision to prosecute is made by a council committee which causes further delays in processing complaints (Jew, 1994: 11). Authorities sometimes have difficulty in discovering the landlord's true identity or address. Prosecutions may also fail because the charges as framed did not convey to the court the real nature of the alleged offence. The significance of a single act, which might appear justifiable when viewed in isolation may only become appreciated when set in the context of all the defendant's activities. (Department of the Environment and Welsh Office, 1988: para. 8).

Where the harassment occurs in a house in multiple occupation, the local authority may use its powers under s. 379, Housing Act 1985 if appears that 'the state or condition of the house is such as to call for the taking of action' and 'the living conditions in the house are such that it is necessary to make [a Control Order] ... to protect the safety, welfare or health of persons living [there]'. See *R* v *Secretary of State for the Environment, ex parte Royal Borough of Kensington & Chelsea* (1987) 19 HLR 161 in which a compulsory purchase order was made in respect of five houses where the tenants had complained of harassment and intimidation.

The low level of fines for successful prosecutions may discourage authorities from instituting criminal proceedings, although heavier fines may well be imposed where there is evidence of financial motivation (Nelken, 1983: 9). In *R* v *Brennan and Brennan* [1979] Crim LR 603, in which the landlord accompanied by a 'very large man and an alsatian dog' evicted a group of students from their rented premises, it was said that 'loss of liberty should be the usual penalty where landlords use threats or force, in the absence of unusual mitigation'. Where the police or local authority are unwilling to initiate proceedings, the individual occupier may bring a private prosecution.

### 7.2.4  Using violence to secure entry to premises

Section 6, Criminal Law Act 1977 makes it an offence for a person without lawful authority (such as a bailiff executing a warrant of possession) to use or threaten violence for the purpose of securing entry to premises upon which, to his or her knowledge, someone is present who is opposed to the entry. It is not necessary that there should be any entry; the crime can be committed even if the intruders are unsuccessful. The violence may be directed against the person or the property. 'Violence' covers 'any application of force to the person, but it carries a somewhat restricted meaning in relation to property. ... [F]orcing a Yale-type lock with a piece of plastic or a window catch with a thin piece of metal, would almost certainly amount to force, but not to violence. ... On the other hand, splintering a door or a window or its frame would be' (Law Commission, 1976: para. 2.61).

Even an excluded tenant or licensee (see **7.5.1**) or a trespasser cannot be evicted whilst actually within the premises. Eviction can only occur through a bailiff or sheriff and with a court order. The landlord or licensor can, however, wait until the occupier leaves the premises, e.g to go to work, and then remove his or her belongings and change the locks. There will be no criminal offence.

### 7.3  CIVIL LIABILITY

The complexity, cost and length of time involved may deter tenants from bringing a civil action. Reductions in the availability of legal aid introduced in April 1993 mean that many tenants cannot afford civil action and the easiest solution is simply to find somewhere else to live.

It was held in *McCall* v *Abelesz* [1976] 1 All ER 727 that what is now s. 1(3), Protection from Eviction Act 1977 did not create a cause of action for breach of statutory duty on the basis of which a residential occupier could take action, e.g. for damages or reinstatement. Instead action had to be taken under other causes, the primary objective of most civil proceedings in this area being to obtain an injunction from the court ordering the landlord to reinstate the residential occupier in the premises.

### 7.3.1   Contract

Where there is a lease, the tenant can sue the landlord for breach of contract, usually the landlord's implied covenant for quiet enjoyment. Although a covenant for quiet enjoyment will not be implied into a mere licence to occupy property, the court may imply some term preventing the landlord from unduly interfering with the licensee's occupation and use of the property. See, e.g. *Smith* v *Nottingham County Council* (1981) *The Times*, 13 November, in which students living as licensees in a hall of residence were unable to study for their exams because of noise and other disturbance caused by urgent building works to another nearby hall.

As regards quiet enjoyment, the traditional view is that the tenant must have suffered physical interference with his or her enjoyment of the property. However, in *Kenny* v *Preen* [1963] 1 QB 499, a breach of covenant was said to occur when anything was done which was an invasion of the tenant's right to remain in possession undisturbed even if it caused no direct physical interference. Here the landlord had served a purported notice to quit on the tenant (an elderly widow), sent her letters threatening to evict her and to put her property into the street, and knocked at her door, shouting threats. The landlord's 'deliberate and persistent attempt' to drive the tenant out by 'persecution and intimidation' was held to constitute a breach of covenant even if there was no direct physical interference with the tenant's possession and enjoyment. In so far as such interference was a necessary element in the breach of covenant, it was present in the form of knocking on the door and shouting threats. Other examples of a breach of the covenant include cutting off the tenant's gas and electricity (*Perera* v *Vandiyar* [1953] 1 WLR 672), and the removal of doors and windows (*Lavender* v *Betts* [1942] 2 All ER 723). These would now amount to the criminal offence of harassment.

Neither exemplary nor aggravated damages (see **7.3.2.1**) can be awarded for breach of contract because it cannot be described as a contract to provide peace of mind or freedom from distress (*Branchett* v *Beaney, Coster and Swale Borough* [1992] 3 All ER 910). Therefore the tenant who can establish a tort may be in a better position.

### 7.3.2   Tort

A tenant or licensee can sue the landlord in tort, the landlord having committed trespass (to the person, land or personal property) and possibly assault and/or nuisance. In *Caruso* v *Owen* (1983) LAG Bulletin 106, the landlord — in the mistaken belief that the tenant had given up possession — burned the tenant's PhD notes on a bonfire. In assessing damages of £3,000 for the loss of the research material (for the tort of wrongful interference with goods) the judge accepted the tenant's evidence that it would take at least another year to redo the work which had been destroyed and that he had been in receipt of a maintenance grant of £3,000 for the year.

### 7.3.2.1 Types of damages   The plaintiff may obtain:

(a)   *general damages*: these are unliquidated damages which can be claimed for, e.g. any personal injury sustained by the plaintiff, loss of enjoyment, and loss of the right to occupy (*Millington v Duffy* (1985) 17 HLR 232). In *Shafr v Yagambrun* (1994) CLY 1450 the landlord told the tenant a month before her 'A' level examinations, that she must leave the house the next day as it was about to be repossessed by the building society. General damages of £3,000 were based in part on the adverse effect the disruption must have had on the tenant's studies.

(b)   *special damages*: the aim of special damages is to compensate the evicted occupier for specific lossess such as reasonable accommodation costs incurred after the eviction, the cost of items taken from the property (*Ramdath v Daley* (1993) 25 HLR 273) and return of any premium paid (*Ayari v Jetha* (1991) 24 HLR 639).

(c)   *aggravated damages*: these are intended to compensate the plaintiff for 'injury to his proper feelings of dignity and pride' (per Nourse, LJ in *Ramdath v Daley* at p. 279), feelings of outrage, indignation and distress, which he or she incurred as a result of the eviction. See, e.g. *Nwokorie v Mason* (1993) 26 HLR 60; *McMillan v Singh* (1984) 17 HLR 120; *Ashgar v Ahmed* (1984) 17 HLR 25.

(d)   *exemplary damages*: these are payable where the defendant has calculated that his or her conduct will make him or her a profit which may well exceed the compensation payable to the plaintiff (see *Ramdath v Daley*; cf. *Sampson v Wilson* (1994) 26 HLR 486). In *Cassell & Co. v Broome* [1972] AC 1027, at p. 1029 Lord Hailsham gave as an example 'the late Mr Rachman, who is alleged to have used hired bullies to intimidate statutory tenants by violence or threats of violence into giving vacant possession of their residences and so placing a valuable asset in the hands of the landlord'. This, he said, amounted to 'a cynical calculation of profit and cold-blooded disregard of a plaintiffs rights'.

The objective of exemplary damages is punitive rather than compensatory and they can properly be awarded 'whenever it is necessary to teach a wrongdoer that tort does not pay' (per Lord Devlin in *Rookes v Barnard* [1964] AC 1129 at p. 1221). Awards of exemplary damages have been upheld in several eviction cases but they have not been particularly high: see, e.g., *Drane v Evangelou* [1978] 1 WLR 455; *Guppy (Bridport) Ltd v Brookling* (1984) 269 EG 846; *Asghar v Ahmed*, ibid.; *McMillan v Singh*, ibid.) Since the claim for damages is at common law, it is irrelevant that the plaintiff may have failed to behave with the utmost propriety. Thus, in *McMillan v Singh*, the fact that the plaintiff had fallen into arrears from time to time had no bearing on his claim for exemplary damages.

**7.3.2.2 Sections 27 and 28, Housing Act 1988**   Section 27, Housing Act 1988 effectively overturns the decision in *McCall* v *Abelesz* (7.3) and creates a new statutory tort. It gives the residential occupier evicted after 9 June 1988 a right to sue his or her landlord, or any person acting on his or her behalf, for committing an act which amounts to a criminal offence under s. 1, Protection from Eviction Act 1977 and which has caused him or her to give up occupation of the premises as a residence. Awards of damages under these provisions have, in some circumstances, been considerable (£31,000 in *Tagro* v *Carfane and Patel* (1991) HLR 250). The remedy provided by s. 27 does not replace the traditional causes of action in tort and contract which can still be used where, e.g. the occupier did not give up occupation or has been reinstated (see *McCormack* v *Namjou* [1990] CLY 1725), or had little or no security of tenure so that the damages recoverable by him or her under s. 28 would be low.

**7.3.2.3 Defences under s. 27**   Three defences are made available to the landlord by s. 27:

(a) Before proceedings are finally disposed of, the plaintiff has been reinstated in the premises, so that he or she becomes again a residential occupier with the full rights of which he or she has been deprived (s. 27(6)(a)). However, 'reinstatement does not consist in merely handing the tenant a key to a lock which does not work and inviting her to resume occupation of a room which has been totally wrecked' (per Lord Donaldson in *Tagro* v *Carfane* [1991] 2 All ER 235 at p. 239). The occupier is not obliged to accept an offer of reinstatement by the landlord but if one is made before proceedings are commenced then an unreasonable refusal thereof by the occupier may result in a reduction of damages awarded (see below). If the occupier is reinstated he or she may still be able to claim damages under the general law.

(b) The plaintiff has requested the court to reinstate him or her and the court has acceded to that request, so that he or she is once more the residential occupier (s. 27(6)(b)).

(c) The landlord believed, and had reasonable cause to believe, that the occupier had ceased to reside in the premises, or that he or she had reasonable grounds for withdrawing or withholding services (s. 27(8)).

Section 27(7) imposes on the plaintiff a statutory duty to mitigate his or her loss but his or her damages will be reduced in two instances only:

(a) if the landlord made an offer of reinstatement prior to the commencement of proceedings which was not taken up by the plaintiff;

(b) where the conduct of the occupier or any person living with him or her in the premises in question was such that it is 'reasonable' to mitigate the damages payable.

**7.3.2.4 The measure of damages**   By s. 28 the measure of damages is the difference in value, as at the date when the residential occupier left the premises, between the property with the occupier in it and the property with vacant possession. In other words, it is the profit which the landlord stood to make by acting unlawfully, whether or not in fact he or she makes it. That which is to be valued is the whole building in which the premises are situated so that the potential gain to, e.g. the last protected tenant of a bedsit in a house with the potential for convesion into flats or resale for owner-occupation, will be considerable as in *Guppys (Bridport) Ltd* v *Brookling* (1984) 14 HLR 1. However, against that must be set the assumptions that the landlord is selling his or her interest in the open market to a willing buyer, that neither the occupier nor a member of the occupier's family want to buy, and that there is no extant 'substantial development' or demolition permission. Thus 'there shall be no increase in the damages because the effect of the tenant being dispossessed is that it enables some very valuable development to take place' (per Lord Donaldson in *Tagro* v *Carfane* [1991] 2 All ER 235 at pp. 242, 243, in which the landlord, himself a business tenant, argued unsuccessfully that the value of his interest was nil because his lease prohibited assignment and sub-letting).

It is the right of occupation which is to be valued so that eviction of someone with a lesser right, e.g. a restricted contract or an assured shorthold tenancy, will produce a lower amount of damages than an assured or protected tenant with full security of tenure. In *Melville* v *Bruton* [1996] EGCS 57, the landlord unlawfully evicted the plaintiff a few weeks after the start of her assured shorthold tenancy. The county court judge awarded damages of £15,000 under ss. 27 and 28, representing the difference in the value of the property immediately before and after the eviction, even though two other people (tenants or licensees) were still living at the property. The Court of Appeal allowed the landlord's appeal on the basis that nothing in ss. 27 and 28 justified disregarding the existence of the other residential occupiers. The tenant's eviction made no difference to the value of the property as it was still encumbered. The purpose of the 1988 Act was not so comprehensive as to provide damages for evicted tenants in all circumstances and it should be interpreted to reflect the fact that the eviction had not materially increased the value of the landlord's interest. The award of £15,000 was set aside and £500 substituted for inconvenience, discomfort and distress.

As stated above, an agent of the landlord can be found guilty of the criminal offences in ss. 1(2), (3) and (3A) of the Protection from Eviction Act 1977 and it follows, therefore, that civil liability under s. 27 can be imposed jointly on a principal and an agent acting within the scope of his or her employment (see *Sampson* v *Wilson* [1995] 3 WLR 455).

## 7.4  FORFEITURE

Section 2, Protection from Eviction Act 1977 provides that 'where any premises are let as a dwelling on a lease which is subject to a right of re-entry or forfeiture, it shall not be lawful to enforce that right otherwise than by proceedings in court while any person is lawfully residing in the premises or part of them'.

This provision is of particular significance for tenants who have no security of tenure. Forfeiture of a protected tenancy under the Rent Act 1977 does not of itself entitle the landlord to possession, and a court order based on a ground for possession must be obtained. Assured tenancies cannot be terminated by forfeiture alone but the presence of a forfeiture clause in a fixed-term assured or assured shorthold tenancy in conjunction with the statutory procedure may enable the tenancy to be brought to an end before the expiry of the term on Grounds 2, 8 and 10 to 15.

## 7.5  EVICTION WITHOUT DUE PROCESS OF LAW

Section 3(1) provides that:

> where any premises have been let as a dwelling under a tenancy which is neither a statutorily protected tenancy nor an excluded tenancy and—
>
> (a)   the tenancy ... has come to an end, but
> (b)   the occupier continues to reside in the premises or part of them,
>
> it shall not be lawful for the owner to enforce against the occupier, otherwise than by proceedings in the court, his right to recover possession of the premises.

By s. 3(2B) of the Rent Act 1977, inserted by the Housing Act 1988, the section is extended to any premises occupied as a dwelling under a licence, other than an excluded licence.

Section 3, as amended, provides a minimum protection for certain residential occupiers who otherwise have no security of tenure. Breach of s. 3 is a tort. The 'statutorily protected' tenancies are listed in s. 8 of the 1977 Act and include, within the residential sector, Rent Act protected tenancies, assured and assured shorthold tenancies under the Housing Act 1988, and long tenancies within Part I of the Landlord and Tenant Act 1954, all of which have their own schemes of protection. Secure tenancies (under Part IV of the Housing Act 1985) and statutory tenancies under the Rent Act 1977 are not 'statutorily protected' tenancies, however, and are subject, therefore, to s. 3. In *Haniff v Robinson* [1992] 3 WLR 875, it was held that the landlord had carried out an unlawful eviction by forcibly entering the premises and removing a statutory tenant, even though he had obtained a possession order and a warrant of execution of the order. The Court of Appeal held that the effect of s. 3 was to protect the occupier until there had been proper execution of the order by the court bailiff. The tenant was awarded damages, calculated in accordance with s. 28.

### 7.5.1  Excluded tenancies and licences

The Housing Act 1988 provides for a new class of 'excluded tenancies and licences' to which s. 3 does not apply. They are set out in s. 3A, Protection from Eviction Act 1977.

**7.5.1.1  Accommodation shared with the owner or a member of the owner's family**  Section 3A(2) provides that:

a tenancy or licence is excluded if—

(a)  under its terms the occupier shares any accommodation with the landlord or the licensor; and

(b)  immediately before the tenancy or licence was granted and also at the time it comes to an end, the landlord or licensor occupied as his only or principal home premises of which the whole or part of the shared accommodation formed part.

Section 3A(3) is worded similarly but refers to 'a member of the family of the landlord or licensor' in place of 'the landlord or the licensor' and contains the additional requirement that 'immediately before the tenancy or licence was granted and also at the time it comes to an end, the landlord or licensor occupied as his only or principal home premises in the same building as the shared accommodation and that building is not a purpose-built block of flats'.

The exception in s. 3A(2) differs from the 'resident landlord' exclusions under the Rent Act 1977 and Housing Act 1988 in that it requires the actual sharing of accommodation. It is not confined to the sharing of living accommodation, but extends to a right to share the use of any accommodation, except storage areas, staircases, passages, corridors or other means of access (s. 3A(5)(a)). Thus, where a tenancy granted before 15 January 1989 falls within the resident landlord provisions of the Rent Act 1977, the tenant will have a restricted contract, which requires a court order for possession under s. 3, Protection from Eviction Act 1977. In the case of a tenancy granted by a resident landlord after the commencement of the 1988 Act, the tenant can have neither a restricted contract nor an assured tenancy. If the conditions of s. 3A are satsified, no court order is required. If they are not, a possession order must still be obtained under s. 3.

If the tenant shares accommodation with a member of the landlord's family, but the landlord himself or herself does not reside at the premises, the tenant may have an assured tenancy, as the resident-landlord rules would not be satisfied. In such a case, neither s. 3 nor s. 3A would apply, recovery of possession being governed by the assured tenancy rules, which require a possession order (and a ground for possession). If, however, the tenant shares accommodation with a member of the landlord's or licensor's family and the landlord occupies as his only or principal home premises in the same building (which is not a purpose-built block of flats), no possession order under s. 3 is required.

**7.5.1.2  Trespassers**  A tenancy or licence is excluded by s. 3A(6) if it was granted as a temporary expedient to a person who entered the premises in question, or any other premises, as a trespasser (whether or not, before the beginning of that tenancy or licence, another tenancy or licence to occupy the premises had been granted to him or her). This provision will be significant mainly to local authorities who may allow trespassers to remain in occupation of its property as a temporary measure.

**7.5.1.3  Holiday occupation**  A tenancy or licence is excluded by s. 3A(7)(a) if it confers on the tenant or licensee the right to occupy the premises for a holiday only. Holiday lettings are excluded from the definition of protected tenancies under the Rent Act 1977 and assured tenancies under the Housing Act 1988. Prior to the enactment of s. 3A of the Protection from Eviction Act 1977, tenants with holiday lettings had the protection of the court order requirement. Such tenants (and licensees) are now denied the opportunity of arguing that the exception has been used as an evasion device unless they are willing themselves to initiate the proceedings.

**7.5.1.4  Rent-free occupation**  A tenancy or licence is excluded if it is granted otherwise than for money or money's worth (s. 3A(8)).

**7.5.1.5  Hostel accommodation**  A licence (but not a tenancy) is excluded if it confers rights of occupation in a hostel, within the meaning of the Housing Act 1985, provided by various specified public bodies such as local authorities, the Housing Corporation, and housing trusts which are either charities or registered housing associations (s. 3A(8)).

## 7.6  NOTICE TO QUIT

A notice to quit is required for the determination of periodic tenancies. At common law it need not be in writing but must be clear and unambiguous (*Gardner* v *Ingram* (1890) 61 LT 729). The length of the notice required depends upon the express terms of the tenancy. If there are none, six months' notice must be given to end a yearly tenancy, one-quarter's notice to end a quarterly tenancy, one month's notice to end a monthly tenancy, and one week's notice to end a weekly tenancy. The appropriate notice must be expressed to expire at the end of the period or on the anniversary date.

Statutory provisions may require longer periods of notice. As regards residential tenancies, s. 5(1), Protection from Eviction Act 1977 provides that a minimum of four weeks' notice to quit must be given in writing. By s. 5(1A) the same rule applies to periodic licences, but not to a licence which is expressed to be terminable with the licensee's employment (e.g. *Norris* v *Checksfield* [1991] 4 All ER 327). Section 5 does not apply to excluded tenancies or licences, nor to tenants at will. A landlord's notice must provide certain information, in accordance with the Notices to Quit (Prescribed Information) Regulations 1988 (SI 1988/2201). Put simply it should inform the occupier that if he or she does not leave the dwelling, he or she cannot be lawfully evicted without a possession order from the court, that the landlord or licensor cannot apply for such an order before the notice to quit or notice to determine has run out, and that if he or she is uncertain of his or her right to remain in possession, information and advice is available from a solicitor, a Citizen's Advice Bureau, a Housing Aid Centre or a Rent Officer. Help with all or part of the cost of legal advice and assistance may be available under the Legal Aid Scheme.

There may be particular problems where a notice to quit is given by one joint tenant, a situation which is most likely to arise in the case of relationship breakdown. The tenant leaving the property will often turn for accommodation to the local authority, which may also be the landlord of the existing accommodation. As a precondition of housing the applicant, the authority will generally require the termination of the existing tenancy, a step which will have the effect of making homeless the tenant who is left. In *Hammersmith and Fulham LBC v Monk* [1992] 1 AC 47, Mr Monk and Mrs Powell were joint tenants of a council flat. Following a domestic dispute, Mrs Powell left the flat and the local authority agreed to rehouse her if she would terminate the tenancy by giving the requisite four weeks' notice to quit. This she did without Mr Monk's knowledge or consent. The authority immediately notified Mr Monk that the tenancy had been determined and, in due course, brought possession proceedings against him. The House of Lords upheld the effectiveness of the notice. It said that, unless the tenancy agreement provides otherwise, a joint tenant can validly determine the tenancy by notice without the agreement of the other joint tenant or tenants. Lord Browne-Wilkinson spoke of 'two instinctive reactions' to the case which lead to 'diametrically opposed conclusions'. The first was that the flat in question was the joint home of Mr Monk and Mrs Powell: it could not be right, therefore, that one of them unilaterally could join with the landlords to put an end to the other's rights in the home. The second view — which the House of Lords favoured — was that Mr Monk and Mrs Powell undertook joint liabilities as tenants for the purpose of providing themselves with a joint home and that, once they no longer wanted to live together, the one who left the home should not be made to continue indefinitely to be liable for the discharge of the obligations to the landlord under the tenancy agreement.

In *Hounslow LBC v Pilling* (1993) 25 HLR 305, the local authority undertook to rehouse any tenant who had experienced domestic violence, provided that the tenant surrendered his or her tenancy. The tenancy agreement required four weeks' written notice 'or such lesser period as the council may accept'. With the landlord's consent, Ms Doubtfire, a joint tenant acting unilaterally, gave three days' notice to quit. The Court of Appeal rejected the notice as inappropriate and therefore ineffective. In relying on the landlord's discretionary acceptance of a shorter period, the tenant had not exercised a power of determination by notice to quit but had instead sought to operate what amounted to a break clause cannot be unilaterally invoked by one joint tenant. In any event, the court held that it was not possible to override the Protection from Eviction Act requirement of at least four weeks' notice.

### References

Burrows, L. and Hunter, N., *Forced Out!*, London: Shelter, 1990.
Carey, S., *Private Renting in England 1993/4*, London: HMSO, 1995.
Department of the Environment and Welsh Office, Joint Circular 3/89, Housing Act 1988: Protection of Residential Occupiers.

Farrand, J.T., *The Rent Act 1977. The Protection from Eviction Act 1977*, London: Sweet & Maxwell, 1978.

Holland, Sir Milner, Report of the Committee on Housing in Greater London, Cmnd. 2605, London: HMSO, 1965.

Home Office, Criminal Statistics, England and Wales 1995, Cm. 3421, London: The Stationery Office, 1996.

Law Commission, Report on Conspiracy and Criminal Law Reform (Law Com. No. 76.) London: HMSO, 1976.

Jew, P., *Law and Order in Private Rented Housing*, London: Campaign for Bedsit Rights, 1994.

Nelken, D., *The Limits of the Legal Process: A Study of Landlords, Law and Crime*, London: Academic Press, 1983.

**Further reading**

Carrott, S. and Hunter, C., *Arden and Partington on Quiet Enjoyment*, London: Legal Action Group, 1990.

Kemp, P., 'The Ghost of Rachman' in *Built to Last* (ed. Grant, C.), London: Roof, 1992, pp. 110–121.

# EIGHT

## The history of social housing

### 8.1  INTRODUCTION

Most social housing in this country is owned and managed by local authorities but, since 1988, housing associations have been thrust into the limelight as the main providers of new social housing and they have also taken over a significant amount of housing which was previously in local authority ownership. Even though the size of the council housing sector has dropped from 32% of all housing in Great Britain in 1979 to 18.9% today, it is still large in comparison with other countries. In Australia, for example, the size of the public sector has hovered around 4 to 7% of the housing stock since 1954 (Van Vliet, 1990: Table 24.2). This chapter considers the origins and development of council housing and concludes with a brief examination of the voluntary housing sector. The decline of council housing is addressed in **Chapters 11** (under the 'right to buy') and **12**.

### 8.2  FROM THE NINETEENTH CENTURY TO THE FIRST WORLD WAR

The nineteenth century was a period of dynamic change in Great Britain. Between 1801 and 1841 the population rose from nine million to 16 million and by 1901 it was twice as large again (Merrett, 1979: 3). Growth was concentrated in the manufacturing towns of the north of England, and cities such as Glasgow, Birmingham and Bristol where opportunities for employment existed. The pollution caused by industrial processes, inadequate drainage and sanitation, the shortage of decent housing and the consequent overcrowding combined to produce appalling living conditions. In 1844, Engels vividly described part of Manchester in which each house was 'packed close behind its neighbour ... all black, smoky, crumbling, ancient, with broken panes and window frames' and where, at the entrance to one courtyard, stood 'a privy without a door, so dirty that the inhabitants can pass into and out of the court only by passing through foul pools of stagnant urine and excrement'. Nearby tanneries filled the neighbourhood with 'the stench of animal putrefaction' while 'the contents of all the neighbouring sewers and privies' found their way into the river into which was also discharged effluent from the 'tanneries, bone mills and gasworks' (Engels, F., *The Condition of the Working Class in England, 1844–5*, quoted in Clayre, 1977). Continuing industrial development produced a demand for more housing but also reduced the existing supply. The new railway system cut a swathe through residential areas into city centres, and the space produced by slum clearance was often filled, not with new homes, but with warehouses, offices, grand new thorough-fares and the civic monuments to commercial success exemplified by law courts and town halls (Wohl, 1977: 26–27; Merret, 1979: 12; Forrest et al, 1991: 18).

The disease caused by overcrowded and insanitary conditions adversely affected labour productivity and profits while the dissatisfaction they engen-dered lead to fears of civil unrest. One response lay in public health legislation and the regulation of new buildings (Merrett, 1979: 6, 9). In 1871 the Local Government Board was set up to oversee local affairs and the Public Health Act 1872 required the formation of sanitary authorities covering the whole country. The Public Health Act 1875 empowered local authorities to make by-laws setting out basic requirements regarding housing standards and amenities, thus preventing the construction of new slums but leaving existing ones untouched.

The Artisans and Labourers' Dwellings Act 1868 (the 'Torrens' Act) gave local authorities the power to close or demolish *individual* unfit dwellings while the Artisans and Labourers' Dwellings Improvement Act 1875 (the 'Cross' Act) enabled them to demolish and clear *areas* of unfit housing. The 1875 Act also, and significantly, imposed an obligation upon local authorities to rehouse on site those households which had been displaced during the clearance. Any housing built in pursuance of this obligation was to be sold within 10 years of its completion. However, the only council housing erected under the 1875 Act appears to have been in Devonport, Liverpool and Nottingham (Merrett, 1979: 20). In most cases the local authorities sold the sites to charitable housing trusts endowed by wealthy philanthropists such as Rothschild, Guiness and Peabody, or to 'model dwelling companies' such as the Improved Industrial Dwellings Company, the 4% Industrial Dwellings Company, and the East End Dwellings Company. These bodies aimed to provide working-class housing with a regular water supply, adequate sewage disposal and proper ventilation, all at an affordable rent, while ensuring a limited return to investors of about 5%. Often, however, the rents payable for the new properties were beyond the reach of the displaced tenants.

The Royal Commission on the Housing of the Working Classes (1884–5) found that overcrowding was on the increase in nearly all the areas of London it surveyed. The model dwelling companies had failed to provide enough working-class homes in central districts, and 'the working-class suburb' was not yet a viable proposition. The Commission emphasised that overcrowding was a housing problem caused by high rents and the need for working people to live near their work. It was not a sanitary problem which could be resolved merely by public health measures. Nor was it the fault of the feckless and undeserving poor since even better paid artisans were the victims of overcrowding. It was, in the words of a memorable phrase employed by the Royal Commission, 'the stye that made the pig' and not the other way round.

The Local Government Act 1888 put in place a unified system of local government, replacing the plethora of ad hoc bodies — improvement commissions, highways boards, health boards and sanitary authorities — which had been set up earlier in the century as and when the need arose and whose functions had gradually been absorbed by councils. The 1888 Act established the county councils, the London County Council and the county borough councils and, in 1894, the urban and rural district councils were formed to take over from the old urban and rural sanitary authorities. This structure remained virtually intact until the major reorganisation of local government in 1974.

The Housing of the Working Classes Act 1890 was largely a consolidating measure which brought together the Torrens and Cross Acts but also enabled local authorities to redevelop a site themselves if no other agency came forward (Part I), and to build, renovate and improve 'working class lodging houses' (Part III). It was 'a qualitative turning point' and a 'quanititative watershed' in the history of British public housing (Merrett, 1979: 26) in that it permitted the construction of public housing quite separately from any clearance operations. It too required properties built to be sold off within 10 years.

The London County Council used Part III more extensively than any other authority, constructing its first four suburban estates at Tooting, Croydon, Tottenham and Acton (Merret, 1979: 24). Public housing was also built in Sheffield, Liverpool and Glasgow but most authorities built no houses at all. Some had no desire to become landlords but even the enthusiastic were deterred by the fact that housing built under these schemes was expected to be self-financing. A subsidy of some sort was needed to to bridge the gap between construction costs and the rents which working class tenants could afford but nothing was forthcoming from central government and, as local government was largely in the hands of local property owners, voluntary subsidies from the rates were out of the question. In consequence, the model dwelling companies retained their role as the main providers of social housing and 'the market model, largely unconstrained by the redistributive influence of the state, dominated housing policy' (Clapham et al, 1990: 40).

The Liberal government which assumed office in 1906 initiated a number of measures which paved the way for the construction of the welfare state but, so far as public housing was concerned, its only contribution was the Housing and Town Planning Act 1909 which brought to an end the requirement that dwellings built under the 1875 and 1890 Acts should be sold after 10 years. By 1914, local authorities owned about 24,000 dwellings (well under half a per cent of the entire housing stock at the time).

## 8.3   THE INTER-WAR YEARS

No recognisable housing policy existed before 1914. Between the wars, it consisted of two main elements: rent control in the private sector and the development of the public sector. Initially, the latter involved the provision of general needs housing, and it emerged as a tenure which served mainly clerks and small tradesmen, skilled and semi-skilled workers with above average wages, average sized families and secure jobs. Towards the end of the 1920s, however, attention turned to the accommodation of people displaced by slum clearance. Throughout this period, housing was a political football kicked to and fro between the opposing parties. The Conservatives supported private enterprise and regarded state intervention merely as a temporary expedient whilst Labour envisaged a permanent role for public housing but was hindered by a lack of political power and economic resources. Even so, there was a high output of new houses in both the private and public sectors. Between 1919 and 1939, 3,998,000 new houses were built: 1, 112,000 by local authorities and 2,886,000 by private enterprise of which 430,000 were subsidised (Burnett, 1978: 242). Most of the properties built by private enterprise were sold to owner-occupiers but as many as 900,000 were added to the private rented sector (Malpass et al, 1994: 48). Housing standards were higher than those which had prevailed in the nineteenth century.

Council housing began in earnest soon after the First World War. The introduction of rent control in 1915 meant that speculative builders could no longer be relied on to provide low-cost housing, when the costs of labour and building materials were rapidly increasing. The low level of building both before and during the war, together with a huge increase in household numbers, resulted in many men returning to housing conditions which were worse than those they had left. Often they had to move in with relatives, to occupy one or two rooms in houses shared with several other families, or to live in various 'temporary dwellings', including wooden shacks, caravans and railway carriages which were totally devoid of any sanitary facilities (Burnett, 1978: 217). Speaking in Wolverhampton on 23 November 1918, Lloyd George declared that 'Slums are not fit homes for the men who have won this war'.

The First World War brought about a major social shake-up, challenging long-established class divisions and highlighting a growing dissatisfaction with pre-war standards of working-class life in general and of housing in particular (Bowley, 1945: 3, 4). The Russian Revolution had only recently taken place and the British labour movement had become much stronger during the war with the growth of the trade unions. 'The money we propose to spend on housing is an insurance against Bolshevism and revolution' pronounced Lord Astor, Parliamentary Secretary to Local Government Board, although he was mindful too of the moral and social casualties inflicted by bad housing and 'the awful havoc upon the morality of young girls' wrought by overcrowding (*Hansard*, HC Debates, vol. 114, col. 1956, 8 April 1919). All of a sudden, housing became a national and party political issue, rather than one in which only isolated groups of social reformers were interested.

### 8.3.1  The Housing and Planning Act 1919

A coalition government of Liberals and Conservatives, led by Lloyd George, took office in November 1919. Dr Christopher Addison was the President of the Local Government Board and, later, the first Minister of Health. The Housing and Planning Act 1919 (the Addison Act) gave local authorities a new, significant role in the provision of housing. It required local authorities to survey the housing needs of their districts and to make and carry out plans to provide the houses which were needed. Ministerial approval was required before the plans were put into practice and for the rents at which the houses were to be let.

The government intended that half a million dwellings should be built in three years. Building on such a large scale, however, necessitated the co-operation of the local authorities and they were reluctant to dig deep into their municipal pockets. Their co-operation was secured by limiting their liability to a penny rate. The difference between the income from rents and the cost of providing houses was to be met by the Exchequer. In effect, therefore, the state had assumed financial responsibility for the provision of working class houses. In their capacity as developers of the new housing, the local authorities were required to compete in the open market for materials and labour and to raise capital as best they could. This meant borrowing from institutional lenders at commercial rates of interest.

The 1919 Act thus set up a framework for the production, financing, and management of council housing which lasted until the end of the 1960s. The only differences over this period were the variations in the levels of subsidy, the purpose for which it was granted (typically general needs or slum clearance), and the period for which it would be paid (Hughes et al, 1995: 14). None the less the subsidy has been a mechanism by which central government has influenced the output of local authority housing and channelled it towards either general needs housing or the rehousing of people displaced by slum clearance, despite the ostensible autonomy which authorities have enjoyed in deciding how much and what sort of housing they should provide.

The Addison Act 'opened the door' for the provision of working-class houses to be treated as 'a sort of social service' (Bowley, 1945: 37). With the benefit of hindsight, it can be seen as having effected 'a minor revolution' in standards of working class housing and living. Hundreds of thousands of people were moved from crowded inner-city areas to new residential districts on the outskirts and, in some cases, to completely new planned communities far from their former homes. The working classes were thus absorbed into the process of suburbanisation which the middle classes had followed since at least the middle of the nineteenth century. A geographical separation was achieved between home and work. By 1921, when all new approvals were stopped, the 214,000 houses for which approval had been given fell far short of the 500,000 target and the scheme was abandoned because of its cost.

### 8.3.2 The Housing Act 1923

When he introduced the Housing Bill in the House of Commons, Neville Chamberlain, then Minister of Health in the new Conservative government, expressed the hope that future state intervention in any form would be unnecessary, and that the building industry would return to its pre-war economic basis. In reply to questions about the housing problems of newly-married couples, he observed that 'they should be so happy that they can enjoy living even in one room' (Burnett, 1978: 222).

The policy of encouraging local authorities to become major providers of working class housing was completely reversed. The main objects of the Housing Act 1923 (the Chamberlain Act) were to encourage speculative building of working-class houses for sale or rental, and to limit local authority activity. Local authorities were permitted to build only if they could convince the Minister of Health that the houses which were needed would not be built by private enterprise. The Act provided for a new subsidy (available for houses built by October 1925) to be paid by the Treasury for any house built, whether by private enterprise or by local authorities, which satisfied certain conditions as to size, etc. No contribution from the rates was required. It was assumed that further subsidies would be unnecessary after October 1925. By then, the housing crisis would be over and houses could again be built by the unsubsidised private sector. Between 1923 and 1929 (the year until which the subsidy was in fact extended) the Chamberlain Act yielded 438,000 houses: 363,000 by private enterprise and only 75,000 by local authorities. The subsidy undoubtedly played some part in stimulating private house-building but of more consequence were falling building costs and an expansion of home-ownership made possible by easier mortgages.

### 8.3.3   The Housing (Financial Provisions) Act 1924

The first Labour government came to power in 1924 but for only nine months. Wheatley was the new Minister of Health. The primary purpose of the Housing (Financial Provisions) Act 1924 (the Wheatley Act) was make local authorities part of the permanent machinery for the provision of working-class housing. Encouragement to greater activity on their part came in the form of new and larger subsidies and the introduction of a long-term housing programme. They were given back their powers to construct houses without first having to prove that they could not be provided by private enterprise.

A new Treasury subsidy was made available for houses built by local authorities which complied with standards as to size, etc. similar to those laid down by the Chamberlain Act (8.3.2). A mandatory rate contribution was related to the amount needed to keep average rents down to the equivalent of controlled rents in the private sector. The Wheatley Act is generally regarded as the most successful of the inter-war housing measures. Although the Labour government was very quickly replaced by a new Conservative administration, the Wheatley subsidies continued in place until 1933 by which time a total of 508,000 houses had been produced under its terms, all but 15,000 provided by local authorities. Even so, council houses could not be brought within the reach of those on low pay, or those whose employment was insecure, or the unemployed who numbered three million by 1931. These people continued to live in old property, much of which was deteriorating into slums (Burnett, 1978: 234).

### 8.3.4   The Housing Act 1930

A Labour government was returned to office in the summer of 1929 with Greenwood as Minister of Health. The Housing Act 1930 (the Greenwood

Act) was passed in the depths of the economic depression 'to deal with the problem of the worst housed sections of the community for whom the ordinary subsidy was of no use' (Bowley, 1945: 45). Once again, public housing was directed towards rehousing the poor, and it was left to private enterprise to provide ordinary working class houses for general needs. The scheme introduced by the 1930 Act did not properly begin until it was adopted by the Housing (Financial Provisions) Act 1933 which also brought to an end the general Wheatley subsidy. The Greenwood Act required local authorities to draw up plans for slum clearance and to rehouse those who were displaced in the process. The Exchequer subsidy was based on the numbers of people displaced and rehoused. The Act marked a return to the 'sanitary' considerations of the later nineteenth century, although this time with a subsidy to ensure that some slum clearance and rehousing actually took place (Malpass et al, 1994: 59; Burnett, 1978: 237). Local authorities were required to set 'reasonable' rents and allowed to operate rent rebate schemes, so that lower rents could be set for poor tenants at the expense of others who would pay more (Malpass et al, 1994: 61). Almost inevitably, the *per capita* subsidy and the need to keep rents affordable for poor families rehoused from slum properties, resulted in housing which was smaller and of a lower standard. Perhaps too there was the desire to reduce the appeal of council housing to people who could afford accommodation in the private sector (Malpass et al, 1994: 46). A special subsidy was made available for flats and, although it formed only a small part of the housing built during the inter-war years, 'multi-storey living began to acquire a less grudging acceptance as a normal means of accommodation in cities' (Bowley, 1945: 241).

The expansion and contraction of local authority activity directly complemented activity in the private sector. When costs were high, local authorities ensured a supply of housing which private enterprise could not have provided. When costs fell, local authorities withdrew from general needs construction, and the private builders moved in. Indeed, as general needs housebuilding by local authorities was abandoned, a massive boom in private housebuilding took place, made possible by the low costs of land, labour and materials and low interest rates, coupled with rising living standards in the more prosperous southern half of the country where most of the new building was located. The highest rates of construction came several years after the removal of the Exchequer subsidies which had been available for private housebuilding in the 1920s, and occured without the sort of state support for home ownership that has become such an integral part of housing policy in more recent years' (Malpass et al, 1994: 46–48).

Until 1935, the rents of each scheme from the Addison Act onwards were calculated as each scheme was completed, taking into account its annual costs (loan charges, repairs and management), and any Exchequer subsidy or contributions from the rate fund. Each scheme was kept separate, and each account had to balance. This meant that significantly different rents might be payable for indentical houses, depending on the scheme under which they had been built. The Housing Act 1935 required each authority to maintain a single Housing Revenue Account for their entire stock. All the outgoings were added together, all the subsidies and rate fund contibutions were deducted and the difference determined the rental income which was required. Eventually, this 'rent-pooling' enabled the local authorites to transfer the subsidies on older, cheaper properties to more modern ones which had cost much more to build. Initially, however, the object of the single account was to facilitate rebates: the subsidies which were brought together could fund rebates to poorer tenants, while the rest paid full, economic rents. Local resistance to rebate schemes persisted, however, and by 1939 only a few authorities were operating them (Merrett, 1979: 58; Malpass et al, 1994: 61–62; Aughton et al, 1994: 27).

## 8.4   1945–1964

Housing policy from 1945 to 1964 has been described as bearing a marked resemblance to policy between the wars. In the first decade after each world war, attention was focused on reducing the severe housing shortage created by the war and, despite the disruption to the economy, the quality of new local authority housing was at its highest. When the immediate problem had been dealt with, the question of slum clearance re-emerged and the quality of new public sector housing fell. The local authorities were edged out of general needs housing, and the private sector moved in (Malpass et al, 1994: 69).

Labour won the general election in July 1945 and Aneurin Bevan was appointed Minister of Health. Not surprisingly, the air raids of the Second World War had wreaked havoc with the housing stock in many parts of Great Britain. Some 450,000 dwellings had been destroyed or made uninhabitable, and an estimated three million damaged to a lesser extent (Malpass et al, 1994: 64). New building had been at a virtual standstill during the war but the population had increased by about one million, and it was predicted that nearly as many houses would be needed to solve the housing crisis created by the war as had been built by the local authorities between 1919 and 1939 (Bowley, 1945: 232–3). In the short-term, temporary housing was produced (often in the form of prefabricated dwellings), severely damaged dwellings were repaired, local authorities and private builders rebuilt houses which bombing had destroyed, existing premises (including houses and war-time hostels built for factory workers) were converted and adapted, empty properties were requisitioned, and use was made of service camps which had been built during the war (Merrett, 1979; 238–9).

The new government possessed the will but not the means to promote new homes. Industry, nationalisation and the welfare state programmes were also strong contenders for state support, and the housebuilding programme fell prey to the balance of trade deficit in the mid-1940s which led to cuts in public spending (Burnett, 1978: 277). The previous limitation, whereby councils could only provide housing for 'the working classes', was removed by the Housing Act 1949 so that account could be taken of the housing conditions and needs of all members of the community. During the Labour government's period of office, over one million dwellings were built (over 80% of them by local authorities) and they were generally of good quality. This represented the first large scale investment in public housing since the Wheatley legislation but the failure to meet the target of 240,000 per year was one of the reasons for the government's electoral defeat.

In October 1951, the Conservatives were returned to power. Sir Winston Churchill became Prime Minister and Harold Macmillan was appointed Minister of Housing and Local Government. At their annual conference in 1950 the Conservatives had settled on a policy of building 300,000 dwellings a year and the grave balance of payment deficit of 1951–2 was not allowed to stand in the way of the new government's target. In 1952 the Exchequer subsidy and the rate fund contribution were increased. In 1953 319,000 new homes were built and, in 1954, a record 348,000. This very high output was achieved at the expense of the building and design standards which Bevan had insisted upon, underlining the Conservatives' residualist attitude towards the public housing sector.

In the 1953 White Paper, 'Houses: the Next Step', the government set out its strategy which, broadly, represented 'a return to the philosophy of Chamberlain and the "golden years" of the 1930s' (Merrett, 1979: 247). First, output was to be stabilised at about 300,000 dwellings per year. Secondly, new general needs housing was to be the responsibility of the private sector and the building of new houses for owner-occupation was to be promoted by all possible means. Owner-occupation was seen to represent one of the best forms of saving and the form of ownership which was 'the most satisfying to the individual and the most beneficial to the nation'. Thirdly, local authority output was to be controlled so that it made up the shortfall of private enterprise activity below the 300,000 target. Finally, large-scale housing renewal was to be stimulated.

A boom in the building industry in 1954 coincided with the ending of building licensing and a reduction in the subsidy for general needs housing. The subsidy was cut by a further 50% by the Housing Subsidies Act 1956 and abolished altogether soon afterwards (by executive order rather than by legislation). A subsidy was retained, however, for the construction of one-bedroomed dwellings for the elderly and for slum clearance. A higher subsidy was made available for flats in blocks which exceeded a certain number of storeys. These consequently found favour with many local authorities in inner city slum clearance areas where space was limited and land was relatively expensive, even though 'the increased construction costs in high-rise building more than outweighed the savings in other costs' (Forrest et al, 1991: 26). So far as tenants were concerned, however, high rise blocks of flats often destroyed communities and damaged family life.

In 1955, the government took a new approach to local authority rents, urging the adoption of 'realistic' rents, and the use of rent-rebate schemes to channel subsidy towards low-income households. The Housing Subsidies Act 1956 removed the obligation on local authorities to contribute to the Housing Revenue Account from the rate fund regardless of their total rent income. This enabled them to raise rents generally (while providing rebates for the needy), and increase their total income (thereby reducing the need for a rate fund contribution). Realistic rents therefore meant higher rents for those who could afford to pay the full economic cost of their housing and lower rents for the poor. Subsidising better-off tenants was seen as a misuse of public money.

As regards general needs housing, the government pinned its hopes on private enterprise and on the Rent Act 1957 which was intended to introduce greater mobility into the housing market by the partial removal of rent control in the private rented sector. By the end of the decade, however, it was clear that a new housing crisis was looming. The 1957 Act had failed to halt the decline of the private rented sector, homelessness was a growing problem and lower-paid workers, immigrant groups and the elderly often lived in very poor conditions. The early 1960s became, therefore, a period of 'policy reconsideration' (Merret, 1978: 252).

The Housing Act 1961 reintroduced subsidies for general needs building and the rate of council-house construction began to recover. Both the Conservative government and the Labour opposition agreed that a very high level of housebuilding was needed. In the event, the Conservative government fell from office in 1964 in a year of record housing output — 374,000, of which 218,000 were built by private enterprise and 156,000 by public authorities (Burnett, 1978: 278).

## 8.5   1964–1979

In its election manifesto, Labour had pledged to build 500,000 houses a year but it was forced to cut back on its building programme as part of the package of public spending cuts which followed the devaluation of the pound in November 1967. Even so, 'the rate of new building under the Labour government continued at a high level, the years 1965–9 inclusive producing approximately 1.8 million houses, almost equally divided between the public and private sectors' (Burnett, 1978: 278).

The 1965 White Paper, 'The Housing Programme 1965–1970', marked a significant change of direction for Labour's attitude towards the relative roles of council housing and owner-occupation. Any government, whatever its political persuasion, would have been compelled to accept the existence and continued growth of owner-occupation which had been on the increase since the 1920s. But the Labour government went much further than this: the expansion of building for owner-occupation was presented as 'normal', reflecting 'a long-term social advance which should gradually pervade every region'. Council housing was relegated to a residualist role, to be provided until Great Britain had overcome 'its huge social problem of slumdom and obsolescence, and met the need of the great cities for more houses let at moderate rents'. With the Housing Act 1969, the emphasis was switched to the private rehabilitation of older properties and local authorities were permitted to make more generous grants.

A Conservative government was elected in June 1970 with Edward Heath at the helm. In July 1971 the newly formed Department of the Environment published a White Paper, 'Fair Deal for Housing', which advocated the establishment of a uniform system of fair rents for all private and public sector tenants. Ministers regarded council rents as being unacceptably low as a result of the machinations of Labour-controlled local councils and a subsidy system which operated across the board, instead of focusing on tenants who were in particular need.

The 'fair rent' system in the private rented sector, introduced by the Rent Act 1965, had led to increases in rent levels and a gap was growing between private sector rents and those in the public sector. The Housing Finance Act 1972 introduced an entirely new rent and subsidy system, removing the autonomy which local authorities had enjoyed since 1923 in setting rents and granting rebates. Henceforth, council rents in England and Wales were to be brought into line — by staged increases — with the fair rents in the private rented sector. Authorities were under an obligation to set provisional fair rents but the final decision rested with an independent committee for each area, the members of which came from same panels of people from which members of Rent Assessment Committees were drawn. For the first time, the link between rents and the costs of providing council houses was broken. A new mandatory rent rebate system was introduced for council tenants on low incomes. All previous subsidies were abolished and a new Exchequer subsidy was introduced, based on the deficit on the Housing Revenue Account after 'reckonable expenditure' on loan charges, repairs and maintenance had been set against rental income.

These reforms 'aroused sharper controversy than at any time since councils first became involved with housing' (Aughton, 1994: 30) as it was clear that the move to fair rents would lead to substantial rent increases and to considerable savings as regards the subsidy from central government. The Labour-controlled council of Clay Cross in Derbyshire refused to implement the Act and councillors were removed from office, personally surcharged for the rent income lost and a commissioner — with whom the authority refused to co-operate — was appointed to run the town's housing service (Malpass, 1992). As it was, the 1972 Act never had the opportunity to operate as planned because the Labour government which came to office in 1974 immediately froze council rents, as part of its counter-inflationary policy. The Housing Rents and Subsidies Act 1975 repealed the fair rent provisions for council housing and restored the freedom to set 'reasonable rents' based on historic costs. Once again local authorities were empowered to make rate fund contributions at their own discretion. The deficit subsidy was replaced with a new temporary subsidy related to the cost of new borrowing and this regime operated until it was replaced by the Housing Act 1980 (Aughton, 1994: 30).

## 8.6   FROM 1979 TO THE PRESENT

Under the leadership of Margaret Thatcher, the Conservatives introduced some major pieces of housing legislation. Particularly notable were the Housing Act 1980 (which introduced the 'right to buy' for council tenants), the Housing Act 1985 (which enabled local authorities to dispose of all their housing stock to the private sector via large-scale voluntary stock transfers), and the Housing Act 1988 (which, in relation to the public sector, introduced the housing action trust and tenants' choice provisions). The object of all of these measures was to privatise public housing. The 'privatisation' of housing has not meant a disengagement of government from housing, rather a greater involvement, especially in the owner-occupied market.

Running parallel to the Housing Act 1988 was the introduction of a new financial regime under the Local Government and Housing Act 1989 which came into force on 1 April 1990. Formerly, capital expenditure (on the acquisition and development of land, building work, vehicles, plant and machinery, capital grants and advances) had been authorised by the annual Housing Investment Programme, and the allocation was normally backed by borrowing approval. Authorities could also use capital receipts (mainly from the sale of council houses under the right to buy and from Large Scale Voluntary Transfers), although only 20% could be used for 'prescribed expenditure' (e.g. for new building) during the year in which the council received the money. 20% of any remaining receipts could be used the next year and so on. Over a period of years, therefore, this 'cascade' effect permitted virtually the whole amount to be spent. The 1989 Act permits only 25% of receipts to be spent on new developments and at least 75% must be used to repay debt, even though councils face huge problems of repair and modernisa-tion. It has been said that this makes as much sense as a householder, faced with a leaking roof, using all his or her available cash to make a premature reduction on his or her mortgage (Aughton et al, 1994: 39). Authorities are no longer able to subsidise the housing revenue account out of other accounts. A requirement that rent increases should reflect differences in capital values led to significant increases in council rents designed perhaps to encourage more tenants to exercise the right to buy or to opt for another landlord.

Production targets were a familiar feature of housing politics in the 1950s and 1960s but in the past three decades they have ceased to be a measure of 'ministerial virility', and have therefore disappeared completely (Malpass et al, 1994: 65). Since 1979 new local authority building has declined to its lowest peacetime level since 1921, central government spending on public housing has plummeted from £165 million in 1980 to only £43 million by 1995 (Driscoll, 1997: 825), general subsidies which benefit all council tenants have been replaced by individual means-tested subsidy, and council rents have risen in real terms to a level greater than at any time since 1945. The role of both council housing and housing policy, informed by taxation and public expendi-ture considerations and a desire to extend the role of the private sector, has become increasingly a residual, welfare one (Malpass et al, 1994: 97).

John Major succeeded Margaret Thatcher as Prime Minister in 1991 and, in 1992, led the Conservatives to a fourth consecutive term. The measures set in process during the Thatcher years were continued (e.g. large scale voluntary stock transfers) and extended (e.g. compulsory competitive tendering). Signifi-cant changes were made to the allocation of social housing and the housing of homeless households. Of great concern, both to the Conservative government and to the Labour opposition, was the issue of anti-social behaviour among tenants.

Since coming to power in May 1997, the Labour government, under Tony Blair, has used delegated legislation to curb some of the worst excesses of the previous administration's legislation on allocations and homelessness. It has promised to release the estimated £5 billion of capital receipts from homes sold under the right to buy scheme and to remove the restrictions which currently limit authorities' spending to 25% of receipts. However, most of the money released will probably be spent on repairing and improving existing stock, rather than on the construction of new homes. It seems unlikely that there will ever be a return to the large-scale building of council houses of the 1950s and 1960s and, indeed, it has been predicted that in 20 years time, all stock previously owned by local authorities will have passed into the hands of housing associations via Large Scale Voluntary Stock Transfers.

## 8.7  HOUSING ASSOCIATIONS

### 8.7.1  What are housing associations?

The 1987 White Paper acknowledged the contribution made by municipal housing to increasing the total housing stock and clearing slums. However, it criticised the 'distant and bureaucratic' housing operations of local authorities in many big cities, and the insensitive design and bad management of some housing. Housing had been badly maintained, tenants alienated, and a wide range of social problems had emerged: an increase in crime and violence; the departure of many people for better opportunities elsewhere; the disappearance of local enterprise and employment; and the welfare dependancy of whole communities. A 'more pluralist and more market-oriented system' was advocated which would ensure that housing supply could respond more flexibly to demand, provide tenants with more choice and allow 'greater scope for private investment and more effective use of public sector money'. Provision of housing by local authorities as landlords should gradually be diminished, and alternative forms of tenure and tenant choice should increase. The government felt that housing associations had a vitally important role to play in the revival of what it described as the 'independent rented sector' (Department of the Environment, 1987: paras. 1.9, 1.11, 1.16, 4.3).

Housing associations are voluntary, non-profitmaking bodies which can take a variety of legal forms. Most of the 4,000 or so housing associations in Great Britain are constituted as idustrial and povident societies, many are registered as companies limited by guarantee and the remainder are trusts, some of them charitable. Some associations can trace their roots back to twelfth century almshouses, while others emerged from the philanthropic housing movement of the nineteenth century. Between them they own over a million homes (4.3% of all housing in Great Britain: Department of the Environment, 1997: Table 9.3). In 1994, 13 housing associations owned more than 10,000 dwellings (25% of all housing association stock) and 1,741 owned fewer than one hundred (*Roof*, January/February 1996: 37). In 1995, 19,369 new housing association homes were completed, compared with 1,359 local authority homes and 149,573 in the private sector (Department of the Environment, 1997: Table 6.1). In 1975, the figures were 14,693, 129,883 and 150,752 respectively (Department of the Environment, 1986: Table 6.1).

Although housing associations are independent organisations, registration with the Housing Corporation or Housing for Wales is an essential prerequisite of eligibility for public grants, not only from the Corporation itself but also from local authorities and other public bodies. Other associations may seek registration if they are negotiating funding from private lenders. Since 1989 they have raised some £10 billion in private loans to fund new housing developments (Driscoll, 1997: 826).

### 8.7.2   The funding of housing associations

The Housing Act 1964 set up the Housing Corporation (an unelected body, the members of which are appointed by the Secretary of State for the Environment) with the duty of encouraging new-style housing societies and old-style housing associations as a response to the nefarious activities of certain private landlords such as Rachman (see **Chapter 7**). Initially, its funding powers were very limited but its role was considerably extended, in terms both of funding and regulatory powers, by the Housing Act 1974. The 1974 Act provided a legislative and financial framework which existed until 1988. A particularly significant measure was the introduction of the Housing Association Grant (HAG — a lump sum provided by central government to housing associations registered with the Housing Corporation) to aid in the renewal of General Improvement and Housing Action areas, covering building and rehabilitation costs. A 'fair rent' (as defined by the Rent Act 1977) was determined for each dwelling by the rent officer. How much of the cost of any project was to be borne by way of a mortgage was determined by however much could be repaid from the rental income after management and maintenance costs were taken into account. The balance was met by the HAG. Under this system, HAG (the amount of which was calculated at the end of the project) accounted on average for about 85–90% of the total scheme cost. Housing associations could develop projects safe in the knowledge that most of their borrowing would be under-written by central government.

However, the 1987 White Paper recommended that private funding from financial institutions should be turned into the main source of funding for housing association projects. In consequence:

> for new lettings all housing associations will let on an assured tenancy basis or on a shorthold basis in the same way as the private rented sector. This should give them the essential freedom and flexibility in setting their rents to enable then to meet the requirements of private sector finance instead of relying on funding from public sources (Department of the Environment, 1987: para. 4.6).

The Housing Act 1988 established a new system of housing association finance. The HAG (rechristened the Social Housing Grant by the Housing Act 1996) is now set in advance as a predetermined amount (in 1996 it was set at an average of 56% of initial costs), and the rent level is adjusted to cover the balance which has to be met by the mortgage. As a result, rents are significantly higher than fair rent levels. A survey conducted in 1995 by MORI found that the average weekly assured rent for housing association properties was £45.03, compared to the average fair rent of £37.93 and local authority rent of £38.32

(*Roof*, Factfile 5, October 1996). As rents have risen, so government subsidy has fallen, from a peak of £2.2 billion in 1992 to a little over £600 million in 1998.

### 8.7.3   The nature and accountability of housing associations

Prior to the Housing Act 1988, housing associations formed part of the public housing sector, complementing the housing function of local authorities by providing low-cost accommodation often for groups with special housing needs: for the elderly, ex-offenders, single homeless, mentally or physically disabled. Like local authority tenants, housing association tenants generally had secure tenancies under the Housing Act 1985. Those who become housing association tenants on or after 15 January 1989 are no longer subject to the same regime as council tenants and their position is more akin to that of tenants in the traditional private rented sector, although subject to the additional protection afforded by the Tenants' Guarantee. While housing associations have been viewed in terms of finance, philosophy and tenant security as being closer to the public then the private sector, they have been described as having moved 'to centre stage' in the early 1990s (Langstaff, 1992: 46). The 1988 Act has pushed them firmly out into 'the more dangerous waters of the open market, of the private sector' (Bridge, 1989: 77) and, '... the ethos of public rented housing is being changed to place more emphasis on market values so as to strengthen the ideological hold of property rights over citizenship rights in the sector' (Clapham et al, 1990: 222). The privatisation of council housing since 1988 has been a significant growth area for housing associations. Not only have they increased in number and taken on a greater amount of stock but they have also assumed new roles: the modernisation and redevelopment of local authority housing estates, the management of council estates as the result of compulsory competitive tendering, the delivery of 'care in the community' by providing care and support previously undertaken by local social services departments.

Some interesting issues are raised by the transformation of housing associations into the main providers of social housing and the extension of their activities. In 1987 the government suggested that a departure from the local authorities' near monopoly of social housing would give tenants a wider choice, and housing associations were seen as possessing the virtues of 'diversity, voluntary input and small size'. Most subsequent development has been carried out, however, by the larger associations and as the management of associations has become more professional, paid staff have assumed a more prominent role in their operations.

The registration process and the registration criteria contained in s. 2, Housing Act 1996 have circumscribed the functions and powers of a social landlord, and the Housing Corporation's increasingly detailed requirements regarding the behaviour of associations has led to the observation that they have been turned into 'hired agents of central government, operating as branch offices of the Corporation' (Langstaff, 1992: 43). Their accountability, therefore, is something of a vexed question. Whether or not they are subject to the rules of judicial review depends on the nature of the activity under consideration. Decisions on eviction flow out of their normal and essential functions as landlords and are, therefore, matters of private law (*Peabody Housing Association Ltd* v *Green* (1978) 38 P & CR 644) but an association which has been formed to take over the stock from a local authority by way of a Large Scale Voluntary Transfer may be subject to judicial review (*R* v *West Kent Housing Association, ex parte Sevenoaks DC* (1994) *Inside Housing*, 28 October 1994). In *R* v *Panel on Take-overs and Mergers, ex parte Datafin plc* [1987] QB 815 the Court of Appeal laid down a two-fold test for establishing whether decisions are subject to judicial review. First, the body must be performing duties in the public interest. Secondly, it must be a body which can be linked with the government proper, i.e. 'but for' its existence, the government itself would have to carry out the activity in question. It is arguable that some decisions made by housing associations might satisfy the *Datafin* tests. 'But for' the existence of housing associations, government would have to provide social housing.

### 8.7.4　Registered social landlords

The Housing Act 1996 introduces the concept of registered social landlords. A body may now apply for registration with the Housing Corporation if it is a registered charity which is a housing association, a society which is registered under the Industrial and Provident Societies Act 1965 or a company registered under the Companies Act 1985 provided that the society or company is non-profitmaking and is established for the purpose of providing housing (s. 2, Housing Act 1996). This paves the way for the development of 'local housing companies', a concept which was first promulgated by the Duke of Edinburgh's Enquiry into British Housing in 1991 and has received support from the Conservatives 'as giving fresh impetus to the break-up of local authority controlled housing' and from Labour as 'an acceptable compromise between council ownership and increased investment' (*Roof*, May/June 1996: 23). Local authority representatives, tenants and other interested parties are included on their controlling boards but local authority nominees must be in the minority so that they do not exercise 'a dominant influence'. In April 1998, 1,800 homes on three estates in Tower Hamlets were scheduled to be transferred to the first local housing company — Poplar Housing and Regeneration Community Association. Proposals in the White Paper to allow profitmaking companies to compete alongside housing associations and non-profitmaking companies for funds to provide social housing were dropped during the parliamentary passage of the Housing Act 1996.

### 8.7.5　Registered social landlords and the right to acquire

The Housing Act 1980 introduced the right to buy for tenants of non-charitable housing associations and the Housing Act 1996 introduces a right for tenants of a registered social landlord to acquire the dwellings of which they are tenants. There are three conditions:

(a)   the tenant must be an assured tenant (other than an assured shorthold tenant or of a long tenancy), or a secure tenant, of the dwelling-house in question;

(b)   the dwelling must have been provided with public money and remained in the social rented sector; and

(c)   the tenant must satisfy any further qualifying conditions applicable under Part V, Housing Act 1985 (the right to buy, see **11.8.5**).

Section 17 empowers the Secretary of State to provide for discounts to be given on the exercise of the right to acquire, and to designate rural areas where the right is not to apply. The right to acquire has been dismissed as 'a decaffeinated right to buy' which 'like too many housing measures since 1980 ... seems designed not so much to solve housing problems but to avoid causing offence by not working'. An uptake of 4,000 per year is expected (Coleman, 1996).

**References**

Aughton, H. and Malpass, P., *Housing Finance: a Basic Guide*, London: Shelter, 1994.

Bowley, M., *Housing and the State, 1919–1944*, London: George Allen & Unwin, 1945.

Bridge, S., *Blackstone's Guide to the Housing Act 1988*, London: Blackstone Press Ltd, 1989.

Burnett, J., *A Social History of Housing, 1815–1970*, Newton Abbott: David & Charles, 1978.

Clapham, D., Kemp, P. and Smith, S., *Housing and Social Policy*, Basingstoke: Macmillan, 1990.

Clayre, A. (ed.), *Nature and Industrialization*, Oxford: Oxford University Press, 1977.

Coleman, D., 'Two cheers for the Act', *Roof*, November/December 1996, p. 10.

Department of the Environment, *Housing and Construction Statistics 1975–1985*, London: HMSO, 1986.

Department of the Environment, Housing: The Government's Proposals, London: HMSO, Cm. 214, 1987.

Department of the Environment, *Housing and Construction Statistics 1985–1995*, London: The Stationery Office, 1997.

Driscoll, J., 'What is the Future for Social Housing: Reflections on the Public Sector Provisions of the Housing Act 1996', *Modern Law Review*, vol. 60, 1997, pp. 823–839.

Forrest, R. and Murie, A., *Selling the Welfare State: the Privatisation of Public Housing*, London: Routledge, 1991.

Hughes, D. and Lowe, S., *Social Housing Law and Policy*, London: Butterworths, 1995.

Langstaff, M., 'Housing Associations: A Move to Centre Stage' in Birchall, J. (ed.), *Housing Policy in the 1990s*, London: Routledge, 1992.

Malpass, P., 'The Road from Clay Cross', in Grant, C. (ed.), *Built to Last: Reflections on British Housing Policy*, London: Roof, 1992.

Malpass, P. and Murie, A., *Housing Policy and Practice*, Basingstoke: Macmillan, 1994.

Merrett, S., *State Housing in Britain*, London: Routledge & Kegan Paul, 1979.

Randolph, B., 'The Reprivatisation of Housing Associations' in Malpass, P. and Means, R., *Implementing Housing Policy*, Buckingham: Open University Press, 1993, pp. 45–6.

Van Vliet, W. (ed), *International Handbook of Housing Policies and Practices*, New York, Westport Connecticut, London: Greenwood Press, 1990.

Wohl, A., *The Eternal Slum: Housing and Social Policy in Victorian London*, London: Edward Arnold, 1977.

# NINE

## The allocation of housing by local authorities

### 9.1 THE LEGAL FRAMEWORK FOR THE PROVISION OF COUNCIL HOUSING

There is an obvious link between the amount of housing which an individual authority has available and the policies it uses to allocate that housing and to allow transfers. It is useful, therefore, to consider the legal position governing the provision of council housing.

Local authorities have a duty to 'consider housing conditions in their district and the needs of the district with respect to the provision of further housing accommodation' (s. 8, Housing Act 1985). As to 'conditions', reviews must be carried out at least once a year to determine what action should be taken in respect of repairs notices, area improvement, slum clearance and houses in multiple occupation (under Parts VI, VIII, IX and XI respectively of the 1985 Act), renewal areas under Part VII, Local Government and Housing Act 1989, and grants, etc. for the renewal of private sector housing under Part I, Housing Grants, Construction and Regeneration Act 1996 (s. 605, Housing Act 1985). The 'needs' of the district are not confined to the needs of the people already living there, but extend to residents in nearby areas who might want to live, or who might be more conveniently housed, there in the future (*Re Havant and Waterloo UDC, CPO (No.4)* [1951] 2 KB 779) as, for example, where the development of new industry in the area is planned. The special needs of the chronically sick and disabled must also be taken into account (s. 3, Chronically Sick and Disabled Act 1970).

In 1980 the duty of local authorities (which had existed since 1919) to prepare and submit plans for the provision of new housing with which to meet the 'needs' referred to in what is now s. 8 was removed. It is now left to the discretion of the individual authority to decide how much and what sort of housing (if any) it will actually provide. Increasingly, however, the financial restraints imposed upon them by central government make it impossible for authorities to provide the housing which they perceive to be necessary, and a number of authorities have disposed of their entire stock (see **Chapter 12**).

By s. 9(1), Housing Act 1985 a local housing authority may provide housing accommodation by way of erection, conversion and acquisition. By s. 9(2) it may alter, enlarge, repair or improve a house it has built, converted or acquired under s. 9(1). The effect of s. 9(5), Housing Act 1985 (inserted by s. 161(1), Local Government and Housing Act 1989 by which time a number of semi-urban and rural districts had already divested themselves of their stock, generally to housing associations), is that a local housing authority is not required to hold any housing land or stock. It should be noted, however, that those authorities who have disposed of all their stock remain housing authorities for a variety of purposes, most importantly with regard to homelessness, in respect of which they have to make appropriate arrangements.

A local housing authority may provide 'furniture, fittings and conveniences' (s. 10), 'meals and refreshments', 'laundry and laundry services' (s. 11) and welfare services (s. 11A) in connection with the housing accommodation it provides. By s. 12, either solely or jointly with another person (such as a private company), it may provide and maintain shops, recreation grounds and other buildings which, in the opinion of the Secretary of State, will serve a beneficial purpose in connection with the requirements of the persons for whom the housing accommodation is provided. In *Conron* v *LCC* [1922] 2 Ch 283 it was held that a beer-house could be provided to the meet the requirements of people living on an estate.

## 9.2  THE TENSION BETWEEN ALLOCATIONS AND HOMELESSNESS

Section 21(1), Housing Act 1985, by which the general management, regulation and control of a local housing authority's houses is vested in and exercised by the authority, appears to give authorities complete freedom in determining how and to whom they should let their housing. However, since 1935, they have been under an obligation to secure that, in the selection of their tenants, a 'reasonable preference' is given to, e.g., people who are occupying insanitary and overcrowded houses, those who have large families or are living in unsatisfactory housing conditions. The homeless were brought into the 'reasonable preference' obligation by the Housing (Homeless Persons) Act 1977, greater attention to social need having been forcefully advocated in the Cullingworth Report. Until the Housing Act 1996 came into force, local authorities were obliged to provide long-term accommodation to people who were unintentionally homeless and in priority need (s. 65, Housing Act 1985). This meant that there were two routes into 'permanent' social housing: one via the waiting list and the other via the homelessness legislation.

In allocating their housing, local authorities have long had to contend with 'fewer houses to rent [in the private rented sector], an increasing dependence upon council housing, more single person and elderly households, [and] a decreasing supply of large family-type houses' (Central Housing Advisory Committee, 1969: para. 447). Recent years have witnessed a decline in rates of council housebuilding, the introduction of the right to buy for public sector tenants and the transfer of council housing stock to other bodies via, e.g., large-scale vountary stock transfers. The most desirable homes have become absorbed into owner-occupation through the right to buy, and the fact that virtually no new council houses have been built since 1980 means that a limited range of inferior and unpopular properties have been left for those who rent. The practice of putting families with children into tower blocks, which was ended in the 1970s on the advice of the then government, has been resurrected in areas of particular housing need (Bright et al, 1995: 159).

Many people, who previously would have been rehoused from the general waiting list, were surfacing as homelessness cases and, by the early 1990s, virtually all of the properties owned by some local authorities were being taken up by homelessness allocations. Research revealed that nationally, homelessness was a factor contributing to the allocation of council houses in 59% of all cases and 78% in London (Department of the Environment, 1994). The government interpreted these figures as indicating a failure by the homelessness legislation to fulfil its original function as a safety net. It was seen rather as a queue-jumping device into social housing, thereby creating 'a perverse incentive for people to have themselves accepted by a local authority as homeless' (Department of the Environment, 1994: 4). According to Shelter, however, 59% of homeless acceptances were made in respect of applicants who were already on the waiting list (Shelter, 1994).

In its 1995 White Paper, the government expressed its commitment to maintaining a safety net (in the form of the homelessness legislation) 'for families and vulnerable people' but asserted that this should be separate from a fair system of allocating long-term accommodation in a house or flat owned by a local authority or housing association. Achieving that separation would be by reforming the homelessness legislation and the introduction of new arrangements for the allocation of social housing. It stated that allocation schemes should reflect 'the underlying values of our society', balancing 'specific housing needs' against 'the need to support married couples who take a responsible approach to family life, so that tomorrow's generation grows up in a stable home environment' (Department of the Environment, 1995: 36).

Part VI, Housing Act 1996 creates a completely new system for the allocation of accommodation by local housing authorities. Section 22, Housing Act 1985 which set out the 'reasonable preference' groups is repealed. Its replacement, s. 167, places greater emphasis on the socio-economic and welfare characteristics of prospective tenants but, until amended by regulations, made no reference to homeless applicants at all. Further, the 1996 Act has reduced the duty owed to those who are unintentionally homeless and in priority need. Where no alternative accommodation is available, the local authority must still secure that accommodation is made available, but now only for two years (although this period may be extended at the discretion of the authority, or on re-application by the individual, if he or she continues to qualify). The purpose of the 1996 Act was to provide a single route into long-term social housing, putting 'all those with long-term housing needs on the same footing, while providing a safety net for emergency and pressing needs'. Soon after coming to power, however, the Labour government restored certain homeless households as reasonable preference groups by means of the Allocation of Housing (Reasonable Preference) Regulations 1997 (SI 1997/ 1902) but, in future, allocations of long-term housing must come from the register.

## 9.3 THE HOUSING REGISTER

Until Part VI, Housing Act 1996 came into force, local housing authorities were under no duty to to operate a housing register. However, those authorities which retained a stock of housing invariably did keep such registers (more commonly known as 'waiting lists') on which general applicants for council housing could register, and from which the authorities made their allocations in accordance with their individual selection schemes. Persons accepted as statutorily homeless could not register but were able to make their way into long-term accommodation by means of the homelessness legislation.

Section 162, Housing Act 1996 obliges every local housing authority to establish and maintain a register of qualifying persons: the 'housing register'. In general, accommodation (whether in the authority's own stock or, through nomination, accommodation held by another person or a registered social landlord) is to be allocated only to people on the housing register. Households accepted as statutorily homeless who are given temporary accommodation by the local authority are able to register and, indeed, the local authority may apply for registration on their behalf.

Section 162(3) allows local authorities to keep their housing register as part of a larger register which is maintained for other housing purposes (e.g. exchanges and transfers), or is maintained in common by the authority and one or more other landlords. Joint housing registers between local housing authorities and housing associations are already quite common. Lettings can be made directly from the register to all the parties to the register, while the local authority makes nominations from the register to, e.g., other housing associations in its district.

### 9.3.1 Information on the register

Regulations provide that, in addition to the applicant's name, address, date of entry on the register, and the most recent date on which an entry was amended, the register shall contain details of the number of other people who normally reside with the applicant as a member of his or her family, or who might reasonably be expected to do so, and the number of people in the household who are:

(a)   under the age of 10 years;
(b)   expecting a child;
(c)   over the age of 60 years.

Otherwise, authorities have a free hand in deciding what information to keep on the register.

Section 166 gives people on the housing register the right to see their entries (and to receive free copies) and to be given such information as will enable them to assess how long it is likely to be before appropriate accommodation is available for allocation to them. According to the Code of Guidance, the authority should at least give an applicant an indication of his or her position in the queue and of the supply of likely properties over the coming year (para. 4.38)

### 9.3.2  Qualifying persons

Section 161 requires a local housing authority to allocate housing only to people who are defined as 'qualifying persons'. Section 163 entitles a person to be put on the register if he or she appears to the authority to be a qualfying person, and s. 163(2) empowers a local housing authority to put a qualifying person on the register without waiting for an application. The authority must notify the person that this has been done. The applicant has the right to require the removal of his or her name unless the applicant is a homeless person to whom duties are owed under ss. 193 and 195.

A person subject to immigration control within the meaning of the Asylum and Immigration Act 1996 is not a qualifying person unless he or she comes within a class prescribed by regulations (s. 161(2)). The Allocation of Housing Regulations 1996 (SI 1996/2753), as amended by the Allocation of Housing and Homelessness (Amendment) Regulations 1997 (SI 1997/631), prescribe that, *inter alia*, people with refugee status and people who have been granted exceptional leave to enter or remain in the UK are qualified to be allocated housing. A person does not qualify to be allocated housing under Part VI if he or she:

(a)  is not habitually resident in the Common Travel Area (i.e., the UK, the Republic of Ireland, the Channel Islands and the Isle of Man); or

(b)  is a national of a country within the European Economic Area and is notified by the Home Secretary that he or she no longer has a right to reside in the UK.

The term 'habitually resident' is not defined in legislation but is intended to convey a degree of permanence in the person's residence in the Common Travel Area. It also operates to determine eligibility for housing benefit. It applies to all housing applicants regardless of their nationality, except:

(a)  a person who has refugee status;

(b)  a person who has exceptional leave to enter or remain;

(c)  a person who is a 'worker' for the purposes of EEC Regulations;

(d)  a person who has a right to reside in the UK under an EEC Council Directive.

Otherwise, it is up to the local authority to decide the eligibility criteria for inclusion on its register. The Code of Guidance encourages authorities not to be too rigid in applying such criteria and to make provision for others to appear on the register if their individual circumstances merit. In other words, the authority must take care not to 'fetter its discretion'. Residence in the district of the authority for a specified period is frequently required, and authorities may impose age requirements or disqualify single people or those who have assets worth more than a certain amount or a high income, unless (in both cases) they are elderly or disabled, or people with a history of anti-social behaviour or rent arrears.

The fact that someone falls within one or more of the 'reasonable preference' categories does not give them an automatic entitlement to register. In *R v Wolverhampton Metropolitan Borough Council, ex parte Watters* (1997) 29 HLR 931, Mrs Watters, her husband and five children were evicted from their council house for non-paymnt of rent arrears. They moved into privately rented housing which the council agreed was statutorily overcrowded. This, together with the size of Mrs Watter's family and the fact that they were living in unsatisfactory housing conditions, brought them within three of the reasonable preference categories. Mrs Watters applied to be placed on the council housing list but her application was turned down because of the council's policy of not registering people with at least two weeks' rent arrears outstanding from previous council tenancies. There was a right of appeal where tenants had made substantial efforts to reduce the arrears, or they had a substantial social or medical need or if other exceptional circumstances existed. The Court of Appeal upheld the dismissal of Mrs Watters' application for judicial review on the ground that the requirement of a 'reasonable' preference (as opposed to an 'absolute' one) envisaged that other factors might weigh against, and so diminish and even nullify, the preference. In fixing the criteria for allocation, the council was entitled to balance the seriousness of the history of behaviour as a tenant, as against the severity of the circumstances identified in s. 22 which applied in the particular case. The weight given to each factor was a matter for the council to determine and the court would only rarely intervene. The council also had a duty to have regard to the financial consequences of its actions, and to balance its housing revenue account (*R v Newham London Borough Council, ex parte Miah* (1995) 28 HLR 279). The existence of the right of appeal meant that it had not fettered its discretion.

### 9.3.3   Refusal of application or removal of name from register

By s. 164, if a local housing authority decides not to put a person on its housing register who has applied to be put on it, or to remove someone from it other than at his or her own request, it must notify the applicant in writing of its decision and the reasons for that decision. It must also inform the applicant of the right to request a review provided that such a request is made within 21 days of receiving notification. Local authorities have a discretion to allow a longer period. The Allocation of Housing and Homelessness (Review Procedures and Amendment) Regulations 1996 (SI 1996/3133) provide that where the review is to be carried out by an officer it must be an officer who was not involved in the original decision, and is senior to the officer who was involved in making that original decision.

An applicant who is aggrieved about the decision on review under s. 164 may complain to a Local Government Ombudsman if he or she considers that unfair treatment has resulted from maladministration, or if, for example, the authority has delayed taking action without good reason, has taken into account irrelevant considerations or ignored relevant ones, has not followed its own rules or complied with the law, has not fulfilled undertakings given to the applicant, has given the applicant the wrong information, or has not reached a decision in the correct way (Code of Guidance, para. 4.31).

## 9.4  ALLOCATIONS UNDER PART VI, HOUSING ACT 1996

### 9.4.1  General principles

Section 159, Housing Act 1996 sets the scene for the allocation of social housing, obliging local housing authorities to comply with the provisions of the Act in 'allocating housing accommodation'. An authority allocates accommodation when:

(a)   it selects someone to be a secure or introductory tenant of one of its dwellings; or
(b)   it nominates someone to be a secure or introductory tenant of another landlord (e.g., a housing action trust); or
(c)   it nominates someone to be an assured tenant of housing held by a registered social landlord (s. 159(2)).

The provisions of Part VI do not apply in cases of succession to tenancies on death (s. 89, Housing Act 1985), mutual exchange (s. 92, Housing Act 1985), orders made on the breakdown of relationships (s. 24, Matrimonial Causes Act 1973, Matrimonial and Family Proceedings Act 1984 and sch. 1, Children Act 1989: s. 134, Housing Act 1996), or allocation to people who are already secure or introductory tenants or assured tenants of registered social landlords or of accommodation already allocated through the local housing authority (ss. 159–160, Housing Act 1996).

### 9.4.2  The allocation scheme

According to the Code of Guidance (para, 5.1), s. 167:

is intended to ensure that social housing meets long-term housing needs but it should also be seen in a wider context. The allocation of housing is not just about meeting housing need. It embraces other objectives such as using stock effectively, reducing the number of empty and underoccupied properties, improving the turnaround time for void properties, maximising rental income, and, where possible, creating balanced communities.

Section 167(1) provides that each local housing authority must have an allocation scheme for determining priorities between applicants which should also set out the procedure to be followed in allocating housing accommodation. 'Procedure' includes all aspects of the allocation process, including the people, or descriptions of people, by whom decisions are to be taken. The Allocation of Housing (Procedure) Regultions 1997 (SI 1997/483) limit the involvement of councillors is certain allocation decisions. In 1969, the Cullingworth Committee recommended that the selection of individual tenants for council houses should in general be undertaken by housing officers. In 1994, it was reported that councillors were involved in decisions about the allocation of properties, directly or in consultation with officers, in 19 out of 37 Welsh local authorities (Stirling, 1994: 12). While councillors can, of course, make a valuable contribution to the allocation process, their involvement carries the risk of discrimination and exploitation of the process for personal or political gain. In *R v Port Talbot BC, ex parte Jones* [1988] 2 All ER 207, a councillor, who lived outside the ward she represented, applied for a council house. In the normal course of events, she would have been allocated a one- or two-bedroomed flat, but the Chair of the Housing Tenancy Committee pressurised the borough officer into offering her a tenancy of a three-bedroomed house in the ward. The court allowed the application by another councillor for judicial review because the decision to allocate the house to her had been made in breach of the council's published allocation rules (and not, therefore, in a lawful and authorised manner) and it was based on irrelevant considerations (that she would be in a better position to fight an election from the house).

### 9.4.3    Types of allocation scheme

Once an applicant's name is on the housing register, the speed at which he or she reaches the top depends on his or her housing needs, as determined by the type of allocation scheme which the authority uses. An authority must not allocate housing accommodation except in accordance with its allocation scheme (s. 167(8)).

In the past, when there was generally less pressure on public housing, date-order schemes were popular. These opperated on a 'first come, first served' basis. Today, the type of scheme most commonly used is the 'points' scheme. Here, applicants are awarded 'points' according to their housing needs and circumstances. Once applicants are registered, the higher the number of points they amass, the sooner they are rehoused. Points may be given for, e.g., overcrowding, having to share facilities (kitchen lavatory, bathroom, hot running water) with another, unrelated household; badly situated facilities (a cooker on the landing, an outside lavatory or a bath or shower in the kitchen); living in temporary or insecure accommodation (with friends or relatives who have asked the applicant to leave, as a lodger sharing facilities with the landlord who has asked the applicant to leave, in a bed and breakfast hotel or hostel, etc.); and medical problems. Additional points may be awarded to reflect time spent on the waiting list while living in particularly difficult housing conditions (e.g., in overcrowded or insanitary accommodation). The factors normally selected for 'pointing' mean that families with children and the elderly have a much higher priority than single people of below retirement age, childless couples, or other adult households. Many authorities use 'quota schemes', setting aside a quota of anticipated allocations for groups with particular characteristics.

As the supply of social housing is insufficient to satisfy demand, the need for housing has to be prioritised. The point on the spectrum at which the definition of need is drawn depends partly on the available resources but it also involves making value judgments. Reporting in 1969, the Cullingworth Committee expressed surprise that some housing authorities:

> took up a moralistic attitude towards applicants: the underlying philosophy seemed to be that council tenancies were to be given only to those who 'deserved' them and that the 'most deserving' should get the best houses. Thus unmarried mothers, cohabitees, 'dirty' families, and 'transients' tended to be grouped together as 'undesirable'. Moral recitude, social conformity, clean living and a 'clean' rent book on occasion seemed to be essential qualifications for eligibility — at least for new houses (Central Housing Advisory Committee, 1969: para. 96).

Today, a less judgmental view may be taken of cohabitees but the use of 'objective' allocation schemes has not prevented the segregation of, and discrimination against, certain types of household. There is, for example, a long and well-documented history of racial discrimination in the allocation of council housing (see Hughes et al, 1978–9; Henderson et al, 1984) and there has also been a tendency to concentrate so-called 'problem families' in particular sections of the housing stock. Such a policy may exacerbate the difficulties of the families involved and the deterioration of the areas in which they are housed while their arrival is resisted by 'existing residents, often struggling themselves with the consequences of local economic decline' (Cole et al, 1994: 141).

Authorities must publish summaries of their allocation schemes and supply a copy free of charge to any member of the public who asks for one (s. 168(1)). Before adopting or altering a scheme, the local housing authority should end a draft scheme, or proposed alteration, to every registered social landlord with which it has nomination arrangements, giving the man opportunity to make comments on the proposals. If alterations are made, the authority must notify everyone on its housing register within a reasonable period of time (s. 168(3)).

### 9.4.4   Reasonable preference

Section 167(2) provides that, in framing their allocation scheme, authorities must ensure that reasonable preference is given to:

(a)   people occupying insanitary or overcrowded housing or otherwise living in unsatisfactory housing conditions;
(b)   people occupying housing accommodation which is temporary or occupied on insecure terms;
(c)   families with dependent children;

(d)  households consisting of or including someone who is expecting a child;

(e)  households consisting of or including someone with a particular need for settled accommodation on medical or welfare grounds;

(f)  households whose social and economic circumstances are such that they have difficulty in securing settled accommodation.

From 1 November 1997, reasonable preference must also be given to:

(g)  people owed a homelessness duty under s. 193 or 195(2), Housing Act 1996;

(h)  people accommodated beyond the two-year period under s. 194;

(i)  people accommodated by means of advice and assistance under s. 197; and

(j)  people who have been provided with advice and assistance within the previous two years.

The effect of (g) to (j) is that reasonable preference in the allocation of housing must be given to any people found by the authority to be unintentionally homeless and in priority need.

A 'reasonable preference' involves giving applicants 'a reasonable head start' (per Judge LJ in *R v Wolverhampton Metropolitan Borough Council, ex parte Watters* (1997) 29 HLR 931) but it may be weighed against other factors which may diminish or even nullify the preference. It implies the power 'to choose between different applicants on "reasonable grounds" [and] it is not unreasonable to prefer good tenants to bad tenants' (*R v Newham LBC, ex parte Miah* (1995) 28 HLR 279).

It is for the local authority to decide how to reflect the categories set out in s. 167(2) in its allocation scheme (subject to any regulations made by the Secretary of State under s. 167(4)). It may, therefore, make provision for other groups not specifically included but authorities 'should not allow their own secondary criteria to dominate their allocations scheme at the expense of factors in the statutory list' (Code of Guidance, para. 5.4).

By s. 167(6) a local housing authority is free to decide the structure of its allocations scheme (i.e. whether it is points-based, date-order, etc.), what indicators to use, and what weighting to give to the categories listed in s. 167(2). Authorities must behave rationally, taking into account all considerations relevant to housing and social needs, and ignoring irrelevant factors. They should not operate 'on a purely formulaic basis' but should establish procedures for dealing with special cases on an exceptional basis (Code of Guidance, para. 5.7).

### 9.4.5  Additional preference

'Additional preference' must be given to households within (e) at **9.4.4** who cannot reasonably be expected to find settled accommodation for themselves in the near future. It means that extra priority must be given where, for example, a carer living with such a person has to provide virtually 24-hour care, or where all members of a household are elderly or infirm. It does not require authorities to allocate the first available property of any sort in such cases, but assumes that people meeting this description will have to be first in line for suitable vacancies (Code of Guidance, paras. 5.9, 5.10).

### 9.4.6   Challenging the authority's decision

The courts are reluctant to intervene in allocation decisions by way of judicial review but will do so if an authority is operating a blanket policy which fetters discretion or has reached a decision which no reasonable authority could have reached (see *Associated Provincial Picture Houses Ltd* v *Wednesbury Corporation* [1947] 2 All ER 680). In *R v Canterbry City Council, ex parte Gillespie* (1987) 19 HLR 7, the applicant and her cohabitee were joint secure tenants of a council house. When their relationship broke down, she moved to accommodation which was both 'overcrowded' and gave rise to 'unatisfactory housing conditions' within what is now s. 167. However, the local authority refused her application to join the waiting list unless she relinquished the secure tenancy. Her landlord authority would not allow her to surrender the tenancy, however, because there were rent arrears outstanding. The authority later admitted her to the waiting list but refused to consider her for allocation of accommodation, again because of its stated policy of debarring those who held secure tenancies elsewhere. The authority's decision was quashed because it constituted 'a rule which was required to be followed slavishly rather than merely a stated general approach which is always subject to an exceptional case and which permits each application to be individually considered'.

The existence of a procedure for dealing with special cases on an exceptional basis enables authorities to reach what often appear to be very harsh decisions. In *R v Bristol CC, ex parte Johns* (1993) 25 HLR 249, the applicant and her husband were the outright owners of a two-bedroomed, two-storey terraced house. The applicant, who was suffering from osteoarthritis, applied unsuccessfully to Bristol City Council for housing. Three years later, she was diagnosed as suffering from multiple sclerosis which progressed to the extent that she was effectively confined to a wheelchair. Bristol changed its allocation policy to the effect that owner-occupiers could not be considered for rehousing under their points scheme unless they were in 'severe difficulties'. An occulational therapist from Avon County Council reported that the applicant was 'housebound and socially isolated' which, together with the unsuitability of the property in which she was living, had resulted in her becoming very depressed. She reapplied unsuccessfully for rehousing and was told that, as an owner-occupier, she could not be considered for rehousing under the points scheme. Her application for judicial review was based on the argument that the authority had fettered its discretion by having this blanket policy. The court dismissed the application because the authority retained some discretion despite the exclusion from the points system of owner-occupiers other than those in severe difficulties.

No duty to give reasons arises from a decision on reasonable preference. This is because the powers of authorities in this context are those of general management and create no rights for individuals (*R* v *London Borough of Newham, ex parte Dawson* (1994) 26 HLR 747).

## References

Bright, S. and Gilbert, G., *Landlord and Tenant: The Nature of Tenancies*, Oxford, Clarendon Press, 1995.

Central Housing Advisory Committee, Housing Management Sub-Committee, *Council Housing: Purposes, Procedures and Priorities*, London: HMSO, 1969.

Cole, I. and Furbey, R., *The Eclipse of Council Housing*, London: Routledge, 1994, pp. 140–144.

Department of the Environment, *Access to Local Authority and Housing Association Tenancies: a Consultation Paper*, London, HMSO, 1994.

Department of the Environment, *Our Future Homes: Opportunity, Choice, Responsibility*, Cmnd. 2901, London: HMSO, 1995.

Henderson, J. and Karn, V., 'Race, Class and the Allocation of Public Housing in Britain, *Urban Studies*, 1984, vol. 21, pp. 115–128.

Hoath, D., *Public Housing Law*, London: Sweet & Maxwell, 1989.

Hughes, D. and Jones, S., 'Bias in the Allocation and Transfer of Local Authority Housing: A Study of the Commission for Local Administration in England', *Journal of Social Welfare Law*, 1978–9, pp. 273–295.

Shelter, *Homelessness in the 1990s — Local Authority Practice*, London: Shelter, 1994.

Stirling, T., 'Blast from the Past', *Roof*, September/October 1994, p. 12.

# TEN

# Secure and introductory tenancies under the Housing Act 1985

## 10.1 INTRODUCTION

Not until the Housing Act 1980 (which introduced secure tenancies) were public sector tenants given 'the same kind of protection from being evicted from their homes without good and sufficient cause as had been enjoyed by tenants in the private housing sector for many decades under the Rent Acts'. It had been thought 'safe and proper to give local authority landlords a complete discretion with regard to the eviction of public sector tenants, and to rely on them to exercise such discretion fairly and wisely (Brandon LJ in *Harrison v Hammersmith & Fulham London Borough Council* [1981] 1 WLR 650, at p. 661). The rights of public sector tenants were governed, therefore, by the common law and the terms of the tenancy agreements employed by the various local authorities. In truth, however, council tenancy agreements simply reflected the imbalance of power between council tenants and their landlords; they contained few undertakings by landlords, offered limited rights to tenants and usually amounted to little more than a list of tenants' obligations (Cole et al, 1994: 39). Statutory intervention was felt necessary by some tenants not only to improve their status in the public eye and the regard with which they were held by local authorities but also to compel local authorities to meet their obligations (Stewart, 1996: 154).

The 1980 Act also introduced a number of other rights for secure tenants (including the 'the right to buy'), collectively referred to as the Tenants' Charter. They were consolidated into Part IV, ss. 79 to 117, Housing Act 1985 and further amended by the Housing and Planning Act 1986 and the Housing Acts of 1988 and 1996.

## 10.2 INTRODUCTORY TENANCIES

Local authorities and housing action trusts (see **Chapter 12**) may elect to operate an introductory tenancy regime under which new periodic tenants and licensees are granted introductory tenancies rather than secure tenancies (s. 124, Housing Act 1996). An introductory tenancy lasts for a trial period of one year beginning with the date the tenancy is entered into or, if later, the date when the tenant is first entitled to possession (s. 125(2)).

A tenancy ceases to be an introductory tenancy if, before the end of the trial period:

(a)   the circumstances are such that the tenancy would not otherwise be a secure tenancy (e.g., the tenant ceases to occupy the dwelling-house as his or her only or principal home); or

(b)   a person or body other than a local housing authority or Housing Action Trust becomes the landlord; or

(c)   there is no-one qualified to succeed on the tenant's death (s. 125(5)).

At the end of the trial period, the tenancy automatically becomes a secure tenancy unless the landlord has already begun possession proceedings and obtains possession either during or after the first year of the tenancy.

Part V, Housing Act 1996 — in which the introductory tenancy appears — is entitled 'Conduct of Tenants'. The 1995 White Paper described the scheme as one for 'tenancies on a probationary basis' to allow landlords at any time during the probationary period to be able to terminate the tenancies of 'the minority of tenants who do not behave responsibly' (Department of the Environment, 1995: 44). It is not clear, however, whether an introductory tenancy or licence can be brought to an end for reasons unconnected with anti-social behaviour, e.g., a change in the landlord's allocation policy, or under-occupation. A court order is necessary if the landlord wishes to bring an introductory tenancy to an end during the trial period (s. 127(1)). There is no need to prove that a ground for possession exists but the court cannot entertain proceedings for possession unless the landlord has served a notice which:

(a)   sets out the landlord's reasons for seeking possession (s. 128(3));

(b)   specifies a date for the beginning of proceedings, which must be no earlier than that of a common law notice to quit (s. 128(4)); and

(c)   informs the tenant or licensee of the right given by s. 129 to seek a review and thereby challenge the reasons given by a landlord for its decision (Introductory Tenants (Review) Regulations 1997, SI 1997/22).

Not surprisingly, an introductory tenancy has a number of features in common with a secure tenancy. Thus, a succession is allowed to the tenancy on the death of the original tenant by a member of his or her family subject to conditions similar to those which apply to secure tenancies (ss. 131–134) and the secure tenants' repair scheme has been extended to introductory tenancies by subordinate legislation (s. 135). Section 134 prohibits the express assignment of an introductory tenancy except:

(a)   in pursuance of court a order made under:

(i)    s. 23A or 24, Matrimonial Causes Act 1973,
(ii)   s. 17(1), Matrimonial and Family Proceedings Act 1984, or
(iii)  sch. 1, para. 1, Children Act 1989, or

(b)  to a person who would be qualified to succeed if the tenant died immediately before the assignment.

## 10.3    SECURE TENANCIES

### 10.3.1  Definition

A secure tenancy is 'a tenancy under which a dwelling-house is let as a separate dwelling . . . at any time when the conditions described in sections 80 and 81 as the landlord condition and the tenant condition are satisfied' (s. 79, Housing Act 1985). Like the Rent Act 1977 and the Housing Act 1988, there must be 'a tenancy' of 'a dwelling-house' which is 'let as a separate dwelling' (see **Chapter 3**). However, a number of differences exist between the public sector and private sector codes. First, secure tenancies specifically include certain licences (s. 79(3)). Secondly, the Housing Act 1985 contains no equivalent provision to s. 22, Rent Act 1977 or s. 3, Housing Act 1988 where the dwelling-house is not 'let as a separate dwelling'. Thirdly, the words 'at any time' in s. 79(1) mean that a tenant can move in and out of secure status.

**10.3.1.1  Licences**  Section 79(3), Housing Act 1985 states that 'the provisions of this Part apply in relation to a licence to occupy a dwelling-house (whether or not granted for a consideration) as they apply in relation to a tenancy'. It should be noted, however, that not all residential licences fall within the statutory regime and that, even where a licensee does enjoy the protection of the 1985 Act, advantage cannot be taken of the right to buy provisions contained in Part V of the Act. There will be no security where:

(a)  the licence is granted as a temporary expedient to a person who entered the dwelling-house as a trespasser (s. 79(4)). This concerns former squatters who may have been granted short-life licences of the properties in which they squatted, or of other properties destined for improvement, conversion or redevelopment; or
(b)  there is no exclusive possession of the premises. The inclusion of licences was originally enacted in s. 48, Housing Act 1980, at a time when some private landlords were granting exclusive possession of residential accommodation at a rent but in the form of a licence. Section 48 was held to afford protection only if the licence conferred exclusive possession on the occupant (*Family Housing Association* v *Miah* (1982) 5 HLR 94; *Royal Borough of Kensington & Chelsea* v *Hayden* (1985) 17 HLR 114). However, in *Family Housing Association* v *Jones* [1990] 1 All ER 385, Balcombe LJ appeared to hold that, in the light of the decisions in *Street* v *Mountford* and *A.G. Securities* v *Vaughan*, s. 79(3) must have been intended to alter the law and confer the status of a secure tenancy on a licensee who did not enjoy exclusive possession.

Such a decision would make it difficult for bodies charged with responsibilities to house the homeless, to enter into any arrangement under which a person was to enjoy exclusive occupation of premises, however temporarily, without conferring security of tenure by virtue of s. 79(3). The result would be 'substantially to reduce the choice of methods available to [such bodies] for dealing with their always limited supplies of housing stock' (per Slade LJ at p. 396).

The point was clarified by the House of Lords in *Westminster City Council* v *Clarke* [1992] 2 AC 288. Mr Clarke was given temporary accommodation in a hostel for single homeless men as the first stage in the council's discharge of its homelessness duties. A resident warden was present during the daytime to supervise the hostel and, if necessary, to assist the occupants (some of whom had personality disorders or physical disabilities). Mr Clarke's 'licence to occupy' gave him no right to exclusive occupation of a particular room or accommodation which might be allotted to him. The licence contained a 'mobility clause' which gave the authority power to change the allotted accommodation and to require Mr Clarke to share accommodation with any other person. The room he occupied was a self-contained bedsitting room with kitchen facilities which included a sink, a small oven, two electric rings and a refrigerator. It had its own lockable door to which both Mr Clarke and the warden had a key. Occupants had to be in their rooms by 11 p. m. and any vistors had to leave by that time. Because of Mr Clarke's unacceptable behaviour, the council gave him notice to determine his rights of occupation on the basis that he had a mere licence which could be revoked at any time. Mr Clarke contended that he was a tenant. The Court of Appeal reluctantly felt bound to follow *Family Housing Association* v *Jones* (ibid.), although Dillon LJ doubted the soundness of that decision in so far as is construed s. 79(3).

Lord Templeman, who delivered the only speech in the House of Lords, pointed out that the 1985 Act was a consolidating Act which gave effect to certain recommendations of the Law Commssion Report on the Consolidation of the Housing Acts (Law Com. No. 144), none of which related to s. 48. In redrafting s. 48 into s. 79(3), the draftsman had no power to alter the law. It did not apply, therefore, to all licences but only to those which granted a right of exclusive possession of a dwelling-house. In deciding that Mr Clarke did not have exclusive possession of any particular room in the hostel, their Lordships took into account the authority's need to retain total control over all rooms in the premises in order to discharge its homelessness duties, the very considerable limitations on the occupier's ability to enjoy any room allotted to him, the need for him to obtain approval before he could entertain guests, and to comply with instructions from resident staff. Lord Templeman pointed out that these provisions in the licence were inserted to enable the council to discharge its responsibilities to the vulnerable persons accommodated at the hostel and not to enable it to avoid the creation of a secure tenancy.

**10.3.1.2 Sharing living accommodation**  A 'separate dwelling' must provide the the necessary facilities for the major activities of life: cooking, eating and sleeping. Therefore, an occupier who shares essential living accommodation (such as a kitchen) cannot be a secure tenant. Unlike s. 22, Rent Act 1977, and ss. 3 and 10, Housing Act 1988, the 1985 Act makes no special provision for tenants who share essential accommodation with others. In *Central YMCA Housing Association Ltd* v *Saunders* (1991) 23 HLR 212, Mr Saunders occupied a room (with a small bathroom attached) in a hostel which comprised 600 furnished rooms in three tower blocks. On each of the floors of the block in which he lived, there were two kitchens, each of which was shared by 12 residents. The occupants were expressly forbidden to cook in their rooms, but Mr Saunders did confess to boiling eggs in his electric kettle! The Court of Appeal held it to be a clear case of sharing. While Mr Saunders might be said to live in part of a house, it was not a separate dwelling. In *Central YMCA Housing Association Ltd* v *Goodman* (1992) 24 HLR 109 Mr Goodman occupied a bedroom with an en suite bathroom and lavatory. There was no kitchen. The letting was subject to the YMCA's regulations which forbade any kind of heating or cooking apparatus in the room. It was held not to be a dwelling-house.

**10.3.1.3 Satisfaction of the landlord and tenant conditions 'at any time'** The tenant will be a secure tenant at any time when the landlord and tenant conditions are satisfied. The section has what has been described as an 'ambulatory effect'so that the tenant can move in and out of protection. In *Basingstoke & Dean Borough Council* v *Paice* [1995] 2 EGLR 9, the local authority let a garage to the tenant for a term of 15 years. In breach of covenant the tenant converted part of the premises into a flat and let it. When the tenant surrendered the unexpired term of the lease to the authority, the occupier of the flat became the authority's direct tenant and, it was held, a secure tenant. See too *Hussey* v *Camden London Borough Council* (1995) 27 HLR 5; *Elvidge* v *Coventry City Council* [1993] 4 All ER 903.

**10.3.2 The landlord condition**

A landlord will satisfy the landlord condition of s. 79(1) if it belongs to the list of bodies set out in s. 80(1):

(a) a local authority,
(b) a new town corporation,
(c) a housing action trust,
(d) an urban development corporation,
(e) the Development Board for Rural Wales, and
(f) a housing co-operative.

Until the Housing Act 1988 came into force, the Housing Corporation, charitable housing trusts and housing associations could all grant secure tenancies. This means that tenancies granted by such bodies before 15 January 1989 will be secure tenancies under the Housing Act 1985, while those granted after 15 January 1989 will be assured tenancies under the Housing Act 1988.

If the landlord's interest is transferred to a landlord who is not listed as satisfying the landlord condition of s. 80, the tenancy ceases to be secure.

### 10.3.3  The tenant condition

By s. 81, Housing Act 1985, the tenant condition is satisfied where:

(a)  the tenant is an individual and occupies the dwelling-house as his or her only or principal home; or

(b)  where the tenancy is a joint tenancy, each of the joint tenants is an individual and at least one of them occupies the dwelling-house as his or her only or principal home.

These issues have already been covered in relation to the private rented sector in **Chapter 3**.

### 10.3.4  Exclusions from secure status under the Housing Act 1985

Schedule 1 to the Housing Act 1985 lists the tenancies which cannot be secure. The exclusions are set out at **10.3.4.1** to **10.3.4.13**.

**10.3.4.1  Long leases (sch. 1, para. 1)**  A long tenancy, i.e., one granted for a term certain exceeding 21 years whether or not it can be determined before the end of the term by a tenant's notice or by forfeiture, is not secure.

**10.3.4.2  Introductory tenancies (sch. 1, para. 1A)**  Introductory tenancies are not secure nor are those which cease to be introductory because there is no-one qualified to succeed (under s. 133(3), Housing Act 1996) or because the residence requirement (s. 125(5), Housing Act 1996) is no longer fulfilled.

**10.3.4.3  Premises occupied in connection with employment (sch. 1, para. 2)**  This exclusion applies where the landlord employs the tenant and the contract of employment requires occupation of the dwelling-house for the better performance of the tenant's duties. Even if the contract of employment did not originally require such occupation, it may subsequently be varied so as to bring the tenant within the exclusion (*Elvidge* v *Coventry City Council* [1993] 4 All ER 903 where, on the tenant's promotion from water bailiff to assistant ranger of a countryside park, his conditions of employment were altered so as to require him to live in the cottage he was already occupying).

In *South Glamorgan County Council* v *Griffiths* (1992) 24 HLR 334, a retired school caretaker was held not to be, and never to have been, a secure tenant, as he was *impliedly* required to live in a house adjacent to the school for the better performance of his duties. His 'insecure' status remained notwithstanding his recent retirement. However, in *Hughes* v *Greenwich London Borough Council* [1993] 4 All ER 577, the House of Lords was not prepared to imply a term into a headmaster's contract of employment to the effect that he was required to occupy a house in the school grounds for the better performance of his duties.

He was therefore a secure tenant with the right to buy. In *Greenfield* v *Berkshire County Council* (1996) 28 HLR 691, a former school caretaker who had been made redundant was allowed to remain in tied accommodation until a house provided with his new job became available. It was held that his continued occupation was not referable to his former employment but to a decision by the council to let him stay there. He had therefore obtained a secure tenancy even though his tenancy was not secure at its commencement.

A dwelling-house which has been let on a tenancy within this exclusion may be kept out of security for a period or periods not exceeding three years even if it is re-let to a non-employee provided that written notice is served on the tenant not later than the grant (sch. 1, para. 2(4)).

**10.3.4.4   Land required for development (sch. 1, para. 3)**   A tenancy cannot be secure if the dwelling-house is on land which has been acquired for development and in the meantime is being used by the landlord as temporary housing accommodation. The purpose of this exception is to make use of land which is awaiting redevelopment. The landlord need not be the person who acquired the land for development (*Hyde Housing Association* v *Harrison* (1990) 23 HLR 57, in which a housing association had granted a temporary weekly licence to occupy a flat on land which the Department of Transport had acquired for a road-widening scheme). An authority may change the nature of the development envisaged without losing the protection of the exception (*Attley* v *Cherwell District Council* (1989) 21 HLR 613) but where permission for development has been refused and no development is subsequently pending, the exemption will not apply (*Lillieshall Road Housing Co-operative Ltd* v *Brennan & Brennan* (1992) 24 HLR 195).

**10.3.4.5   Accommodation for homeless persons (sch. 1, para. 4)**   A tenancy granted in pursuance of any duty discharged under Part VII, Housing Act 1996 (which deals with homelessness) is not a secure tenancy unless the local housing authority concerned has notified the tenant that the tenancy is to be regarded as secure. People accommodated as homeless will remain insecure, therefore, unless and until the authority decides otherwise. Authorities may house under the full duty for a maximum period of two years, unless the accommodation is a hostel or privately leased (s. 207, Housing Act 1996). Notification that the tenancy will be secure amounts to an allocation under Part VI, Housing Act 1996. This exemption also applies to a temporary letting by a housing association discharging the authority's duty by arrangement (*Family Housing Association* v *Miah* (1982) 5 HLR 94).

**10.3.4.6   Temporary accommodation for persons taking up employment (sch. 1, para. 5)**   The purpose of this provision is to provide temporary accommodation for people moving jobs. Four conditions must be satisfied:

(a)   the tenancy must be granted to a person who, immediately before the grant, did not live in the local housing authority's district; and

(b)   prior to the grant of the tenancy, the tenant obtained employment, or an offer thereof, in the district or in its surrounding area; and

(c)   the tenancy was granted to meet the tenant's need for temporary accommodation in the district or its surrounding area in order to work, and to enable the tenant to find permanent accommodation there; and

(d)   the landlord notified the tenant in writing of the circumstances in which this exception applies.

If the landlord is a local housing authority, the tenancy becomes secure on notification. Otherwise, it is not secure for one year from its grant unless the landlord notifies the tenant that it is secure.

**10.3.4.7   Short-term arrangements (sch. 1, para. 6)**   The tenancy is not secure if:

(a)   the dwelling-house has been leased to the landlord with vacant possession for use as temporary housing accommodation; and

(b)   the terms on which it has been leased provide for the head landlord (which is not a body capable of granting secure tenancies) to obtain vacant possession from the landlord on the expiry of a specified period or when required, e.g. pursuant to a break clause in the lease; and

(c)   the landlord has no interest in the dwelling-house other than under the lease in question or as a mortgagee.

Despite the use of the word 'leased' in para. 6, this exception includes the situation in which the owner of a house makes it available to the local authority under a licence agreement (*Tower Hamlets London Borough Council* v *Miah* (1992) 24 HLR 199).

**10.3.4.8   Temporary accommodation made available to the tenant (sch. 1, para. 7)**   A tenancy is not secure if the dwelling-house has been made available to the tenant or to a predecessor in title (who is not a secure tenant) while works are carried out to his or her principal home. This exception will come into play where, for example, the tenant's home is subject to compulsory improvement works.

**10.3.4.9   Agricultural holdings (sch. 1, para. 8)**   This exception is identical to s. 10, Rent Act 1977 and is designed to exclude from security farm-managers, whether they work for the landlord or for a tenant of the landlord.

**10.3.4.10   Licensed premises (sch. 1, para. 9)**   This provision, which is derived from s. 11 Rent Act 1977, applies only to on-licensed premises such as a public house.

**10.3.4.11   Student lettings (sch. 1, para. 10)**   A tenancy is not secure if it was granted to enable the tenant to attend a designated course at an educational establishment and the landlord has served an appropriate written notice before the grant of the tenancy. Paragraph 10(2A), (2B) and (3) set out the circumstances in which the tenancy may become secure.

**10.3.4.12   Business tenancies within Part II, Landlord and Tenant Act 1954 (sch. 1, para 11)**

**10.3.4.13   Almshouses (sch. 1, para. 12)**   A licence to occupy an alms-house is not a secure tenancy if the licence was granted by a charity which has no power under the provisions which establish it as a charity to grant a tenancy of the almshouse.

### 10.3.5   Termination of the secure tenancy by the tenant

The Housing Act 1985 restricts only the landlord's rights to end a secure tenancy. It can still be terminated by the tenant by use of a notice to quit (for periodic tenancies) or by surrender or exercise of a break clause (for fixed-term tenancies).

Apparent abandonment of the premises is a problem commonly encountered by local housing authorities. Whether this points towards a surrender by operation of law (see **6.2.2**) depends on the facts. If the tenant leaves owing substantial arrears of rent, the court may, after a lengthy absence, infer that the landlords have impliedly accepted the tenant's offer to surrender the tenancy (*Preston Borough Council* v *Fairclough* (1982) 8 HLR 70). Such inference will be easier to make where the landlord peaceably re-enters, changes the locks of the premises and relets them to a different tenant, in other words has altered its position in reliance upon the supposed surrender (*R* v *London Borough of Croydon, ex parte Toth* (1988) 20 HLR 576).

### 10.3.6   Termination of the secure tenancy by the landlord

**10.3.6.1   Procedural requirements: fixed-term tenancies**   Where the landlord wishes to bring a tenancy to an end during the currency of the fixed term, the tenancy agreement must contain a provision for re-entry or forfeiture and the landlord must apply to the court under s. 82(3) for an order terminating the tenancy. This will necessitate compliance with the notice procedure set out in s. 83 unless the court considers it 'just and equitable' to dispense with the requirement of such a notice.

Where a fixed-term secure tenancy comes to an end (whether by effluxion of time or by an order of the court under s. 82(3)), a statutory periodic tenancy arises by virtue of s. 86(1) unless the landlord grants the tenant a further secure tenancy of the same dwelling-house (whether for a term certain or periodic) to begin on the termination of the original tenancy. The statutory periodic tenancy will be on the same terms as those of the original tenancy, in so far as they are compatible with a periodic tenancy and do not include any proviso for re-entry or forfeiture (s. 86(1)). To recover possession, the landlord must apply for a court order using the procedure outlined below.

**10.3.6.2 Procedural requirements: periodic tenancies** A secure periodic tenancy, whether it be contractual or statutory, cannot be ended by a landlord's notice to quit. The landlord must obtain a court order for possession of the dwelling-house and the tenancy will come to an end on the date specified in that order. A 'notice of seeking possession' must be served on the tenant (s. 83). The court may dispense with the need to serve a notice if it considers it just and equitable to do so (s. 83(1)(b), Housing Act 1985).

**10.3.6.3 The notice of seeking possession** The court cannot entertain proceedings for possession unless a notice of seeking possession has been served. Such a notice must be in the prescribed form (Secure Tenancies (Notices) Regulations 1987, SI 1987/755), and

(a)  specify the ground on which the court will be asked to make an order for possession of the dwelling-house or for the termination of the tenancy; and
(b)  give particulars of that ground; and
(c)  (in the case of a periodic tenancy), state the date after which proceedings may be begun (s. 83(2)).

The notice lapses 12 months after the specified date (s. 83(4)). The specified date cannot be earlier than the date on which the tenancy could be brought to an end by notice to quit. Where the ground (or one of the grounds) specified in the notice is Ground 2 (nuisance or other anti-social behaviour), the notice must state that possession proceedings may be begun immediately and specify the date sought by the landlord as the date on which the tenant is to give up possession (s. 83(3)). The court cannot allow the landlord to bring a claim for possession until after the specified date has passed and the notice remains in force (s. 83A(1)).

The purpose of the notice is to give the tenant an opportunity to rectify any breaches under the tenancy. Sufficient particulars must therefore be given of the ground on which the landlord intends to seek possession to enable the tenant to put matters right. In *Torridge DC* v *Jones* (1987) 19 HLR 526 a statement that 'the reasons for taking this action are non-payment of rent' did not suffice. The court held that the notice of seeking possession is a 'warning shot across the bows', the purpose of which is to enable the tenant to know what he or she has to do to put matters right before proceedings are commenced.

Minor errors in the prescribed form of the notice will not be fatal provided that the notice is substantially to the same effect as that required by s. 83 (Secure Tenancies (Notices) Regulations 1987, para. 2(1)). Similarly, the notice will not be invalidated by a mistake in the particulars if the landlord has in good faith stated the ground and given the particulars at the time the notice was served (see *Dudley Metropolitan Borough Council* v *Bailey* (1990) 22 HLR 424).

Where the tenant breaks the terms of a suspended possession order, the order becomes effective and the tenancy is terminated from that moment. The landlord is not obliged to take any further steps to notify the tenant of its intention to seek a warrant for possession (*Thompson* v *Elmbridge BC* (1987) 19 HLR 526).

**10.3.6.4  Substantive requirements**  Once a notice seeking possession has been served under s. 83, or the court has dispensed with the need for service of such a notice, the landlord may enter the case into court by applying for a summons to be issued. A court is only entitled to grant the landlord possession on one or more of the statutory Grounds 1–16 set out in sch. 2, Parts I–III, Housing Act 1985. It cannot make an order for possession based on a ground which is not specified in the landlord's s. 83 notice but the grounds which are specified may be altered or added to with the leave of the court (s. 84(3), as substituted by the Housing Act 1996, s. 147(2)). In *Camden LBC* v *Oppong* (1996) 28 HLR 701, the Court of Appeal held that the power to alter or add grounds imports a power to alter or add to particulars. The court cannot order possession to take effect any earlier than the date specified in the landlord's notice (s. 84(4)).

**10.3.6.5  Grounds for possession**  Unlike the Rent Act 1977 and the Housing Act 1988, there are no mandatory grounds. The grounds for possession are divided into three categories:

(a)  Part I (Grounds 1–8): an order for possession will be made only if the court considers it reasonable to make the order;

(b)  Part II (Grounds 9 to 11): the court will make an order for possession only if it is satisfied that suitable alternative accommodation will be available for the tenant when the order takes effect;

(c)  Part III (Grounds 12–16): the court will make an order for possession only if it both considers it reasonable to make the order and it is satisfied that suitable alternative accommodation will be available for the tenant when the order takes effect.

Many of the grounds contained in sch. 2 to the Housing Act 1985 are identical, or similar, to grounds and cases already dealt with in the context of the Rent Act 1977 and the Housing Act 1988. Reasonableness too has already been considered, and reference should be made to **Chapter 6**. Where proceedings are brought on any of the grounds contained in Part I or Part III, the court has a discretion to adjourn those proceedings, or stay or suspend the execution of any order or postpone the date of possession for such period or periods as it thinks fit (s. 85). Where a secure tenancy has come to an end by the granting of an order for possession, the tenant can apply to the court under s. 85 to make an order postponing the date given for possession at any time until the order is executed, thereby reviving the tenancy (*Burrows* v *Brent LBC* [1996] 4 All ER 577).

**Part I   Grounds on which an order for possession may be made if the court considers it reasonable**

*Ground 1   Rent arrears or breach of obligation of tenancy*
Rent lawfully due from the tenant has not been paid or an obligation of the tenancy has been broken or not performed.

*(a)   Rent arrears*   A postal survey of all local authorities carried out by the Department of the Environment in 1986 found that the overwhelming majority of actions for possession concerned rent arrears; only 1 to 2% were based on other grounds. Grounds 2 to 16 were scarcely used at all (Leather et al, 1989: 13). Almost half of local authority and housing association tenants are behind with their rent (Gray et al, 1994). This ground bears a close resemblance to Case 1 under the Rent Act 1977 and the same considerations apply (see **6.8.2.1**).

The present procedure for recovering possession on grounds of rent arrears has been subject to some criticism (Woolf, 1996: paras. 20–22). Fixed-date hearings are usually a mere formality because the majority of defendants do not attend and those who do are rarely represented (Nixon et al, 1996). They are wasteful, therefore, of both court time and legal costs. Further, the objective of the procedure tends not to be possession of the property but the payment of arrears. In theory, the landlord may recover what is owed by a claim for debt against the tenant or the 'archaic' remedy of distress (*Abingdon RDC* v *O'Gorman* [1968] 2 QB 811), but neither of these are really satisfactory: it is not worth bringing an action in debt against a tenant who seemingly cannot afford to pay the rent, and the amount yielded by distraint is often inadequate to cover arrears. The threat of possession is, therefore, the only effective weapon landlords have against recalcitrant tenants but, because possession is not really in the interests of either party, judges often give the tenant a last chance by making a possession order suspended so long as the current rent is paid and a further sum is paid off the arrears (unless, for example, the tenant makes no proposals for paying off serious rent arrears (*Haringey London Borough Council* v *Stewart* [1991] 2 EGLR 252)). A large money judgment payable by small weekly instalments will result in the possession order being suspended for lengthy periods — possibly years.

If the order is not suspended, or the conditions are not met by the tenant, the local authority may apply for a warrant to obtain possession. This is issued by the court bailiff and, at the same time, an eviction date is fixed. Even at this stage, however, an eviction may be cancelled or suspended by the plaintiff (usually if a payment of arrears is made) or by the court on an application by the defendant. Few warrants are executed: most are suspended by the local authority, or the eviction is made purely technical when the tenant voluntarily gives up possession (Leather et al, 1989: 14). However, because a secure tenancy determines as soon as there is a breach of the terms of a suspended order (*Thompson* v *Elmbridge Borough Council* (1987) 19 HLR 526), tenants and their families who are subject to such orders live in a curious social and legal limbo. Eviction is effectively at the landlord's discretion (subject to an appeal by the tenant for the suspension of the warrant) and the tenant's rights, therefore, depend 'more on the exercise of administrative discretion than on definable legal rights' (Driscoll, 1988: 376). As failure to comply with the terms of a suspended order may result in the loss of the tenancy and, given that the households most likely to be in arrears are families with children, eviction may simply result in the local authority having to rehouse.

The usual reasons for arrears are illness, unemployment, relationship breakdown and the late payment of housing benefit. If the proceedings are defended, these matters will be taken into consideration when addressing the issue of reasonableness. In *Woodspring* v *Taylor* (1982) 4 HLR 95, the Court of Appeal dismissed an appeal against a refusal by the county court to grant an outright order against the tenants even though the arrears amounted to more than £550 by the date of the hearing. The tenants had been satisfactory tenants for almost 20 years and had fallen into arrears only because of illness and unemployment.

*(b)    Breach of tenancy obligation*    The tenancy agreement has been described as 'the landlord's strongest tool for dealing with nuisance and anti-social behaviour, and possession proceedings under this part of Ground 1 are invariably concerned with anti-social behaviour. 'Nuisance clauses' are increasingly used by social landlords to attempt to modify tenants' behaviour. They can cover general harassment, racial, sexual and homophobic harassment, domestic violence, criminal behaviour, the abuse of housing staff, drug dealing, noise nuisance including loud music, the keeping and behaviour of dogs and other animals, rubbish and litter dumping, untidy gardens, the repair of cars and other vehicles in the street and their unsocial parking.

In considering whether or not it is reasonable to make the order, the court must take into account all the circumstances, including the seriousness of the breach, whether it is capable of remedy, whether it is likely to happen again, and the availability of other remedies such as an injunction. In *Wandsworth London Borough Council* v *Hargraves* [1994] EGCS 115, one of the conditions of the tenancy was that the tenant should 'not permit to be done anything which may increase the risk of fire'. A visitor brought a can of petrol into the tenant's flat, made petrol bombs and threw them out of the window, damaging a car parked outside. A fire started in the flat from some spilt petrol. The Court of Appeal upheld the decision at first instance that, even though the terms of the tenancy had been broken, it was not reasonable to make an order for possession. The tenant had not taken an active part in the events leading to the fire and there had been no misconduct on his part since the event. In *Sheffield City Council* v *Jepson* (1993) 25 HLR 299, however, the Court of Appeal overturned a county court judge's decision that it could not be reasonable to make an order for possession against a tenant who had kept a dog in breach of covenant, because the breach was deliberate and persistent.

A term will not be implied into the tenancy agreement that the landlord will enforce the nuisance clause in other tenancy agreements. Nor is a duty of care owed by a landlord to enforce a clause in a tenancy agreement, for the benefit of another tenant (*O'Leary* v *Islington LBC* (1983) 9 HLR 81).

*Ground 2    Nuisance or anti-social behaviour*
Ground 2 applies where:

the tenant or a person residing in *or visiting* the dwelling-house—

(a)    has been guilty of conduct causing or likely to cause a nuisance or annoyance to a person *residing, visiting or otherwise engaging in a lawful activity in the locality*; or

(b)   has been convicted of

(i)   using the dwelling-house or allowing it to be used for immoral or illegal purposes; or
(ii)   *an arrestable offence committed in, or in the locality of, the dwelling-house.*

The meaning of 'nuisance' and 'annoyance' has already been considered in **6.8.2.3.** The changes made to Ground 2 by the Housing Act 1996 are shown in italics. The following points should be noted:

(a)   The nuisance or annoyance can be caused by a person visiting the premises, even without the occupier's consent.
(b)   An actual nuisance or annoyance is not required if it can be shown that one is likely to be caused.
(c)   The ground formerly required a nuisance or annoyance to 'neighbours'. The category has been extended to include a person residing, visiting or otherwise engaging in a lawful activity in the locality (such as housing or police officers or someone carrying out repairs).
(d)   'Locality' is designed to cover as wide an area as possible: the common parts of blocks of flats, other parts of an estate and even where tenants do not have the same landlord (see *Hansard,* HC, Standing Committee G, 27 February 1996, cols. 382–3).

Possession will be ordered on Grounds 1 and 2 only if it is *reasonable* to do so (s. 84(2), Housing Act 1985). In *Camden LBC v Hawkins* [1988] March *Legal Action* 18, the Court of Appeal dismissed an appeal by the council against a refusal to order possession, one of the reasons being that it would not have been reasonable to order possession against a tenant of 24 years' standing by reason of the activities of her teenage son. In *Ealing Family Housing Association v Taylor* [1987] December *Legal Action* 15, the judge declined to order possession despite the fact that evidence had been given by two neighbours, an arresting police officer and a visitor to the premises who had been assaulted, and statements made by two officers of the plaintiff association. The judge found the evidence to be grossly exaggerated, holding that if there had been a nuisance, it was 'slight in all the circumstances'. However, in *Kensington & Chelsea RBC v Simmonds* (1996) 29 HLR 507, the Court of Appeal rejected a submission that some degree of fault on the part of the tenant must be shown before an order for possession can be made. If that submission were right, repossession could not be sought from the parents of an ill-disciplined and uncontrollable child, too old to control but too young to be put out of the house, who had caused the nuisance and annoyance. An order for possession was upheld, therefore, against the tenant whose 12-year-old son had subjected neighbours to racial harassment. Again, the seriousness of the nuisance and annoyance will be relevant and it may be appropriate to order possession if the tenant makes no assurance as to future behaviour (e.g., *Woking BC v Bistram* (1995) 27 HLR 1, where the tenant had allegedly used 'vile and abusive language' in respect of race and sexual orientation and there was no evidence that she intended to mend her ways).

*Conviction for illegal or immoral user*   Subject to the issue of reasonableness, a possession order can now be made against a tenant if he or she, another resident or visitor, is convicted of committing an arrestable offence in the premises or its locality. The extension of the 'conviction' limb was a response to Opposition amendments to strengthen local authorities' powers to deal with drug dealers who operate in the common parts of the estate rather than in a person's home (*Hansard*, HC, 30 April 1996, Report Stage). It extends far beyond drug dealing, however, as arrestable offences include murder, theft, handling stolen goods, criminal damage, taking a motor car without consent and various sexual offences (s. 24, Police and Criminal Evidence Act 1984).

No longer does the landlord have to wait for at least four weeks before issuing possession proceedings based on Ground 2. Instead, the notice of seeking possession will state:

(a)   that proceedings may be begun immediately; and
(b)   the date by which the tenant is required to give up possession (s. 83(3), Housing Act 1985, inserted by s. 147(1), Housing Act 1996).

*Injunctions against anti-social behaviour*   Some landlords may decide as a general policy not to intervene in disputes, perhaps because they do not really know how to deal with them. Alternatively, there may be 'half-hearted intervention', the landlord asking offenders to modify behaviour and making 'vague threats' about the legal consequences if such modification does not occur. A survey carried out between 1989 and 1992 encountered landlords who were unwilling to intervene unless blame could clearly be attributed to one of the parties or who responded to disputes by seeking voluntary rehousing for one or other of the parties (usually the complainant). Such a step may simply transfer the problem to a new set of neighbours (Hughes et al, 1994: 204). A local authority is not generally liable for nuisance committed by one of its tenants (*Smith* v *Scott* [1972] 3 All ER 645).

Since 1994, many local authorities have used injunctions in an attempt to combat nuisance and annoyance, e.g. joyriding, on their estates. Injunctions have been sought under a variety of provisions: tenancy agreements, ss. 111 and 222, Local Government Act 1972, actions for trespass as landowner, nuisance, and duties under the Race Relations Act 1976. Section 152, Housing Act 1996 is designed to provide an express power which dispenses with the need to rely on these other powers which were not originally intended to deal with the anti-social behaviour of tenants. Only a local authority can apply for such an injunction and not, e.g. a registered social landlord.

Section 152, Housing Act 1996 provides that, on an application by the local authority, the county court or High Court may grant an injunction prohibiting anyone from:

(a)   engaging or threatening to engage in conduct causing or likely to cause a nuisance or annoyance to a person residing in, visiting or otherwise engaging in a lawful activity in residential premises or the locality of such premises; or

(b)   using or threatening to use residential premises for immoral or illegal purposes; or

(c)   entering residential premises or the locality of such premises.

Section 152(2) defines 'residential premises' as:

(a)   dwelling-houses held under secure or introductory tenancies from the local authority;

(b)   accommodation provided by the local authority under their duties to the homeless (Part VII of the 1996 Act).

The injunction cannot be granted unless:

(a)   the respondent has used or threatened to use violence against any person residing in, visiting or otherwise engaging in a lawful activity in residential premises or their locality; and

(b)   there is a significant risk of harm to that person or a person of a similar description if the injunction is not granted (s. 152(3)).

In relation to a person aged 18 or over, 'harm' is defined as 'ill-treatment or the impairment of health'. Where a child is involved, it means 'ill-treatment or the impairment of health or development' (s. 158(1)). The court may attach a power of arrest to one or more of the provisions of an injunction which it intends to grant (s. 152(6)). There is no need to notify the respondent of the proceedings where it is just and convenient to make (or vary) the injunction (s. 152(7)) (e.g. where to give notice might provoke retaliation by the respondent) but the respondent must then have an opportunity to make representations at an *inter partes* hearing as soon as is just and convenient.

*Power of arrest*   Section 153(1) provides that where a social landlord seeks an injunction to enforce the terms of its tenancy against a tenant, the court may attach a power of arrest to any part of the injunction order. However, this power can only be used when the breach or anticipated breach of the tenancy terms consists of:

(a)   engaging or threatening to engage in conduct causing or likely to cause a nuisance or annoyance to a person residing, visiting or otherwise engaging in a lawful activity in the locality;

(b)   using or threatening to use the premises for immoral or illegal purposes; or

(c)   allowing any sub-tenant or lodger of his or hers or any other person residing (whether temporarily or otherwise) on the premises or visiting them to act as mentioned above.

Under s. 153(6) the court must be of the opinion that:

(a)   the respondent or any sub-tenant, lodger or other resident has used or threatened violence against a person residing, visiting or otherwise engaging in a lawful activity in the locality, and

(b)   there is a significant risk of harm to that person or a person of a similar description if the power of arrest is not attached to one or more provisions of the injunction immediately.

Where a court attaches a power of arrest to any provision of an injunction, it may provide that the power has effect for a shorter period than the other provisions of the injunction (s. 157(1)).

### Ground 2A    Domestic violence by partner
This ground was introduced by the Housing Act 1996. It can be used where the dwelling-house was occupied (whether alone or with others) by a married couple or a couple living together as husband and wife (one of whom is the tenant) and one of them has left because of the violence of one to the other or to a child residing with that person immediately before his or her departure. The court must be satisfied that the person who has left is unlikely to return.

### Ground 3    Deterioration of premises or common parts
This ground may be used where the condition of the dwelling-house or any of the common parts has deterioriated owing to acts of waste by, or the neglect or default of, the tenant or a person residing in the dwelling-house and, where the tenant's lodger or sub-tenant is responsible, the tenant has failed to take such steps as ought reasonably to have been taken for that person's removal. This ground is virtually identical to Case 3 under the Rent Act 1977.

### Ground 4    Deterioration of furniture
The wording of this ground is very similar to the that of the previous one but it applies instead to furniture provided by the landlord.

### Ground 5    Grant of tenancy induced by tenant's false statement
Ground 5 comes into play where the tenant is the person, or one of the persons, to whom the tenancy was granted and the landlord was induced to grant the tenancy by a false statement made knowingly or recklessly by the tenant, e.g. where a secure tenant of a housing association obtained housing from the local authority by stating on her application form that she was currently living with family and friends (*Rushcliffe BC* v *Watson* (1991) 24 HLR 124). In deciding the question of reasonableness, the court can take into account, *inter alia*, the nature and degree of the untrue statements, and the tenant's attitude when the deception is discovered (*Shrewsbury & Atcham BC* v *Evans* (1997) 30 HLR 123).

### Ground 6    Premium paid in connection with assignment
This ground may be used where a premium was paid in connection with the assignment of the tenancy (under s. 92, Housing Act 1985) to:

(a)   the tenant; or
(b)   a predecessor in title who is a member of the tenant's family and is residing in the dwelling-house.

A 'premium' in this context means any fine or other sum and any other pecuniary consideration in addition to rent. This provision is designed to prevent the exploitation of s. 92 which permits secure tenants to exchange tenancies.

*Ground 7    Premises let in connection with employment*
This ground may be utilised where:

the dwelling-house forms part of, or is within the curtilage of, a building which, or so much of it as is held by the landlord, is mainly held for purposes other than housing purposes, and consists of accommodation other than housing accommodation, and—

(a)   the dwelling-house was let to the tenant or a predecessor in title in consequence of the tenant or predecessor being in the employment of the landlord, or of—

a local authority
a new town corporation
a housing action trust
an urban development corporation,
the Development Board for Rural Wales, or
the governors of an aided school, and

(b)   the tenant or a person residing in the dwelling-house has been guilty of conduct such that, having regard to the purpose for which the building is used, it would not be right for him to continue in occupation of the dwelling-house.

The purpose of this ground, which is peculiar to the Housing Act 1985, is to enable a landlord to regain possession where an employee of the landlord (or other body specified in (a)) who lives within a building used for non-housing purposes (e.g. a school or hospital) is guilty of misconduct which makes continued occupation inappropriate.

*Ground 8    Temporary accommodation*
The dwelling-house was made available for occupation by the tenant (or a predecessor in title) while works were carried out on the dwelling-house which the tenant previously occupied as his or her only or principal home and:

(a)   the tenant (or predecessor) was a secure tenant of the other dwelling-house at the time when he or she ceased to occupy it as his or her home,

(b)   the tenant (or predecessor) accepted the tenancy of the dwelling-house of which possession is sought on the understanding that he or she would give up occupation when, on completion of the works, the other dwelling-house was again available for occupation under a secure tenancy, and

(c)   the works have been completed and the other dwelling-house is so available.

## Part II   Grounds on which the court may order possession if suitable alternative accommodation is available (Grounds 9–11)

The requirements of suitable alternative accommodation under the Housing Act 1985 are similar to those contained in the Rent Act 1977. The court cannot make an order for possession under s. 84(2)(b) unless a member of the tenant's family who lives in the premises has been joined as a party to the proceedings (*Wandsworth LBC* v *Fadayomi* [1987] 3 All ER 474).

Accommodation will be suitable if it consists of premises:

(a)   which are to be let as a separate dwelling under a secure tenancy; or

(b)   which are to be let as a separate dwelling under a protected tenancy, not being a tenancy under which the landlord might recover possession under one of the Cases in Part II of sch. 15 to the Rent Act 1977 (cases where court must order possession); or

(c)   which are to be let as a separate dwelling under an assured tenancy which is neither an assured shorthold tenancy, within the meaning of Part I, Housing Act 1988, nor a tenancy under which the landlord might recover possession under any of the Grounds 1–5 in sch. 2 to the 1985 Act;

and, in the opinion of the court, the accommodation is reasonably suitable to the needs of the tenant and his or her family (sch. 2, Part IV, para. 1).

In determining whether the alternative accommodation is suitable the court shall have regard to:

(a)   the nature of the accommodation which it is the practice of the landlord to allocate to tenants with similar needs;

(b)   the distance of the accommodation available from the place of work or education of the tenant or any members of his or her family;

(c)   its distance from the home of any member of the tenant's family if proximity to it is essential to that member's or the tenant's well-being;

(d)   the needs (as regards extent of accommodation) and means of the tenant and his or her family;

(e)   the terms on which the accommodation is available and the terms of the secure tenancy;

(f)   if furniture is provided by the landlord for use under the secure tenancy, whether furniture is to be provided for use in the other accommodation, and if so the nature of the furniture to be provided.

It will be observed that, unlike the private sector provision, the Housing Act 1985 makes no reference to the character of the proposed accommodation, so that no account may be taken of environmental factors.

In *Enfield LBC* v *French* (1985) 17 HLR 211, it was held that although a garden can qualify as one of the 'needs' of a tenant, accommodation may none the less be regarded as reasonably suitable even if one particular need cannot be met. A one-bedroomed flat constituted suitable accommodation for a bachelor, even though it had no garden and he was a dedicated gardener who had created 'a beautiful garden' out of a 'wilderness' at his existing home, with fish in a pond and birds in an aviary.

## Ground 9   Overcrowding
The dwelling-house is overcrowded, within the meaning of Part X, in such circumstances as to render the occupier guilty of an offence.

## Ground 10   Demolition or reconstruction
The landlord intends, within a reasonable time of obtaining possession of the dwelling-house:

(a)   to demolish or reconstruct the building or part of the building comprising the dwelling-house; or
(b)   to carry out work on that building or on land let together with, and thus treated as part of, the dwelling-house;

and cannot reasonably do so without obtaining possession of the dwelling-house.

This ground is similar to the provisions for assured tenancies contained in Ground 6 of the Housing Act 1988 (see **6.8.4.1**).

## Ground 10A   Dwelling-house in redevelopment area
This ground, added by s. 9, Housing and Planning Act 1986, may be used where the whole or part of the dwelling-house is in an area which is subject to a redevelopment scheme approved by the Secretary of State or the Housing Corporation in accordance with sch. 2, Part V and the landlord intends, within a reasonable time of obtaining possession, to dispose of the dwelling-house in accordance with the scheme and for that purpose reasonably requires possession of the dwelling-house.

## Ground 11   Landlord is a charity
The landlord is a charity and the tenant's continued occupation of the dwelling-house would conflict with the objects of the charity.

**Grounds on which the court may order possession if it considers it reasonable to do so and suitable alternative accommodation is available (Grounds 12–16)**

*Ground 12   Dwelling-house required for employee*
The dwelling-house forms part of a building which is mainly used for non-residential purposes or is situated in a cemetery and the landlord requires it for an employee.

*Ground 13   Dwelling-house suitable for occupation by a physically disabled person*
The dwelling-house has features which are substantially different from those of ordinary dwelling-houses and which are designed to make it suitable for occupation by a physically disabled person who requires accommodation of a kind provided by the dwelling-house and:

(a)   there is no longer such a person residing in the dwelling-house; and
(b)   the landlord requires it for occupation (whether alone or with members of his or her family) by such a person.

These features must be of a type not normally in an ordinary dwelling, e.g. ramps instead of steps, cooking surfaces at a special height, but not an additional downstairs lavatory (*Freeman* v *Wansbeck* [1984] 2 All ER 746).

*Ground 14   Dwelling-house required by housing association or trust*
The landlord is a housing association or housing trust which lets dwelling-houses only for occupation (whether alone or with others) by persons whose circumstances (other than merely financial circumstances) make it especially difficult for them to satisfy their need for housing, and:

(a)   either there is no longer such a person residing in the dwelling-house or the tenant has received from a local housing authority an offer of accommodation in premises which are to be let as a separate dwelling under a secure tenancy; and
(b)   the landlord requires the dwelling-house for occupation (whether alone or with members of his or her family) by such a person.

*Ground 15   Dwelling-house required for person with special needs*
The dwelling-house is one of a group of dwelling-houses which it is the practice of the landlord to let for occupation by persons with special needs and:

(a)   a social service or special facility is provided in close proximity to the group of dwelling-houses in order to assist persons with those special needs;
(b)   there is no longer a person with those special needs residing in the dwelling-house; and
(c)   the landlord requires the dwelling-house for occupation (whether alone or with members of his or her family) by a person who has those special needs.

*Ground 16    Over-occupation*
The accommodation afforded by the dwelling-house is more extensive than is reasonably required by the tenant who, as a member of the previous tenant's family, succeeded to a *periodic* tenancy by virtue of s. 89, Housing Act 1985. Notice that possession is being sought must have been served under s. 83, or proceedings for possession begun, between six and 12 months after the date of the previous tenant's death. In determining whether it is reasonable to make an order on this ground, the court must take into account:

   (a)   the tenant's age;
   (b)   the period during which the tenant has occupied the dwelling-house as his or her only or principal home; and
   (c)   any financial or other support given by the tenant to the previous tenant.

**References**

Cole, I. and Furbey, R., *The Eclipse of Council Housing*, London: Routledge, 1994.

Department of the Environment, *Our Future Homes: Opportunity, Choice Responsibility*, Cmnd. 2901, London: HMSO, 1995.

Driscoll, J., 'Rent Arrears, Suspended Possession Orders and the Rights of Secure Tenants', *Modern Law Review*, vol. 51, 1988, pp. 371–377.

Gray, B., Finch, H., Prescott-Clarke, T., Cameron, S., Gilroy, R., Kirby, K. and Mountford, J., *Rent Arrears in Local Authorities and Housing Associations in England*, London: HMSO, 1994.

Hughes, D., Karn, V. and Lickiss, R., 'Neighbour Disputes, Social Landlords and the Law', *Journal of Social Welfare and Family Law*, 1994, vol. 16, pp. 201–228.

Leather, P. and Jeffers, S., *Taking Tenants to Court: a Study of Possession Actions by Local Authorities*, London: HMSO, 1989.

Nixon, J., Smith, Y., Wishart, B. and Hunter, C., *Housing Cases in County Courts*, York: The Policy Press, 1996.

Stewart, A., *Rethinking Housing Law*, London: Sweet & Maxwell, 1996.

Woolf, H., *Access to Justice: Final Report to the Lord Chancellor on the Civil Justice System in England and Wales*, London: HMSO, 1996.

# ELEVEN

## Rights and duties of secure tenants

Quite apart from security of tenure, secure tenants have a number of other rights which are incorporated in the so-called 'Tenants' Charter'. Rights of succession and rights relating to rent and repairs are dealt with in **Chapters 13** and **16.2.6** respectively but the others are considered here. Of most significance is the 'right to buy'.

### 11.1  ASSIGNMENT

Because the allocation of social housing is generally based on need, it is important that public sector landlords are able to control the occupation of their housing. Therefore, s. 91, Housing Act 1985 prohibits assignment except in the following circumstances:

(a)    under the 'right to exchange' provisions contained in s. 92;
(b)    by court order in cases of relationship breakdown; or
(c)    to a person who would be qualified to succeed if the tenant died immediately before the assignment (s. 91(3)(c)).

### 11.1.1  Exchange

Section 92 implies a term into every secure tenancy that the tenant may assign the tenancy:

(a)    to another secure tenant; or
(b)    to an assured tenant whose landlord is either the Housing Corporation, Housing for Wales, a registered social landlord, or a charitable housing trust.

The assignee must have the landlord's written consent to assign either to the first-mentioned tenant or another secure tenant (thus permitting three-way or multiple exchanges). Consent can be withheld only on one or more of the following grounds which are set out in sch. 3 to the Housing Act 1985:

(a)    the assignee is already obliged by a court order to give up possession;

(b)    a notice of seeking possession under s. 83 has been served, or proceedings for possession have begun, on any of Grounds 1–6 in sch. 2;

(c)    the accommodation afforded by the dwelling-house is substantially more extensive than is reasonably required by the proposed assignee;

(d)    the extent of the accommodation is not reasonably suitable to the needs of the proposed assignee and his or her family;

(e)    the accommodation has been let to the tenant in consequence of employment, related to non-housing purposes;

(f)    the landlord is a charity and the proposed assignee's occupation of the dwelling-house would conflict with the charity's objects;

(g)    the dwelling-house is adapted for a disabled person;

(h)    occupation of the dwelling-house by the proposed assignee would conflict with the purposes of a specialist housing association or trust;

(i)    the dwelling-house is one of a group of houses which the landlord lets for the occupation of people with special needs;

(j)    the proposed assignee refuses to become a member of the tenants' housing association which is managing the property.

Within 42 days of the tenant's application for consent, the landlord must serve on the tenant a notice specifying and giving particulars of the ground on which consent is withheld (s. 92(4)). If it is withheld for any reason other than one of the grounds set out in sch. 3, the tenant may treat it as having been given (s. 92(3)). Consent can be made conditional upon the tenant paying any outstanding rent or remedying any breach of obligation (s. 92(5) and (6)).

### 11.1.2   Relationship breakdown

Assignment of a secure tenancy is possible by virtue of court orders made under:

(a)    ss. 23A or 24, Matrimonial Causes Act 1973;

(b)    s. 17(1), Matrimonial and Family Proceedings Act 1984; or

(c)    sch. 1, para. 1, Children Act 1989.

On granting a decree of divorce, nullity or judicial separation, the court can make a property adjustment order under s. 23A or 24, Matrimonial Causes Act 1973 transferring the tenancy from one spouse to another. An assignment of the tenancy by the tenant is necessary to give effect to the court's order. In deciding whether or not to make an order under the 1973 Act, the court should take into account the policy of the local housing authority with regard to housing need and its effect on the parties concerned and the circumstances of security of tenure. In *Jones* v *Jones* [1997] 2 WLR 373, the wife had access to a loan which would probably enable her to find accommodation in the private rented sector. The husband's need to retain the tenancy was greater as he was disabled and the property was particularly suited to his needs. It was also felt that he should have priority, given that he had been the tenant for 20 years and his wife had only lived in the flat for the 15 months of the couple's marriage. The Family Law Act 1996 extends the power to transfer between cohabitants and former cohabitants whose relationship has broken down. When considering whether to transfer a tenancy, the court must have regard to all the circumstances, e.g. the parties' respective housing needs and resources, their financial resources and their suitability as tenants (sch. 7, para. 5). Further, the transferee may be ordered to pay compensation to the transferor for the loss of his or her rights under the tenancy (sch. 7, para. 10).

In its report which paved the way for the Family Law Act 1996 (Law Commission, 1992), the Law Commission overlooked the problem which arises where the sole tenant leaves the property, intending never to return. It will be recalled that the occupation of the dwelling as a residence is an essential prerequisite of a statutory tenancy under the Rent Act 1977, and that occupation by the tenant as his or her only or principal home is necessary to keep alive an assured tenancy under the Housing Act 1988 and a secure tenancy under the Housing Act 1985. Until the making of a decree absolute, an exception is made to the normal rules governing statutory residence to the effect that occupation by the departed tenant's spouse is deemed to maintain occupation by the tenant himself or herself. On the making of the decree absolute, or the permanent departure of a sole cohabitant tenant, the tenancy ceases to be statutory, assured or secure as the case may be and there is nothing left to transfer.

### 11.1.3 Assignment to a successor

This provision may be used where the tenant wishes, e.g., to pre-empt any dispute which may arise upon his or her death between the potential successors, or to assign to a potential successor and then leave the premises. In *Peabody Donation Fund* v *Higgins* [1983] 1 WLR 1091, the tenancy agreement contained an absolute prohibition against assignment. The tenant, intending to retire to Ireland, executed an assignment by deed in favour of his daughter (who would have qualified to succeed upon the tenant's death). It was, therefore, an effective assignment but, because it was contrary to the terms of the tenancy, there was nothing to prevent the landlord from starting proceedings afresh to recover possession on Ground 1 (breach of a term of the tenancy).

To be effective, the assignment must be by deed (s. 52, Law of Property Act 1925), even if writing was not necessary for the tenancy itself because it is for less than three years. Thus, in *Crago* v *Julian* (1991) 24 HLR 306, a wife's appeal against a possession order was unsuccessful where her husband had given a written undertaking to transfer the weekly tenancy to her within 14 days of the granting of their decree absolute, but had failed to incorporate the assignment in a deed. In *City of Westminster* v *Peart* (1991) 24 HLR 389, Sir Christopher Slade doubted, obiter, that Parliament had intended to impose the formality and expense of executing a deed upon those who wished to take advantage of s. 91(3)(c) but the approach taken in *Crago* was confirmed by the

Court of Appeal in *London Borough of Camden* v *Alexandrou* (1997) 74 P & CR D33.

## 11.2 TAKING IN LODGERS AND SUBLETTING

It is a term of every secure tenancy that the tenant—

(a) may allow any persons to reside as lodgers in the dwelling-house, but
(b) will not, without the landlord's written consent, sub-let or part with possession of part of the dwelling-house (s. 93(1), Housing Act 1985).

If a secure tenant parts with possession of the dwelling-house or sub-lets the whole of it (or sub-lets part of it and then the remainder), the secure status of the tenancy is lost and cannot subsequently be resurrected (s. 93(2)).

Consent to sub-letting must not be unreasonably withheld. If it is withheld unreasonably it will be treated as given. A tenant must always seek consent before sub-letting but it may be validly given even after the sub-lease has been granted (s. 94(4)). If consent is refused, the landlord must give the tenant a written statement of the reasons for refusal (s. 94(6)). The burden of proof is on the landlord to show that the withholding of consent was not unreasonable (s. 94(2)). In determining the matter of reasonableness, the court should take into account whether granting consent would lead to overcrowding of the dwelling-house within the meaning of Part X of the 1985 Act (see **16.6**), or whether the landlord proposes to carry out works on the premises which would affect the accommodation likely to be used by the sub-tenant (s. 94(3)(a) and (b)).

## 11.3 IMPROVEMENTS

The improvement programmes of local authority landlords have been severely affected by cuts in capital spending. Theoretically, this highlights the significance of the right given to secure tenants to carry out improvements but most secure tenants cannot afford to do so (Stewart, 1996: 153).

It is a term of every secure tenancy that the tenant will not make improvement without the written consent of the landlord (s. 97(1), Housing Act 1985). 'Improvement' means any alteration in, or addition to, a dwelling-house, and includes any addition or alteration to the landlord's fixtures and fittings or connected with the provision of services to the dwelling-house, the erection of a wireless or TV aerial, and the carrying out of external decoration (s. 97(2)).

Consent to improvements must not be unreasonably withheld. If it is withheld unreasonably it will be treated as given (s. 97(3)). The burden of proof will be on the landlord to show that consent was not withheld unreasonably (s. 98(1)). In determining whether consent has been withheld unreasonably, the court should consider the extent to which the improvement would be likely:

(a)   to make the dwelling-house, or any other premises, less safe for the occupiers;

(b)   to cause the landlord to incur expenditure which it would be unlikely to incur if the improvement were not made; or

(c)   to reduce the price which the dwelling-house would fetch if sold on the open market or the rent which the landlord would be able to charge on letting the dwelling-house (s. 98(2)).


Consent to an improvement may be made subject to conditions (s. 99(1)), but if the condition is not reasonable, consent will be taken to have been unreasonably withheld (s. 99(2)). A secure tenant who fails to satisfy a reasonable condition will be treated as having breached an obligation of the tenancy (s. 99(4)).

If the improvements have added to the value of the property or the rent that the landlord can charge, the tenant may be entitled to compensation. Depending on whether the improvements were begun before or after 1 February 1994, compensation will be governed by s. 100, Housing Act 1985 or ss. 99A and 99B which were inserted into the 1985 Act by s. 122, Leasehold Reform, Housing and Urban Development Act 1993.


## 11.4   VARIATION


There are only three ways in which the terms of a secure tenancy may be varied:


(a)   by agreement between the landlord and tenant (s. 102(1)(a), Housing Act 1985);

(b)   by the landlord or tenant in accordance with a provision in the lease or tenancy agreement, or in an agreement varying it, provided that the variation relates to rent or to payments in respect of rates, council tax or services (s. 102(1)(b));

(c)   in accordance with s. 103, Housing Act 1985.


Terms which have been implied by statute cannot be varied (s. 103(3)(a)).

By s. 103, which applies only to secure periodic tenancies, the landlord who wishes to vary the terms of a secure tenancy must serve on the tenant a preliminary notice which:


(a)   informs the tenant of the landlord's intention to serve a notice of variation;

(b)   gives details of the proposed variation and its effect; and

(c)   invites the tenant to comment on the proposed variation within a specified time (s. 103(2)). The landlord must consider any comments made by the tenant.

## 11.5  INFORMATION

Tenancy agreements need not be in writing but s. 104, Housing Act 1985 requires landlords to publish information about their secure tenancies, explaining in simple terms the effect of:

(a)  the express terms of their secure tenancies;
(b)  the provisions of Part IV (Secure Tenancies and Rights of Secure Tenants) and Part V (the right to buy);
(c)  the provisions of ss. 11–16, Landlord and Tenant Act 1985 (landlord's repairing obligations; see **15.6.2**).

They should also ensure that, so far as is reasonably practicable, the information so published is kept up to date (s. 104(1)) and should make available a statement of the tenancy terms in so far as they are neither expressed in the written tenancy agreement (if any) nor implied by law (s. 104(2)(b)). Where the landlord is a local housing authority, it should supply its secure tenants with a copy of the information required by s. 104(1)(b) and (c) at least once a year (s. 104(3)). Section 106 requires landlords to publish information about housing allocation.

## 11.6  CONSULTATION

Section 105, Housing Act 1985 requires landlords who fulfil the landlord condition to maintain such arrangements as they consider appropriate to enable secure tenants who are likely to be substantially affected by a matter of housing management:

(a)  to be informed of proposed changes and developments; and
(b)  to make their views known to their landlord within a specified time.

A matter is one of 'housing management' if, in the landlord's opinion:

(a)  it relates to the management, maintenance, improvement, or demolition of municipal dwellings, or to the provision of services or amenities to such dwellings; and
(b)  it represents a new programme of maintenance, improvement or demolition, or some change in the landlord's practice; and
(c)  it is likely substantially to affect either its secure tenants as a whole or a group of them. A group is defined as a group of secure tenants who form a distinct social group, or who occupy dwelling-houses which constitute a distinct class, whether by reference to the kind of dwelling, or the housing estate or larger area in which they are situated. Thus, in *Short* v *London Borough of Tower Hamlets* (1986) 18 HLR 171, the Court of Appeal held that a decision taken 'in principle' to dispose of an estate to a private developer was not a matter of 'housing management' requiring consultation nor, in *R* v *London*

*Borough of Hammersmith & Fulham ex parte Beddowes* [1987] 1 All ER 369, was the identity of the prospective developer.

The authority has a duty to consider any representations made by secure tenants before making any decisions on a matter of housing management.

Section 106A gives a right to secure and introductory tenants whose local authority landlord is intending to dispose of their dwellings to a private sector landlord, to be consulted prior to the disposal.

Section 27BA imposes a duty on a local housing authority to consult with tenants with respect to the management of their housing management functions.

## 11.7  MANAGEMENT

A local housing authority may, with the Secretary of State's approval, transfer specified management functions over specified houses to 'another person' (s. 27, Housing Act 1985). Such delegation is by way of a management agreement which sets out the terms on which the authority's functions are exerciseable by the manager and must contain such provisions as are prescribed by regulations made by the Secretary of State. 'Another person' can mean the tenants or, since the advent of compulsory competitive tendering, other professional managers such as housing associations. The management functions which can be delegated under these powers are widely defined and include maintenance, repair, allocation of tenancies and rent collection.

Local authorities were slow to use their powers to delegate housing management. By 1993, only 62 estates had passed to tenant management organisations (about 2% of all local authority housing). In a series of consultation papers produced in the early 1990s, the government proposed that certain tenant organisations would have the right to insist on delegation. Since 1993, tenant management organisations have had the 'right to manage', i.e., a right to insist that a local authority delegates its housing management functions to them in defined circumstances (s. 27AB, Housing Act 1985, inserted by s. 132(1), Leasehold Reform, Housing and Urban Development Act 1993). For a description of the procedure involved in exercising the right to manage see Driscoll, 1994.

## 11.8  THE RIGHT TO BUY

### 11.8.1  Introduction

The sale of council houses to tenants has been possible throughout the history of council housing. It really took off, however, with the Housing Act 1980 which gave the 'right to buy' to secure tenants who fulfilled the qualifying period. Since 1979, 1.5 million local authority and housing association (public sector) tenants have bought their homes, 1.25 million of them under the right to buy (Department of the Environment, 1995: 14). In previous periods of high discretionary sales, the amount of new building was considerably higher than disposals but since the introduction of the right to buy, hardly any local authority housing has been built. This so-called 'sale of the century' has resulted in the largest ever transfer of public assets into the private sector, the receipts from council house sales having contributed almost as much in terms of capital receipts as the rest of the government's privatisation programme put together (Inquiry into British Housing, 1991: 71). When the right to buy was introduced, it was assumed that sales would be spread evenly across the country. In fact, the pattern of sales has been uneven, both geographically and socially. It is typically in those areas where home ownership was already high that it has grown the most (Forrest et al, 1992: 144–146).

### 11.8.2   Council house sales before 1980

When local authorities were first empowered to build houses, they were not intended to remain the owners of those houses for ever. The Artisans and Labourers' Dwellings Improvement Act 1875 and the Housing of the Working Classes Act 1890 both provided that housing constructed by local authorities should be sold within 10 years of its completion but very little council housing was produced under this legislation, and the obligation to sell was in any case removed by the Housing and Town Planning Act 1909. Local authorities were still permitted to sell council houses with ministerial consent but, even though the inter-war years witnessed council house building on an unprecedently large scale, the volume of sales was small. Where sales did take place, they had to be for the best price obtainable.

A refusal of consent to the sale of council houses during the Second World War was maintained after 1945 by the Labour government which considered that in the current circumstances as many houses as possible should be kept available for letting to people who were most in need of them (*Hansard*, 1947–8, vol. 445, col. 1167; 1948–9, vol. 468, col. 186). There was also the view that 'where public money and public facilities have been found to provide houses for letting to those in the greatest need, those houses should [not] now be sold to others merely because they have the money to buy them. (*Hansard*, 1947–8, vol. 445, col. 1167). By contrast, the Conservative party leadership promised to increase home-owning as part of their plan to create 'a property-owning democracy', a phrase coined in 1946 by Anthony Eden, then deputy leader of the Opposition.

Following the election victory of the Conservatives in 1952, the requirement that local authorities obtain ministerial consent to sales was removed. Instead the 'general consent', contained in Circular 64/52 issued by the Ministry of Housing and Local Government, allowed them to sell their housing and simply to notify the Minister on completion. No longer were local authorities obliged to obtain the best price for the houses they sold. For pre-1945 houses, the price was to be at least 20 times the net annual rent. For post-war houses, the price was to be not less than the all-in cost of providing the house. Circular 64/52 (subsequently incorporated into the Housing Act 1952) also required authorities to impose conditions on sale, limiting the resale price for a period of five years and reserving a right of pre-emption so that they could buy back the property at its original price if the purchaser resold it within five years. Between 1953 to 1959 local councils sold an annual average of only 2,003 houses, which included houses built for sale was well as those bought by sitting tenants (Merrett, 1979: 119). Obviously demand was limited.

The next general consent was given by a Conservative government in 1960. Circular 5/60 stated that the terms of the 1952 Circular were minima which should not be regarded as the norm, and cautioned authorities not to sell at 'sacrificial' prices. It also asked them to consider carefully the effect that sales would have on the ability of authorities to accommodate poorer families at rents within their means.

In the lead-up to the 1964 general election it was Labour which made the running on housing and home ownership. The new Labour government let the general consent on sales issued in 1960 continue in force and actively supported council house sales in the new towns in order to achieve a social and economic balance. The encouragement of home ownership was desirable but was 'primarily a matter for the private sector to deal with' (Hansard, 1967, vol. 740, col. 1336). In the private rented sector, the government's Leasehold Reform Act 1967 gave long-leaseholders the right to purchase freeholds or extend leases by 50 years. At the same time, however, the government increased building targets and specified that 50% of new building should be by local authorities for letting. The number of council house sales was not sufficiently high to pose a threat to the government's housing programme (Forrest et al, 1991a: 47).

The rate of sales stayed at around 2,000 to 3,000 per year until the late 1960s when the Conservatives won control of many major local authorities (notably Greater London and Birmingham) and began to mount enthusiastic sales campaigns. Circular 24/67 was a response to this substantial development of sales in certain areas. It replaced the 1952 minima and, for the first time, required sale prices to be based on market valuations. Because of the problems involved in making valuations and the restrictions on resale, authorities were allowed to reduce values by up to 20% below the vacant possession market value provided that no loss on the sale was incurred. It attempted to dissuade local authorities from selling accommodation in areas where there was a pressing social need for rented housing.

In 1968 over 8,000 sales were recorded despite the Labour government's circular (MHLG Circular 42/68) which imposed a limit on the proportion of municipal stock to be sold annually in the major conurbations. On the return of a Conservative government in 1970, these restrictions on sales were removed and a general consent was given to local authorities that houses could be sold at full market value, or at a discount of up to 20% on condition that the house was offered back to the council if it was re-sold within five years (MHLG Circular 54/70). Sales figures rose by what was then quite a dramatic rate, peaking at 45,000 in 1972 when the government issued a circular stating that applications to buy should only be refused in exceptional local circumstances. A further circular issued in 1973 enabled councils to increase the discount to 30% but only with ministerial consent.

During the 1973/4 parliamentary session, a Conservative MP introduced a Private Member's Bill to give tenants a statutory right to buy. This policy was adopted by the party and the 1974 election manifesto contained a commitment that 'subject to the right of appeal to the local authority to the Secretary of State on clearly specified grounds, we shall ensure that, in future, established council tenants are able, as of right, to buy on reasonable terms the house or flat in which they live' (Craig, 1975: 386). In the event, however, a Labour government — which had pledged to provide every family with 'a decent home' — was returned. Circular 70/74 maintained that in general local authorities should not sell council houses in areas where there were substantial needs to be met for rented dwellings, as in large cities. While the sale of council houses into owner-occupation might be appropriate in some areas to achieve a better housing balance, this should not be done where there was an unmet demand for rented accommodation. The general consent was reissued, however, although the government's apparent lack of concern may be explained by the dominance of Labour in the large urban authorities (Forrest et al, 1991a: 54). Certainly, annual sales did not exceed 5,000 between 1974 and 1976.

The rise in the number of council house sales during the late 1970s was attributable to Conservatives regaining control of many urban local authorities. In March 1979, therefore, the Labour Secretary of State for the Environment announced restrictions to prevent 'indiscriminate and irresponsible' sales of stock at discounts by some Conservative-controlled authorities. There was a tension in the Labour Party, however, between those with a traditional allegiance to council housing and those who supported owner-occupation.

**Table 11.a  Local authority dwellings sold 1970–79 (England and Wales)**

| | |
|---|---|
| 1970 | 6,231 |
| 1971 | 16,851 |
| 1972 | 45,058 |
| 1973 | 33,720 |
| 1974 | 4,153 |
| 1975 | 2,089 |
| 1976 | 4,582 |
| 1977 | 12,020 |
| 1978 | 29,100 |
| 1979 | 40,550 |

Source: Department of the Environment, 1981: Table 82.

In 1979, the Conservatives won the general election, having made clear in their manifesto their commitment to the sale of council houses. In the Debate on the Queen's Speech in 1979, the new Prime Minister, Margaret Thatcher, spoke enthusiastically about the 'thousands of people in council houses and new towns [who] came out to support us for the first time because they wanted a chance to buy their own homes' and of making 'a giant stride towards making a reality of Anthony Eden's dream of a property-owning democracy' (*Hansard*, 1979, vol. 967, cols. 79–80). The government lost no time in putting its pre-election promises into effect. During the Second reading of the Housing Bill (which was to go on to confer the right to buy), Michael Heseltine, then Secretary of State for the Environment, spoke of the 'deeply ingrained desire for home ownership' which 'ensures the spread of wealth through society, encourages a personal desire to improve and modernise one's home, enables parents to accrue wealth for their children and stimulates the attitudes of independence and self-reliance that are the bedrock of a free society'. The proposed legislation, he said, laid the foundations 'for perhaps as profound a social revolution as any of our history' (*Hansard*, 1980, vol. 976, cols. 1444–5).

The Housing Act 1980 provided for a system of centrally directed, compulsory sales with a more generous level of discount. Tenants of three years' standing were entitled to an immediate 33% discount and for every additional year of tenancy a further 1% discount was added, up to a maximum of 50% of the property valuation. The discount was justified on two grounds: it was common practice to give discounts to sitting tenants in the private sector who bought their homes and it was claimed that tenants should be entitled to compensation for past rent payments. The Housing and Building Control Act 1984 reduced the residence qualification and increased the maximum discount, leading to the observation that the discount rate has become simply 'a balancing act between providing sufficient incentive to maintain sales and generating a certain level of capital receipts' (Forrest et al, 1992: 141). The current provisions regarding the discount to which the tenant may be entitled are dealt with in **11.8.8**.

It has been said that council housing should have become 'the Marks and Spencer of housing'. Instead, it was claimed, council housing was monolithically insensitive, lacked choice of dwellings, tenants had little hope of mobility in or between authorities, and transfers were frequently confined to households of special need (Kilroy, 1979: 453). While it was undoubtedly the case that problems such as 'poor management, bureaucratic incompetence and petty restriction' did exist, they were probably not widespread, and could have been rectified by measures other than the disposal of council stock: the extension of tenant participation, greater self-management and maintenance among tenants, and improved transfer and allocations policies' (Lansley, 1979: 173). The eager take-up by tenants of the right to buy probably owes less to their dissatisfaction with their local authority landlords than to the opportunity they were given to buy — at knock-down prices — generally well-built and maintained housing which would almost certainly appreciate and which they could pass on to their children. Whether or not 'the encouragement of working-class owner occupation is, at least, partly motivated by the desire to subvert revolutionary and militant activity' (Jacobs, 1981) is a moot point. A survey of people who had bought their council houses between 1968 and 1973 provided no evidence either way that moving into owner-occupation had influenced their political loyalties (Forrest et al, 1991b).

## 11.8.3   Council house sales since 1980

**Table 11.b   Local authority dwellings sold under right to buy scheme, 1980–93 (England and Wales)**

| | |
|---|---|
| 1980 | 81,416 |
| 1981 | 102,720 |
| 1982 | 202,045 |
| 1983 | 138,406 |
| 1984 | 103,175 |
| 1985 | 92,290 |
| 1986 | 88,187 |
| 1987 | 98,769 |
| 1988 | 147,188 |
| 1989 | 160,780 |
| 1990 | 105,553 |
| 1991 | 58,495 |
| 1992 | 50,982 |
| 1993 | 49,290 |
| 1994 | 51,261 |
| 1995 | 38,265 |

Source: Department of the Environment, 1996: Table 9.6.

Not surprisingly, sales of local authority housing accelerated rapidly after the right to buy provisions came into force and the Conservative government's support for the extension of the 'property owning democracy' continued throughout the 1980s. Its commitment to home ownership was reaffirmed in its election manifesto of 1987 and, in the 1987 White Paper, one of its four main objectives for future housing policy was stated to be the 'spread [of] home ownership as widely as possible, through encouraging suitable market conditions, continuing tax relief on mortgage interest, and pressing on with the right to buy' (Department of the Environment, 1987: para. 1.4).

Rising real incomes for households in employment, lower levels of unemployment and rising rents ensured the continuation of high levels of council house sales in 1988 and 1989 despite an escalation in house prices and rising interest rates followed by a general recession in the property market. Moreover, high discounts helped cushion right to buy purchasers from rising prices and mortgage interest rates, and the uncertainty over the future of council housing raised by various provisions in the Housing Act 1988 and the Local Government Act 1989 may also have encouraged tenants to move into home ownership (Forrest et al, 1992: 142). From 1990 onwards, however, sales have fallen off.

The right to buy has expanded the socio-economic base of home ownership, extending to many tenants an opportunity they would not otherwise have had to enter owner occupation. However, the large number of repossessions by mortgagees in recent years (falling from their peak of 75,500 in 1991 to 49, 410 in 1995 — *The Guardian*, 6 March 1996) bears witness to the fact that home ownership has become much more hazardous than in previous decades. Unemployment, the spread of atypical employment, high interest rates, cuts in mortgage interest tax relief and in income support for unemployed borrowers have serious affected the ability of many people to enter or maintain owner-occupation, particularly in areas where sales have traditionally been high. There are also those who now find themselves saddled with properties which are virtually worthless, design defects having come to light since the purchases took place, or facing drastic increases in service charges (see *The Guardian*, Society, 9 August 1995). Moreover, the fact that the more desirable, better-maintained dwellings have been sold off has compounded the process of 'residualisation', whereby the disadvantaged have become increasingly concentrated in council housing — ironically at the same time as this sector has been starved of investment funds and subsidies, housebuilding has decreased to a very low levels, whilst rents (and by necessity means-tested benefits) have increased (see Malpass et al, 1994: 146–151).

In its 1995 White Paper, the government expressed its full commitment to 'the continued growth of sustainable home ownership, which gives people more opportunities and choice' (Department of the Environment, 1995: 12). One way of continuing the growth of home ownership is made possible by the Housing Act 1996, ss. 16 (which was brought into force on 1 April 1997) and 17 (1 August 1996) which extends the rights to buy to tenants of registered social landlords (see **Chapter 8**).

### 11.8.4  The subject-matter of the right to buy

Secure tenants have either the right to buy the freehold or to be granted a long lease of the dwelling-house in which they are living. If the dwelling-house is a house and the landlord owns the freehold, the tenant will acquire the right to purchase the freehold. If the dwelling-house is a house and the landlord does not own the freehold, or if the dwelling-house is a flat, the tenant will acquire the right to be granted a long lease (s. 118(1)). This will usually be for a minimum term of 125 years at a rent not exceeding £10 per annum.

### 11.8.5  The 'qualifying tenant' and the 'qualifying period'

The right to buy can only be enjoyed by a secure *tenant* and not, therefore, a licensee who has acquired statutory protection under s. 79(3), Housing Act 1985. The tenant must satisfy the 'qualifying period, ' as defined by sch. 4, Housing Act 1985. This means that he or she must have held a public sector tenancy (i.e. one where the 'landlord condition' and the 'tenant condition' are satisfied) for at least two years (s. 119). The period does not have to be a continuous period (sch. 4, para. 1), and it need not immediately precede the tenant's exercise of the right to buy (sch. 4, para. 2(a)). The tenant need not have had the same landlord for the whole of the period, nor the tenancy of one particular dwelling-house. Where the secure tenancy is a joint tenancy, the qualifying period has only to be satisfied with respect to one of the joint tenants

(s. 119(2)). Secure tenants of local authorities who are transferred to the private sector following a voluntary transfer, for example, retain a 'preserved right to buy, even though they are no longer secure tenants (see s. 171, Housing Act 1985).

If the secure tenancy is a joint tenancy, the right to buy belongs jointly to all of the tenants, or to such one or more of them as they may agree, provided that the person or at least one of the persons to whom the right to buy is to belong occupies the dwelling-house as his or her only or principal home (s. 118(2)). Where there is only one secure tenant, he or she may require that the right to buy is shared with not more than three members of the tenant's family who occupy the dwelling-house as their only or principal home (s. 123). This applies only to:

(a)   the tenant's spouse (or a person who lives with the tenant as his or her husband or wife); or

(b)   a family member who has been residing with the tenant throughout the period of 12 months ending with the giving of notice; or

(c)   a family member who does not satisfy the residence requirement, provided the landlord consents.

The joint purchasers will then be treated as joint tenants of the property.

By virtue of s. 121 the right to buy cannot be exercised:

(a)   if the tenant is obliged to give up possession of the dwelling-house in pursuance of an order of the court or will be so obliged at a date specified in the order; or

(b)   if the purchaser, or one if them if it is a shared purchase, has a bankruptcy petition pending aginst him or her, or is an undischarged bankrupt, or has made a composition or arrangement with creditors which has not been finalised.

Under s. 82 a secure tenancy lasts until the date when the secure tenant is ordered by the court to give up possession but even if a tenant has claimed to exercise the right to buy, the landlord may become entitled to possession at any time up to completion on any of the grounds contained in sch. 2 to the Housing Act 1985. This is because the exercise of the right to buy is not a once and for all step but a continuing process; the right is 'exercised' each and every time the tenant takes any step towards the implementation of his or her right to purchase (*Enfield London Borough Council* v *McKeon* [1986] 1 WLR 1007). However, 'as soon as all matters relating to the grant and to the amount to be left outstanding or advanced on the security of the dwelling-house have been agreed or determined' in accordance with s. 138(1), the tenant is entitled have the freehold conveyed or the lease granted and can seek an injunction under s. 138(3) or a decree of specific performance.

Thus, in *Dance* v *Welwyn Hatfield DC* [1990] 1 WLR 1097, the tenants had served a notice stipulating a date for completion. Four days after the date specified in the notice, the authority served a notice of seeking possession on the ground that it intended to demolish the property. Distinguishing *McKeon*, the Court of Appeal held that the tenants' entitlement under s. 138(1) had arisen, at the latest, on the date fixed for completion. There was no impediment, therefore, to the granting of an enforcment injunction. In *Taylor* v *Newham LBC* [1993] 2 All ER 649, the conditions of s. 138(1) had been satisfied. It was held that the tenant purchaser was entitled as of right to an injunction to enforce the council's duty to convey the house to her on the terms agreed and the court had no discretion to refuse to grant the injunction because of the tenant's racial harassment of her neighbours. *Bristol City Council* v *Lovell* [1996] NPC 1930 underlined the principle that the right to buy conferred on a secure tenant can only be extinguished by virtue of s. 121 if the tenant is obliged to give up possession under a court order prior to seeking an injunction under s. 138(3).

### 11.8.6   Properties excluded from the right to buy

Section 120, Housing Act 1985 provides that the right to buy will not arise in the following cases, which are set out in sch. 5 to the Act (**11.8.6.1 to 11.8.6.7**).

**11.8.6.1   Charities**   The right to buy does not arise if the landlord is a charitable housing association or housing trust (sch. 5, para. 1).

**11.8.6.2   Certain housing associations**   The right to buy does not exist where the landlord is a co-operative housing association or a housing association which has at no time received public funds (sch. 5, paras. 2, 3).

**11.8.6.3   Landlord with insufficient interest in the property**   There is no right to buy where the landlord does not own the freehold or does not have an interest sufficient to grant a lease (21 years for a house and 50 years for a flat.)

**11.8.6.4   Dwelling-houses let in connection with employment**   There is no right to buy if the dwelling house forms part of a building which is held by the landlord mainly for non-housing purposes, or is situated in a cemetery, and it was let to the tenant because he or she was employed by the landlord or by another body which satisfies the 'landlord condition' (see **10.3.2**) or by the governors of an aided school.

**11.8.6.5   Certain dwelling-houses for the disabled**   No right to buy arises:

   if the dwelling-house has features which are substantially different from those of ordinary dwelling-houses and are designed to make it suitable for occupation by physically disabled persons and—

(a)   it is one of a group of dwelling-houses which it is the practice of the landlord to let for occupation by physically disabled persons, and

(b)   a social service or special facilities are provided in close proximity wholly or partly for the purpose of assisting those persons (sch. 5, para. 7).

In *Freeman* v *Wansbeck DC* [1984] 2 All ER 746 it was held that the introduction of an indoor downstairs lavatory was not a feature 'substantially different' even though introduced by the use of powers contained in the Chronically Sick and Disabled Persons Act 1970 for the benefit of the tenants' daughter who suffered from spina bifida. 'Designed' was held to refer to the architectural process; it does not mean 'intended'.

Schedule 5, para. 9 makes similar provision for dwelling-houses occupied by people who are suffering, or have suffered, from a mental disorder. There is no requirement for physical adaptation of the property. Only grouped accommodation will qualify.

**11.8.6.6   Elderly persons' dwellings**   By para. 10(1) of sch. 5, the right to buy does not arise if the dwelling-house is one of a *group* of dwelling-houses:

(a)   which are particularly suitable, having regard to their location, size, design, heating systems and other features for occupation by elderly persons; and

(b)   which it is the practice of the landlord to let for occupation by persons aged 60 or more, or for occupation by such persons and physically disabled persons.

By para. 10(2) the services of a resident warden must be provided or a non-resident warden, a system for calling and the use of a common room in close proximity to the group of dwelling-houses. Paragraph 11, added by s. 106 of the Leasehold Reform, Housing and Urban Development Act 1993, excludes *individual* dwelling-houses for elderly persons from the right to buy.

**11.8.6.7   Dwelling-houses held on Crown tenancies**

**11.8.7   The purchase price**

The price payable for the dwelling-house is its market value at the time when the tenant serves notice under s. 122 claiming to exercise the right to buy, less the discount to which the purchaser is entitled (s. 126, Housing Act 1985). If a dispute arises as to the value of the dwelling-house, it must be referred to the district valuer for determination under s. 128.

The value of the dwelling-house is the price it would realise if sold on the open market by a willing vendor. Section 127 sets out the assumptions that should be made in reaching a valuation. If the freehold is to be conveyed the assumptions are:

(a)    that the vendor was selling an estate in fee simple with vacant possession;

(b)    that neither the tenant nor a member of the tenant's family residing with him or her wanted to buy; and

(c)    that the dwelling-house was to be conveyed with the same rights and subject to the same burdens as it would be in pursuance of Pt V of the Housing Act 1985 (s. 127(2)).

If a lease is to be granted the assumptions are:

(a)    that the vendor was granting a lease with vacant possession for a term of 125 years (or if the the landlord's interest is less than 125 years, for a term of five days less than the length of the landlord's term);

(b)    that neither the tenant nor a member of the tenant's family residing with him or her wanted to take the lease;

(c)    that the ground rent would not exceed £10 per annum; and

(d)    the grant was to be made with the same rights and subject to the same burdens as it would be in pursuance of Part V, Housing Act 1985 (s. 127(3)).

Any improvements made by the tenant will be disregarded, as will a failure by the tenant to keep the dwelling-house in good internal repair (s. 127(1)(b)). Service charges or improvement contributions will be assumed not to be less than the amounts specified in the landlord's notice under s. 125 (s. 127(1)(c)).

### 11.8.8    The discount

The amount of the tenant's discount depends on the length of the 'qualifying period', i.e. the amount of time that the tenant has been a public sector tenant (see above). For a house, the discount is 33% plus 1% for each complete year by which the qualifying period exceeds two years, up to a maximum of 60%; for a flat, it is 44% plus 2% for each complete year by which the qualifying period exceeds two years up to a maximum of 70% (s. 129(2)). Originally, the same discount rates applied to both flats and houses, but the disproportionately poor take up of flats led to the introduction of a preferential discount. The maximum discount is £50,000 (Housing (Right to Buy) (Maximum Discount) Order (SI 1989/513)). Where joint tenants are seeking to exercise the right to buy, the discount is calculated by reference to the joint tenant who satisfies the longest qualifying period (s. 129(3)). A full discount is not available where the tenant has exercised the right to buy on a previous occasion (s. 130).

Where, before completion of the sale, another person become the secure tenant other than by way of exchange under s. 92, 'the new tenant shall be in the same position as if the notice had been given by him and he had been the secure tenant at the time it was given' (s. 136). In *McIntyre* v *Merthyr Tydfil District Council* (1989) 21 HLR 320, the Court of Appeal held that the new tenant is in the same position as if he or she had been the secure tenant, with all the secure tenant's qualities and characteristics. The secure tenant's daughter (who succeeded to the tenancy on her mother's death) was thus entitled to the same discount as her mother, rather than a lesser one based on her own period of residence.

### 11.8.9   Discount repayment on premature, non-exempted disposal

The right to buy is not intended to give tenants the opportunity of making a quick profit by buying at a discount and then selling the property on at a full market price. Section 155 of the 1985 Act therefore provides that, where the dwelling-house has been purchased at a discount, the purchaser must covenant to repay some or all of the discount to the landlord if there is a 'relevant disposal' within three years of the conveyance or grant. A 'relevant disposal' is:

(a)   a further conveyance of the freehold or an assignment of the lease; or
(b)   a grant of a lease or sub-lease for more than 21 years otherwise than at a rack rent, whether the disposal is of the whole or part of the dwelling-house (s. 159(1)).

The amount that must be repaid is one-third of the discount for each complete year which has elapsed since the conveyance or grant (s. 155(2)). The liability to make a repayment does not arise in the case of exempt disposals, e.g. on the vesting of the property under a will or on intestacy, or a disposal under s. 23, 24 or 24A, Matrimonial Causes Act 1973, s. 17(1) Matrimonial Homes and Family Proceedings Act 1984 or para.1 of sch. 1 to the Children Act 1989. Where, however, the property is sold pursuant to an order of the court in matrimonial proceedings, the sale is not an exempt disposal (*R v Rushmoor BC, ex parte Barrett* (1988) 20 HLR 366).

### 11.8.10   Right to acquire on rent to mortgage terms

Secure tenants with a right to buy originally had a right to a mortgage which covered the purchase price (i.e. the value less the discount), together with the council's costs incurred in providing a mortgage, and such of the secure tenant's costs as the council had agreed to defray on the tenant's behalf.
There was no obligation, however, to provide a mortgage which exceeded a specified multiplier of the secure tenant's 'available annual income' and even when the discounts were taken into account, many council tenants could not afford to exercise the right to buy. Shared ownership leases, designed to encourage lower income council tenants into home ownership, were introduced by the Housing and Building Control Act 1984. This scheme enabled tenants who could not afford to buy their properties, even with a mortgage, to purchase a slice of a long lease (of 99 years or more), and to continue to pay a rent (reduced according to the size of the slice acquired) on the landlord's remaining interest. Having bought the initial share, the tenant could purchase additional 'slices' as and when his or her finances permitted until the whole had been acquired. Shared ownership leases were never popular, however. The rights to a shared ownership lease and to a mortgage were withdrawn by s. 107,

Leasehold Reform, Housing and Urban Development Act 1993 and replaced with a new 'rent to mortgage' scheme.

Under the rent to mortgage scheme, the tenant makes an initial payment, usually financed by a building society mortgage, the repayments under which are equivalent to the tenant's current rental payments (s. 143B(3), (4)). The difference between the valuation less the discount and the initial payment is dealt with as an interest-free loan by the landlord (s. 147). This loan is also secured by a mortgage on the property. The building society mortgage has priority over the landlord's mortgage, provided that it is granted by an approved lending institution (s. 151B). The tenant may pay off the landlord's mortgage in full or in part at any time; it must be redeemed in full if the dwelling is sold or the tenant dies (s. 151A, sch. 6A). Further shares may be acquired by additional payments which also attract discount (sch. 6A, paras. 2, 6 and 7). A tenant who has been in receipt of housing benefit during the past 12 months (s. 143A) or can afford to exercise the full right to buy (s. 143B) is excluded from the rent to mortgage scheme. As with any other right to buy application, a tenant cannot buy on rent to mortgage terms if, e.g., he or she is an undischarged bankrupt (s. 121, see **11.8.5**).

On completion of the rent to mortgage procedure, the tenant acquires the freehold (if the dwelling is a house) or a leasehold interest (if the dwelling is a flat) (s. 150). The tenant ceases to be a secure tenant (s. 151(2)) and assumes the rights and obligations of a full owner-occupier, including the responsibility for repairs. The purchaser retains some rights, such as the right to be consulted on certain matters of housing management under s. 27, Housing Act 1985, but loses other rights, including the right of exchange conferred by s. 92.

In the financial year 1996/7 just four properties in England and Wales were sold under the rent to mortgage scheme (Department of the Environment, 1997). Evidently it has been no more successful than the right to a shared ownerhip lease in extending home ownership to the lower paid.

## 11.8.11   The right to buy procedure

A tenant wishing to exercise the right to buy must serve a notice on the landlord (s. 122, Housing Act 1985). This notice, which can be withdrawn at any time before completion, must be in the form prescribed in the Housing (Right to Buy) (Prescribed Forms) Regulations 1986 (SI 1986/2194 as amended). The landlord has four weeks in which to serve a written notice in reply either:

(a)   admitting the right to buy, or
(b)   denying it and stating the reasons why, in the landlord's opinion, the tenant does not have the right to buy (s. 124).

The tenant can apply to the county court for a declaration if the landlord denies the tenant's right to exercise the right to buy (s. 181).

If the landlord admits the tenant's right to buy, or approval is given by the county court, the landlord must serve notice upon the tenant in accordance with s. 125. This notice should be served within eight weeks if the tenant has the right to acquire the freehold, or within 12 weeks if the tenant has the right to be granted a lease (s. 125(1)). Where the right to buy was first claimed on or after 11 October 1993, the notice must, *inter alia*, describe the dwelling-house, state the price payable and show how that price was arrived at, contain estimates of service charges or improvement contributions (where appropriate), state the provisions which, in the opinion of the landlord, should be contained in the conveyance or grant, and contain a description of any structural defect known to the landlord (s. 125, as amended by the Leasehold Reform, Housing and Urban Development Act 1993).

Within 12 weeks of receiving the s. 125 notice, the tenant must serve a further notice on the landlord stating whether the tenant intends to pursue his or her claim to exercise the right to buy, or to withdraw the claim (s. 125D). Alternatively, the tenant may serve notice under s. 144 claiming to exercise the right to acquire on rent to mortgage terms.

As soon as all the matters relating to the purchase of the freehold or the grant of the lease have been agreed or determined, the landlord is under a duty to complete (s. 138(1)). A similar obligation arises under s. 150, Housing Act 1985 (inserted by s. 115, Leasehold Reform, Housing and Urban Development Act 1993) where the tenant has claimed to exercise the right to acquire the property on rent to mortgage terms. The tenant can withdraw from the process at any time up to the completion or grant by serving written notice on the landlord (s. 122(3)). If all relevant matters have been agreed or determined, the landlord can serve a notice at any time on the tenant requiring completion within a specified period of not less than 56 days (s. 140). If the tenant fails to comply with this preliminary notice, the landlord may serve a further and final notice (s. 141). If the tenant fails to comply with the second notice within the specified time (which must be at least 56 days) the right to buy is deemed to have been withdrawn.

### 11.8.12   Enforcing the right to buy

There are a number of ways in which the landlord's duty to complete the purchase or grant the lease can be enforced. The following are the most important:

(a)   The tenant can pursue the matter in the county court; the duty to complete the transaction is enforceable by injunction (ss. 138(3) and 150(3)).

(b)   The tenant can utilise the self-help remedy contained in ss. 153A and 153B, Housing Act 1985 (inserted by s. 124, Housing Act 1988). The tenant must serve an initial notice of delay followed by an 'operative notice of delay' if the landlord fails to serve a counter-notice within the time allowed. Thereafter, all future payments of rent can be credited against the eventual purchase price.

(c)   The Secretary of State has extensive default powers to intervene when it is apparent that 'tenants generally, a tenant or tenants of a particular landlord have or may have difficulty in exercising effectively or expeditiously the right to buy' (s. 164). The Secretary of State may directly vest the freehold or long-leasehold interest, recover the costs with interest from the local authority (ss. 165–166) and provide assistance to the tenant, including legal assistance and arranging legal representation (s. 170). The decision to intervene under the default powers can only be challenged on judicial review. In *Norwich City Council* v *Secretary of State for the Environment* [1982] 1 All ER 737, the Court of Appeal described them as coercive and draconian and deliberately framed by Parliament to maximise the minister's power and to minimise any power of review by the court.

Within the first year of the Housing Act 1980 coming into force, Norwich City Council received some 900 applications claiming the right to buy. The council, with a long history of Labour control, was opposed to the sale of council houses and had not used its powers voluntarily to dispose of its purpose-built council housing. Its members were not, however opposed to the expansion of home ownership and, in the past, the council had sold some acquired council dwellings. In most cases, the council admitted the right to buy within the prescribed four-week period but then there were complaints of delay, particularly with regard to valuation of the properties and obligatory counselling interviews arranged by the council for all would-be purchasers.

From May 1981 the Department of the Environment took the matter up with Norwich City Council which led, after correspondence, negotiation and meetings, to a demand by the Secretary of State that all outstanding valuations be completed by February 1982. The council would not promise to complete them before June 1982. The Secretary of State exercised formal powers and Norwich applied unsuccessfully to the Divisional Court for an order of *certiorari* the quash the decision to intervene. The Court of Appeal dismissed Norwich's appeal. Lord Denning MR held that intervention should occur only if the authority's default was unreasonable or inexcusable. The remainder of the Court of Appeal, however, held that the Secretary of State could intervene whenever it appeared that tenants have or may have difficulty in exercising right to buy effectively or expeditiously, regardless of whether or not the authority's behaviour was reasonable, provided that the Secretary of State's own decision was one to which a reasonable man might come in accordance with normal administrative law principles (see Malpass et al, 1990: 223–229, for an account of the so-called 'Battle for Norwich').

## References

Balchin, P., *Housing Policy: An Introduction*, London: Croom Helm, 1985.

Craig, F. (ed.), *British General Election Manifestos 1900–1974*, London and Basingstoke: Macmillan Press, 1975.

Department of the Environment, *Housing and Construction Statistics, 1970–1980*, London: HMSO, 1981.

Department of the Environment, *Housing: The Government's Proposals*, Cm. 214, London: HMSO, 1987.

Department of the Environment, *Our Future Homes: Opportunity, Choice, Responsibility*, Cmnd. 2901, London: HMSO, 1995.

Department of the Environment, *Housing and Construction Statistics, 1985–1995*, London: The Stationery Office, 1996.

Department of the Environment, *Local Housing Statistics, England and Wales, No. 122*, London: The Stationery Office, 1997.

Driscoll, J., 'Leasehold Reform, Housing and Urban Development Act 1993: The Public Sector Housing Provisions', (1994) 57 *Modern Law Review*, pp. 788–798.

Forrest, R., and Murie, A., *Selling the Welfare State: The Privatisation of Public Housing*, London: Routledge, 1991a.

Forrest, R. and Murie, A., 'Transformation through Tenure: the Early Purchasers of Council Houses, 1968–1973', *Journal of Social Policy*, 1991, vol. 20, pp. 1–25.

Forrest, R. and Murie, A., 'The Right to Buy', in Grant, C. (ed.), Built to Last, London: Shelter, 1992.

Inquiry into British Housing, chaired by HRH The Duke of Edinburgh: Second Report, York: Joseph Rowntree Foundation, 1991.

Jacobs, S., 'The Sale of Council Houses: Does it Matter?', *Critical Social Policy*, 1981, vol. 4, issue 3, pp. 35–48.

Kilroy, B., 'Labour's Housing Dilemma', *New Statesman*, 28 September 1979, pp. 451–453.

Lansley, S., *Housing and Public Policy*, London: Croom Helm, 1979.

Law Commission, 'Domestic Violence and Occupation of the Family Home', No. 207, 1992, London: HMSO.

Malpass, P and Murie, A., *Housing Policy and Practice*, Basingstoke: Macmillan, 1994.

Merrett, S., *State Housing in Britain*, London: Routledge & Kegan Paul, 1979.

Stewart, A., *Rethinking Housing Law*, London: Sweet & Maxwell, 1996.

**Further reading**

Cole, I. and Furbey, R., *The Eclipse of Council Housing*, London: Routledge, 1994.

Cooper, S., *Public Housing and Private Property 1970–1984*, Aldershot: Gower, 1985.

Saunders, P., *A Nation of Home Owners*, London: Unwin Hyman, 1990.

# TWELVE
## The privatisation of council housing

### 12.1 INTRODUCTION

The privatisation of housing by Conservative governments in recent years has taken broadly two forms:

(a) the sale of council houses to their tenants, and
(b) the disposal of council stock to housing associations, trusts and private companies — either for renting or for re-sale.

The sale of council houses was considered in **Chapter 11**. This chapter deals with the different methods by which councils have been forced or encouraged to dispose of the whole or parts of their stock to other landlords, and to delegate their housing management functions.

The government set out its agenda for public sector housing in its 1987 White Paper. Taking the view that local authorities had been inefficient and bureaucratic managers of their housing, that tenants had been deprived of choice, that public investment in housing had been at the expense of other public sector spending programmes and that party political considerations had often operated at local level to the detriment of housing (Department of the Environment, 1987a: para. 1.11) the government sought to change their role. No longer were they to be the main providers of social housing; instead '[they] should increasingly see themselves as enablers who ensure that everyone in their area is adequately housed; but not necessarily by them' (ibid., para. 1.16). Theirs was to be strategic role which included 'identifying housing needs and demands' and 'encouraging innovative methods of provision by other bodies to meet such needs' (ibid., para. 5.1). Registered housing associations, once regarded as part of the public sector, were henceforth to be the main providers of social housing, their housing projects being financed mainly by private funding from financial institutions.

Housing Action Trusts (to take over areas of run-down local authority housing) and Tenants' Choice (providing for the acquisition of local authority housing by other landlords) were identified as the means by which housing stock was to be transferred out of local authority control. Tenants' Choice (also known as 'Pick a Landlord') was presented in the White Paper as a scheme which would offer a remedy to tenants who received a poor service from their council. Even those who chose not to transfer would, it was said, benefit from a better general standard of services resulting from the exposure of councils to 'healthy competition'. If tenants wished to transfer, they could decide when to set the process in motion (Department of the Envrionment, 1987a: para. 5.9). They would need to identify a new landlord willing to take them on and arrangements would be made to put tenants and prospective new landlords in touch. Landlords — established housing associations, commercial landlords, tenants' co-operatives — would require formal approval by the Housing Corporation or Housing for Wales to ensure that they were 'financially stable and capable of managing their homes to a high standard while giving value for money' (Department of the Environment, 1987b: para. 16).

The White Paper placed the emphasis on tenants taking the initiative but the scheme which emerged in Part IV, Housing Act 1988 appeared, by contrast, to confer something resembling a 'predatory private landlord's choice' (Hoath, 1989: 372) which gave tenants very little choice indeed. Any approved person or body could acquire the fee simple in any relevant buildings occupied by qualifying tenants of a public sector landlord. Various categories of property were excluded from the scheme. A detailed and lengthy procedure culminated in affected tenants being balloted on their wishes. If:

(a)   less than 50% of eligible tenants responded; or
(b)   a majority voted against the proposal,

the application could not proceed. If, however, at least 50% responded, an 'inertia' vote in favour of the proposed acquisition was deemed to have been registered by any tenant who failed to respond, or who indicated no strong feelings either way. All existing tenants would then be transferred to the new landlord and would become assured tenants but with a preserved right to buy. Given the unusual system of inertia voting involved in the scheme, the effective exercise of such choice as there was — the right to reject given applicants — would, it was said, require 'an extraordinarily high degree of organised resistance to the proposals concerned', requiring 'meticulous planning, forceful campaigning and careful organisation' (Bridge, 1989: 107, 118).

In its passage through Parliament, Part IV was 'the most politically controversial and potentially divisive part of the whole statute' (Bridge, 1989: 106). Critics believed it could lead to the complete dismantling of council estates. However, despite the fears it provoked, only 982 tenants actually transferred to the private sector by way of Tenants' Choice (Driscoll, 1997: 824) and (save for applications which had been made before 1 October 1996) the scheme was finally laid to rest by the Housing Act 1996.

## 12.2  LEGAL ROUTES TO THE PRIVATISATION OF COUNCIL HOUSING

Apart from the right to buy, there are basically three methods whereby tenanted council properties may be 'privatised':

(a)  voluntarily, at the instigation of the council itself by means of large scale voluntary transfers;

(b)  compulsorily, at the instigation of the Secretary of State for the Environment under the 'Housing Action Trust' scheme;

(c)  compulsory competitive tendering.

## 12.3  LARGE SCALE VOLUNTARY STOCK TRANSFERS

Throughout the history of council housing, local authorities have been empowered, subject to ministerial consent, to dispose of housing land and stock to the private sector. The powers to carry out transfers — called voluntary transfers, or large scale voluntary transfers where an authority's entire housing stock is sold — are contained in ss. 32–34 and 43, Housing Act 1985. Consultation provisions were added by the Housing and Planning Act 1986 and restrictions on large scale voluntary transfers imposed by the Leasehold Reform, Housing and Urban Development Act 1993. Large scale voluntary transfers were not, therefore, among the mechanisms identified in the 1987 White Paper to extend housing choice to council tenants but were promoted by local authorities themselves and the changes made by the Housing Act 1988 were simply a response to the local government initiatives already under way. The first transfer took place in 1988 — before the 1988 Act came into force — when Chiltern District Council in Buckinghamshire transferred its stock to the newly created Chiltern Hundreds Housing Association. By 1995, 41 councils around the country had transferred nearly 185,000 homes to 45 landlords. In all but one case, the transfers were to housing associations registered with the Housing Corporation (Department of the Environment, 1995: 28). When a voluntary transfer take place, the new landlord takes over all the stock involved. The tenants whose homes have been transferred cease to be secure tenants and if, as is usually the case, the transfer is to a housing association, they become assured tenants (s. 38, Housing Act 1988). They do, however, retain the 'preserved right to buy' (s. 171A–H, Housing Act 1985) and are subject to the 'Tenants' Guarantee', drawn up by the Housing Corporation after the Housing Act 1988, to give assured tenants of housing associations similar rights to those of secure tenants. The legislation is supplemented by guidance issued by the Department of the Environment, the Housing Corporation and Housing for Wales.

While some authorities made use of the voluntary transfer mechanism to rid themselves of the burden of housing provision and management, many early transfers were attempts to circumvent the proposals contained in the 1987 White Paper (especially those concerned with Tenants' Choice), and the effects of the new financial regime introduced by the Local Government and Housing Act 1989. Transfers — generally to housing associations specifically set up by the authorities to receive their housing stock — meant that the existing stock could be preserved as new tenancies would be excluded from the right to buy. There was the additional advantage that housing associations, free of the borrowing constraints to which local authorities are subject, could raise money for the building of new houses from the banks and other lending institutions, using the asset base of the stock as security. Authorities also believed that they would be able to retain control over their former housing but guidance issued by the Department of the Environment in 1988 made it clear that ministerial consent would be forthcoming only where the proposed transfers were to bodies which were independent of their local authorities. There would be (and still is) a 20% ceiling on local authority representation on the purchasing body, and a prohibition on the provision of services by the council (e.g. payroll, computers, etc.) after a transitional period, and the automatic redeployment of council staff to the new association (Mullins et al, 1993: 172).

In determining whether or not to give consent to the transfer, the Secretary of State may have regard to the extent to which:

(a)  the intending purchaser is controlled or influenced by members or officers of the authority; and
(b)  the proposed disposal would result in the intending purchaser becoming the predominant or a substantial owner in any area of housing accommodation let on tenancies or subject to licences (s. 34(4A), Housing Act 1985).

The idea is not 'to replace one large, mostly anonymous landlord with another' (Bright et al, 1995: 539). Generally, local authorities may dispose of the property on such conditions as they think fit but, by s. 33(2), Housing Act 1985, the Secretary of State's consent is required for the inclusion of any of the following terms:

(a)  a condition limiting the resale price;
(b)  in the case of a sale, a condition reserving a right of pre-emption (i.e. a requirement that the purchaser cannot sell the property or grant a lease on it without giving the vendor authority one month to refuse, or fail to accept, an offer of sale or lease-back);
(c)  on the grant of a lease, a condition which prohibits assignment or the grant of a sub-lease.

## 12.3.1  Consultation

Only exceptionally will a local authority seek to transfer property with vacant possession. Where the purchaser plans to carry out redevelopment, the court will order possession under Ground 10A (sch. 2, Part II, Housing Act 1985) to enable the transfer to proceed. The court must be satisfied that suitable alternative accommodation is available for the displaced tenants and that the local authority will dispose of the properties in accordance with the development scheme within a reasonable time of obtaining possession. Before a landlord applies to the Secretary of State for the approval of a redevelopment scheme, it must consult the secure tenants of any dwelling-houses affected by the proposal and consider their views (sch. 2, Part V, Housing Act 1985). In considering whether or not to approve such a scheme, the Secretary of State must also have regard to the tenants' representations, as well as:

(a)  the effect of the scheme on the extent and character of housing accommodation in the neighbourhood;
(b)  the period of time over which it is proposed that the disposal and redevelopment will take place; and
(c)  the extent to which the scheme includes provision for housing provided under the scheme to be sold or let to existing tenants or persons nominated by the landlord.

The tenants concerned must also be consulted where the local housing housing authority is seeking to dispose of dwelling-houses subject to secure or introductory tenancies and the proposed disposal is to a landlord which does not fulfil the 'landlord condition' of s. 80 (see **10.3.2**) (s. 106A, sch. 3A, Housing Act 1985). These provisions replace the normal consultation requirements contained in s. 105. There is no requirement to consult, however, where the local authority has acquired the property by means of a compulsory purchase order which provides for onward disposal to a registered social landlord, and the disposal is made within a year of the acquisition (s. 106A(3), Housing Act 1985).

The authority must serve written notice on the tenant, informing him or her of:

(a)  such details of the proposal as the authority considers appropriate, but including the identity of the purchaser;
(b)  the likely consequences of the disposal for the tenant (e.g. changes in security of tenure and in rent);
(c)  the effect of the consultation provisions;
(d)  the effect of the preserved right to buy; and
(e)  the right to make representations to the authority within a reasonable, specified time (sch. 3A, para. 3(1), (2)).

The authority must then consider the representations and serve a further notice on the tenant of any significant changes to the plan, the right to make representations to the Secretary of State, and the duty of the Secretary of State to withhold consent if a majority of the tenants are opposed to the scheme. The Secretary of State may require the authority to carry out further consultation with its tenants. Consent must not be given if it appears to the Secretary of State that a majority of the tenants concerned do not wish the disposal to proceed (sch. 3A, para. 5). It is important, therefore, that tenants opposed to the sale make their objections known. Circular 6/88 issued by the Department of the Environment requires that the consultation process should involve, *inter alia*, a formal test of tenant opinion. This requirement has been met in all cases by a ballot of tenants. Most authorities have employed a straight majority voting system but a few have used the system of 'intertia voting' devised for Tenants' Choice ballots (Mullins et al, 1993: 179, 180; Stewart, 1996: 171).

Transfer proposals have been attractively packaged in order to secure support from existing tenants for the proposed transfer. Usually this has been accomplished by offering rent guarantees at a few percentage points above inflation, together with an assurance of improvements in service directed particularly towards repairs and maintenance. 'Tenancy agreements have also been used to place on a contractual basis some of the statutory rights which would have been lost in the move from secure to assured tenancies' (Mullins et al, 1993: 181). Not only does the consultation process enable tenants to express their views on the proposed transfer but it also gives them a degree of power to negotiate advantageous terms.

### 12.3.2 Restrictions on large scale voluntary transfers

The popularity of large scale voluntary transfers has had a significant impact on public sector costs. As a result of changes made to local authority housing revenue accounts by the Local Government and Housing Act 1989, some authorities now obtain negative housing subsidy because the housing revenue account subsidy does not fully compensate for the payments they make by way of housing benefit. Once the stock moves out of local authority ownership on a voluntary transfer, the cost of the housing benefit must be met by the Department of Social Security, thereby placing a much greater burden on the Exchequer (Stewart, 1996: 173), especially if the tenants transferred are required to pay higher rents than those payable whilst they were local authority tenants (Driscoll, 1994: 792). These Exchequer implications spurred the government into imposing restrictions on large scale voluntary transfers. The Secretary of State is now empowered to prepare a disposals programme limiting the number of voluntary transfers which will be allowed each year, and based on an estimate of the Exchequer costs of the disposal, including any increase attributable to housing benefit (s. 135, Leasehold Reform, Housing and Urban Development Act 1993). Further, a one-off levy of 20%, in favour of the Secretary of State, may be charged on on any capital receipt arising from a large scale voluntary transfers, as a way of recouping some of the extra housing benefit cost (s. 136).

The valuation of the stock to be transferred takes into account the need to pay for management, maintenance, repairs and improvements, the future rental income and the fact that transferring tenants retain their right to buy. Invariably, therefore, the price paid by the new landlord is much lower than the amount which the houses would fetch if sold individually under the right to buy (Aughton et al, 1994: 37). Where the properties are in relatively good repair, the authority obtains a substantial capital receipt. The London Borough of Bromley raised £117 million from the sale of its housing stock to Bromleigh Housing Association and were able to wipe out the authority's capital debts in one fell swoop. However, at least 75% of the net capital receipts generated by housing transfers must be set aside to pay off any outstanding loans and only 25% may be used for capital expenditure.

## 12.4  HOUSING ACTION TRUSTS

The Conservative party was returned to government in 1987 having pledged in its manifesto to revive the inner cities. Earlier attempts to target certain underprivileged areas had been made in the introduction of urban development corporations in London, Merseyside and elsewhere, and enterprise zone authorities. Urban development corporations were devised to tackle largely derelict industrial areas in need of regeneration, while enterprise zones aimed to encourage private sector commercial and industrial expansion. Recognising that some council estates were so run down that Tenants' Choice could not be implemented, the government stated in the 1987 White Paper its proposal to establish bodies similar to urban development corporations in designated areas. The new bodies, to be known as housing action trusts, would take over responsibility for local authority housing, renovate it and pass it on new owners, including housing associations, tenants' co-operatives, and approved private landlords. As well as improving housing conditions, they would act as 'enablers and facilitators' for the provision of other community needs such as shops, workshops and advice centres, and for encouraging local enterprise (Department of the Environment, 1987a: para. 6.3). Areas suitable for housing action trust treatment were identified in a consultation paper produced by the Department of the Environment as those containing large numbers of poor quality public sector dwellings in deprived environments with high vandalism rates and other social problems such as unemployment, a high proportion of residents in receipt of state benefits, poor estate design, and general decay.

The initiative to establish a housing action trust over a particular area comes from the Secretary of State who is empowered by s. 60, Housing Act 1988 to 'designate an area of land for which, in his opinion, it is expedient that a . . . housing action trust . . . should be established'. In deciding whether an area should be so designated, the Secretary of State must have regard to 'such matters as he thinks fit', but is prompted to have regard to:

(a)   the extent to which the housing accommodation in the area as a whole is occupied by tenants or owner-occupiers and the extent to which it is local authority housing;

(b)   the physical state and design of the housing accommodation in the area and any need to repair or improve it;

(c)   the way in which the local authority housing in the area is being managed; and

(d)   the living conditions of those who live in the area, its social conditions and general environment (s. 60(4) and (5)).

Section 61 of the 1988 Act imposes a duty on the Secretary of State to consult with every local housing authority, any part of whose district is to be included in the proposed designated area, whether or not it is intended that their housing should be taken over by the housing action trust. It was initially proposed that tenants too would merely be *consulted* but s. 61 also obliges the Secretary of State to give secure and introductory tenants of houses in the proposed designated area the right to be *ballotted* before any transfer takes place. The Secretary of State cannot proceed if 'a majority of the tenants, who, on that ballot or poll, express an opinion about the proposal . . . are opposed to it' (s. 61(4)).

Theoretically, housing action trusts, are an important means whereby central government can interfere in local government issues. In practice, however, proposals to set up housing action trusts for certain areas have met with considerable resistance by tenants and, by October 1995, six housing action trusts had been established (in Waltham Forest, Liverpool, Hull, Castle Point, Tower Hamlets and Stonebridge (Brent LBC)) and it is unlikely that there will be many more.

### 12.4.1 Composition and functions of a housing action trust

Each housing action trust has a chair and between five and 11 members, all of whom are appointed by the secretary of state, in consultation with the local authority, on the basis of their special knowledge of the housing action trusts designated area (s. 62, schs. 7, 8, Housing Act 1988). Housing action trusts are not seen as being providers of housing and housing repair for the indefinite future. Each housing action trust is required to use its best endeavours to secure that its objects are achieved as soon as practicable. It will then be dissolved by the Secretary of State (s. 88). In addition to income from rents and sales, housing action trusts are financed partly by grants and loans from central government, and partly by loans from the private sector. They have the same broad rent-fixing discretion as that enjoyed by local authorities under s. 24, Housing Act 1985 (s. 85, Housing Act 1988).

Once it has been set up, a housing action trust's first task is to prepare a statement of its proposals regarding the exercise of its functions. It must consult any affected local housing authority or county council and take appropriate steps to ensure that its proposals are adequately publicised and that people who live in the designated area are made aware of their opportunity to make representations to the trust and, when the time comes, that they are actually given that opportunity (s. 64). Section 63(1) sets out the primary objectives of a housing action trust in relation to the designated area for which it is established. They are:

(a) to secure the repair and improvement of housing accommodation for the time being held by the trust;

(b) to secure its proper and effective management and use;

(c) to encourage a greater diversity of tenure and in the identity of landlords; and

(d) generally to improve the living conditions of those living in the area, and the area's social conditions and general environment.

In order to achieve these objectives, the housing action trust may (by s. 63(2), (3)):

(a)  provide and maintain housing accommodation;
(b)  facilitate the provision of shops, advice centres and other community facilities;
(c)  acquire, hold, manage, reclaim and dispose of land;
(d)  carry out building and other operations;
(e)  seek to ensure the provision of main services; and
(f)  carry on any business or undertaking.

Section 65 empowers the Secretary of State to grant a housing action trust the powers of the local housing authority in the area (either with or instead of the authority), except in relation to homelessness and it may also be designated as a planning authority (s. 67) and given specified public health functions of a local authority (s. 68).

Section 74 which, together with s. 61, is probably the most important section in this part of the 1988 Act, empowers the Secretary of State to order the transfer from a local housing authority to a housing action trust of:

(a)  all or any of the authority's local authority housing situated in the designated area, and
(b)  any other land held or provided in connection with that local authority housing.

The transfer will be on such terms as the Secretary of State thinks fit. This may include payment *from* an authority to a housing action trust.

## 12.4.2  Disposal of housing by housing action trusts

Section 79, Housing Act 1988 gives housing action trusts wide powers to dispose of land, subject to ministerial consent. Houses subject to secure or introductory tenancies may only be disposed of to:

(a)  a registered social landlord, or
(b)  a local housing authority or other local authority.

Subsequent disposals by registered social landlords are also subject to ministerial consent under s. 81. Some disposals are exempt, e.g the disposal of a dwelling-house to a person having the right to buy it under Part V, Housing Act 1985, and the grant of an assured tenancy. Subsequent disposals are also subject to consultation requirements involving affected tenants.

Since at least some of the responsibility for the decline of the inner cities was laid at the door of the local authorities, and the first step in the rejuvenation process was 'to remove the areas of greatest concern out of their hands altogether', it was predicted that homes removed from public sector control would not be returned to it once purposes of the housing action trust had been accomplished (Bridge, 1989: 90, 91). Such a move would be at odds with the 'diversity of landlord and ownership' sought by the 1987 White Paper and incorporated in s. 63(1)(c) of the 1988 Act. In fact, however, the law was altered to allow the local authority to repurchase the stock on the dissolution of the housing action trust. Section 84, Housing Act 1988, as amended by the Leasehold Reform, Housing and Urban Development Act 1993, applies where a housing action trust proposes to dispose of one or more dwellings let on secure or introductory tenancies to 'another person' who is not a local housing authority or other local authority. Before applying for the Secretary of State's consent, the housing action trust must inform any local housing authority within its area of the proposed disposal and require the authority to serve a notice, within not less than 28 days, informing the housing action trust of the likely consequences for the tenants if the authority were to acquire their houses. The housing action trust must then serve notice on the tenants informing them of:

(a)  the proposed disposal and the name of the person to who disposal is to be made;
(b)  any other details of the disposal as the housing action trust considers appropriate;
(c)  the consequences of the disposal for secure or introductory tenants and, if appropriate, of the effects of ss. 117A–171H (the preserved right to buy);
(d)  the likely effect of acquisition by the authority; and
(e)  the tenant's right to make representations to the Secretary of State if the tenant wishes to become a tenant of the authority; and
(f)  the tenant's right to make representations to the housing action trust about the proposed disposal within a specified period.

Any general representations must be taken into account. More importantly, if the tenant of a house, or the majority of tenants in a block of flats make representations that they wish to become tenants of the local housing authority, the Secretary of State must by order transfer the house or block of flats from the housing action trust to the local housing authority. Any transfer is on such terms, including financial terms, as the Secretary of State thinks fit, which may include payments to or from the local housing authority (s. 84A(4), (5)).

## 12.5  COMPULSORY COMPETITIVE TENDERING AND BEST VALUE

Throughout the 1980s, attempts to dismantle the near monopoly enjoyed by local authorities in the ownership and management of social housing focused on ownership. While that approach continues and has been given an added impetus in the form of housing companies, attention has also shifted to the separation of ownership and management through the Compulsory Competitive Tendering for housing management services, a concept which 'is based on the assumption that it is appropriate or possible to manage public sector stock on a commercial basis' and 'marginalises the social collective elements of public housing' (Stewart, 1996: 177).

Local authorities have always had the power to contract with the private sector for the provision of services. Until the introduction of compulsory competitive tendering by the Local Government, Planning and Land Act 1980, core services were usually provided by directly employed council staff and the private sector was invited to tender only for specialist work or to assist at times of high demand. It was generally agreed by central and local government, and across the party political divide, that this was the most effective way to deliver public services. Compulsory competitive tendering for the supply of goods and materials to local authorities, and the execution of works, was well-established, and the 1980 Act applied to a relatively small, albeit important, area of authorities' activities. Only gradually did the government come to realise the potential of competitive tendering, as part of its broader, political strategy of privatisation. The public justification for competitive tendering hinged on the maintenance of standards and the reduction of costs, but it appealed to the government on other grounds including the encouragement of businesses in the service sector and the reduction of public expenditure. The reluctance of most local authorities voluntarily to subject themselves to competitive tendering led to the enactment of Local Government Act 1988 which significantly extended compulsory competitive tendering and was specifically designed to make it very difficult for authorities to circumvent the Act's provisions (Radford, 1988: 747–749). The 1988 Act specified household and commercial refuse collection, cleaning of buildings, street cleansing, school, welfare and other catering, ground maintenance and the repair and manintenance of vehicles as the 'defined activities' which had to be put out to tender. The Local Government Act 1992 gave central government the power to extend compulsory competitive tendering to other local authority services by way of statutory instrument (s. 9).

The housing management functions which became subject to compulsory competitive tendering (from 1 April 1994), and must therefore be put out to tender, are set out in the Local Government Act 1988 (Competition) (Defined Activities) (Housing Management) Order 1994 (SI 1994/1671). Broadly, they include rent and service charge collection; letting of properties; dealing with vacant properties; repairs and maintenance; caretaking and cleaning. Local authority landlords are required to specify and cost the services involved and can continue to provide these services only if their own in-house management teams win the contract following a compulsory competitive tendering exercise with other would-be providers. Where the contract in question exceeds £140,000, the authority must also comply with the EC public procurement requirements which require authorities to advertise a contract in the *Official Journal*, and then to adopt one of the public procurement contractor selection exercises as appropriate (Public Services Contract Regulations 1993, SI 1993/3228). Functions which authorities can continue to exercise themselves (without putting them out to tender) include: setting the council's housing strategy, its housing investment programme, rent setting, allocation policies, tenancy conditions, maintenance, waiting lists, assessing housing need and allocating tenancies. Tenant consultation and the giving of advice or information to tenants are not defined and are not therefore subject to compulsory competitive tendering (Driscoll, 1994: 794–796). Small authorities, where the annual value of the defined activities is £500,000 or less, are exempt from housing-management compulsory competitive tendering because of high set-up costs and minimal savings which would be involved. Allegations have been made (and strenuously denied by the Chartered Institute of Housing) that councils have deliberately under-valued contracts so that they are caught by these so-called '*de minimis*' rules (Blake et al, 1996: 23). The consultation paper produced by the Department of the Environment in 1996 proposed, *inter alia*, the phasing out of the *de minimis* threshold altogether.

It was predicted that the introduction of compulsory competitive tendering to the management of local authority housing was likely to have a profound impact in relation to local authority housing management functions, potentially transforming the landlord and tenant relationship (Stewart, 1996: 176) and resulting both in 'a fragmentation of ownership and enhanced complexity' (Driscoll, 1994: 796). Such fragmentation could occur in a number of ways. First, tenant management organisations might initiate the procedure under s. 27AB, Housing Act 1985 which obliges the local authority to delegate the management of the housing concerned to them (see **11.7**). Secondly, local authorities might delegate housing management functions voluntarily, in which case the tenants affected must be consulted. Thirdly, if local authorities wish to retain their housing management functions, they must go through a compulsory competitive tendering procedure. If this latter route is taken, s. 27BA, Housing Act 1985 gives the Secretary of State the power to make regulations ensuring that local authorities consult tenants, or to consider representations from them with respect to:

(a)   the terms of a written specification to be prepared by the authority of functions proposed to be exercised by the authority or another person;

(b)   a proposal of the authority to exercise management functions themselves;

(c)   any person whom the authority propose to invite to submit a bid to exercise any of their management functions;

(d)   the standards of service for the time being achieved by the authority or (as the case may be) the person with whom they have entered into a management agreement;

(e)   a proposal to enforce the standards of service required by a management agreement.

The full introduction of housing-management compulsory competitive tendering was scheduled to be phased in over a period of three years in order to allow the larger authorities time to complete the tendering exercises, and the first round of housing-management compulsory competitive tendering, which ended in the Spring of 1996, resulted in councils losing only 16 contracts (generally to housing associations). Ninety five per cent of those tendered remained in-house. This suggests that the effects of compulsory competitive tendering may not be as far-reaching as originally feared. The change of government in May 1997 also casts doubt over the future of compulsory competitive tendering. While in opposition, the Labour Party expressed the view that councils should be allowed to put services out to tender if they wish, but should not be forced to do so. Two preferred methods of 'setting targets, achieving standards and monitoring costs' would be the formulation with tenants of 'local performance programmes', setting out a council's new quality/costs targets and monitoring past performance, and the publication by district auditors of performance indicators comparing the performances of different councils. Grant for central government could include a 'standards incentive', rewarding councils which performed well (Blake et al, 1996: 23).

Since coming to power, the Labour Government has announced that compulsory competitive tendering is to be replaced by a new duty for local authorities to achieve 'Best Value' for their services. Authorities will also be required to publish local performance plans with targets for service improvement. There is no presumption that services must be privatised and once the regime is in place, authorities will not be obliged to put their services out to tender. Thirty five local authorities in England and three in Wales have been chosen to take part in a pilot best value scheme. The pilot projects are expected to run for two to three years so that compulsory competitive tendering and best value will operate in parallel until the details concerning the abolition of compulsory competitive tendering have been finalised and the appropriate legislation enacted.

**References**

Aughton, H. and Malpass, P., *Housing Finance: a Basic Guide*, London: Shelter, 1994.
Blake, J. and Dwelly, T., 'Left in the Starting Blocks', *Roof*, September/October 1996, pp. 23–25.
Bridge, S., *Blackstone's Guide to the Housing Act 1988*, London: Blackstone Press, 1989.
Bright, S. and Gilbert, G., *Landlord and Tenant: the Nature of Tenancies*, Oxford: Clarendon Press, 1995.
Department of the Environment, *Housing: the Government's Proposals*, Cm. 214, London: HMSO, 1987a.
Department of the Environment, *Tenants' Choice: the Government's Proposals for Legislation*, London: HMSO, 1987b.
Department of the Environment, *Our Future Homes: Opportunity, Choice, Responsibility*, Cmnd. 2901, London: HMSO, 1995.
Driscoll, J., 'The Leasehold Reform, Housing and Urban Development Act 1993: The Public Sector Housing Provisions', (1994) 57 *Modern Law Review* 788.
Driscoll, J., 'What is the Future for Social Housing: Reflections on the Public Sector Provisions of the Housing Act 1996', (1997) 60 *Modern Law Review* 823–839.
Hoath, D.C., *Public Housing Law*, London: Sweet & Maxwell, 1989.

Mullins, D., Niner, P. and Riseborough, M., 'Large-Scale Voluntary Transfers', in Malpass, P. and Means, R. (eds), *Implementing Housing Policy*, Buckingham: Open University Press, 1993, pp. 169–184.

Radford, M., 'Competition Rules: the Local Government Act 1988', 1988 51 *Modern Law Review*, 747–767.

Stewart, A., *Rethinking Housing Law*, London: Sweet & Maxwell, 1996.

# THIRTEEN

## The regulation of rents

### 13.1 THE PRIVATE RENTED SECTOR: LEGISLATIVE BACKGROUND

As indicated in **Chapter 2**, there have been three generations of rent regulation. The first, which existed from 1915 until 1965, consisted of compulsory, *national* control. The Increase in Rent and Mortgage Interest (War Restrictions) Act 1915 froze rents at the free market level operative at the outbreak of war and only staggered increases were subsequently permitted. Some decontrol followed in the 1920s and 1930s, but control was reimposed in 1939 for all but highest value properties. Extensive decontrol took place in 1957, but for the most part on a piecemeal basis, as and when properties subject to controlled tenancies were vacated.

The second generation of rent regulation emerged from the Rent Act 1965 which provided for voluntary, *individual* rent regulation, thereby separating regulation of rent from security of tenure. It has been described as 'a watershed in governmental policy towards the private rented sector' which ended 'the violent swings between control and decontrol dictated by party political ideology' and marked 'an implicit acceptance' by the Labour government that the appropriate mechanism for setting private rents is generally the market, with regulation to prevent the exploitation of scarcity by the charging of exorbitant rents (Watchman, 1985: 199). However, as stated in **Chapter 2**, rent control has been perceived by a number of commentators (and recent Conservative governments) as a main reason for the decline of the private rented sector and for the poor condition of much housing in the sector. Somewhat ironically, while rent control may operate to reduce supply, it can push up the demand for rented housing by bringing it within the reach of a greater proportion of the population. People who would otherwise have been forced by their financial circumstances to live together, are tempted to break away to form new separate households. Its critics also argue that it discourages mobility of labour — an important point in this age of the flexible workforce, the members of which are expected to move to wherever jobs are available. The existence of what has been described as a 'stationary housing subsidy' prompts 'a greater mismatching of workers to jobs'. People pass up opportunities for better jobs which are more suited to them, or may even prefer to remain unemployed, if taking up a new job necessitates their moving out of property which is subject to a fair rent to one for which a market rent is payable. For the same reason, rent control is said to encourage an inefficient use of house space because it gives tenants an incentive to stay where they are, rather than to adjust their housing consumption to changes in their circumstances, e.g. the birth of children, children growing up and leaving home, the death of a family member, the need to house and look after an elderly relative (Albon et al, 1988: 12, 18). The point may also be made that rent control is inherently unfair. Whether it be by blanket control (as was the case until 1965) or individual control (as under the Rent Act 1977), it places the cost of housing subsidy on landlords, regardless of the financial means of the parties and the lack of evidence that, in general terms, tenants are poor and landlords are rich. The current provisions, which are contained in the Rent Act 1977, are considered in 13.2.

The Housing Act 1988 (the relevant provisions of which are considered in 13.3), dispenses with rent control for assured tenancies and provides for only limited regulation for assured shorthold tenancies. It is left to the market to determine the level at which rents should be set, the aim being to restore the appeal of rented property as an investment so that existing landlords are dissuaded from leaving the sector and prospective landlords are persuaded to make accommodation available for letting.

The removal of control is seen in some quarters as the reason why the supply of housing in the private rented sector has increased since 1988. Such a view presupposes that, before 1989, fair rents had been determined in relation to most properties which came under the Rent Acts. The point has already been made, however, that landlords had become adept at circumventing the Rent Acts by the use of, e.g., so-called 'holiday lets' or 'licences', and an 'informal process of deregulation' had already been taking place. Further, the decline of the private rented sector was not the outcome of rent control alone but of a 'complex web of historical circumstances'. It is worth remembering that the nearest Great Britain has come to a free market in rented housing was during the first half of the nineteenth century. By the end of the nineteenth century, it had failed to provide satisfactory housing for a large part of the population despite the efforts of the philanthropic bodies to provide decent housing for the 'labouring classes', and the public health legislation aimed at eradicating the worst conditions (Ivatts, 1988: 200).

'Market rent' is a 'problematic concept' which raises 'complex issues of distributive justice and social policy'. Free market theory dictates that 'property rents should provide a satisfactory return in relation to the capital value of the house'. That value is affected by the local availability of 'services, transport facilities and communications networks' (which are mostly paid for out of the public purse), and it reflects planning constraints (including the preservation of the 'green belt') and the resultant land shortages. A market rent means, therefore, that the landlord is profiting from that part of the rent which is attributable to the value of public investment and that tenants are paying rents which include an element relating to the 'artificial restrictions upon land use for housing and commercial development in the most economically active regions in the country' (Ivatts, 1988: 198–199). The geographical distribution of the private rented sector is uneven, with high concentrations in some areas (notably, in central London and in some of the northern and western London suburbs, in coastal resort areas, in certain rural areas and in Oxford and Cambridge) and little in others. A disproportionately high amount is substandard and, in many cases, the rents paid represent poor value for money, compared with property in the public rented sector and owner-occupied housing. The problem is compounded by the fact that many of those who are most dependent on the private sector are those with the fewest resources and the least able to afford market rents. This has significant implications for housing benefit.

## 13.2    FAIR RENTS UNDER THE RENT ACT 1977

### 13.2.1    Introduction

Rent regulation under the Rent Act 1977 applies to protected and statutory (i.e. regulated) tenancies. It is slowly dying out as (apart from a few exceptions) no new protected tenancies have been created since 15 January 1989 (the date when Part I, Housing Act 1988 came into force). The 1994/5 Survey of English Housing found that about 170,000 regulated tenancies had a registered rent (Green et al, 1996: 57).

If no rent is registered for a dwelling-house subject to a regulated tenancy, the parties are free to agree on whatever rent they like, but either the landlord or the tenant, or both jointly, may apply at any time for the registration of a fair rent. Application is made to a rent officer, who must act within the statutory guidelines. Once a fair rent has been determined, the rent officer must enter details in an area register which is available for public inspection (s. 66, Rent Act 1977). Both parties have a right to appeal to a Rent Assessment Committee from the rent officer's decision; the appeal is by way of a re-hearing. Appeal from the decision of the Rent Assessment Committee lies to the High Court on a point of law (Tribunals and Inquiries Act 1992). An application for judicial review may also be made, e.g., where the reasons given for the determination are inadequate.

Where a rent for a dwelling-house is registered, 'the rent recoverable for any contractual period of a regulated tenancy of the dwelling-house shall be limited to the rent so registered' (s. 44(1), Rent Act 1977). The registration operates to determine the maximum rent payable for premises until:

(a)    the demised premises undergo such a change in their structure as to render them no longer the dwelling-house referred to in s. 44 (see, e.g., *Solle* v *Butcher* [1950] 1 KB 671 in which internal structural alterations and improvements and the addition of a garage were held not to have changed the identity of the dwelling-house for the purposes of s. 44); or

(b)    there is a cancellation of the registration under s. 73; or
(c)    a new registration results from a fresh application under s. 67(3).

Generally, once a fair rent has been registered, it cannot be altered within two years from the effective date of registration (s. 72(1)). Exceptionally, applications seeking different rents may be made during that period where there has been (s. 67(3)):

such a change in—

(a)    the condition of the dwelling-house (including the making of any improvement therein);
(b)    the terms of the tenancy;
(c)    the quantity, quality or condition of any furniture provided for use under the tenancy (deterioration by fair wear and tear excluded); or
(d)    any other circumstances taken into consideration when the rent was registered or confirmed, as to make the registered rent no longer a fair rent.

### 13.2.2    Determination of a fair rent

**13.2.2.1    Matters to be taken into account**    Section 70(1), Rent Act 1977 provides that:

in determining ... what rent is or would be a fair rent under a regulated tenancy of a dwelling-house, regard shall be had to all the circumstances (other than personal circumstances) and in particular to—

(a)    the age, character, locality and state of repair of the dwelling-house, and
(b)    if any furniture is provided for use under the tenancy, the quantity, quality and condition of the furniture.

Of course not all circumstances will be relevant to the question of how much rent should be payable. As to those which *are* relevant, the courts have said that regard must be had 'to the sorts of factors which tend to push rents up or down on the market' (per Lord Widgery CJ in *Metropolitan Properties* v *Finegold* [1975] 1 WLR 349 at p. 351). Such circumstances could include, e.g. any restrictions in the tenancy as to use of the premises, or the quantity and quality of any services provided for the tenant by the landlord, whether expressly under the tenancy or under a separate agreement.

As far as the state of repair of the dwelling-house is concerned, there is persuasive authority that a nil or nominal rent should be determined in respect of a property which is unfit for human habitation (*Black* v *Oliver* [1978] QB 870, CA) but in *Williams* v *Khan* (1982) 43 P & CR 1, it was held that the Rent Assessment Committee are not bound to assess a nil rent because the property is subject to a closing order. That the landlord cannot afford to keep the property in repair is a 'personal circumstance' which should be disregarded.

There is uncertainty as to whether the possibility of inflation over the two-year period may be taken into account when the rent is initially determined. A rent which was fair when the determination was made will soon become unfair in times of rapid inflation. In *Metropolitan Properties Co. (FGC) Ltd* v *Lannon* [1968] 1 WLR 815, Lord Widgery suggested that some anticipation of inflation is appropriate if sufficient information on inflation trends is available. However, in *Guppys (Bridport) Ltd* v *Carpenter* (1973) 228 EG 1919, he stated that 'it is not the duty of a rent assessment committee necessarily to assume inflation in the ensuing [two] years or to make provision for it'. In *Wareing* v *White* (1984) 270 EG 851, it was held that while account could be taken of inflation, it would be quite wrong for the court to lay down principles as to how the question of inflation should be approached.

**13.2.2.2 Disregards** The Rent Act 1977 makes it quite clear that the following matters should not be taken into account in determining a fair rent:

(a)   personal circumstances (s. 70(1));
(b)   scarcity value (s. 70(2));
(c)   the tenant's defects or improvements to the dwelling-house (s. 70(3)).

*(a) Personal circumstances*   The parties' gender, sexual orientation, age, health, ethnicity, religion, and financial standing should all be disregarded as 'personal circumstances'. Security of tenure is also a 'personal circumstance' (per Lord Reid in *Mason* v *Skilling* [1974] 1 WLR 1437 at p. 1440) unless lettings of assured tenancies are being relied on as comparables (*Spath Holme Ltd* v *Greater Manchester and Lancashire Rent Assessment Committee* (1995) 28 HLR 107).

*(b) Scarcity*   By s. 70(2) rent officers, and Rent Assessment Committees must assume that 'the number of persons seeking to become tenants of similar dwelling-houses in the locality on the terms (other than those relating to rent) of the regulated tenancy is not substantially greater than the number of such dwelling-houses in the locality which are available for letting on such terms'.

If demand for rented accommodation is greater than the available supply, the market rent will be higher than would be the case if supply and demand were evenly balanced. The effect of s. 70(2) is that where there is an imbalance, the rent officer or the Rent Assessment Committee must determine a rent on the assumption that supply and demand are equal. In contrast to the owner of other commodities, the landlord cannot take advantage of shortages in order to increase the rent (Martin, 1995: 173). Implicit in both s. 70(1) and (2) is the notion that the level at which the rent is fixed represents the level of rents if only the current (temporary) housing shortage did not exist. Lord Widgery explained it thus:

> It seems to me that what parliament is saying is this. If the house has inherent amenities and advantages, by all means let them be reflected in the rent under subs. (1); but if the market rent would be influenced simply by the fact

that there is a shortage, and in the locality rents are being forced up beyond the market figure, then that element of market rent must not be included when the fair rent is being considered. Parliament, I am sure, is not seeking to deprive the landlord of a proper return on the inherent value and quality of his investment in the house, but parliament is undoubtedly seeking to deprive a landlord of a wholly unmerited increase in rent which has come about simply because there is a scarcity of houses in the district and thus an excess of demand over supply (*Metropolitan Property Holdings* v *Finegold* [1975] 1 WLR 349 at p. 352).

In *Metropolitan Property Holdings* v *Finegold* the presence of a school in St John's Wood which restricted entry to children of American families in London made the district more attractive to American families and rents went up. The tenant argued that this introduced a scarcity element, which should be disregarded. It was held, however, that the word 'locality' should be interpreted broadly and does not mean the immediate locality. Thus, the scarcity test should be applied over a substantial area, ignoring local scarcity caused by a particular amenity.

*(c)   Failure to repair by the tenant or the tenant's improvements to the dwelling-house*   By s. 70(3) the Rent Officer or Rent Assessment Committee must disregard:

(a)   any disrepair or other defect attributable to a failure by the tenant under the regulated tenancy or any predecessor in title to comply with any terms thereof; and

(b)   any improvement carried out by the tenant under the regulated tenancy or any predecessor in title, otherwise than in pursuance of the terms of the tenancy. A similar provision applies to any improvement to or deterioration in the condition of any furniture which is provided. The word 'improvement' means something more than repair and maintenance and, in this context, includes the replacement of any fixture or fitting (s. 70(4)).

In the case of 'any disrepair or other defect', there must be evidence of negligence or other breach of the terms of the tenancy by the tenant. In *McGhee* v *London Rent Assessment Panel* (1969) 113 SJ 384, five fires on the demised property, allegedly caused by the activities of a poltergeist, were held not to have been caused by the tenant's negligence or by any failure to comply with the terms of his tenancy. Accordingly the rent officer's reduction in rent from £6 per week to 5/- (25p) was restored in place of the Rent Assessment Committee's £4. It makes no difference that the landlord has failed to enforce the tenant's repairing covenant (*Metropolitan Properties Co. Ltd* v *Wooldridge* (1969) 20 P & CR 64).

**13.2.2.3   Methods of determining a fair rent**   Section 70(1) leaves it up to the rent officer or Rent Assessment Committee to adopt any method of ascertaining a fair rent provided that it is not unlawful or unreasonable (*Mason* v *Skilling* [1974] 1 WLR 1437, p. 1439).

(a)   Market rent less scarcity factor   This has been described as 'a well recognised and thoroughly reputable route' (*Metropolitan Holdings* v *Laufer* (1974) 233 EG 1011) but it has sometimes proved difficult to put into practice. As the number of registrations increased after 1965, evidence of market rent comparables became increasingly difficult to find. More recently, there has been the problem of ascertaining what degree of scarcity, if any, exists. The Francis Committee was of the opinion that 'the assessment of the scarcity element in the rent ... is incapable of measurement except by way of an intelligent guess' (Francis, 1971: 58) and, in *Metropolitan Holdings* v *Laufer*, Lord Widgery said that it depended on 'personal professional opinion and experience', there being no obligation on the part of the rent officer or Rent Assessment Committee to quantify any element of scarcity allowed. This method seems to have regained favour with landlords since the Housing Act 1988 came into force and evidence as to market rents has become more widely available.

*(b)   Registered comparables*   As registration of rents became more widespread, the registered comparables test replaced the market rent less scarcity test as the most commonly used method of determining a fair rent. This method, in which regard is had to the recently registered rents of comparable properties in a locality, was described in the House of Lords as 'the most obvious and direct method' of ascertaining a fair rent (per Lord Reid in *Mason* v *Skilling* [1974] 1 WLR 1437 at p. 1439. See too Lord Brightman in *Western Heritable Investment Co. Ltd* v *Husband* [1983] 3 WLR 429 at p. 436). The use of comparables does have limitations in that a true comparable rarely exists unless it is an identical flat in the same block, or a corresponding house on a housing estate of similar properties. Even then, there will always be some differing factors.

Since it is based on existing registered rents, the registered comparables method contains a built-in scarcity deduction. In *London RAC* v *St George's Court Ltd* (1984) 48 P & CR 230, the Court of Appeal stated that the rent assessed for a comparable property had to be regarded as 'the best evidence of the rent which would be a fair rent for the property under consideration' unless it could be shown that had been arrived at upon a fundamental misapprehension. Thus, although rents already registered will be presumed to have been have been correctly ascertained, either party may show that those comparable rents have been determined on a wrong basis (per Lord Reid in *Mason* v *Skilling*, ibid., at p. 1439).

The relaxation of controls by the Housing Act 1988 and the entry into the private rented sector of 'slump landlords' (homeowners who grant tenancies of properties which they cannot sell) have combined to reduce scarcity. There is evidence that there has been a steep increase in registered rents, over and above inflation, since the 1988 Act came into force. In 1990 the average weekly rent (excluding housing association tenancies) was £61 for assured tenancies, £66 for assured shorthold tenancies, £27 for regulated tenancies with a registered rent and £33 for regulated tenancies with a non-registered rent (thus suggesting that many non-registered rents for regulated tenancies were not set at 'market levels' but 'in the shadow' of registered rent levels (Davey, 1992:

500). In England, the average annual rate of increase on re-registration between 1989 and 1995 ranged from 18% to 25% (Department of the Environment, 1996: Table 11.6).

Does it follow that:

(a)   the absence of scarcity in a particular locality results in increasing registered rents to market levels; and

(b)   fair rents can be based on rents for comparable properties which are let on assured tenancies (i.e. market rents which make no allowance for the fact that accommodation may be in short supply)?

In *BTE Ltd* v *Merseyside and Cheshire RAC* [1992] 16 EG 111, the High Court held that in a climate where there is no scarcity of comparable rented accommodation, the fair rent is the 'fair market rent' and that the rents obtained for properties let on assured tenancies should be taken into account when determining a fair rent. In *Spath Holme Ltd* v *Greater Manchester and Lancashire Rent Assessment Committee* (1995) 28 HLR 107, the Court of Appeal accepted the proposition that security is a personal circumstance to be disregarded where the capital value/fair yield method is used because the value will depend on the tenant's personal attributes (e.g. age or likely successors). It should not be disregarded, however, where the method adopted involves comparable rents under assured tenancies. The Rent Assessment Committee had erred in its determination that discounted market rents could not be used to determine a fair rent, as a market rent adjusted for security is precisely what a fair rent is required to be. See too *Curtis and Others* v *London RAC* [1997] 4 All ER 842 in which the Court of Appeal made it clear that where close market comparables were available, they should be used in preference to registered fair rents.

*(c)   The capital value/fair yield method*   While seemingly expressing a preference for the registered comparables method, the House of Lords in *Mason* v *Skilling* [1974] 1 WLR 1437 none the less recognised that 'a fair rent should be fair to the landlord as well as fair to the tenant and it can be regarded as fair to the landlord that he should receive a fair return on his capital' (at p. 1440). Under this method (sometimes known as the 'contractor's method' and, not surprisingly put forward by landlords, rather than tenants), the fair rent is calculated as a percentage return on capital outlay.

A lease may be viewed as a form of investment by the landlord; if the landlord's capital were not tied up in the property being let, it would be invested elsewhere and producing a return. When this method of determining a fair rent is employed, a capital value is put on the premises and an appropriate rate of interest applied to give a basic figure upon which the fair rent can be determined. It is the value with vacant possession (i.e. without any sitting tenant) which is used. In the case of new buildings, the capital value may be arrived at by putting a valuation in the site, adding the cost of construction, and applying a rate of interest to the total. In *Western Heritable Investment Co.* v

*Husband* [1983] 2 AC 849 at p. 857, the House of Lords criticised this method as being 'notoriously unreliable' and in *Anglo-Italian Properties Ltd* v *London Rent Assessment Panel* [1969] 1 WLR 730, in which a double deduction for scarcity had been made, the case was sent back to the Rent Assessment Committee with an indicated preference for the registered comparable method.

*(d)   The outgoings plus profit method*   This method involves a calculation of the landlord's outgoings (i.e. repair and maintenance, insurance, management, services, etc.), and adding an appropriate sum for profit. A 'reasonable' profit should effectively mean that scarcity has been eliminated, in the sense that the sum decided upon would tend to exclude any element attributable to shortage alone. A landlord might reasonably expect to make at least a quarter of the rent as profit.

In May 1998 the Government issued an Consultation Paper proposing that increases in fair rents are limited to the Retail Price Index plus 10% for the first re-registration and to the Retail Price Index plus 5% for subsequent re-registrations. It emphasises that there are no plans to change the legislative framework for assured and assured shorthold tenancies (Department of the Environment, Transport and the Regions, 1998).

## 13.3   RENTS UNDER THE HOUSING ACT 1988

### 13.3.1   Assured tenancies

The policy of the Housing Act 1988 — a measure which 'shattered the 20-year-old political consensus on rent regulation' (Davey, 1992: 497) — is to allow feedom of contract to prevail and to limit the degree of statutory intervention. It is left to the parties, therefore, to agree on the level of rent and and make provision for rent reviews in appropriate cases. In contrast to the Housing Act 1957, the 1988 Act did not deregulate any existing lettings but provided that, as a general rule, no new registered tenancies could be created on or after 15 January 1989. The only external influences provided for by the 1988 Act operate through the s. 13 review procedure for assured periodic tenancies (see **13.3.1.1** to **13.3.1.3**) and via referrals to the Rent Assessment Committee by assured shorthold tenants (see **13.3.1.4**). The aim of these provisions is not to limit rents but to set rents at a market level.

**13.3.1.1   Fixed-term tenancies**   The parties to a fixed-term tenancy may agree on whatever rent they like. Unless there is a rent review clause, a landlord who wishes to increase the original rent will have to wait until the fixed-term tenancy ends and a statutory periodic tenancy arises. The landlord will then be able to serve a notice of increase under s. 13.

**13.3.1.2   Statutory periodic tenancies**   A statutory periodic tenancy arises on the termination of an assured fixed-term tenancy (by expiry of the term (s. 5(2)) or the operation of a break clause by the landlord) and also where the tenant has succeeded to a tenancy which was previously regulated by the Rent Act (s. 39(6)(f)). The rent payable will continue at the same level as before (s. 5(3)) but the landlord will now have the right to propose a rent increase under s. 13. The general requirements as to the service of a notice apply, but the rent increase may be sought as from expiry of the term certain; the landlord does not have to delay the start of the period for the proposed new rent for one year from the commencement of the periodic tenancy — which he or she must do where a periodic tenancy was granted (s. 13(1)(b)). The landlord must serve the notice during the final year of the fixed-term assured tenancy, giving a 'minimum period' for the coming into effect of the new rent. The length of the minimum period will depend on the intervals at which rent is payable under the tenancy. Further increases in rent will be governed by the provisions which apply to periodic tenancies.

**13.3.1.3 Periodic tenancies** The landlord may increase the rent of a periodic or statutory periodic assured tenancy by serving notice under s. 13. However, any provision in the tenancy agreement for rent review will govern rent increases to the exclusion of the statutory procedure (s. 13(1)(b)). Alternatively, the landlord and tenant may agree to vary the rent, regardless of the provisions of ss. 13 and 14 (s. 13(5)). The statutory procedure allows for rent to be increased annually.

The landlord must serve a notice in the prescribed form, proposing a new rent to take effect as from a 'new period of the tenancy specified in the notice' (s. 13(2)). The form advises the tenant of his or her right to refer the rent to a Rent Assessment Committee under s. 13(4). There is no earliest date when the notice can be served, but the increase cannot take effect any earlier than:

(a)   the minimum period after the date of service of the notice; and
(b)   the end of the first anniversary of the date in which the first period of the tenancy began (s. 13(2)(b)).

If the rent has previously been increased by a s. 13 notice or a s. 14 determination by a Rent Assessment Committee, no further notice of increase can be served until one year after the increased rent takes effect (s. 13(2)(c)).

By s. 13(2) and (3), the 'minimum period', from which the new rent is payable, is not to begin earlier than:

(a)   in the case of a yearly tenancy, six months;
(b)   in the case of a tenancy where the period is less than a month, one month;
(c)   in any other case, the period of the tenancy.

Once the period specified in the notice expires, the new rent takes effect as specified in the notice, unless the tenant has referred the notice to a Rent Assessment Committee, by an application in the prescribed form, or the parties have agreed on a different rent, or have agreed that no increase is called for

(s. 13(4)). Of course, a periodic tenant who is unwilling or unable to pay a new rent may determine the tenancy by a notice to quit.

### 13.3.1.4 Determination by a Rent Assessment Committee

There is no procedure which allows a tenant to take the initiative in referring a matter to a Rent Assessment Committee; its jurisdiction arises exclusively on a landlord's attempt to secure an increase. Where there are joint tenants, the application must be made by all of them unless they all authorise one tenant to act as their agent.

The referral must be in a prescribed form and must take place before the beginning of the 'new period' specified in the notice (s. 13(4)). Otherwise the new rent specified in the notice will become payable, however high or unreasonable it may be. The Committee must consider the reference under s. 14. Committees are empowered to obtain from both the landlord and the tenant such information as they may reasonably require for the purposes of their functions (s. 41) and the President of every rent assessment panel must keep and make publicly available specified information as to the rents of assured and assured shorthold tenancies (s. 42). Both parties may give written notice that they no longer require a determination (s. 14(8)). Rent does not include a variable service charge (s. 14(4)), but the Committee must consider sums payable for furniture and for services, repairs, maintenance or insurance of the landlord's costs of management, whether or not they are separate from the rent, and whether they are payable under the tenancy or under separate agreements.

The Rent Assessment Committee must determine the rent at which they consider the dwelling-house might reasonably be expected to be let in the open market by a willing landlord under an assured tenancy on the assumption that (s. 14(1)):

(a)   the tenancy is periodic with the same periods as the tenancy to which the notice relates;

(b)   it begins at the beginning of the period from which the new rent specified in the notice is payable;

(c)   the terms are those of the tenancy to which the notice relates (other than that relating to the amount of rent); and

(d)   where appropriate, notices under sch. 2, Grounds 1–5 have been given to the tenant.

The rent determined by a Rent Assessment Committee takes effect as from the date specified in the landlord's s. 13 notice, unless the Committee considers that this would cause undue hardship to the tenant, in which case they may substitute a later date which cannot be any later than the date of their decision (s. 14(7)).

### 13.3.1.5 Statutory disregards

While the rent must be determined as a market rent, the Committee must make the following disregards (s. 14(2)):

(a)   The fact that there is a sitting tenant.

(b)   Any increase in the value of the dwelling-house attributable to certain improvements carried out by the person who, at the time they were carried out, was the current tenant.

Any improvement carried out pursuant to a contractual obligation will generally be disregarded. Voluntary improvements cannot be disregarded unless they were carried out either during the current tenancy, or under an earlier tenancy, provided that (s. 14(3)):

(i)   they were carried out no more than 21 years before the date of service of the notice; and

(ii)   at all times since then, the dwelling-house has been let under an assured tenancy; and

(iii)   on the coming to an end of an assured tenancy at any time during that period, the tenant (or one of the joint tenants) did not quit the property.

(c)   Any reduction in the value of the dwelling-house attributable to a failure by the tenant to comply with the terms of the tenancy. Where á person became an assured tenant by succession under s. 39, Housing Act 1988, a failure by the tenant's predecessor to comply with the terms of the tenancy cannot be taken into account as s. 14(2)(c) applies only to the defaults of the *current* tenant (*N & D (London) Ltd* v *Gadsden* [1992] 1 EGLR 112).

### 13.3.2   Assured shorthold tenancies

The 1987 White Paper which paved the way for the Housing Act 1988 stated that for all new lettings under the proposed Act, landlords should be able to choose either:

(a)   to let on the assured tenancy basis with rents freely negotiated between landlord and tenant; or

(b)   to let on the shorthold basis, with no security beyond the period of the tenancy but with the right for either party to seek registration of an aprropriate rent.

(Department of the Environment, 1987: para. 3.11.) The impression given was that because assured shorthold tenancies carry no security of tenure, assured shorthold tenants would pay less rent. What has happened in fact is that because most lettings have been assured shorthold tenancies, the rent payable under an assured shorthold tenancy has become the market rent and does not reflect the tenant's lack of security.

#### 13.3.2.1   Periodic assured shorthold tenancies   The tenant who, after 28 February 1997, is granted a periodic assured shorthold tenancy has a right to refer the rent to the Rent Assessment Committee but only during the first six months of the tenancy. The landlord can use the s. 13 procedure to increase the rent.

**13.3.2.2   Fixed-term assured shorthold tenancies**   By s. 22, Housing Act 1988 an assured shorthold tenant may apply to the Rent Assessment Committee to determine the rent 'which, in the committee's opinion, the landlord might reasonably be expected to obtain'.

Where the tenancy was granted after 28 February 1997, the tenant cannot refer the rent if more than six months have elapsed since the beginning of the tenancy (s. 22(2)(aa), as amended by s. 100(1), Housing Act 1996) or, in the case of a replacement tenancy, since the beginning of the original tenancy. The tenant cannot in any case refer the rent if a rent has previously been determined under s. 22 (s. 22(2)(a)).

The Rent Assessment Committee can only make a determination if, by s. 22(3) they consider that:

(a)   there is a sufficient number of similar dwelling-houses in the locality let on assured tenancies (whether shorthold or not); and

(b)   the rent payable under the assured shorthold tenancy in question is 'significantly higher' than the rent which the landlord might reasonably be expected to be able to obtain under the tenancy, having regard to the level of rents payable under the tenancies of similar dwelling-houses in the locality.

The rent, as determined by the Rent Assessment Committee, takes effect from whatever date the Committee directs, but no earlier than the date of the application (s. 22(4)(a)). The landlord cannot serve notice of an increase of rent under s. 13(2) until after the first anniversary of the date on which the determination takes effect (s. 22(4)(c)).

## 13.4   HOUSING ASSOCIATION RENTS

### 13.4.1   Tenancies granted before 15 January 1989

Part VI, Rent Act 1977 provides for the registration of 'fair' rents for dwellings let by housing associations, housing trusts and the Housing Corporation before 15 January 1989.

### 13.4.2   Tenancies granted on or after 15 January 1989

Tenancies granted by housing associations on or after 15 January 1989 are assured tenancies. During the passage of the Housing Act 1988 through Parliament, the government rejected the argument made by representatives of the housing association movement that, because most housing associations were created to provide low-cost housing, there should be a separate regime for housing association rents. Rents for housing association tenancies created since the Housing Act 1988 came into force are determined in the same way as other private sector tenancies but the 'Tenants' Guarantee' produced by the Housing Corporation urges housing associations to set rents affordable for people in low-paid employment. Cuts in grants from central government and the consequent need to turn to private funding make this objective difficult to achieve.

## 13.5   THE SIGNIFICANCE OF HOUSING BENEFIT

The housing benefit scheme is administered by local authorities under the central direction of the Department of Social Security. Housing benefit is a means-tested or income-related payment which gives low income tenants and licensees, whether in or out of work, help with their rent. Only the main provisions are outlined here.

For private sector and housing association tenants, payment is in the form of a rent allowance, which is a direct cash payment, whether to the tenant or direct to the landlord (usually where the tenant has rent arrears). For local authority tenants, housing benefit takes the form of a rent rebate. The framework of the housing benefit scheme is contained in the Social Security Contributions and Benefits Act 1992 and the Social Security Administration Act 1992. The detailed rules on entitlement, the calculation of benefit, claims and payments are in the Housing Benefit (General) Regulations 1987 and the Rent Officers (Additional Functions) Order 1995.

**Table 13.a   Housing benefit recipients: Great Britain**

|      | Local authority tenants (000s) | Regulated tenants tenants (000s) | Deregulated tenants (000s) | Housing Association tenants (000s) |
|------|------|------|------|------|
| 1992 | 2,981 |       |       |       |
| 1993 | 3,049 | 359   | 689   | 375   |
| 1994 | 3,045 | 309   | 826   | 484   |
| 1995 | 2,992 | 263   | 886   | 590   |
| 1996 | 2,918 | 230   | 933   | 694   |
| 1997 | 2,823 | 198   | 894   | 762   |

Source: Department of Social Security, *Social Security Statistics 1997*, London: The Stationery Office, 1997, Table A301.

When the housing benefit scheme first came into existence, local authorities were reimbursed by central government the full cost of paying benefit on reasonable rents. However if:

(a)   the accommodation was deemed to be larger than was reasonably needed for the occupier and anyone who also occupied the accommodation; or

(b)   the rent was unreasonably high compared with that for suitable accommodation elsewhere within the area;

the local authority was required to meet the full cost of the difference. Financial incentives existed, therefore, for local authorities not to pay out full benefit on unreasonable rents so that claimants had either to find the difference themselves or try to persuade landlords to reduce the rent. Safeguards existed for certain vulnerable claimants (the elderly, disabled and families with children) and the courts were sometimes prepared to exercise some control over landlords (see, e.g. *R* v *Manchester City Council, ex parte Baragrove Properties Ltd* (1991) 23 HLR 337).

In January 1996 the regulations were amended in relation to new claims made by private sector and most housing association tenants so that payments of housing benefit are now limited to a 'maximum rent'. The authority applies to the rent officers for a determination, and the maximum rent is then fixed in the light of that determination. The rules of the new regime are extremely complex and readers are referred to Partington, 1997 for further details. Generally, rent officers will be asked to determine a 'local reference rent' (arrived at by adding the highest rent which, in the rent officer's opinion, a landlord might have been able to obtain for the dwelling in question, to the lowest rent, and dividing by two). Councils can meet 50% of the difference between local reference rents and their 'market' equivalents (i.e. the maximum amount that non-claimant tenants would willingly pay). The previous safeguards for vulnerable claimants have been removed, leaving only local authorities' general powers to make provision in cases of exceptional hardship. Rent officers are also empowered to make pre-tenancy determinations of the maximum eligible rent at the request of prospective tenants, the idea being that, given such information, tenants can then seek to renegotiate the asking rent.

Since October 1996, the amount of housing benefit payable to many single people under the age of 25 living in private sector accommodation has been severely restricted and covers only the 'average' cost of shared accommodation (Housing Benefit (General) Amendment Regulations 1996, SI 1996/965). The policy behind this change was to dissuade young people from occupying self-contained accommodation, freeing it up for families. Plans to extend this restriction to all single people between the ages of 25 and 59 were scrapped by the new Labour government.

The introduction of market rents and the phasing out of fair rents has, not surprisingly, led to significant increases in rent levels in the private rented sector. Given that many people who rely on the private rented sector are elderly, or on low incomes or unemployed, the housing benefit bill has escalated over the past decade. The restrictions on housing benefit introduced since January 1996 are intended in part, therefore, to put a brake on private sector rents but it is unrealistic to expect tenants to be able to negotiate lower rents with their landlords, particularly when, in many areas, it is a 'sellers' market'.

## 13.6   LOCAL AUTHORITY RENTS

Local authorities have always enjoyed a wide discretion in fixing their own rents but their discretion has been significantly affected by the financial regime established under the Local Government and Housing Act 1989.

Section 24, Housing Act 1985 empowers a local housing authority to make 'such reasonable charges as they may determine for the tenancy or occupation of their houses'. By s. 24(2), 'the authority shall from time to time review rents and make such changes, either of rents generally or of particular rents, as circumstances may require'. In deciding whether a charge is 'reasonable' the courts have held that local authorities must strike a balance between the ratepayers and the tenants (*Belcher* v *Reading Corporation* (1950) 1 Ch 380) and are entitled to approach it as a matter of social policy (*Luby* v *Newcastle-under-Lyme Corporation* [1965] 1 QB 214). They are neither obliged to relate their rents to market rents nor to seek to make a profit (*Evans* v *Collins* [1965] 1 QB 580). Although these principles are still good law they must be viewed in the light of the 'ring-fencing' of the Housing Revenue Account which prohibits authorities from making payments to the Housing Revenue Account from any other revenue account, e.g. the General Fund. Local authorities are under a duty to prevent a debit balance on the Housing Revenue Account (s. 79, Local Government and Housing Act 1989) and, as one of the major sources of income to the account is the rental income, the rent levels set will necessarily reflect this duty. Furthermore, the other major source of income — housing subsidy — is now calculated on the account on the basis of the assumed, rather than actual, rent levels and of reasonably efficient management (s. 80).

In exercising their functions under s. 24, local authorities must 'have regard in particular to the principle that the rents of houses of any class or description should bear broadly the same proportion to private sector rents as the rents of other houses of any other class or description' (s. 24(3)). 'Private sector rents' are the rents which would be recoverable if the 'houses of any class or description' were let on assured tenancies within the meaning of the Housing Act 1988 by a person other than the authority (s. 24(4)). The effect of this provision is that the differential between the rents charged for different types of housing in the public sector should be broadly the same as that in the private sector. Thus, if under an assured tenancy, the rent for a three-bedroom flat is roughly three times the rent charged for a one-bedroom flat, the local authority should try to maintain the same ratio between its own three-bedroom and one-bedroom flats.

Unlike the Rent Act 1977, the Housing Act 1985 contains no formal machinery for challenging the rent payable. Theoretically, the tenant can seek judicial review of the local authority's exercise of its discretion but, in practice, such a course of action is unlikely to be successful. The discretion given to a local authority is such that the court can interfere only if the tenant can prove that it has been exercised in a manner which no reasonable person could consider justifiable. In only one reported case has the authority's discretion been overturned (see *Backhouse* v *Lambeth BC* (1972) *The Times*, 14 October).

## References

Albon, R and Stafford, D.C., 'Rent Control: its Costly Repercussions', *Social Policy and Administration*, 1988, vol. 22, pp. 10–21.

Davey, M., 'Rent Control: a Farewell to Fair Rents', *Journal of Social Welfare and Family Law*, 1992, vol. 14, pp. 497–510.

Department of the Environment, *Housing: The Government's Proposals*, Cm. 214, London: HMSO, 1987.

Department of the Environment, *Housing and Construction Statistics 1985–1995*, London: HMSO, 1996.

Department of the Environment, Transport and the Regions, *Limiting Fair Rent Increases: A Consultation Paper*, London: The Stationery Office, 1998.

Francis, H.E., Report of the Committee on the Rent Acts, Cmnd. 4609, London: HMSO, 1971.

Green, H., Thomas, M., Iles, N. and Down, D., *Housing in England 1994/95*, London: HMSO, 1996.

Ivatts, J., 'Rented Housing and Market Rents: a Social Policy Critique', *Social Policy and Administration*, 1988, vol. 22, pp. 197–209.

Martin, J., *Residential Security*, London: Sweet & Maxwell, 1995.

Partington, M., 'The Re-introduction of Rent Control? The Effect of Changes to the Housing Benefit Scheme, 1996 and 1997', *Journal of Housing Law*, 1997, vol. 1, pp. 8–11.

Watchman, P.Q., 'Fair Rents and Market Security', *The Conveyancer*, 1985, vol. 49, pp. 199–216.

**Further reading**

Lee, R., 'Rent Control — The Economic Impact of Social Legislation', *Oxford Journal of Legal Studies*, 1992, vol. 12, pp. 543–557.

# FOURTEEN

## Succession

### 14.1 INTRODUCTION

At common law, where there is a joint tenancy and one of the joint tenants dies, the rule of survivorship applies. Otherwise, a tenancy (whether it be periodic or fixed-term) is an estate in land which passes on the tenant's death to the person who is entitled under the tenant's will or on intestacy. This may be of some value in the case of a fixed-term tenancy which still has some time to run, but the transmission on death of a periodic tenancy is of little practical use as it can generally be terminated by notice. However, the common law rules have been modified extensively by statute.

### 14.2 SUCCESSION UNDER THE RENT ACT 1977

Succession rights for Rent Act tenants were first conferred by s. 12(1)(g), Increase of Rent and Mortgage Interest (Restrictions) Act 1920. As originally drafted, the prospective legislation confined succession to the widow of a male tenant. A few Members of Parliament recognised that this restriction might present a problem in the 'great number of cases of women who earn their living all over the country, journalists and others, who sometimes have old mothers living with them or young sisters. . . . It would be hard if [the tenant] died and the mother or sister might be turned out' (HC Debs, 1920, vol. 130, cols. 1929–30).

Section 12(1)(g) therefore defined the word 'tenant' to include 'the widow of a tenant dying intestate who was residing with him at the time of his death' or, where the tenant:

(a)   died intestate leaving no widow, or
(b)   was a woman,

'such member of the tenant's family so residing as aforesaid . . .' It was soon established that a widower was a member of his wife's family (*Salter* v *Lask*

[1925] 1 KB 584). A six-months residence requirement for members of the tenant's family was added in 1933 and a second succession was added by the Rent Act 1965. The Rent Act 1977, which it will be remembered is a consolidating Act, allows for two possible successions — the first to the spouse (or, if none, to a member of the tenant's family), and the second to a member of the tenant's family. The policy underlying these provisions was said to derive from 'the middle-class ideal of owning your own home and garden' which 'so infused English thinking that those who cannot afford to buy their homes are given the next best things: security for one, two or three lives'. At the same time it was recognised that 'it is such a serious inroad on the right of the landlord that it runs close to expropriation, at least of the present owner's effective interest' (Honore, 1982: 59).

By conferring long-term security of tenure, the Rent Acts give tenants far greater protection than they would have enjoyed by virtue of their own contractual arrangements. The security conferred by the Act was designed not merely to ensure that the tenant had a roof over his or her head, but also — perhaps mainly — to provide the tenant with enough security to establish a family home (Zuckerman, 1980: 263). Further, 'it would be inequitable to deny such protection to those whose lives are intimately bound up with that of the statutory tenant, and who would reasonably be expected to share his day-to-day life and home'. In consequence, 'the [Rent] Act gives security to such people at the time when they are most vulnerable (after the tenant's death) by allowing them to "inherit" the protection granted to the tenant' (Berkovits, 1981: 95). Significant changes were made to the rules regarding succession to Rent Act tenancies by the Housing Act 1988 and these are dealt with in **14.2.2** and **14.2.5**.

A successor may have a claim to a statutory or assured tenancy on the death of a regulated tenant. If there is no successor, a statutory tenancy will come to an end but a protected tenancy will devolve under the will or intestacy of the tenant. Succession under the statutory provisions takes precedence over the rights of any person entitled under the tenant's will (*Moodie* v *Hosegood* [1952] AC 61), or on the tenant's intestacy. Such rights are suspended until the succession rules have run their course.

### 14.2.1  Death of the original tenant before 15 January 1989

The Rent Act 1977, in its original form, allowed two successions. Either the tenant's spouse or (if the tenant had no spouse) a 'member of the original tenant's family' could become a statutory tenant by succession. A spouse was entitled to succeed if he or she was 'residing in the dwelling-house immediately before the death of the original tenant'; a member of the tenant's family was entitled only if he or she had been 'residing with' the tenant 'at the time of and for the period of six months immediately before [the tenant's] death'. The Housing Act 1988 extended the length of the residence requirement to two years where the original tenant dies on or after 15 January 1989. Similarly, the circumstances of the second succession depend on whether the death of the first successor occurs before or after 15 January 1989 or on or after that date (see **14.2.4** and **14.2.5**).

**14.2.1.1  Spouses and cohabitees**  There is no definition of 'spouse' in the Rent Acts but, in effect, it has been interpreted as a person who has gone through a legal ceremony of marriage with the tenant.

Until the Housing Act 1988 amended the succession provisions of the Rent Act, the tenant's unmarried cohabitee was not regarded as a spouse and, in order to become a stautory tenant by succession, had to prove that he or she was a member of the tenant's family. The first occasion on which the Court of Appeal was faced with the issue was in *Gammans* v *Ekins* [1950] 2 All ER 140, in which the defendant had lived with the deceased tenant for 20 years or so 'in close, but unmarried, association'. He had adopted her name and posed as her husband. The couple had no children. The court held that no ordinary man could on the facts answer 'yes' to the question of whether the surviving partner was a member of the tenant's family. The court took a somewhat censorious view of the relationship. Asquith LJ thought it 'anomalous that a person can acquire a "status of irremoveability" by living or having lived in sin . . . To say of two people masquerading as these two were as husband and wife . . . that they were members of the same family seems to be an abuse of the English language' (at pp. 141, 142). The presence of children in such a case appears to have been significant in creating a family unit. Thus, in *Hawes* v *Evendon* [1953] 2 All ER 737 the claimant who had lived with the tenant for 12 years and had borne him two children was successful.

In *Dyson Holdings* v *Fox* [1976] QB 503, the Court of Appeal departed from *Gammans* v *Ekins* and found for the claimant (who had lived with the as his wife for 21 years until his death but had no children with him) on the ground that the popular meaning of 'family' had changed. Bridge LJ spoke of the 'complete revolution in society's attitude to unmarried partnerships of the kind under consideration' which had occurred between 1950 and 1975. 'Such unions', he said 'are far commoner than they used to be' and 'the social stigmas that once attached to them has almost, if not entirely, disappeared' (at p. 512). He felt some hesitation as to whether the court could give effect to the change in social attitude without doing violence to the doctrine of judicial precedent but in the end decided it would be unduly legalistic to allow this consideration to defeat the claim.

In *Helby* v *Rafferty* [1979] 1 WLR 13, a man who had cohabited with the tenant for five years was held not entitled to succeed to a statutory tenancy on the ground that the relationship lacked the permanence and stability over a long period necessary to constitue a family relationship. The couple shared expenses, went to shows and the cinema and did the shopping together. When the tenant became ill, the defendant nursed her as a loving husband might have done. However, the parties had no intention of marrying and did not hold themselves out as married. Neither had taken the other's name. In *Watson* v *Lucas* [1980] 1 WLR 1493, a majority of the Court of Appeal upheld the claim because relationship was permanent (the couple had lived together for 19 years) even though the woman had not adopted the man's name and the claimant had a wife and children elsewhere. In *Chios Property Investment Co. Ltd v Lopez* (1988) 20 HLR 120 — described as a 'most exceptional case' — the woman had lived with the tenant for two years with ultimate intention of marrying him as soon as financial circumstances permitted. She was held entitled to succeed despite the comparative brevity of their relationship and the absence of children. The Court of Appeal noted that there could be no hard and fast rule as regards the necessary length of the relationship, although the longer it had lasted, the easier it would be to infer permanence.

The situation with regard to same-sex partners is dealt with in 14.2.3.

### 14.2.2 Death of original tenant on or after 15 January 1989

As before, the spouse of the deceased tenant is entitled to be the first successor provided that he or she was residing in the dwelling-house immediately before the tenant's death. However, the term 'spouse' has been extended to cover those living together as husband and wife (sch. 1, para. 2(2), Rent Act 1977, inserted by sch. 4, para. 2, Housing Act 1988) which means that cohabitants no longer have to to try to establish that they are members of the same family. Where the successor is the spouse or a cohabitant, he or she is entitled to a statutory tenancy under the Rent Act 1977.

In the absence of a spouse or a cohabitant, the first successor is a member of the tenant's family. The residence requirement is increased from six months to two years. A member of the tenant's family succeeds to an assured periodic tenancy under the Housing Act 1988, rather than a statutory tenancy under the Rent Act 1977 and no further succession is possible (s. 17(2)(c), Housing Act 1988).

#### 14.2.2.1 Who is 'a member of the original tenant's family'?   None of the Rent Acts has included a definition of the word 'family'. In *Salter v Lask* [1925] 1 KB 584, at p. 587 Salter J predicted that 'it may have to be determined some day what limit is to be put on these words "tenant's family", whether they are equivalent to "household" or whether they are limited as meaning blood relations'. The issue has indeed come before the courts on many occasions, membership of a family being nowhere near as clear cut as would appear at first glance.

In *Brock v Wollams* [1949] 2 KB 388, Cohen LJ said that in deciding whether the claimant to the tenancy was a member of the tenant's family, the test should depend upon the opinion of the 'ordinary man'. However, in *Carega Properties SA v Sharratt* [1979] 1 WLR 928, at p. 932 Viscount Dilhorne observed that the ordinary man approach was 'not likely to exact any more than the judge's personal view', and in *Watson v Lucas* [1980] 1 WLR 1493, at p. 1507, Sir David Cairns expressed his doubt as to the value of the test, admitting that on the facts of the case he had no idea what an ordinary man would say.

It has been said that the term 'family' requires 'a broadly *de facto* familial nexus' which may be 'found and recognised as such by the ordinary man' where the link would be 'strictly familial had there been a marriage, or where the link is through adoption of a minor, *de jure* or *de facto*, or where the link is "step-", or where the link is "in-law" or by marriage' (per Russell LJ in *Ross* v *Collins* [1964] 1 WLR 425). Not surprisingly, it has been held to include brothers and sisters (*Price* v *Gould* (1930) 143 LT 333), and a grandchild (*Collier* v *Stoneman* [1957] 1 WLR 1108).

The courts will take the surrounding circumstances into account and the fact that the claimant is related by blood to the deceased tenant does not necessarily mean that he or she is a member of the tenant's family for the purposes of the Rent Act. *Langdon* v *Horton* [1951] 1 All ER 60 concerned the tenant's two cousins, the three women having lived together for many years. It was not their consanguinity which was regarded as decisive, but the fact that they were living together for reasons of convenience. It was thought that the ordinary man would not regard as members of the same family two middle-aged women who decided to live together, or if one accepted an invitation to live in the house of the other, even if they were cousins and remained together for many years.

In *Jones* v *Whitehill* [1950] 2 KB 204 the tenant's niece by marriage, having acted out of natural love and affection, was held to have assumed the duties and offices peculiarly attributable to members of a tenant's family, by looking after her uncle and aunt for between 18 months and two years until their deaths. Sir Raymond Evershed MR made it clear, however, that not all nephews and nieces by marriage should be regarded as members of the tenant's family. Caring for the tenant, even for a very long time, and thus performing some of the duties associated with family membership does not, in the absence of consanguinity or a relationship by marriage or *de facto* adoption, suffice. In *Ross* v *Collins* [1964] 1 WLR 425 a housekeeper who regarded the tenant as an older relative — partly elder brother, partly father — was held not to be a member of the tenant's family. She had performed all household duties for him, nursed him and arranged his holidays. In return, he had provided her with free accommodation. In *Carega Properties SA* v *Sharratt* [1979] 1 WLR 928, the defendant lived with the tenant for 18 years until her death at the age of 94. He was some 50 years her junior. The tenant had no children of her own and at one stage had wanted to call the defendant her son. Since his mother was still alive, they reached a compromise: he called the tenant 'Aunt Nora' and she called him 'Bunny'. They were not related in any way. The judge at first instance described their relationship as 'sensitive, loving, intellectual and platonic'. Through their mutual devotion, he concluded, they had achieved 'what must surely be regarded in a popular sense, and in common sense, as a familial nexus'. The Court of Appeal and the House of Lords thought differently. 'The line must be drawn somewhere', warned Browne LJ in the Court of Appeal (echoing the sentiments of Asquith LJ in *Gammans* v *Ekins* [1950] 2 All ER 140, at p. 141). If the relationship between the deceased tenant and the defendant were held to constitute a family it would be 'difficult, if not impossible, to exclude the cases ... of two old cronies sharing a house'. In rejecting the defendant's claim, the House of Lords made it clear that the only *de facto* relationships which were recognised for succession purposes were the 'common law' spouse and the 'parent/child' relationship where the child had joined the tenant's household at a young age but had never been legally adopted. Accordingly, in *Sefton Holdings Ltd* v *Cairns* [1988] 14 EG 58 the claimant was unsuccessful despite having lived with the tenant's family for 45 years and having been treated as a daughter. It was significant that she had moved in with the tenant's family at the age of 23.

### 14.2.3 Same-sex partners

*Fitzpatrick* v *Sterling Housing Association Ltd* [1997] 4 All ER 991 was the first case to consider the question of whether the homosexual partner of a protected tenant lived 'with the original tenant as his or her wife or husband' or was 'a member of the tenant's family' for the purposes of the Rent Act 1977, although the issue had already been raised in relation to a secure tenancy in the public sector (*Harrogate BC* v *Simpson* (1984) 17 HLR 205; see **14.4.2**). In *Fitzpatrick* v *Sterling Housing Association Ltd*, the tenant and his partner, Mr Fitzpatrick, lived together in a permanent and stable homosexual relationship for 18 years until the tenant's death.

In the Court of Appeal, Waite LJ (delivering the majority judgment) said there would be no doubt about the case at all if 'endurance, stability, interdependence and devotion were the sole hallmarks of family membership'. Mr Fitzpatrick and the tenant were 'devoted and faithful, giving each other mutual help and support in a life which shared many of the highest qualities to be found in heterosexual attachments, married or unmarried'. To interpret the statute in such a way that allowed all sexual partners, whether of the same or opposite sex, to succeed to tenancies protected by the Rent Acts would be consistent not only with social justice but also with 'the respect accorded by modern society to those of the same sex who undertake a permanent commitment to a shared life'.

However, problems would flow from the extension of succession rights to same-sex partners in a sexually based relationship. Would it then be right to continue to exclude platonic friends? If friends were to be included, how could the stability and permanence of their household be defined? There was also the question of fairness to home-owners whose rights to possession of their property would be more deeply invaded by an enlargement of the class of potential successors to rent-controlled tenancies. Reconciling these competing social priorities might in the end require a political judgment and was a task better suited to the legislative function of Parliament than to the interpretative role of the courts.

### 14.2.4 Death of the first successor before 15 January 1989

It will be recalled that where the original tenant died before 15 January 1989, the tenant's spouse or a member of the tenant's family (who satisfied the residence requirements) became a statutory tenant by way of succession. If, by the time of the first successor's death, he or she was still a statutory tenant, the tenancy devolved to the first successor's spouse or a member of his or her family (who satisfied the residence requirements). On the death of the second successor (whenever it occurs), the statutory tenancy comes to an end, and the landlord is entitled to recover possession.

A statutory tenant by succession is protected by the Rent Act 1977 'if and so long as he [or she] occupies the dwelling-house as his or her residence' (s. 2(1)(a)).

### 14.2.5  Death of the first successor on or after 15 January 1989

Where the first successor was a statutory tenant by way of succession, a further succession is possible but the conditions to be satisfied are stricter than those which apply to deaths before the 1988 Act came into force. The second successor must be a member of the original tenant's family *and* a member of the first successor's family *and* he or she must have resided with the first successor in the dwelling-house for a period of at least two years immediately before the first successor's death. The second successor takes as an assured periodic tenant. These rules are designed to deal with the situation where the claimant is the child of the original tenant and the first successor.

There can be no second succession where the first successor was a member of the tenant's family who succeeded to an assured periodic tenancy. The landlord may recover possession under Ground 7 of the Housing Act 1988 where an assured periodic tenancy devolves under the will or intestacy of the tenant.

In the event of there being more than one eligible claimant, the county court can decide who becomes the statutory tenant if the parties themselves fail to agree (s. 2(1)(b); sch. 1, Part I, paras. 2, 3, Rent Act 1977). In *Dealex Properties Ltd v Brooks* [1966] 1 QB 542, it was held, *per curiam*, that a statutory tenancy cannot be transmitted to a number of persons jointly, but only to one person who fulfils the necessary qualifications.

## 14.3  SUCCESSION UNDER THE HOUSING ACT 1988

### 14.3.1  Introduction

The Housing Act 1988 permits one succession to an assured tenancy and that to the tenant's spouse only. As stated in **Chapter 3**, all new private sector lettings are now effected by assured shorthold tenancies unless steps are taken expressly to create an assured tenancy. Since an assured shorthold tenancy can be brought to an end by two months' notice, the issue of succession becomes academic. All in all, the aim of establishing a measure of security sufficient to encourage and support the formation of a family by the tenant has all but disappeared for the vast majority of Housing Act tenants in the private rented sector. However, most housing association tenants are assured tenants and they, therefore, are the real beneficiaries of the succession provisions of the Housing Act 1988.

### 14.3.2  Fixed-term assured tenancies

Unlike the Rent Act 1977, the Housing Act 1988 makes no special provision for succession to fixed-term tenancies. When a fixed-term assured tenant dies, the remainder of the term will pass to whoever is entitled under the tenant's will or on intestacy. That person will become the assured tenant provided that he or she satisfies the requirements of an assured tenancy, e.g. he or she occupies the dwelling-house as his or her only or principal home. If not, the tenancy will cease to be assured and the landlord may recover possession at the end of the term.

### 14.3.3 Periodic assured tenancies (contractual or statutory)

Under the general law, the tenancy will pass under the tenant's will or on intestacy but, in order to prevent the tenancy continuing indefinitely, Ground 7 provides a mandatory ground for succession on the death of a periodic assured tenant. The only exception is to be found in s. 17 which prevails over any devolution under the tenant's will or intestacy. It provides for a statutory transfer of the tenancy to a surviving spouse who, immediately before the tenant's death, was 'occupying the dwelling-house as his or her only or principal home'. The right is limited to sole tenants. In the case of a joint tenancy, the survivor is treated as a successor, so that there can be no further succession on his or her death (s. 17(2)). Section 17(4) extends succession rights to 'a person who was living with the tenant as his or her wife or husband'. If more than one person fulfils the condition relating to the spouse in occupation in s. 17(1) they may agree, or if they do not agree the court may decide, who is to be treated as the spouse. As with Rent Act tenancies, a joint succession is not possible. Only one succession is permitted under s. 17.

## 14.4   SUCCESSION TO SECURE TENANCIES

### 14.4.1   General principles

Limited rights of succession exist on the death of a tenant who is not a 'successor'. By s. 88, the tenant is a successor where:

(a)   the tenancy vested in the tenant by virtue of s. 89 (succession to a periodic tenancy); or

(b)   the tenant was a joint tenant and has become a sole tenant; or

(c)   the tenancy arose by virtue of s. 86 (periodic tenancy arising on the ending of a term certain) and the first tenancy there mentioned was granted to another person or jointly to him or her and another person; or

(d)   he or she became the tenant by virtue of an assignment under s. 92 and was a succesor in relation to the tenancy which he or she assigned. If the assignment was made in pursuance of an order made under:

(i)    s. 23A or 24, Matrimonial Causes Act 1973;

(ii)   s. 17(1), Matrimonial and Family Proceedings Act 1984; or

(iii)  sch. 1, para. 1, Children Act 1989;

the tenant is a successor only if the other party to the marriage was a successor;

(e)   the tenancy vested in the tenant on the death of the previous tenant; or

(f)   the tenancy was previously an introductory tenancy and the tenant was a successor to the introductory tenancy.

### 14.4.2   Who is entitled to succeed?

Under s. 87, Housing Act 1985, the successor must fulfil two conditions:

(a)   the dwelling-house must have been his or her 'only or principal home at the time of the tenant's death'; and

(b)   the successor is *either*;

(i)   the tenant's spouse; *or*

(ii)   is another member of the tenant's family and has resided with the tenant throughout the period of 12 months ending with the tenant's death.

'Member of the tenant's family' is defined by s. 113, Housing Act 1985 to include those who 'live together as husband and wife', and those who are the parents, grandparents, children, grandchildren, brothers, sisters, uncles, aunts, nephews and nieces of the deceased. Relationships by marriage are treated as relationships by blood, the half-blood as the whole, step-children as children and illegitimate children as legitimate children of their mothers and reputed fathers.

The county court recently declined to follow the first instance decision in *Reading BC* v *Isley* [1981] CLY 1323 that members of the tenant's family include children whom the tenant has fostered throughout their childhood and has always treated as his or her natural children. It was pointed out that s. 113(1) and (2) define exhaustively the relationships which can qualify and it was not the intention of Parliament to include a foster child (*Hereford City Council* v *O'Callaghan* [1996] CLY 3831).

The category of those 'living together as husband and wife' does not include same sex partners. In *Harrogate BC* v *Simpson* (1985) 17 HLR 205, 'the essential characteristic of living together as husband and wife, ' said Ewbank J (at p. 210), 'is that there should be a man and a woman and that they should be living together in the same household'. It did not suffice that the tenant and the claimant (a lesbian couple who had lived together for three years), had regarded and described themselves as husband and wife, nor that they had behaved in some ways as though they were, the tenant being the masculine partner who wore men's clothing and the claimant being 'the female counterpart'. During the passage of the Housing Act 1996 through Parliament, an attempt to expand the definition of wife or husband to include same-sex partners was overturned on the Third Reading in the House of Commons. However, guidance has been issued to local authorities requiring them to grant joint tenancies to same-sex partners so that the rule of survivorship operates on the death of one of the joint tenants.

### 14.4.3   Periodic tenancies

Succession to periodic tenancies is governed by s. 89, Housing Act 1985. Where more than one person is qualified to succeed, the tenant's spouse is to be preferred to another family member. Where two or more other members of the tenant's family qualify and cannot agree between themselves, the successor is to be selected by the landlord (s. 89(2)(b)).

If there is no person qualifed to succeed to the tenant, the tenancy will be disposed of under the terms of the tenant's will or according to the intestacy rules. It ceases to be a secure tenancy unless the the vesting or disposal of the tenancy is in pursuance of an order made under:

(a)   s. 24, Matrimonial Causes Act 1973 (property adjustment orders in connection with matrimonial proceedings);

(b)   s. 17(1), Matrimonial and Family Proceedings Act 1984 (property adjustment orders after overseas divorce); or

(c)   sch. 1, para. 1, Children Act 1989 (orders for financial relief against parents).

### 14.4.4   Fixed-term tenancies

A fixed-term tenancy will be disposed of under the terms of the tenant's will or according to the intestacy rules. It will cease to be secure unless:

(a)   the vesting or disposal of the tenancy is in pursuance of an order made under:

(i)   s. 24, Matrimonial Causes Act 1973 (property adjustment orders in connection with matrimonial proceedings);

(ii)   s. 17(1), Matrimonial and Family Proceedings Act 1984 (property adjustment orders after overseas divorce); or

(iii)   sch. 1, para. 1, Children Act 1989 (orders for financial relief against parents); or

(b)   the vesting or disposal is to a person qualified to succeed the tenant (s. 90(3), Housing Act 1985).

## 14.5   SUCCESSION TO INTRODUCTORY TENANCIES

Section 131, Housing Act1996 provides that a person is qualified to succeed to a tenancy on the death of an introductory tenant if that person occupies the tenant's house as his or her only or principal home at the time of the tenant's death and was either the tenant's spouse or another member of the tenant's family and has resided with the tenant throughout the 12 months prior to the tenant's death. If the tenant who has died was a successor, no statutory succession can take place. Section 132 sets out the circumstances in which a tenant is himself or herself a successor. Section 133 provides for the succession to an introductory tenancy. Where more than one person is qualified to succeed, the tenant's spouse is to be preferred to another family member. Where there is no agreement between two or more other members of the tenant's family, the successor is to be selected by the landlord. An introductory tenancy comes to an end where there is no person qualified to succeed.

## 14.6  RESIDENCE WITH THE TENANT

As has already been pointed out, a member of the tenant's family who is claiming to succeed to what was originally a tenancy regulated under the Rent Act, must have been 'residing with' the tenant for two years immediately before the tenant's death. In the case of succession to a secure or introductory tenancy, the tenant's spouse or a member of the tenant's family must have been 'residing with the tenant throughout the period of 12 months ending with the tenant's death'. The question arises, therefore, as to what is meant by 'residing with' the tenant.

In *Edmunds v Jones* [1957] 1 WLR 1118 the tenant had sub-let two rooms in the house to her daughter and the two of them shared a kitchen. It was held that the words 'residing with' must be given their ordinary popular meaning. The person claiming to succeed to the tenancy must have lived in, and shared for living purposes, the whole of the premises to which he or she claimed to have succeeded. Since the daughter had no right to go into any part of the house beyond the confines of her own tenancy and the kitchen, she could not be said to have been residing with her mother at the time of her mother's death.

In *Collier v Stoneman* [1957] 1 WLR 1108 the plaintiff's grandmother was the statutory tenant of a flat consisting of two rooms and a kitchen. One room was occupied by the tenant as her bedroom and other by the plaintiff and her husband. They all shared the kitchen. The tenant kept very much to her own room and did most of her own shopping and cooking, eating only occasionally with the plaintiff and her husband in the kitchen. The Court of Appeal held that the plaintiff (and her husband) were residing with the grandmother up to the date of her death. *Edmunds v Jones* was distinguished. In that case, the daughter was legally entitled to exclusive posession of the two rooms comprised in her subtenancy; she could not be said to be residing in them with her mother for she was, in fact, residing in them to the exclusion of her mother. In *Collier*, the fact that the parties led largely independent lives was irrelevant. It might have been otherwise if they had lived 'wholly separate lives without mutual meetings or domestic co-operation' (per Romer LJ at p. 1118).

In *Foreman v Beagley* [1969] 1 WLR 1387 the tenant spent the last three years of her life in hospital. Her son came to the flat to air the premises and he lived there for the year immediately preceding her death. The Court of Appeal held he had not been 'residing with' her as he had only moved in as caretaker without any indication of establishing a joint household. The phrase 'residing with' requires some factual community of family living and companionship. There had never been any 'community of living' with his mother. Had he lived in the flat with her before her illness and had continued to live there during her absence, the residence requirement would probably have been satisfied.

*Foreman* v *Beagley* was distinguished in *Hedgedale Ltd* v *Hands* (1991) 23 HLR 158 in which a young man moved into his grandmother's flat in order to help care for her. Soon afterwards, she broke her arm and went to stay with her daughter. After about three months, she returned to the flat where she lived with her grandson for the remaining five months of her life. The young man was held to have resided with her for the requisite period, despite her absence, since he had at all material times the intention to form a family unit with her in the flat.

The issue of residence with the deceased tenant becomes more problematic where the claimant has a home elsewhere. Of course, the Rent Acts recognise that a person may have two homes but it is only rarely that a claimant with his or her own home will be successful. In *Morgan* v *Murch* [1970] 1 WLR 778, a man left his wife and children in a council house to live with his mother. On her death, six-and-a-half months later, the son was held entitled to remain as a successor since he had made his home with her. He had not attempted any reconciliation with his wife, and there was no immediate prospect of his returning to the matrimonial home. In *Swanbrae* v *Elliott* (1987) 19 HLR 87, the claimant slept three or four nights a week at the home of her sick mother and spent the other nights in her own house where her adult son continued to live. It was held that she was not residing with her mother. The fact that she had a permanent home of her own was not necessarily fatal to her claim but made it more difficult for her to satisfy the test of residence with her mother. She had move in for a limited time and for a limited purpose, i.e. to stay with her mother for so long as was necessary. In *Hildebrand* v *Moon* (1989) 37 EG 123, a woman moved back to nurse her sick mother. She kept her own flat on but contemplated selling it a few months before her mother's death. The Court of Appeal held that, in contrast to the daughter in *Swanbrae* v *Elliott* she had made her home with her mother and was entitled, therefore, to succeed to her statutory tenancy.

The Rent Act 1977 Act did not originally specify whether the whole of the qualifying period of residence with the tenant must have taken place in the dwelling-house to which succession was claimed, provided that they had lived together for the required six-month period. However, the amendments made by the Housing Act 1988 provide that the two-year period of residence must have been 'in the dwelling-house' (sch. 4, Housing Act 1988). Where succession to a secure tenancy (and, presumably an introductory tenancy) is involved, the period of residence does not need to be in the same property throughout the relevant period (*Waltham Forest LBC* v *Thomas* [1992] 2 AC 198).

## References

Berkovits, B., 'The Family and the Rent Acts: Reflections on Law and Policy', *Journal of Social Welfare Law*, 1981, pp. 83–100.

Honore, T., *The Quest for Security: Employees, Tenants, Wives*, London: Stevens, 1982.

Zuckerman, A.A.Section , 'Formality and the Family — Reform or Status Quo', *Law Quarterly Review*, 1980, vol. 96, p. 248 (esp. pp. 260–271).

# FIFTEEN

## The responsibility for repairs

### 15.1  INTRODUCTION

Many properties in the private rented sector were built around the beginning of the century and now require extensive and frequent repairs. In the public sector, a significant number of relatively modern properties suffer problems as a result of poor design, unproven building techniques and bad workmanship. The proportion of council housing in a sub-standard condition has increased since the 'right to buy' provisions introduced in 1980 creamed off the better quality properties into owner-occupation. Around one in twenty homes have severe problems with condensation or mould, and one in a hundred suffer seriously from damp. Around 500,000 need more than £2,000 of repairs (Department of the Environment, 1995: 34). Not surprisingly, given the sums of money which may be involved, liability for the repair and maintenance of rented property provides a rich source of disputes between landlords and tenants.

At common law, no covenant is implied by the landlord of an unfurnished house or flat that it is, or will be, reasonably fit for habitation or that the landlord will carry out any repairs during the course of the tenancy. In the absence of express agreement, the landlord is not liable to the tenant for defects in the demised premises which make the premises dangerous or unfit for occupation, nor for personal injury to the tenant caused by such defects even though the landlord knows of their existence (*Lane* v *Cox* [1897] 1 QB 415). There is no duty to warn the tenant of them. There may be situations in which there is no repairing obligation imposed either expressly or impliedly on anyone in relation to a lease (*Demetriou* v *Robert Andrews (Estate Agencies) Ltd* (1990) 62 P & CR 536, at pp. 544–5, per Stuart Smith LJ), resulting in deadlock between the parties. The principle of *caveat emptor* ('let the buyer beware') applies and it is up to the prospective tenant to inspect the property, to satisfy himself or herself as to its condition and — despite the inequality of bargaining power between landlords and the majority of tenants — to negotiate an appropriate contract. By contrast, Scottish law implies an obligation on the landlord of an urban house (but not a farmhouse) to give the tenant a habitable house and to maintain it in that condition (*Cameron* v *Young* [1908] AC 176) and similar law is implied in certain states of the USA.

There are a number of instances where a repairing obligation or an obligation as to fitness is either implied against a landlord or imposed by statute. Local authorities too play an important role in ensuring that residential property is in a habitable condition. The oft-quoted statement that 'fraud apart, there is no law against letting a tumble-down house' (*Robbins* v *Jones* (1863) 15 CB(NS) 221, at p. 240) is subject to important exceptions. However, the law has developed in a haphazard and piecemeal fashion and the Law Commission have recently recommended extensive reform by the enactment of a new statute, on the ground that there is 'a public interest in seeing that there is an adequate stock of usable rented property, properly maintained and repaired . . . and that residential property should be reasonably fit to live in' (Law Commission, 1996: para. 1.27).

## 15.2  EXPRESS OBLIGATIONS

Usually the parties will make express provision as regards liability for repairs. A long lease normally contains covenants by the tenant to keep the demised premises in repair during the term of the lease and to repair defects within a specified time of being requested by the landlord to do so. These will generally be coupled with a covenant by the tenant to permit the landlord or the landlord's agents to enter and view the state of repair. 'Clear' leases are commonly used by private landlords where the premises are let to several tenants. The landlord covenants for the repair of the structure, exterior and common parts but the individual tenants bear all the costs of repairing and maintaining by way of service charges so that the rent reaches the landlord clear of all expenses and overheads. The tenant's express covenant for repair will normally extend only to the inside of the premises. Otherwise landlords usually enter into express repairing covenants only where short leases are granted.

## 15.3  THE MEANING OF 'REPAIR'

### 15.3.1  The distinction between repair, renewal and improvement

Repair 'connotes the idea of making good damage so as to leave the subject as far as possible as though it had not been damaged' (per Atkin LJ in *Anstruther-Gough-Calthorpe* v *McOscar* [1924] 1 KB 716, at p. 734) but it may also involve taking steps so as to prevent damage from occurring, or to prevent recurrence where damage has already occurred (*Stent* v *Monmouth DC* (1987) 19 HLR 269).

In *McDougall* v *Easington DC* (1989) 58 P & CR 193, the Court of Appeal identified three tests which the courts have used in determining whether the works required consitute repair or something more:

(a)   whether the alterations went to the whole or substantially the whole of the structure or only to a subsidiary part;

(b)   whether the effect of the alterations was to produce a building of a wholly different character than that which had been let; and

(c)   the cost of the works in relation to the previous value of the building and their effect on the value and lifespan of the building.

These tests may be applied separately or concurrently, but must all be approached in the light of 'the nature and age of the premises, their condition when the tenant went into occupation, and the other express terms of the tenancy'.

The traditional approach has been to distinguish between a repair on the one hand and a renewal or an improvement on the other. In *Lurcott* v *Wakely & Wheeler* [1911] 1 KB 905, at p. 924 Buckley LJ described repair as 'the resoration by renewal or replacement of subsidiary parts of a whole'. Renewal, he said, is 'the reconstruction of the entirety, meaning by entirety not necessarily the whole but substantially the whole subject-matter under discussion'. Repair always involves the renewal of subsidiary parts but if a house is in such poor condition that substantially the whole of it needs to be renewed, the works cannot properly be described as 'repairs'. Improvement involves rectifying defects by substituting something qualitatively different from, and better than, the original.

### 15.3.2   The relative costs

A new approach was adopted in *Ravenseft Properties Ltd* v *Davstone (Holdings) Ltd* [1980] QB 12, in which Forbes J said (pp. 21–22) that whether or not the works amount to repair is always a question of degree, bearing in mind the cost of the disputed work relative to the value or cost of the whole premises. This test was adopted and applied in *Elmcroft Developments Ltd* v *Tankersley-Sawyer* (1984) 15 HLR 63 in which the replacement of a defective damp-proof course in a flat in a high-class fashionable residential area of London was held to constitute repair. By contrast, in *Wainwright* v *Leeds City Council* (1984) 270 EG 1289 (in which *Ravenseft* was not cited), it was held that the insertion of a damp-proof course, where none had existed before, in a run-down back-to-back terraced house in a poor part of Leeds would involve giving back something wholly different from that demised, and would not, therefore, be a repair.

### 15.3.3   Inherent defects

Poor housing conditions are often the outcome of inherent defects brought about by design faults, bad workmanship, etc. Inherent defects fall into two categories: those which cause damage to the demised premises and those which do not. In the former case, repairs may be necessary to put the matter right, as where condensation results in damage to plaster-work, or causes window frames to rot, or where rising damp makes it necessary to repoint a basement wall (*Pembery* v *Lamdin* [1940] 2 All ER 434, or a slate damp-proof course put in too low leads to rising damp (*Elmcroft* v *Tankersley-Sawyer*, ibid.). In the latter case, the inherent defect may have caused the property to have become uninhabitable but a repairing covenant has no application since no damage has been done. In *Quick* v *Taff-Ely BC* [1985] 3 All ER 321, specific performance was sought of the local authority landlord's repairing obligation under what is now s. 11, Landlord and Tenant Act 1985. The house had single-glazed metal-framed windows and a central-heating system based on warm air ducts. Severe condensation — caused largely by lack of insulation around the concrete window lintels, and sweating from the windows — made the house virtually unusable during the winter and rotted the tenant's furniture and furnishings. However, the Court of Appeal held, reluctantly, that the landlord was not bound to replace the metal windows nor to insulate the lintels; although they were inherently defective, neither item was damaged or in want of repair, and had caused no damage to the demised premises. The key factor, said Dillon LJ, 'is that disrepair is related to the physical condition of whatever has to be repaired, and not to questions of lack of amenity or inefficiency'. Had the authority failed in its appeal it would have cost £9 million to rectify similar defects in all its properties.

## 15.4   THE STANDARD OF REPAIR

The standard of repair must be sufficient to enable the premises to be used not only with safety but with reasonable (although not excessive) comfort by the appropriate class of persons (*Belcher* v *M'Intosh* (1839) 2 Mood & R 186 at p. 189). It is such 'as having regard to the age, character and locality of the house, would make it reasonably fit for the occupation of a reasonably minded tenant of the class likely to take it' (per Lopes LJ in *Proudfoot* v *Hart* (1890) 25 QBD 42, 55). As Lord Esher explained in *Proudfoot* v *Hart*, a 200-year-old house cannot reasonably be expected to be in the same condition as a house recently built, and the character of the house is relevant in that the class of repair appropriate to a palace would be inappropriate to a cottage. As regards locality, the state of repair necessary for a house in Grosvenor Square would be totally different from that necessary for a house in Spitalfields.

  The standard of repair is judged by the condition of the property at the commencement of the lease and is not raised by any improvement in its tenants or its neighbourhood, nor lowered by their deterioration (*Anstruther-Gough-Calthorpe* v *McOscar* [1924] 1 KB 716).

## 15.5   LANDLORDS' CONTRACTUAL OBLIGATIONS IMPOSED BY COMMON LAW

### 15.5.1   Letting of furnished accommodation

It is an implied condition of a letting of furnished accommodation that it will be reasonably fit for habitation when the tenancy begins. If this condition is not fulfilled, the tenant may treat the contract as repudiated and quit the premises without any liability for rent. Alternatively, the tenant may sue the landlord for breach of contract.

The covenant imposes no obligation upon the landlord to *keep* the premises fit for human habitation (*Sarson v Roberts* [1895] 2 QB 395). The landlord will be liable, however, if the premises were unfit for human habitation at the start of the tenancy but their lack of fitness did not become apparent until later on. Examples of defects which have been held to render premises unfit for habitation in this context include infestation by bugs (*Smith v Marrable* (1843) 11 N & W 5), defective drains (*Sarson v Roberts*, ibid.), and recent occupation by a person with an infectious disease (*Collins v Hopkins* [1923] 2 KB 617). Note, however, that the obligation is confined to fitness for habitation and that the implied term does not require the landlord to ensure that the premises are in structural repair when let.

### 15.5.2    Obligation to repair common or essential parts

Where the tenancy is of a dwelling-house which forms only part of a building and is granted on or after 15 January 1989 for a term of less than seven years, a term will be implied that the landlord will keep in repair the structure and exterior of any part of the building in which the landlord has an estate or interest (s. 11(1A), Housing Act 1985, as supplemented by s. 116(1), Housing Act 1988). Thus the landlord will generally be under a statutory duty to keep in repair the structure and exterior (including the common parts) of a block of flats.

For those tenants whose tenancies were granted before 15 January 1989, other terms may be implied into the contract unless they are excluded by express terms to the contrary.

Where the landlord retains part of a building, maintenance of which in proper repair is necessary for the protection of the demised premises or the tenant's safe enjoyment of them, there is implied an obligation on the landlord to take reasonable care to maintain the retained parts so as to not to cause damage to the tenant or the premises let. Thus a landlord who retains control of the roof and gutters is obliged to repair them so as to prevent damp getting into the flat (*Cockburn v Smith* [1924] 2 KB 119).

Where the landlord retains control of essential means of access to the demised premises, the insertion of a term may be necessary to give business efficacy to the contract. In *Liverpool City Council v Irwin* [1976] 2 All ER 39, the House of Lords held that the local authority landlord was under a contractual obligation to take reasonable care to maintain lifts, stairways and rubbish chutes serving upper-storey lettings in a 15-storey high-rise block of flats. Their Lordships emphasised that this was not an absolute obligation. The council was held to have discharged its obligation; it had spent large sums of money to repair the lifts, stairs, etc. and the subsequent — almost immediate — disrepair was due to vandalism. The court cannot imply terms it considers reasonable; it is a question of what is necessary so that failure to imply the term will render the contract 'futile, inefficacious and absurd' (per Lord Salmon at p. 51). No contractual obligation could be implied therefore where the lease itself provided for a perfectly workable scheme of repairs (*Duke of Westminster* v *Guild* [1984] 3 All ER 144).

Because the common parts are deemed to be within the landlord's control, the tenant is not required to give notice of disrepair before the obligation to repair arises.

### 15.5.3   Correlative obligations

In some circumstances, the courts may imply an obligation on the landlord to match a correlative obligation expressly imposed on the tenant (*Duke of Westminster* v *Guild* [1985] QB 688, p. 697). Thus in *Barrett* v *Lounova (1982) Ltd* [1989] 1 All ER 351, the lease provided that the tenant would 'carry out all inside repairs . . . and at the expiration of the tenancy . . . leave the inside of the said premises and fixtures in good repair order and condition. . . '. Neither party was under an express duty to keep the outside of the property in repair. Water penetration had damaged internal plasterwork and timbers. It was obvious, said Kerr LJ, that sooner or later the covenant imposed on the tenant (which was clearly intended to be enforceable throughout the tenancy) could no longer be complied with unless the outside has been kept in repair. In his view it was therefore necessary, as a matter of business efficacy to make the agreement workable, that an obligation to keep the outside in repair must be imposed on someone. And that someone, he said, was clearly the landlord.

### 15.5.4   Houses in the course of construction

In a lease of a house which is still in the course of construction, there is implied a warranty that it will be built with proper materials in a workmanlike manner and fit for human habitation when completed (*Perry* v *Sharon Development Co. Ltd* [1937] 4 All ER 390). This is because the tenant is in no position to check the physical state of the premises in accordance with the principle of *caveat emptor*.

## 15.6   LANDLORDS' CONTRACTUAL OBLIGATIONS IMPOSED BY STATUTE

In general, an express covenant will override or displace an implied one. This is particularly so with implied covenants which derive from case law. However, some of the statutory obligations imposed upon landlords cannot be contracted out of and will apply despite any provision to the contrary.

### 15.6.1   Premises let at a low rent

Regardless of any express stipulation to the contrary, s. 8, Landlord and Tenant Act 1985 implies in certain contracts for the letting of a house:

    (a)   a condition that at the commencement of the tenancy the house is fit for human habitation; and
    (b)   an undertaking that the landlord will keep it so during the tenancy.

As well as the house, the duty embraces 'any yard, garden, outhouse and appurtenances belonging to the house or usually enjoyed with it' (s. 8(6)). However, there are important qualifications to this provision:

(a)   It applies only to houses let at very low rent (£80 per annum in London and £52 elsewhere). The provision was first included in the Housing of the Working Classes Act 1885 to deal with insanitary and overcrowded housing and appears to have encompassed a substantial proportion of leased accommodation. Parliament's failure to increase these rent levels (which have remained unchanged since 1957) is explained by a number of factors: the extension of local authority housing, the decline in the private rented sector, the rise in owner-occupation, and the introduction of the implied repairing obligation in 1961 of what is now s. 11, Landlord and Tenant Act 1985, all of which appeared to make the implied term redundant and out-dated (Law Commission, 1996: para. 4.13). There can be very few lettings, if any, to which s. 8 applies. It was not available to the tenant in *Quick* v *Taff Ely BC* [1985] 3 All ER 321, even though he was unemployed and lived in a small council house. If the upper levels for the implied obligation of fitness were to be restored to a position equivalent to those which applied in 1957, they would be well over £3,000 per annum (Law Commission, 1996: para. 4.12).

(b)   Section 8 does not apply if the house is let for a term of not less than three years upon the terms that the tenant puts it into a condition reasonably fit for human habitation, and the lease is not determinable by either party within three years.

(c)   The landlord's obligation under s. 8 is restricted to cases where the house is capable of being rendered fit for habitation at a reasonable expense (*Buswell* v *Goodwin* [1971] 1 All ER 418).

Section 10 provides that in determining whether a house is unfit for human habitation regard should be had to repair, stability, freedom from damp, internal arrangement, natural lighting, ventilation, water supply, drainage and sanitary facilities, facilities for the preparation and cooking of food, and the disposal of waste water. The test is whether the state of the house is such that by ordinary user the occupier might be injured in limb or in health (*Morgan* v *Liverpool Corporation* [1927] 2 KB 131). In *Summers* v *Salford Corporation* [1943] AC 283, a broken sashcord in the only window of one bedroom was held to be a breach of the undertaking but in *Stanton* v *Southwick* [1920] 2 KB 642 an invasion of the house by rats did not constitute a breach because liability arises only in relation to the defects *within* the premises let to the tenant.

The landlord's obligation is limited to defects of which he or she has notice and the landlord may, on giving 24 hours' notice in writing to the occupier, enter to view the condition of the premises (s. 8(2)). Breach of the condition makes the lease voidable. Breach of the undertaking gives rise only to a claim to damages or specific performance.

### 15.6.2   Sections 11–16, Landlord and Tenant Act 1985

The implied covenant to repair now contained in s. 11, Landlord and Tenant Act 1985 was first enacted in 1961:

(a)   to stop unscrupulous landlords from imposing unreasonable repairing obligations on tenants under short leases; and

(b)   for public policy reasons, to make someone responsible for getting repairs done.

(Law Commission, 1996: para. 5.11.) It is frequently invoked and is particularly useful to local authority tenants who cannot utilise the repair notice procedure under the Housing Act 1985, *but* tenants have found it 'exceptionally difficult' to use s. 11 to 'counter under-funded or inadequate council repairs programmes' (Stewart, 1996: 153). Landlord of secure tenants are required to publish information about the effect of ss. 11 to 16 (s. 104, Housing Act 1985).

Section 11 imposes repairing obligations on landlords of dwelling-houses where the lease was granted after 24 October 1961 and is for a term of less than seven years. This includes periodic tenancies. The term 'dwelling-house' includes 'a building or part of a building' (s. 16(b)). Section 11 can apply to a flat or bedsit, therefore, as well as a whole house.

Section 11(1) implies a covenant by the landlord:

(a)   to keep in repair the structure and exterior of the dwelling-house (including drains, gutters and external pipes); and

(b)   to keep in repair and proper working order the installations in the dwelling-house for the supply of water, gas and electricity and for sanitation (including basins, sinks, baths and sanitary conveniences but not, except as aforesaid, fixtures, fittings and appliances for making use of the supply of water, gas or electricity); and

(c)   to keep in repair and proper working order the installations in the dwelling-house for space heating and heating water.

The landlord's obligation to effect repairs carries with it an obligation to make good any consequential damage to decorations (*Bradley* v *Chorley BC* (1985) 17 HLR 305).

The landlord is not liable (s. 11(2)):

(a)   for repairs attributable to the tenant's failure to use the premises in a tenant-like manner;

(b)   to rebuild, or reinstate the premises as a result of damage by fire, tempest, flood or other inevitable accident;

(c)   to repair or maintain any tenant's fixtures.

**15.6.2.1  To 'keep in repair'**   A covenant to 'keep in repair' obliges the covenantor:

(a)   to put the premises into repair at the outset (if necessary); and

(b)   to keep the premises in repair at all times during the currency of the tenancy (*Luxmore* v *Robson* (1818) 1 B & Ald 584).

Liability arises as soon as the premises fall into disrepair and the covenantee can compel repair work to be done during the course of the tenancy.

**15.6.2.2  Structure and exterior**  The 'structure' consists of 'those elements of the overall dwelling-house which give it its essential appearance, stability and shape'. It does not extend to 'the many and various ways in which the dwelling-house will be fitted out, equipped and decorated and generally made to be habitable' (per Mr Recorder Thayne Forbes QC in *Irvine v Moran* [1991] 1 EGLR 262 at p. 262).

The 'exterior' has been held to include the dividing wall between a house and the one adjoining it (*Green v Eales* (1841) 2 QB 225), and steps and a flagstone path leading to, and demised with, the house (*Brown v Liverpool Corporation* [1969] 3 All ER 1345) but not paving slabs in the back yard of a house or a passageway to the rear of the property which was not included in the lease (*Hopwood v Cannock Chase DC* [1975] 1 All ER 796). 'Structure and exterior' also includes windows (*Irvine v Moran*, ibid.).

**15.6.2.3  Installations**  The obligation to keep installations in proper working order refers to their mechanical condition and may require the landlord to remedy an inherent defect which prevents them from working properly. A landlord was not in breach for failing to lag the pipes so that they burst during a spell of very cold weather (*Wycombe Health Authority v Barnett* (1982) 264 EG 619).

**15.6.2.4  The effect of the Housing Act 1988**  Where the lease was entered into before 15 January 1989, the repairing obligation applies only to the dwelling-house in question. In *Campden Hill Towers v Gardner* [1977] 1 All ER 739, it was held that where the dwelling-house — typically a flat — formed part of a larger building, the obligation to repair the structure and exterior did not apply to the whole building, but only to that of the particular part included in the lease. Thus, the roof of a block of flats would not form part of the structure and exterior of a ground floor flat, but might do as regards a top floor flat (*Douglas-Scott v Scorgie* [1984] 1 WLR 716). The obligation to keep installations in repair and proper working order was limited to the repair of installations within the physical confines of the dwelling. It would not cover the central heating boiler which supplied hot water to all the flats in the block and was located in the basement.

Section 11(1A) (inserted by s. 116, Housing Act 1988) reverses the effect of *Campden Hill Towers v Gardner* (ibid.) so that:

(a)  the obligation to repair the structure and exterior now applies to any part of the building in which the landlord has an estate or interest; and

(b)  the obligation in relation to installations apply to those which directly or indirectly serve the dwelling-house and which either form part of the building in which the landlord has an estate or interest, or are owned by the landlord or are under his or her control.

These extended obligations apply only if the disrepair or failure to maintain affect the tenant's enjoyment of the dwelling-house or any common parts which he or she is entitled to use (s. 11(1B)).

If the necessary work requires access to a part of a building or an installation to which the landlord does not have a sufficient right of access, it is a defence if the landlord can prove that 'he used all reasonable endeavours to obtain such rights as would be adequate to enable him to carry out the works or repairs' (s. 11(3A)). The landlord may, however, be able to obtain an access order under the Access to Neighbouring Land Act 1992.

**15.6.2.5 Standard of repair** In determining the standard of repair required by the landlord's repairing covenant, regard must be had to 'the age, character and prospective life of the dwelling-house and the locality in which it is situated' (s. 11(3)). In taking acount of the property's prospective life, this differs from the standard of repair in *Proudfoot* v *Hart* (1890) 25 QBD 42 and means that a landlord may not be obliged to carry out repairs which do not make economic sense. In *Newham LB* v *Patel* [1978] 13 HLR 77, the tenant spent five years in a house which had been condemned as both unfit for habitation and a statutory nuisance. The Court of Appeal found no breach of s. 11 as the house had been scheduled for redevelopment and carrying out repairs on it would have been a waste of money. Alternatively, the council had charged the tenant only a very low rent because of the property's poor condition and, even if a breach were established, the tenant could not have the benefit both of a low rent and an award of damages.

Liability under s. 11 does not arise unless the landlord has actual notice of the want of repair (see *O'Brien* v *Robinson* [1973] 1 All ER 583) and is only in breach of covenant if, after a reasonable time from being given notice, he or she fails to remedy the defect. The landlord, or a person authorised by the landlord in writing, may view the state of repair of the premises, at reasonable times of the day and on giving 24 hours' written notice (s. 11(6)).

The landlord can only contract out of these obligations with the tenant's consent and the approval of the court (s. 12). Otherwise any repairing covenant by the tenant (including any covenant to put in repair or deliver up in repair, to paint, point or render or to pay money in lieu of repairs by the tenant or on account of repairs by the landlord) is ineffective in so far as it relates to the obligations imposed by s. 11(1) (s. 11(4)).

The landlord who is in breach may be subject to action by the tenant or the local authority.

## 15.7    OBLIGATIONS ARISING IN TORT

### 15.7.1    Nuisance

The habitability of the demised premises may occasionally be affected by a nuisance for which the landlord is liable. However, this will generally be the case only where that nuisance emanates from property retained by the landlord. In *Habinteg Housing Association* v *James* (1994) 27 HLR 299 infestation by cockroaches was finally eliminated after six years following the service of an abatement notice on the landlord housing association under what is now s. 80, Environmental Protection Act 1990. There were no common parts in the block of which the flat in question formed part and no proof that the cockroaches entered the flat from any property controlled by the housing association. The situation was distinguishable from *Sharpe* v *City of Manchester* (1977) 5 HLR 712 in which the tenant successfully sued his landlords for the nuisance caused by an infestation of cockroaches which had come into the flat throught service ducts situated in the common parts of a block of flats.

### 15.7.2   Negligence

At common law, the landlord owes no duty towards the tenant's family or visitors to ensure that the premises are in a safe condition at the time of the letting (*Tredway* v *Machin* (1904) 91 LT 310) or during its currency (*Lane* v *Cox* [1897] 1 QB 415). No liability in negligence arises even where the landlord knows of, or is responsible for, any defect or disrepair in the premises which makes them dangerous or unsafe. As the landlord is liable only for breach of a repairing covenant, those who are not parties to the letting — the tenant's family and visitors — are completely unprotected. While the courts have increasingly imposed liability on the suppliers of goods and services, they have preserved this rule of general immunity in relation to landlords, even though occupiers have been seriously injured or even killed (*Cavalier* v *Pope* [1906] AC 428). The one exception is where a local authority landlord constructs an unfurnished dwelling-house to its own design and specification (*Rimmer* v *Liverpool City Council* [1984] 1 All ER 930).

However, the common law position has been extensively altered by statute. It was s. 4, Occupiers Liability Act 1957 which first imposed on the landlord a tortious duty of care in respect of danger arising from failure to comply with repairing obligations under the lease. This was replaced and significantly extended by the Defective Premises Act 1972.

### 15.7.3   Occupiers' Liability Act 1957

The occupier of premises owes to all lawful visitors the 'common duty of care', i.e., a duty to take such care . . . that visitors will be reasonably safe in using the premises for the purposes for which they were invited or permitted to be there' (s. 2, Occupiers'Liability Act 1957). 'Occupation' in this context focuses on 'control' (*Wheat* v *Lacon* [1966] 1 All ER 582). Thus, the landlord who retains control over any part of the building, e.g. entrance hall, lifts, forecourt or other common parts, will be the occupier for the purposes of the 1957 Act and and will be liable for injury caused by any defects in that part. The landlord who has let the whole of the premises, retaining no control over any part, ceases to be the occupier for the purposes of the 1957 Act but the Defective Premises Act 1972 will then come into play. An owner who grants a licence, rather than a tenancy, and still has the right to do repairs may be regarded as being sufficiently in control for the purposes of the 1957 Act (see, e.g., *Hawkins* v *Coulsdon & Purley UDC* [1954] 1 QB 319, in which the landlord was held liable to a visitor who fell on the defective step to the front door, and *Greene* v *Chelsea BC* [1954] 2 QB 127, in which the defective ceiling fell on the occupier's wife).

The landlord may try to restrict, modify or exclude this statutory duty by agreement, notice or any other means. However, any such exclusion or modification must be shown to be reasonable (ss. 1, 2(1), Unfair Contract (Terms) Act 1977), and any purported exclusion or restriction of liability for death or personal injury will be ineffective (ss. 1, 2(2)). The 1977 Act applies to business liability only and a domestic occupier is perfectly free to modify, restrict or exclude liability for negligence.

### 15.7.4  Section 4, Defective Premises Act 1972

This section imposes a duty of care on the landlord who, under the terms of the tenancy, is under an obligation to the tenant for the maintenance or repair of the premises. The obligation may arise from an express term in the lease or may be implied by statute, e.g. s. 11, Landlord and Tenant Act 1985. The duty encompasses 'all persons who might reasonably be expected to be affected by defects in the state of the premises'. It is a duty to take such care as is reasonable in all the circumstances to see that they are reasonably safe from personal injury or from damage to their property caused by a defect within the repairing obligation. Although s. 4 was primarily intended to protect third parties — members of the tenant's household, visitors, neighbours, passers-by and even trespassers — the duty of care it imposes is also owed to tenants (*Smith* v *Bradford Metropolitan Council* (1982) 44 P & CR 171). It arises if the landlord knows, or ought to have known, of the defect (s. 4(2)) but where the landlord has an express or implied right to enter premises and carry out repairs, the duty of care laid down in s. 4(1) is owed in the same way as if there was an obligation to carry out such work (s. 4(4)).

Significantly, the duty of care under s. 4 arises only where there is some hazard which makes the property unsafe rather than unfit. It does not extend, therefore, to damp in the premises which discolours decorations, leads to the growth of mould, and causes the tenant's children to suffer coughs and colds (see *Sandra Kay McNerny* v *Lambeth London Borough Council* (1988) 21 HLR 188).

## 15.7  TENANTS' OBLIGATIONS

### 15.7.1  Tenant-like user

There is an implied obligation on every tenant to use the premises in a tenant-like manner. According to Denning LJ in *Warren* v *Keen* [1953] 2 All ER 1118, at p. 1121:

. The tenant must take proper care of the place. He must, if he is going away for the winter, turn off the water and empty the boiler. He must clean the chimneys, when necessary, and also the windows. He must unstop the sink when it is blocked by his waste. In short, he must do the little jobs about the place which a reasonable tenant would do.

A tenant from year to year must keep the premises wind and water-tight (*Wedd* v *Porter* [1916] 2 KB 41). In *Wycombe Health Authority* v *Barnett* (1982) 264 EG 619 the tenant was held not to have breached her duty to use the premises in a tenant-like manner in leaving unattended a house with unlagged pipes for two nights during which time the pipes froze and burst.

### 15.7.2 Doctrine of waste

'Waste' is a tort. Technically, it is any act which alters the premises for better or for worse. It is of two main types: voluntary and permissive. Voluntary waste is the commission of any act which alters or destroys the premises, e.g. a failure to make good damage caused by the tenant's lawful removal of fixtures (*Mancetter Developments Ltd* v *Garmanson Ltd and Givertz* [1986] 1 All ER 449). Permissive waste is an omission to take action to prevent damage to the premises, e.g. allowing a house to decay; permitting foundations to rot through failing to clear drains (*Herne* v *Bembow* (1813) 4 Taunt 463. All tenants are liable for voluntary waste. All tenants, apart from weekly tenants, tenants at will and tenants at sufferance, are liable for permissive waste. A defence is available where the tenant can show that his or her use of the premises was reasonable (*Manchester Bonded Warehouse Co.* v *Carr* (1880) 5 CPD 507).

If a tenant commits waste, the landlord may either:

(a)  bring an action for damages; or
(b)  in the case of voluntary waste only, seek an injunction.

An injunction will not be granted in respect of permissive waste as it involves supervising the tenant to ensure that omissions are corrected'. Damages for waste are based on the damage to the value of the reversion, and not the actual cost of making good the damage to the premises (*Whitham* v *Kershaw* (1886) 16 QBD 613). Thus, if the tenant alters the premises by, e.g. building an extension, an action in damages may well fail since it will be difficult to show that the alteration has diminished the value of the reversion. The Law Commission has recommended that the doctrine of waste be abolished.

### References

Department of the Environment, *Our Future Homes: Opportunity, Choice, Responsibility*, Cmnd. 2901, London: HMSO, 1995.

Law Commission, *Landlord and Tenant: Responsibility for State and Condition of Property*, Law Com. No. 238, London: HMSO, 1996.

Madge, N., 'Disrepair Cases', *New Law Journal*, 1998, vol. 148, p. 238.

Stewart, A., *Rethinking Housing Law*, London: Sweet & Maxwell, 1996.

### Further reading

Luba, J., *Repairs: Tenants' Rights*, London: Legal Action Group.

# SIXTEEN

## Remedies for disrepair, overcrowding and houses in multiple occupation

### 16.1  INTRODUCTION

A number of remedies are available to the tenant where the landlord is in breach of a repairing obligation. A lack of resources on the tenant's part makes it likely, however, that he or she is in no position to pursue those remedies. For this reason, the involvement of local authorities in ensuring the maintenance of minimum housing standards is of considerable importance. Overcrowding does not concern disrepair *per se* but it does, of course, impinge on housing conditions and is, in any case, relevant to issues of security of tenure (see **5.5.1**) and homelessness (see **18.4.2.2**). Houses in multiple occupation provide accommodation for a large number of people and often pose a significant fire risk. However, only those aspects of the law relating to houses in multiple occupation which concern 'repair' (from the viewpoint of fitness and over-crowding) are outlined below.

### 16.2  TENANTS' REMEDIES

#### 16.2.1  Damages

The tenant can claim damages whenever the landlord is in breach of a repairing obligation. The measure of damages is:

(a)  the difference in value to the tenant between the house in its unrepaired condition and the house in the condition in which it would be had the obligation been fulfilled; and

(b)  any damage to the tenant's property during that period caused by the landlord's default.

The aim is not to punish the landlord but to put the tenant in the position he or she would have been in had the breach not occurred. Damages may be awarded for the cost of alternative accommodation while the demised property is uninhabitable, reasonable expenditure on redecoration, discomfort, loss of enjoyment and ill-health, the cost of storing furniture while the tenant is in temporary accommodation and the cost of clearing debris and clearing up after repair work has been done (*Calabar Properties v Stitcher* (1983) 268 EG 697, *McGreal v Wake* (1984) 269 EG 1254). In *Chiodi v de Marney* (1988) 41 EG 80, the tenant had been in poor health, had spent much of her time in the property because of unemployment, and had been unable to escape from the effects of damp and cold since all parts of the flat were affected. £5,460 for inconvenience and distress was awarded at a rate of £30 per week over three years even though the registered rent was only £8 per week.

### 16.2.2    Self-help/set-off against rent

If the landlord fails to respond within a reasonable time to notice of the breach, the tenant may carry out the repairs and withhold rent to recover the money spent (*Lee Parker v Izzet* [1971] 1 WLR 1688). Where set-off applies, it will be a defence to an action for non-payment of rent.

### 16.2.3    Specific performance

This is an exception to the rule that a court will not compel performance of an obligation which requires supervision.

Specific performance is not available to the landlord to enforce the tenant's repairing obligations (*Hill v Barclay* (1810) 16 Ves 402) and it was assumed by analogy that the same applied to the tenant. It was not until Pennycuick V-C's decision in *Jeune v Queens Cross Properties Ltd* [1974] Ch 97 that it became clear that specific performance was available to a tenant to enforce a landlord's repairing obligations. In this case the breach complained of was failure to reinstate a first-floor stone balcony.

In addition, s. 17, Landlord and Tenant Act 1985 provides that in any proceedings in which a tenant of a dwelling alleges a breach on the part of the landlord of a repairing covenant relating to any part of the premises in which the dwelling is comprised, the court may, in its discretion, order specific performance of that covenant, whether or not the breach relates to a part of the premises let to the tenant, and notwithstanding any equitable rule restricting the scope of that remedy. It extends to obligations to repair and maintain common parts.

### 16.2.4    Appointment of a receiver

Section 37, Supreme Court Act 1981 allows for an application to be made to the court for the appointment of a receiver where it is just and convenient to do so, to carry out some of the functions of the landlord, e.g. *Hart v Emelkirk* (1983) 267 EG 946. This remedy cannot be used, however, in relation to local authority landlords (*Parker v Camden LBC* [1985] 2 All ER 141).

Sections 21 to 24, Landlord and Tenant Act 1987, which deal with the appointment of a manager, apply to premises consisting of the whole or part of a building containing two or more flats except where the landlord is an exempt landlord (e.g. a local authority or registered social landlord) or a resident landlord in a non purpose-built block of flats. The court may make an order appointing a manager to carry out such functions in connection with the management of the premises or of a receiver, or both, as the court thinks fit (s. 24). It must be satisfied that either:

(a)    the landlord is in breach of a management obligation (i.e. repair, maintenance, insurance) under the lease; or
(b)    would be so (but it has not been reasonably practicable for the tenant to give the appropriate notice);

and that it is just and convenient to make the order in all the circumstances. Before an application is made for an order under s. 24, the tenant must serve notice on the landlord (s. 22).

### 16.2.5   Repudiatory breach

In *Total Oil Great Britain Ltd* v *Thompson Garages (Biggin Hill) Ltd* [1972] 1 QB 318 Lord Denning said, obiter, that a lease was not capable of determination by repudiation and acceptance. His view was attributable in part to the fact that a lease was not then capable of determination by frustration so that contractual remedies in other cases could not apply. By acknowledging that a lease could be frustrated, the House of Lords in *National Carriers* v *Panalpina* [1981] 1 WLR 728 effectively paved the way for the application of ordinary contractual principles to leases.

In *Hussein* v *Mehlman* [1992] 2 EGLR 87, the county court held that a repudiatory breach of a letting is possible. A three-year assured tenancy of a house was subject to the landlord's obligation, implied by s. 11, Landlord and Tenant Act 1985, to keep in repair the structure and exterior and the installations for the supply of utilities and space and water heating. After 15 months of the tenancy, one bedroom was uninhabitable owing to the collapse of the ceiling, the sitting room was letting in rainwater and part of its ceiling was bulging dangerously, the outside lavatory was unusable, the hall-well was damp, and the doors and windows were ill-fitting. The landlord refused to carry out repairs so the tenant returned the keys to the landlord's agents, vacated the property and sued the landlord for breach of contract.

Assistant recorder Sedley QC (now Sedley J) held that the landlord's breach of the implied repairing covenant amounted to a repudiatory breach of the lease. The landlord had made it clear that he was not going to comply with the covenant and the house as a whole was unfit for habitation. By vacating the premises, the plaintiffs had accepted that the repudiation had terminated the lease and were entitled to damages.

The decision in *Hussein* brings English law into line with other Commonwealth jurisdictions in which it has been held that a lease my be terminated by repudiation and acceptance (see e.g. the Canadian case of *Highway Properties* v *Kelly* (1971) 17 DLR 3d 710 and, from Australia, *Progressive Mailing House Pty* v *Tabah Pty* (1985) 157 CLR 17 and *Wood Factory Pty* v *Kiritos Pty* (1985) 2 NSWLR 105). It is important to remember, however, that not every breach of covenant amounts to a repudiatory breach. It must be one where 'the party evinces an intention no longer to be bound by the contract or ... to fulfil the contract only in a manner substantially inconsistent with his obligations and not in any other way' (per Melon J in *Progressive Mailing* at p. 33).

### 16.2.6    The right to repair scheme for secure and introductory tenants

A right to carry out repairs and recover certain sums from the landlord was introduced in the Housing and Building Control Act 1984. The original unsuccessful scheme has been replaced by another under the Leasehold Reform Housing and Urban Development Act 1993 which has been extended, by regulations, to introductory tenants. The new scheme has proved no more useful than its predecessor and has been described as 'a dead letter', the problem being 'tenants' lack of confidence and competence when challenging their landlords' (Madge, 1998: 238).

Section 96, Housing Act 1985 (as substituted for the previous s. 96 by s. 121, Leasehold Reform, Housing and Urban Development Act 1993) empowers the Secretary of State to introduce regulations entitling secure tenants of local housing authorities to have 'qualifying repairs' carried out. A 'qualifying repair' is a repair which the landlord is obliged by a repairing covenant to carry out. The Secure Tenants of Local Housing Authorities (Right to Repair) Regulations 1994, as amended, provide that where a secure tenant applies to the landlord to have a qualifying repair carried out, the landlord must issue a repair notice specifying the nature of the repair, the identity of the contractor and the date by which the work should be carried out. If the work is not carried out by this date the tenant will be entitled to compensation'.

## 16.3    LANDLORDS' REMEDIES

### 16.3.1    Damages

Depending on the wording of the tenant's repairing covenant (whether it is, e.g., to 'keep in repair or 'to leave in repair'), the landlord may start an action for damages for disrepair during the currency of the tenancy or after its expiry. During the term, the damages may amount to the diminution in the value of the reversion but thereafter it will be the actual cost of the repair. Section 18(1), Landlord and Tenant Act 1927 imposes a limit on damages for disrepair on all covenants to put, keep or leave in repair. Whether the action is commenced during the term or at its end, the landlord cannot recover more than the amount of diminution in value of the reversion, and no damages are recoverable for failure to put or leave the premises in repair at the termination of the lease if it is shown that the premises are at, or shortly after, termination to be demolished or altered so as to render the repairs valueless. The onus of proof is on the tenant.

## 16.3.2 Forfeiture

The lease must contain a proviso for re-entry and forfeiture. The landlord must serve a notice on the tenant specifying the breach, the remedy and compensation (if required) (s. 146, Law of Property Act 1925). If the lease is for a term of seven years or more, of which three or more remain, the Leasehold Property (Repairs) Act 1938 applies. Not less than one month before bringing the action, the landlord must serve a s. 146 notice indicating that the tenant may, within 28 days, serve on the landlord a counter-notice claiming the benefit of the 1938 Act. Should the tenant do this, the landlord cannot proceed further without leave of the court which will not be granted unless the landlord shows, e.g. an immediate remedy is required to prevent a substantial drop in the value of the reversion, or to give effect to a by-law or court order or any other Act, or to protect another occupier, or would involve relatively smaller cost than if it were postponed, or the special circumstances make it just and equitable to grant leave.

## 16.3.3 Self-help

The landlord may enter the premises and undertake the repairs provided that the right to do so is reserved in the lease. It is a condition of a statutory tenancy under the Rent Act 1977 and an implied term of every assured tenancy that the tenant shall afford the landlord access and 'all reasonable facilities' to execute such repairs as the landlord is entitled to execute (s. 3(2), Rent Act 1977; s. 16, Housing Act 1988). The cost of the repairs may be recovered from the tenant.

## 16.4  PUBLIC LAW REMEDIES: ENVIRONMENTAL PROTECTION ACT 1990

### 16.4.1  General principles

Since the mid-nineteenth century, public health legislation has been the mechanism by which Parliament has sought deal with the worst effects of slum housing (i.e. disease, overcrowding and dangerous buildings). These early measures were largely consolidated into the Public Health Act 1936, ss. 91 to 100 of which are replaced by Part III, Environmental Protection Act 1990, as amended by the Noise and Statutory Nuisance Act 1993. The 1990 Act came into force on 1 January 1991. The relevant law is contained in ss. 79 to 82.

The aim of the public health legislation is to eliminate housing conditions, in both the private and public sectors, which amount to a 'statutory nuisance'. The existence of a statutory nuisance may be proved even though there has been no breach of the landlord's repairing obligations (*Birmingham City DC v Kelly* [1986] 2 EGLR 239) but the legislation is a way of compelling landlords to carry out repairs and improve the condition of their property.

Responsibility for dealing with statutory nuisances rests with the local authority but, where the premises in question are owned by the local authority, or where the local authority declines to intervene, an individual occupier may institute proceedings under the Act. Where local authority landlords are concerned, however, the courts have urged magistrates to act with sense and discretion and to bear in mind that the local housing authorities have many responsibilities and burdens, especially in times of recession and large scale homelessness (see *Salford City Council* v *McNally* [1976] AC 379; *Birmingham DC* v *Kelly* (1985) 17 HLR 572).

### 16.4.2   Statutory nuisances

'Statutory nuisances' include 'any premises in such a state as to be prejudicial to health or a nuisance' (s. 79(1)(a), Environmental Protection Act 1990). 'Prejudicial to health' means 'injurious, or likely to cause injury, to health' (s. 79(7)), i.e. such as would cause a well person to become ill or the health of person who is already ill to deteriorate further (*Malton Urban Sanitary Authority* v *Malton Farmers Manure Co.* (1879) 4 Ex D 302). A mere want of internal decorative repair is not sufficient (*Springett* v *Harold* [1954] 1 All ER 568). Premises which are 'prejudicial to health' for the purposes of the Environmental Protection Act 1990 are most likely to be those which are suffering from the effects of serious dampness, whether due to water penetration (as in *Salford CC* v *McNally* [1976] AC 379) or condensation which gives rise to extensive mould growth and dampness (*GLC* v *London Borough of Tower Hamlets* (1983) 15 HLR 54). This is particularly useful, given that condensation may not be attributable to any want of repair by the landlord (see *Quick* v *Taff-Ely BC* [1985] 3 All ER 321).

The Environmental Protection Act does not define 'nuisance' but it is clear that the act or default complained must be either a private or public nuisance (*National Coal Board* v *Thorne* [1976] 1 WLR 543). Thus, a statutory nuisance cannot arise if what has taken place affects only the person or persons occupying the premises where the nuisance is said to have taken place. The problem must therefore emanate from some external source.

### 16.4.3   Enforcement

#### 16.4.3.1   Service of an abatement notice   The Environmental Health Department of the local authority can either act on its own intitiative, or in response to a complaint made to it by a person living within its area.

If, after investigations, the authority is satisfied that a statutory nuisance exists, or is likely to occur or recur, it must serve an abatement notice requiring (s. 80(1));

(a)   the abatement of the nuisance or prohibiting or its occurrence or recurrence;
(b)   the execution of such works, and the taking of such other steps, as may be necessary for any of those purposes.

The notice must be served on the person responsible for the nuisance, except where the nuisance arises out of a structural defect, or where the person responsible cannot be found, in which case the owner is to be served (s. 80(2)).

The notice may require substantial works of renovation, such as the installation of central heating, rewiring, insulation, or the renewal of defective windows. On the other hand, only minimal works are likely to be specified if the premises in question face imminent demolition. It is only possible to comply with a s. 80 notice by taking some remedial action. Thus, the removal of occupants from premises which are in such a state as to be prejudicial to health or a nuisance does not consitute an abatement of the nuisance (*Lambeth LBC v Stubbs* (1980) LGR 650), nor does the fact that a house has been left unoccupied unless it has been effectively rendered incapable of occupation, e.g. by having all the services permanently disconnected and being boarded up prior to demolition (*Coventry City Council v Doyle* [1981] 2 All ER 184).

The person upon whom the notice is served may appeal to a magistrates' court within 21 days from the date of service of the notice (s. 80(3)). Failure to comply with the terms of the notice amounts to a criminal offence punishable by a fine. A compensation order can also be made. It is a defence to a prosecution under s. 79 to show that there was a 'reasonable excuse' (s. 80(4)).

**16.4.3.2  Remedy of defects by local authority**   Where a local authority considers that an unreasonable delay would result if it proceeded by way of an abatement notice under the Environmental Protection Act 1990, it may serve a notice on the appropriate person stating that it intends to remedy the defective state and specifying the defects it intends to remedy (s. 76(1), Building Act 1984).

**16.4.3.3  Action by tenants and other occupiers**   By s. 82 a person aggrieved by a statutory nuisance may complain direct to a magistrates' court. The complainant must give at least 21 days' written notice of intention to bring proceedings (s. 82(7)). If the court is satisfied that a statutory nuisance exists, it must make an order in terms similar to an abatement notice and fine the defendant. The court has a wide discretion as to the precise terms of such an order (*Nottingham Corporation v Newton* [1974] 2 All ER 760). Costs must be awarded in favour of the complainant where it is proved that the alleged nuisance existed at the date of the complaint, whether or not it has ceased to exist, or has been abated, by the time of the hearing (s. 82(12)).

## 16.5  PUBLIC REMEDIES: PART VI, HOUSING ACT 1985

A local housing authority is under a duty to carry out periodic reviews of housing conditions in its area in order to decide whether and what action it should take under Part VI, Housing Act 1985 if a property is unfit for human habitation (s. 605). It must also to take account of written reports made to it by its officers concerned with unfit housing.

### 16.5.1  The fitness standard

In deciding whether a particular dwelling is unfit for human habitation, the local authority must have regard to the fitness standard which was introduced by the Local Government and Housing Act 1989 substituting a new s. 604. The first is a general standard which is applicable to a 'dwelling-house'. Such a property will not be fit for human habitation if, in the opinion of the local authority, it is not reasonably suitable for occupation because it fails to meet one or more of the following requirements: structural stability, freedom from serious disrepair, freedom from damp prejudicial to the health of the occupants (if any), adequate provision of lighting, heating and ventilation, an adequate piped supply of wholesome water, satisfactory facilties for preparing and cooking food (including a sink with a satisfactory supply of hot and cold water), a suitably located water-closet for the exclusive use of the occupants (if any), a suitably located fixed bath or shower and wash hand basin (each with a satisfactory supply of hot and cold water) for the exclusive use of the occupants, and an effective system for the draining of foul, waste and surface water.

Once the authority have decided that the property is unfit, it must then decide on the most satisfactory course of action by taking into account the Code of Guidance issued by the Secretary of State for the Environment. This requires consideration of, *inter alia*, the cost and the longer-term socio-environmental implications of the various courses of action (see *R* v *Southwark, ex parte Cordwell* (1994) 26 HLR 107).

### 16.5.2   Action under s. 189

If a local authority is satisfied that a dwelling-house or house in multiple occupation is already unfit for human habitation, it *must* serve:

(a)   a repair notice (s. 189(1)); or
(b)   a closing order (s. 264(1)); or
(c)   a demolition order (s. 265(1)).

Alternatively, the authority can designate the area in which the property is situated as 'clearance area' (s. 289).

A s. 189 notice must be served on the person having control of the property or, in the case of a house in multiple occupation, the manager, and a copy must also be served on anyone having an interest in the property. It must specify the work to be done, the starting date (no sooner than 28 days after the date of service of the notice), and the period of time within which the work should be completed. A right of appeal against a repair notice lies to the county court (s. 191(1)).

### 16.5.3   Action under s. 190

A local authority *may* serve a repair notice under s. 190 where it appears that a particular dwelling is reaching the stage where it is unfit for human habitation. The power under s. 190 was first introduced by the Housing Act 1969, at a time when a number of landlords were deliberately allowing properties to fall into such a state of disrepair that they were condemned as unfit human habitation. Protected tenants could then be evicted, the property repaired and sold at a considerable profit. Meanwhile the local authority would be under an obligation to rehouse the dispossessed tenant (see *Hillbank Properties Ltd* v *Hackney LBC* [1978] QB 998, pp. 1010–1011).

If a local authority consider that a dwelling house or house in multiple occupation is not unfit for human habitation, but either that:

(a)  substantial repairs are necessary to bring it up to a reasonable standard, having regard to its age, character and locality; or
(b)  its condition is such as to interfere materially with the tenant's personal comfort,

the authority may serve a repair notice on the person having control of the house (or the manager of the house in multiple occupation as the case may be) and also on anyone who has an interest in it (s. 190). The dwelling must be occupied or situated in a renewal area covered by Part VII, Local Government and Housing Act 1989. The person on whom the notice is served is required to execute the works specified in the notice within a specified period. In the event of non-compliance, the local authority can undertake the work itself and recover the cost of so doing from the person on whom the notice was served (s. 193). If that person agrees to pay, the authority can itself do the work required under a s. 189 or s. 190 notice even before any default on the notice has occurred (s. 191A).

There are, however, limitations on s. 190. First, it has no application to premises controlled by the local authority (*R* v *Cardiff CC, ex parte Cross* (1982) 6 HLR 1). Tenants of council accommodation must use either private remedies, or the procedure for abatement of a statutory nuisance under the Environmental Protection Act 1990. It will be recalled that secure tenants, whose landlord is a local housing authority, have a statutory right to have repairs carried out on application where the landlord is liable under an express or implied repairing obligation (s. 96, Housing Act 1985, substituted by s. 121, Leasehold Reform, Housing and Urban Development Act 1993) and compensation is payable if the repairs are not carried out within a specified period.

Secondly, if the local authority fails to take action under s. 190, an aggrieved occupier's only remedy is judicial review.

Thirdly, a landlord may successfully appeal against a s. 190 notice if the notified works cannot be carried out at reasonable expense. This limitation is not specified in the statute but see *Hillbank Properties Ltd* v *Hackney LBC* (ibid.).

### 16.6   PART X, HOUSING ACT 1985: OVERCROWDING

Overcrowding is dealt with generally in Part X, Housing Act 1985. Specific provisions relating to overcrowding in houses in multiple occupation are contained in Part XI. Both sets of provisions apply equally to licensees and tenants.

A dwelling is overcrowded when the number of persons sleeping in the same dwelling contravenes either the room standard or the space standard (s. 324).

The room standard is contravened when the available sleeping accommodation is such that two people of opposite sexes over the age of ten years and who are not living as husband and wife must sleep in the same bedroom (s. 325). The space standard is contravened whenever the number of persons sleeping in the dwelling exceeds the permitted number. The permitted number is arrived at by a formula set out in s. 326(3) and depends on either the number of rooms or the floor area. In this calculation, no account is taken of children under the age of one year; and children between the ages of one and ten years each count as half a person (s. 326(2)).

The local housing authority has power to require from an occupier information about the number, ages and sexes of the people sleeping in the dwelling (s. 335) and the power of entry to determine the permitted number of people (s. 337).

If a particular dwelling is overcrowded within the meaning of Part X, the local housing authority can serve a notice on the occupier, requiring that the overcrowding be brought to an end within 14 days. If, within three months from the expiry of the 14 days, the person on whom the notice was served or a member of that person's family is still in occupation and the dwelling is still overcrowded, the local housing authority can take its own proceedings in the county court for possession to be given to the landlord, and recover its expenses from the landlord (s. 338). The occupier will be classed as a homeless person and can apply to the local housing authority to be housed under the homelessness legislation.

By s. 331, the offence of 'causing or permitting overcrowding' is committed where:

(a)   the landlord or a person who effected the letting on the landlord's behalf had reasonable cause to believe that the dwelling would become overcrowded; or

(b)   the landlord or a person who effected the letting on the landlord's behalf failed to make inquiries of the proposed occupier as to the number, ages and sex of those who would be sleeping there;

(c)   the landlord has failed to take reasonable steps to abate overcrowding following the service of an abatement notice.

Overcrowding is permitted where:

(a)   The occupier has obtained a licence under s. 330 from the local housing authority permitting overcrowding for a period not exceeding one year because of exceptional circumstances (e.g. a seasonal increase of population).

(b)   The overcrowding results from temporary use of the dwelling by members of the occupier's family (s. 329).

(c)   A child has reached a relevant age and the occupier has sought alternative accommodation from the local housing authority (s. 328). The overcrowding will become illegal if the offer of alternative accommodation is unreasonably refused, or the occupier fails to require the removal of a member of the household, who is not a member of the occupier's family, the removal being reasonably practicable having regard to all the circumstances (including the availability of suitable alternative accommodation for that person.)

## 16.7   HOUSES IN MULTIPLE OCCUPATION

### 16.7.1   What is a 'house a multiple occupation'?

Part XI, Housing Act 1985, as amended by the Local Government and Housing Act 1989 and the Housing Act 1996, contains a number of powers and duties in relation to houses in multiple occupation). A house in multiple occupation is 'a house which is occupied by persons who do not form a single household' (s. 345(1), Housing Act 1985). Whether a house consists of more than one household is a question of fact and degree, and reference should be made to the criteria laid down by Sir Thomas Bingham MR in *Barnes* v *Sheffield CC* (1995) 27 HLR 719. It is estimated that there are over 300,000 houses in multiple occupation in England. They include bedsits, shared houses, and hostels and tend to be associated with poor housing conditions. A particular problem is the increased risk of fire and the absence of adequate fire precautions.

### 16.7.2   Registration

There have been repeated calls for a national mandatory licensing system for houses in multiple occupation. At the moment, however, local authorities have merely the power to set up registration schemes authorising the compilation and maintainance of registers of houses in multiple occupation in their areas (s. 346). Not all authorities have established schemes. Registration is for a period of five years from the date of first registration and may be renewed, on application, for further periods of five years at a time (s. 346A). A local authority may determine that a house cannot lawfully be an house in multiple occupation unless it is registered, and the number of households or persons occupying it does not exceed the number registered for it. It may prohibit the person in control or manager of the house from allowing any more people to occupy it and, either on first registration or renewal, may refuse the application on the grounds that the house is unsuitable and cannot be made suitable, or refuse registration on the ground that the person in control or the manager is not a fit and proper person, or require works to be carried out as a condition of registration, and impose conditions relating to the management of the house.

### 16.7.3   General works notices

Local housing authorities have the power to serve a notice requiring the execution of necessary works where a house in multiple occupation fails to meet one of the requirements of s. 352(1A) as a result of which the property is not considered to be reasonably suitable for occupation by the number of persons or households accommodated on the premises. Section 352(1A) requirements include satisfactory facilities for the storage, preparation and cooking of food, an adequate number of baths, showers and WCs, etc., an adequate means of escape from fire, and other adequate fire precautions.

### 16.7.4   Duty to keep premises fit for the number of occupants

Section 353A, Housing Act 1985 (inserted by s. 73, Housing Act 1996) imposes a duty on the person having control of the house and the person managing the property to take such steps as are reasonably practicable to prevent the occurrence of a state of affairs calling for the service of a s. 352 notice. A tenant, other occupant, or any other person who suffers loss, damage or personal injury as a consequence of the breach may bring an action in damages. In addition, a person who fails to comply with the duty commits a criminal offence and is liable on conviction to a fine not exceeding level 5 on the standard scale.

### 16.7.5   Management

The Housing (Management of Houses in Multiple Occupation) Regulations 1990 (SI 1990/830) require the manager of a house in multiple occupation to 'ensure the repair, maintenance, cleansing and good order' of all means of water supply and drainage in the house, all means of escape from fire and all apparatus, systems and other things provided by way of fire precautions, kitchens, bathrooms and WCs in common use, common staircases, corridors and passage ways, and outbuildings, yards and gardens in common use. If, in the opinion of the local housing authority, the condition of a house in multiple occupation is defective in consequence of neglect to comply with the regulations, it can serve on the manager a notice specifying the works which in its opinion are required to make good the neglect (s. 372). A right of appeal lies to the county court (s. 373). Failure to comply with the notice constitutes a criminal offence and conviction carries a fine not exceeding level 5 on the standard scale (s. 376).

Where the living conditions in the house are so poor as to represent a danger to the safety, health or welfare of the people living in it, the local authority may make a control order (s. 379). This gives the authority the right to run the property itself (s. 381) and may eventually lead to its acquiring the property via a compulsory purchase order.

### 16.7.6   Execution of works by local authority

If a notice under s. 352 or s. 372 is not complied with, the local housing authority may itself do the work specified in the notice (s. 375) and recover the expenses it incurs from the person having control of the house or the manager (sch. 10, para. 2).

### 16.7.7   Overcrowding

In the case of a house in multiple occupation, an 'overcrowding notice' may be served on the occupier or on the person who is responsible for its management and control, where it appears that the house in multiple occupation is already accommodating, or is likely to accommodate, an excessive number of people (s. 358). The notice should specify the maximum number of people who are allowed to sleep in each room, and specify which rooms are considered as unsuitable for sleeping accommodation (s. 359). A right of appeal lies against such a notice (s. 362). A person who contravenes an overcrowding notice commits a summary offence and is liable on conviction to a fine.

**References**

Madge, N., 'Disrepair Cases', *New Law Journal*, 1998, vol. 148, p. 238.

# SEVENTEEN

## Homelessness: definitions, causes and historical context

### 17.1 DEFINITIONS OF HOMELESSNESS

Housing can be viewed as a continuum with outright, mortgage-free ownership at one end and sleeping rough at the other. In between is a large grey area which includes hostels, residential hotels, staying with friends and relatives, licences and insecure tenancies in the private rented sector, accommodation provided by employers, protected and assured tenancies, mortgaged accommodation, and tenancies granted by housing associations and local authorities. The definition of homelessness which is chosen (i.e. where the line of homelessness is drawn on this continuum), has implications for housing policy and provision. Obviously the further it is drawn from the 'rooflessness' end of the continuum, the larger the problem appears to be (Watson et al, 1986: 9.13).

Homelessness is a socially determined and relative concept, definitions of which change with the passage of time and depend on, e.g. the availability of housing generally and the quality of that housing. Mention has already been made in **Chapter 1** of the different approaches taken to housing by those who advocate a market-oriented approach towards welfare provision and those who favour the social democratic model. As regards homelessness, the former 'favour an absolute definition that tends towards rooflessness'. The latter 'extend the concept further along the continuum to embrace a more relative definition in which homelessness begins once the social rights associated with shelter are infringed upon' and might regard as homeless, for example, a woman living in an unsatisfactory relationship who wants to leave her home but cannot afford to do so, or a person living in housing which is in a poor state of repair or lacks certain basic amenities (Clapham et al, 1990: 115). The statutory definition of homeless (now contained in s. 175, Housing Act 1996) was originally to be found towards the narrower end of the spectrum although it did provide that a person would be homeless if he or she had accommodation but it was probable that occupation of that accommodation would lead to domestic violence or threats of violence. The definition was further extended as a result of the House of Lords decision in *R* v *Hillingdon London Borough Council, ex parte Puhlofer* [1986] AC 484 so that regard may now be had to whether it is reasonable for the applicant to continue to occupy existing accommodation (see **18.4.2**).

There is, therefore, no universally accepted definition of homelessness but the recognised definitions have been identified as follows below (Watchman et al, 1996: 10–16).

### 17.1.1  Rooflessness

This, the narrowest definition which equates homelessness with sleeping rough, was the definition accepted by government until the early 1970s (Watchman et al, 1996: 9). A proposal to restore this narrow definition in the Housing Act 1996 (Department of the Environment, 1994: paras. 5 and 8) was dropped at Committee Stage. The single homeless and childless couples are most likely to be roofless, as households with children are generally able to secure accommodation of some sort, even though it may be unsatisfactory.

### 17.1.2  Houselessness

This definition includes not only those who sleep rough but also those who occupy:

(a)  emergency accommodation; or
(b)  accommodation which is not strictly of an emergency nature but offers little more than a bed,
(c)  accommodation which, for a limited period, provides special support; and
(d)  other forms of short stay accommodation such as night shelters, local authority reception centres, model lodging houses, working men's hostels, and alcoholic recovery units.

Pressure groups such as MIND have argued that the definition of 'homelessness' should include people who are admitted to mental hospitals and other long-term institutions simply because they have nowhere else to go. Such people may find themselves on a 'circuit of homelessness' which also embraces prisons, sleeping rough and night shelters. The policy of care in the community of the mentally ill (especially since the passing of the National Health Service and Community Care Act 1990) has shifted the problem: people are no longer detained in hospital and some may be 'discharged to unsupported families or left to fend for themselves ... Homelessness or prison have become the unacceptable outcomes for growing numbers of discharged people' (Braisby et al, 1988: 5). Even where housing authorities accept former psychiatric patients for re-housing, the lack of follow-up support and the consequent inability to cope may lead to their either being evicted as difficult tenants or abandoning their tenancies of their own accord (Allen, 1995).

### 17.1.3  Insecure accommodation

This category includes those with no or limited security of tenure, e.g. occupying squats, 'holiday' or out of season lets, or tied accommodation, living with relatives, sharing with the landlord, residing in lodgings or under licences or non-exclusive occupation agreements (see **Chapters 3** and **5**). By s. 167(2)(b), Housing Act 1996 every local housing authority is obliged to give reasonable preference in the allocation of housing to 'people occupying housing which is temporary or occupied on insecure terms' (see **9.4.4**) but this does not include assured shorthold tenancies which have been enthusiastically embraced by private landlords and have become even easier to create since s. 96, Housing Act 1996 came into force (see **4.5**). People living in insecure accommodation will not be 'homeless' within the meaning of the Housing Act 1996 but s. 167 may give them a better chance of acquiring accommodation in the public rented sector (via the housing register) than other applicants.

### 17.1.4  Intolerable housing conditions

For some time, Shelter has argued that the definition of homelessness should include people who live in overcrowded accommodation or accommodation which is unsatisfactory in that it lacks basic amenties such as a hot water supply, fixed bath or inside WC, or is unacceptably damp (Bailey et al, 1972: 9). This definition acknowledges the importance of a 'home' in providing accommodation of a decent standard. To some extent it is recognised by s. 175(3), Housing Act 1996 which provides that 'a person shall not be treated as having accommodation unless it is accommodation which it would be reasonable for him to continue to occupy'. The physical conditions of the property which an applicant for housing has vacated may also be taken into account in deciding whether he or she left it intentionally. Further, s. 167(2)(a), Housing Act 1996 obliges local authorities to give reasonable preference in the allocation of accommodation to 'people occupying insanitary or overcrowded housing or otherwise living in unsatisfactory housing conditions'. However, as has been pointed out in **Chapter 9**, allocations are to be made henceforth from the housing register, and a household will not automatically be regarded as 'homeless', therefore, simply because it occupies unsatisfactory accommodation. In 1991, some 1.5 million dwellings in England (7.6% of the total housing stock) were found to be unfit for human habitation. Some of these properties are vacant but over 1.3 million are occupied (Department of the Environment, 1993: Table A7.1). To extend the official definition of homelessness to people falling into this category would impose an intolerable burden on local authorities.

## 17.2  CAUSES OF HOMELESSNESS

The causes of homelessness have been described as 'complex, multi-dimensional and obscure'. (Watchman et al, 1996: 26) although the reasons officially given have been fairly consistent:

**Table 17.a    Reasons for homelessness — England, first quarter, 1989, 1991, 1993, 1994**

|                                                                                             | 1989 % | 1991 % | 1993 % | 1994 % |
|---------------------------------------------------------------------------------------------|--------|--------|--------|--------|
| Parent(s), relative(s) or friends no longer able/willing to accommodate                     | 44     | 42     | 40     | 36     |
| Breakdown of relationship with partner                                                      | 18     | 17     | 18     | 20     |
| Mortgage arrears                                                                            | 7      | 8      | 8      | 9      |
| Rent arrears                                                                                | 3      | 4      | 2      | 2      |
| Loss of private rented dwelling for other reasons, including termination of assured tenancy | 16     | 14     | 16     | 18     |
| Other                                                                                       | 12     | 13     | 16     | 18     |

Source: DoE Homelessness statistics, quoted in Newton, 1994: Table 108

It should be noted, however, that the data in **Table 17.a** does not reflect the wider picture — the extent to which the housing shortage, high rents and low incomes lead to rent arrears and subsequently homelessness or how far the tenant's behaviour is the precipitating cause (Greve et al, 1971). The immediate cause often disguises the real reason why someone becomes homeless:

> Homelessness is caused by processes occurring at many different levels: the individual level, the family level, the social group level and the societal level. Housing and labour market factors, migration, demographic and socio-cultural factors interact to create the preconditions of . . . homelessness in the mismatch of housing and job supply and demand. Social and health factors, life-cycle and personal crises cause some people to be more vulnerable to these preconditions (Drake et al, 1981: 12).

At societal level, the fundamental problem is the critical shortage of decent, affordable accommodation, a situation which is progressively worsening. Three 'key and mutually reinforcing factors' have played an important role in contributing towards homelessness since 1979. They are:

(a)    the sharp reduction in council-house building;

(b)    a massive switch in finance away from new building to other forms of incentive and support; and

(c)    the vigorous campaign by Conservative governments (backed by some of the financial incentives just mentioned) to compel local authorities to sell council houses to individual tenants under the right to buy policy.

Government reliance on market-oriented policies, including financial incentives to owner-occupiers and private landlords, 'has serious limitations when matched against the pattern of housing needs, general income levels and demographic factors — notably the rate at which new households are being formed' (Greve, 1991: 21).

For those unable to buy their own homes, the problem is primarily one of access. Even in a locality in which there is no especially acute housing problem, the private rented sector does not cater for families (see Morgan, 1996), and the public sector does not cater for single people and childless couples. As **Table 17.b** shows, there is, in crude terms, a surplus of housing but some of it is situated in areas where there is no work, and many properties stand empty because they are either dilapidated or in serious disrepair. Others await incoming tenants or purchasers, or are second homes.

**Table 17.b    Dwellings and households by tenure at mid-1991 (000s)**

|  | Owner-occupied | Private rented sector | Local authority/ housing association | All tenures |
|---|---|---|---|---|
| Occupied main residences | 12,860 | 1,658 | 4,442 | 18,960 |
| Occupied secondary residences | 97 | 96 | — | 193 |
| Vacant | 401 | 159 | 97 | 657 |
| All dwellings | 13,358 | 1,193 | 4,539 | 19,801 |
| Households (a) | 12,873 | 1,866 | 4,456 | 19,215 |

(a)   includes 20,000 families temporarily resident in hostels, etc. and not included in the tenure tables.

Source: Holmans, 1995: Table 3.

Poverty, low wages, unemployment, changing patterns of work and cuts in entitlement to welfare benefits all make it increasingly difficult to obtain and to maintain housing and are commonly part of a sequence of events which involve illness, family crisis and debt. Homelessness due to mortgage default (itself brought about by changes in the nature of work, cuts in benefits, etc.) has increased since the late 1970s. The number accepted by local authorities would be higher were it not for the fact that people who accumulate mortgage arrears may be treated as being intentionally homeless, thereby disqualifying them from other than very limited housing assistance. (see **18.7**). Some people become homeless when they are forced to leave accommodation over which they have no security of tenure; changes in the law since 1988 mean that those moving into the private rented sector are most likely to be granted assured shorthold tenancies which carry virtually no security of tenure (see **6.9**).

Social factors may also lead to homelessness: domestic disputes, family breakdown and the unwillingness or inability of relatives and friends to continue to provide accommodation. Young people increasingly want to set up home on their own or with friends rather than stay with their parents. Recent research, covering nearly 16,000 young people in inner London and six other major British cities, suggested that that 140,000 people aged between 16 and 25 may be homeless in a year. Two-fifths had slept rough at some point, a quarter had been in care and most had left home because of household friction, eviction and violence (*Guardian*, 10 December 1996).

## 17.3  WHO ARE THE HOMELESS?

Some MPs who contributed to the debates on the Housing (Homeless Persons) viewed the homeless as queue-jumpers, feckless or nomadic Scots and Irish. In fact, homelessness is experienced by people from all walks of life, although men are more likely than women to be long-term homeless and many single homeless also suffer from physical or mental disabilities. A survey of the single homeless carried out in 1981 found that they had 'not inconsiderable levels' of education and skill. Two-fifths had education beyond school leaving age and over a half had skills or some form of job training (Drake et al, 1981: 127). According to a recent survey by the St Mungo Association, 10% of people in projects for the homeless have a degree and a further 10% have A-levels (reported in (1996) 45 Housing Review 63). Many of the single homeless are low-paid casual workers, often in the catering trade.

A mythology has developed that homelessness is caused by the irresponsible behaviour of homeless people themselves. Young people flock to London and the south-east of England from other parts of the country, encouraged by 'overliberal' housing and social security policies, families deliberately make themselves homeless so that they can jump the social housing queue, and teenage girls get themselves pregnant in order to obtain council housing. The real causes of homelessness are masked by these 'pejorative stereotypes and myths' which stigmatise homeless people and dismiss them as undeserving. More responsible behaviour is prescribed both as 'a prevention and a cure' for homelessness (Greve, 1991: 30).

Certainly, a disproportionate number of of the statutorily homeless are lone parents (43%, compared with 10% of of households in general: Prescott-Clarke et al, 1994). However, 'sinister manoeuverings' on the part of teenage girls may be less to blame than the declining availability of rented accommodation (in both the private and public sectors), and policies encouraging owner-occupation. Home ownership has spread more widely among income groups but to the detriment of people who are single and separating, especially women. The statutory provisions on priority need (see **18.6**) mean that 'pregnancy and parenthood are privileged' and, given the way that local authorities define housing need, two-parent families are more likely to obtain accommodation via the waiting while one-parent families are 'driven into homelessness' (Pascall et al, 1996: 196, 197). An alternative view is that while early motherhood does increase the chance of entering social housing substantially, young mothers usually have a partner with them when they get their home (Ermisch, 1996: 19). None the less, the phenomenon of young single mothers entering social housing was seized upon by the Conservative government in the later part of 1993 as part of its 'Back to Basics' campaign. The fundamental change in policy towards the homeless latched on to the 'moral panic' generated by this campaign and led eventually to the Housing Act 1996 (Cowan et al, 1994: 613).

## 17.4 HOW MANY PEOPLE ARE HOMELESS?

Since the Housing (Homeless Persons) Act 1977 was passed, the number of households accepted for rehousing by local authorities increased each year until 1993.

**Table 17.c  Local authority homelessness acceptances, by country: Great Britain, 1978–1993**

| Year | England | Wales | Scotland | Great Britain |
|------|---------|-------|----------|---------------|
| 1978 | 53,110 | 3,204 | 6,699 | 63,003 |
| 1979 | 57,200 | 4,676 | 8,356 | 68,562 |
| 1980 | 69,920 | 5,446 | 8,105 | 73,951 |
| 1981 | 70,010 | 5,462 | 8,149 | 80,601 |
| 1982 | 74,800 | 5,611 | 9,303 | 86,534 |
| 1983 | 78,240 | 5,008 | 8,919 | 89,397 |
| 1984 | 83,190 | 4,999 | 9,727 | 95,226 |
| 1985 | 93,980 | 5,371 | 12,406 | 108,787 |
| 1986 | 102,980 | 5,965 | 13,349 | 119,804 |
| 1987 | 112,730 | 5,683 | 12,637 | 127,490 |
| 1988 | 113,770 | 6,818 | 12,601 | 133,189 |
| 1989 | 122,180 | 7,805 | 14,391 | 144,376 |
| 1990 | 140,350 | 9,963 | 15,056 | 165,369 |
| 1991 | 144,780 | 10,394 | 16,324 | 171,498 |
| 1992 | 142,890 | 10,722 | 19,334 | 172,946 |
| 1993 | 134,190 | 11,221 | 14,563 | 159,974 |

Source: DoE Quarterly Homelessness returns, 1979–93, quoted in Newton, 1994: Table 107.

The slower rate of increase in the early 1990s and the drop in 1993, is likely to be a reflection of a more stringent gatekeeping response by local authorities to the financial pressures they face rather than of any underlying improvement in the housing supply conditions, or an indication that the problem of homelessness has been successfully addressed (Newton, 1994: 119). Furthermore, the statistics show only those who are 'officially homeless', i.e. who are accepted by local authorities as homeless under the homelessness legislation. There are a great many people who are not rehoused by local authorities, either because they do not bother to apply in the first place or, if they do, because they do not fall into one of the priority need groups. Homeless single (non-elderly) people and childless couples are not usually provided with accommodation under the legislation. These 'able-bodied' households are expected to be able to fend for themselves in the market-place' (Clapham et al, 1990: 137). The precise number of households affected by this so-called 'access crisis' is unknown. There are also the 'hidden homeless' who occupy inadequate or unsatisfactory accommodation.

Owing to the diminution in size of council stock, the proportion of those households statutorily rehoused but placed in temporary accommodation rose dramatically up until 1993 but is now declining, paralleling the decline in homeless acceptances. The three main types of temporary accommodation are bed and breakfast, hostels and private sector leasing. The use of bed and breakfast as temporary accommodation has been widely criticised as being detrimental to the family's health, safety, general well-being and the children's ducation (see Power et al, 1995). It is also expensive. Private sector leasing is a scheme under which housing is leased by local authorities from private landlords under short, fixed-term leases (for a maximum of three years) and the authorities then sub-let it to homeless households on a non-secure basis. A second type of private sector leasing is the 'housing associations as managing agents' scheme, under which housing associations lease properties from private owners for reletting to local authorities for the accommodation of homeless households. Private sector leasing was pioneered as an alternative form of temporary housing in the 1970s by a handful of councils such as Eastbourne, and the London boroughs began to make substantial use of it in the late 1980s. While private sector leasing may well have provided a high standard of accommodation a few years ago, it is likely that its recent rapidly increased usage has led to a lower standard of property being leased (Edwards, 1995: 67).

## 17.5  THE HISTORICAL CONTEXT

### 17.5.1  The Poor Law

State intervention to assist the poor, including the homeless, originated in the sixteenth century. First, begging was authorised, then gifts for the succour of the needy were encouraged and then, in 1563, parishes were allowed to introduce a weekly tax for the same purpose. The Elizabethan Poor Law, administered by JPs, Overseers of the Poor, and vestry officials, established a dual structure of poor relief: domiciliary (or 'outdoor') relief for families who continued to live in the community, and institutional care (Glastonbury, 1971: 27). The poor fell into two groups: the 'impotent' poor, such as the very old, the very young, the sick, the crippled, the blind and the insane, who were in no position to maintain themselves, and the 'able-bodied' poor who had no work (Longmate, 1974: 14). Whether or not help would be forthcoming depended on whether the poor or homeless person was a local citizen with a right to settle in the district (Donnison, 1982: 264). Each parish had a duty under the Poor Law to maintain its own aged and infirm and to provide the able-bodied with means of making a livelihood, if necessary maintaining them in the workhouse (Gaudie, 1974: 33). Those who had no right to settle in the district could be punished or ejected under the Vagrancy Acts. Vagrants were regarded by both central and local authorities as 'the lowest of the undeserving poor' (Wood, 1991: 127) and successive statutes, from 1531 onwards, empowered parish officials to deal with them by, e.g. having them tied to the tail of a cart and whipped 'until the blood streams from their bodies'. These statutes were strictly applied as increased poverty and a growing population made the Poor Law system unworkable 'or rather, made it so much resented by those on whom fell the burden of paying the poor-rates, that they were unwilling to maintain it efficiently or interpret it charitably' (Gauldie, 1974: 33).

The Poor Law Amendment Act 1834 took the administration of the Poor Law out of the hands of parish officials and passed it to a central authority. The Act aimed drastically to reduce outdoor relief by allowing help only to those willing to enter the workhouse. Supporting a family in its own home cost less than providing it with minimal standards of care in an institution but it increased the demand for relief, and led to accusations that the system was being exploited by those who were in no real need of funds (Glastonbury, 1971: 28).

In accordance with the principle of 'less eligibility', conditions in workhouses were deliberately made worse than those of the poorest labourer outside. It was believed that 'every penny bestowed that tends to render the condition of the pauper more eligible than that of the independent worker is a bounty on indolence and vice' (Report of the Royal Commission on the Poor laws, quoted in Wood, 1991: 68). Such punitive measures were designed to separate the indigent from the working poor. The workhouse system was intended to encourage self-help. 'Those who were genuinely in dire need would accept the workhouse rather than starvation. Those who were not in such straits would prefer to remain independent and thus avoid contracting the morally wasting disease of pauperism' (Rose, 1972: 8). The workhouse became known as a 'refuge for undesirables' and being an inmate carried a considerable stigma. The attempt to put the 1834 Act into operation and 'the fear of the workhouse ... was an important step in driving the country poor into the towns, there to increase the overcrowding, the unemployment and the disease of fast-growing town populations' (Gauldie, 1974: 68).

Under the New Poor Law, the punishment of vagrants took a different form from that previously inflicted upon them. They were put in the casual wards — the dirtiest accommodation which often lacked even the most basic facilities. Such meagre assistance as there was — bare boards and a diet of bread and gruel — had to been earned, e.g. by breaking stones, grinding corn or picking oakum. Only when they had completed their appointed tasks were they to be released to search for work elsewhere. A casual had to move on after two nights to another ward, often a considerable distance away.

While the harsh and unattractive conditions were intended to act as a deterrent, the workhouse did provide shelter, clothing, regular food and companionship. The census of 1911 recorded a population of 258,000 people in the Poor Law institutions of England and Wales. These included 25% of all single men and 5% all single women aged 65 or over (Donnison et al, 1982: 264). This widespread reliance on the workhouse is not surprising given the social conditions prevailing at the time. Only very limited welfare provision existed for older people, the unemployed, sick and disabled. The labour market was subject to marked seasonal and cyclical fluctuations. Nearly all rented housing was provided by private landlords and it was common for tenants to be evicted for non-payment of rent (Wohl, 1977). The first public sector housebuilding schemes in Britain were deliberately not directed towards the needs of the poor and the homeless. They aimed instead to provide housing for the families of industrious artisans who would be able to afford the, generally unrebated, rents charged for the accommodation (see **Chapter 8**). The concept of a 'comprehensive' housing service emerged only at a much later stage and was only being actively propagated by the time of the Cullingworth Report in the late 1960s (Raynsford, 1986: 39). The introduction of unemployment benefit under the National Insurance Scheme in 1911 removed the 'able-bodied poor' from the ambit of the Poor Law which none the less lingered on until the passing of the National Assistance Act 1948. Despite its official demise, however, the Poor Law regime has had a lasting influence on homelessness law and policy. The two principles of local connection and less eligibility have been carried over, and the attitude of many councils to the homeless has been described as 'ambiguous and, at times, distinctly punitive' (Clapham, 1990: 114).

### 17.5.2  The National Assistance Act 1948

The National Assistance Act 1948 — an Act shaped by 'post-war optimism' — was a significant development in state provision for the homeless which 'heralded the dawn of a more humane approach to the problems of vagrancy and homelessness' (Watchman, 1989: 27). It was a time when 'full employment, the new free health services and more generous social security payments were enabling more and more people to maintain independent households, and more and more of their houses were built and subsidised by local authorities' (Donnison et al, 1982: 264).

The 1948 Act abolished the Poor Law. Most remaining casual wards were closed although the National Assistance Board retained some as short-stay reception centres in order to meet its obligation under the Act to provide shelter for those without 'a settled way of living'. The Act further obliged the National Assistance Board and local authority welfare departments (now social services departments) to provide permanent residential care for the people 'who by reason of age, infirmity or any other circumstances are in need of care and attention which is not otherwise available to them' (s. 21(1)(a)) and temporary accommodation for 'persons who are in urgent need thereof, being need arising in circumstances which could not reasonably have been foreseen or in other such circumstances as the authority may in any case determine' (s. 21(1)(b)). The Ministry of Health Circular No. 87/48 made it clear that the latter provision was not intended to deal with the 'inadequately housed' but to assist people made homeless through an emergency such as flood, fire and (significantly) eviction.

In the immediate post-war period, there was, not surprisingly, an overall shortage of properties fit for residential occupation. Hundreds of thousands of houses had been destroyed or made uninhabitable by bomb damage, and new housebuilding had been at a virtual standstill throughout the war. The first post-war Labour government initiated a major building programme and from

1945 to 1948 local authority completions increased from 2,000 units to 190,000 (Merrett, 1979: 239). At the time the 1948 Act was passed, homelessness was seen as a diminishing and residual problem. It was assumed that households accommodated under s. 21(1)(b) would soon be able to make alternative arrangements, and there was a failure to recognise that most households were homeless as a result of eviction, rather than as the result of flood, fire or some other emergency. After a brief 'honeymoon period' during which evicted families were accepted much as the bombed-out families had been, local authorities resorted to Poor Law practice. For at least 15 years after the passing of the 1948 Act, the old workhouses were used as hostels to accommodate families, supplemented by temporary structures erected during the war and, increasingly, inadequate hostel and bed and breakfast accommodation. The standard of accommodation provided, in terms of privacy, basic comfort and facilities for cooking and washing, was poor. Stays of any length of time were thus discouraged by policies of 'deterrence' and 'less eligibility' reminiscent of the Poor Law (Glastonbury, 1971: 40; Burke, 1981: 65).

The 1948 Act gave local authorities much discretion in interpreting the legislation. It gave no guidance as to the meaning of 'temporary', 'urgent need' and 'reasonably foreseeable' and, in consequence, there were considerable variations in the ways in which different councils met their obligations. Requiring the need for assistance to be unforeseen meant that the concept of need was generally qualified by the notion of 'intentionality', a notion which has been carried through into the current homelessness legislation. It implied that those who anticipated possible homelessness but took no steps to avoid it would not deserve assistance. A circular in 1966 stated that any distinction between foreseeable and unforeseeable homelessness was 'artificial' (see Berry, 1974) but when the extent of the duty was under s. 21(1)(b) was tested in *London Borough of Southwark* v *Williams* [1971] 2 All ER 175, the Court of Appeal held that a family which had moved to London could have foreseen that it would have become homeless and was not entitled, therefore, to temporary accommodation under the Act. The court decided that, in any event, individuals could not pursue any remedy under the Act, apart from one already provided for in the legislation, viz., the default powers given to the Minister by s. 36(1).

Placing the responsibility to accommodate homeless households on welfare, rather than housing, departments placed an intolerable strain on the little accommodation they were able to offer. Faced with a problem with which they were ill-equipped to deal, many authorities interpreted 'urgent need' to apply exclusively to homeless families, or more precisely the mother and children of homeless families, rather than to homeless persons in general. As a result, families were split up (Glastonbury, 1971: 17), and the children sometimes taken into care. The effects of these policies has been described as 'inhumane, inefficient, expensive and of doubtful legality' (Watchman et al, 1989: 28). A report by the society SHAC in 1974 showed that most London boroughs would not accept responsibility for pregnant applicants before the pregnancy had reached seven months, and the London Boroughs of Croydon, Ealing and Lewisham would not usually accept responsibility until the woman had given birth (Raynsford, 1986: 46). Generally, housing departments were unwilling to house homeless people, as they were seen as undeserving and irresponsible and it was considered contrary to waiting list principles. People who lost their homes as the result of an emergency were clearly acknowledged as both homeless and in need of support. Those who did so in non-emergency circumstances were generally assessed according how far they were to blame for the loss. 'The decision on blameworthiness was an arbitrary one, and there were large variations between different officers and different local authorities' (Glastonbury, 1971: 17). Co-operation between welfare and housing departments (where they existed) was poor. Differences in local authority practices meant that geography played a large part in determining a homeless household's chances of getting help.

The 1948 Act placed the wrong powers in the wrong hands. Instead of imposing duties on the Ministry of Housing and local housing departments to provide permanent housing for large numbers, it imposed obligations on the Ministry of Health and the county welfare departments to provide temporary shelter for small numbers (Donnison et al, 1982: 271). The result was a serious policy vacuum at central government level, explicable in part by the prejudices which still attached to the homeless but, probably more importantly, to the perceived conflict of interest between the homeless and those on the council house waiting lists, who were assumed to be competing against each other for the limited supply of council lettings (Raynsford, 1986).

The housing boom in the 1950s, coupled with the relaxation of rent controls in the private rented sector, led to an increase in the supply of housing. A consequent fall in the number of persons admitted to local authority temporary accommodation obscured the fact that the housing needs of many people remained unmet. Public housing policy favoured and reinforced nuclear family households. Local authorities focused on the construction of three-bedroomed family dwellings, a policy which continued throughout Labour's term of office, and under the Conservatives until 1953 (Watson et al, 1986: 49). Those most likely to be neglected were:

> returning servicemen, immigrants and other mobile people who had not spent long enough in any one place to get onto the waiting-lists or to the head of the queue, unmarried mothers and fugitive wives who were expected to stay with their relatives or fend for themselves, and single and childless people who had little chance or being rehoused unless their homes were pulled down in clearance programmes. Most of these found somewhere to live but some could not (Donnison et al, 1982: 265).

The late 1950s witnessed an unexpected rise in the numbers of families rehoused by the welfare authorities in temporary accommodation. The relaxation of controls by the Rent Act 1957, the rapid growth in sales of what had been rented housing for owner-occupation, the reduction in council house building for general needs, the greater confidence with which people threatened with homelessness demanded help from local authorities, all played a part. Most people who sought help with housing were not victims of an emergency, but of the housing shortage. They needed permanent homes which welfare departments, with no permanent housing stock, were unable to provide. However, homelessness was a subect 'on which government expressed concern, commissioned research, set up working parties and issued guidance and advisory circulars, but did not legislate' (Raynsford, 1986).

Homes were also lost through the renewed expansion of slum-clearance programmes and road building schemes. The evictions and harassment which followed the Rent Act 1957 first drew public attention to the homeless, and subsequently to the condition of homeless-family accommodation (Burke, 1981: 65, 66). 'Cathy Come Home', a TV drama documentary which gave a moving portrayal of a homeless family's despair and eventual disintegration, touched the public imagination and turned homelessness into a media issue. Towards the end of its life, s. 21(1)(b) was described as offering 'last-ditch support for families who have not been effectively covered by housing provisions and the growing body of preventive services' (Glastonbury, 1971: 15).

Homelessness continued to grow through the 1960s into the 1970s. In 1966 there were 2,558 households in temporary accommodation, by 1970 there were 4,926 and by 1976 there were 10,270. The decline of the private rented sector through the transfer of investment from residential properties to commercial development or selling for owner-occupation, illegal evictions, the growth of public-sector activity in slum clearance and redevelopment, and the continued rise in the cost of renting or buying were all contributing factors (Burke, 1981: 66). A sharp increase in the value of housing land and construction costs occurred in the early 1970s (Merrett, 1979: 263). Cuts in public expenditure led to cuts in the construction of council housing. Council house 'starts' were at a lower level in 1970 than at any time since 1962. Local authorities made increasing use of bed and breakfast accommodation to house homeless families.

Throughout the 1960s and early 1970s, the case for reform mounted. Two particularly important and, ultimately, influential studies were Glastonbury's study of homelessness in South West England and South Wales and Greve's on homelessness in London, both of which provided extensive documentary evidence of the inadequacies of the 1948 Act. Around the same time, a number of important committees demanded a radical reappraisal of government policy towards the homeless. The 1968 Seebohm Report (Committee on Local Authority and Allied Personal Services, Cmnd. 3703, 1968) the 1969 Cullingworth Report (Council Housing, Purposes, Procedures and Priorities, HMSO, 1969), the Greve Report (1971) commissioned by the DHSS on Homelessness in London, the Finer Report (1974) (Committee on One-parent Families, Cmnd. 5629, 1974, para. 6.60) and, in Scotland, the Morris Committee's Report (Housing and Social Work: A Joint Approach, HMSO, 1975) all emphasised homelessness as a housing, not a welfare, problem and recommended the transfer of statutory responsibility from social services to housing departments. The Seebohm Committee also recommended that housing departments be made responsible for securing permanent accommo-dation to preserve families and prevent children being taken into care. In

1974/5, 2,800 children in England and Wales were placed in care solely because of homelessness (Richards, 1992: 130).

As the private rented sector continued to decline, the supply of immediate access housing dried up and the 1970s witnessed a marked growth in the number of households provided with temporary accommodation by local authorities in England and Wales. The lack of co-operation between welfare and housing departments was exacerbated by local government reforms in 1972 which gave the responsibility for personal social services to county councils and metropolitan district councils, and housing to district councils. Yet, despite evidence that the 1948 Act was not working and homelessness was in fact increasing, s. 195, Local Government Act 1972 reduced the duty to provide temporary accommodation to a discretionary power, with effect from April 1974. This prompted Shelter, the Catholic Housing Aid Society, the Campaign for Homeless and Rootless, SHAC and the Child Poverty Action Group, to form the Joint Charities Group with the aim of amending the Local Government Bill 1974 so as to restore the statutory duty. Although they were unsuccessful, their campaign roused considerable sympathy from MPs on all sides of the house and the Secretary of State for Social Services was obliged to issue a joint DoE/DoH/Welsh Office Circular No. 18/74 which took effect at the same time as local government reorganisation. This circular formed the blueprint for the Housing (Homeless Persons) Bill and the Code of Guidance. It acknowledged that homelessness was an 'extreme form of housing need' and recommended that housing authorities take over homelessness duties from social services. It also introduced the concept of priority groups, advocating that where the housing situation was particularly difficult, authorities should give priority to families with dependent children, and to single people who were homeless through emergency, or vulnerable because of old age, disability, pregnancy or other special reasons. On 1 February 1974, however, the Secretary of State issued DHSS Local Authority Circular No. 13/74 which reimposed the duty on social service authorities to provide temporary accommodation. Chaos ensued, the existence of a duty on social services authorities encouraging some housing authorities to ignore DoE Circular No. 18/74 (Hughes et al, 1995: 240).

A Labour government was returned in the general election of February 1974 but, despite its pre-election pledges, homelessness legislation was not high on its list of priorities. The following year it produced a consultation paper which indicated a clear reluctance to legislate. A survey carried out by the Department of the Environment into the implementation of Circular 18/74 revealed that by April 1975 most authorities had failed to adopt the priority group criteria and only a third of housing departments had accepted sole responsibility for the homeless. In some areas, neither housing nor social services would accept responsibility, with the result that families were shunted backwards and forwards. Even in the early 1970s it was still not unknown for homeless families to be transported across local authority boundaries, and 'dumped' in another 'parish' (Raynsford, 1986: 36).

Homelessness was a growing political embarrassment and, by late October 1975, the government had conceded that legislation was necessary after all. In

1976, around 33,700 households were accepted by authorities in England — more than double the number in 1971. Faced with pressure from all sides for reform, it was clear that Circular 18/74 would only be implemented if it had the force of the law and, in the Spring of 1976, the Department of the Environment began separate but parallel consultation meetings with the local authority associations and the Joint Charities Group to consider proposals for legislation The government's lack of commitment to the legislation became apparent when it dropped the Homeless Persons Bill from the 1976 Queen's Speech, ostensibly because of insufficient parliamentary time. It was introduced to the House of Commons as a private member's bill, with government support, by Stephen Ross, Liberal MP for the Isle of Wight. The Bill itself was actually the Department of the Environment's own draft.

The objective of the Bill in its original form was to give legislative power to Circular 18/74. It provided a statutory definition of homelessness and gave housing authorities duties to secure accommodation for people in priority need and to advise and assist others. It fell short, therefore, of the demands of the Joint Charities Group which also wanted a statutory right of appeal, default powers for the Secretary of State, the extension of priority need to cover single people and a requirement that the accommodation provided be reasonably suitable for the person's needs. Moreover, the Act was passed at a time when a new complacency about housing policy was becoming apparent, the Housing Policy Review Green Paper (Department of Environment, 1977) presenting the housing problem as a localised and essentially residual problem which affected some areas and a limited number of disadvantaged groups, rather than one of national significance. From this perspective the need to provide immediate accommodation for a small number of 'deserving' homeless families could be acknowledged without recognising or taking responsibility for a wider problem of housing market or policy failure. 'Homelessness was portrayed and responded to as an isolated problem faced by a few unfortunate individuals' (Clapham et al, 1990: 120).

The Association of County Councils was largely in favour of the provisions contained in the Housing (Homeless Persons) Bill, but the Association of District Councils and the Association of Metropolitan Authorities were concerned about the cost of putting it into practice and the loss of local autonomy. They opposed a legal definition of homelessness, and a statutory right to housing, preferring a general duty on housing authorities to give homeless people advice and help to secure accommodation. Their vehement opposition to the proposed legislation led to a significant dilution of its potential effectiveness.

## 17.5.3 Housing (Homeless Persons) Act 1977

The Housing (Homeless Persons) Act 1977 has been described as 'a landmark in British housing policy' (Richards, 1992: 129) and 'one of the last reforming measures of the social democratic consensus . . . reflecting the belief — soon to be overturned by the Thatcher era — that public authorities should express social obligations' (Pascall et al, 1996: 190). It demonstrated that 'significant concessions can be won for the poor and the powerless [who have to rely on pluralistic bargaining and democratic pressure to further their interests], even in a society increasingly dominated by corporate groups' (Clapham et al, 1990: 120). It marked a significant turning point in the legislative response to homelessness and constituted 'an important advance towards securing citizenship rights in an area of social welfare in which the rights of private property are paramount' (ibid.). For first time certain groups of homeless people were given a statutory right to be rehoused by their local authority.

However, the Act has also been criticised. The passage of the Bill through Parliament was obstructed by the local authority lobby which attacked it as a Scroungers' Charter, alleging that 'hoardes of misplaced miscreants from the hinterlands of Britain and abroad . . . would descend on seaside resorts and areas which major seaports, airport and rail termini clamouring to be housed' (Watchman et al, 1996: 44). Although the Labour government supported the Bill, its slim majority at Westminster forced it to concede to pressure from the local authorities. The Act thus became 'a series of obstacles to be negotiated before the right to be rehoused could be claimed' (Watchman et al, 1981). It was thus transformed from a rights-based measure to a discretionary one, representing a compromise between 'the needs of the most vulnerable and the prejudices of an uninformed legislature' which legitimised the restriction of help to local people, and discriminated between the 'deserving' and the 'undeserving' (Clapham et al, 1990: 120). No additional funding was provided by central government to assist the local authorities in meeting their new duties. In 1985 the 1977 Act was codified with the rest of the housing legislation and became Part III of the Housing Act 1985.

### 17.5.4   The Housing Act 1996

Another steep increase in the number of households claiming to be homeless occurred during the 1980s (see **Table 17.c**), although the peak had passed by 1993. At the same time, there were major changes in government housing policy. Subsidies for new public housing were cut, and there was a massive thrust towards home ownership. Neither housing associations nor the private rented sector were able to step in and fill the gap (Malpass et al, 1994: 118).

The homelessness legislation was subjected to reviews in 1982 and 1989. Neither proposed any significant changes but some additional funding was made available, most of which was targeted on the renovation of empty homes and some on cash payments to help tenants into owner-occupation, thereby releasing properties for homeless people (Government's Expenditure Plans 1990–91 to 1992–93, Cmnd. 1008, p. 5). In late 1992 housing associations were given funds to provide extra housing to accommodate the homeless (*Guardian*, 12 December 1992, p. 33). Not surprisingly, the obligations to homeless applicants under the 1985 Act imposed an overwhelming strain on resources. In January 1994, the government published their Consultation Paper, Access to Local Authority and Housing Association Tenancies (Department of the Environment, 1994). Despite large-scale protests to the changes it proposed (see Shelter, 1994), the government's proposals found their way into the 1995 White Paper (Department of the Environment, 1995) but were subject to some modification before they reached the statute book in the form of the Housing Act 1996. It has been argued that the new legislation was unnecessary, much of the agenda contained in the Consultation Paper having already been achieved by 'indefensibly restrictive judicial interpretations' of the existing legislation in, e.g. *R* v *Oldham Metropolitan Borough Council, ex parte Garlick* [1993] 2 WLR 609; *R* v *London Borough of Newham, ex parte Dada* [1995] 1 FLR 842; *R* v *Bristol City Council, ex parte Bradic* (1995) 27 HLR 398; and *R* v *London Borough of Brent, ex parte Awua* [1995] 3 WLR 215 (Loveland, 1996).

The Housing Act 1996 repeals the homelessness provisions in Part III, Housing Act 1985 and replaces them with a new statutory code (Part VII, ss. 175–218, Housing Act 1996). Some of the old provisions are replicated (e.g. s. 189, priority need) or re-enacted with only minor amendments (e.g. ss. 175–177, definition of homelessness, s. 188, interim duty to accommodate, ss. 198–199, local connection, and ss. 211–212, protection of property). The Act is supported by a Code of Guidance issued by the Department of the Environment, to which local authorities are to 'have regard' (s. 182, Housing Act 1996), but need not follow slavishly (*De Falco* v *Crawley BC* [1980] QB 460).

## 17.6  OTHER HOMELESSNESS LEGISLATION

The Housing Act 1996 is not the only piece of legislation which deals homelessness. It operates alongside the legislation discussed below.

### 17.6.1  Section 21(1)(a), National Assistance Act 1948

Section 21(1)(a), National Assistance Act 1948 (as amended) empowers (and where the Secretary of State for Health directs, requires) local social services departments to provide 'residential accommodation for persons aged 18 or over who by reason of age, illness, disability or any other circumstances are in need of care and attention which is not available to them'. This power has recently been used to provide accommodation for asylum seekers who did not claim asylum immediately upon their arrival in the UK and are thereby excluded from rights to public housing or welfare benefits (see s. 11 and sch. 1, Asylum and Immigration Act 1996; *R* v *Hammersmith & Fulham LBC, ex parte M and Others* (1997) *The Times*, 19 February; *R* v *Newham LBC, ex parte Medical Foundation for the Care of Victims of Torture* (1997) *The Times*, 26 December).

### 17.6.2  Section 67(2), National Health Service and Community Care Act 1990

Section 67(2), National Health Service and Community Care Act 1990 extends the above duty to those in need of care by reason of illness or disability.

## 17.6.3   Children Act 1989

Section 20(1), Children Act 1989 requires social services authorities to provide accommodation for 'children in need' within their areas who appear to require accommodation because no-one has parental responsbility for them, or they are lost or have been abandoned, or whoever has been caring from them (whether or not permanently and for whatever reason) is prevented from providing suitable accommodation and care. Subsection (3) obliges them to house children over the age of 16 whose welfare will otherwise be 'seriously prejudiced'. Under s. 27 of the 1989 Act, a local social services authority can ask a local housing authority to help in delivering services for children in need, and the housing authority must comply with such a request to the extent that it is compatible with its own statutory duties and other obligations, and does not unduly prejudice the discharge of any of its own functions. In *R v Northavon DC, ex parte Smith* (1994) 26 HLR 659 the House of Lords held that s. 27 cannot be used to obtain permanent accommodation for an applicant and his or her children when a housing authority has already determined that the applicant was intentionally homeless. The 1989 Act imposes a duty of co-operation between the authorities, both of which must their best in carrying out their respective responsibilities for children and housing but judicial review is not the way to obtain co-operation.

## References

Allen, C., 'Caught in between the Acts', *Roof*, January/February 1995, p. 12.

Bailey, R. and Ruddock, J., *The Grief Report*, London: Shelter, 1972.

Berry, F., *Housing, the Great British Failure*, London: Charles Knight, 1974.

Braisby, D., *Changing Futures: Housing and Support Services for People Discharged from Psychiatric Hospitals*, London: King's Fund Publishing Office, 1988.

Burke, G., *Housing and Social Justice*, London and New York: Longman, 1981.

Clapham, D., Kemp P. and Smith, S., *Housing and Social Policy*, Basingstoke: Macmillan, 1990.

Cowan, D. and Fionda, J., 'Back to Basics: the Government's Homelessness Consultation Paper', *Modern Law Review*, 1994, vol. 57, pp. 610–619.

Department of the Environment, *English House Condition Survey 1991*, London: HMSO, 1993.

Department of the Environment, *Access to Local Authority and Housing Association Tenancies*, London: HMSO, 1994.

Department of the Environment, *Our Future Homes: Opportunity, Choice Responsibility*, Cmnd. 2901, London: HMSO, 1995.

Donnison, D. and Ungerson, C., *Housing Policy*, Harmondsworth: Penguin, 1982.

Drake, M., O'Brien, M. and Biebuyck, A., *Single and Homeless*, London: Department of the Environment, 1981.

Edwards, R., 'Making Temporary Accommodation Permanent: The Cost for Homeless Families', 1995, *Critical Social Policy*, vol. 15, issue 1.

Ermisch, J., Di Salvo, P. and Joshi, H., *Household Formation and Housing Tenure Decisions of Young People* (Occasional Papers of the ESRC Research Centre on Micro-Social Change), Occasional Paper 95–1. Colchester: University of Essex, 1996.

Fraser, D., *The Evolution of the British Welfare State*, London: Macmillan, 1973.

Gauldie, E., *Cruel Habitations: a History of Working Class Housing, 1780–1918*, London: Allen & Unwin, 1974.

Glastonbury, B., *Homeless near a Thousand Homes: a Study of Families without Homes in South Wales and the West of England*, London: Allen & Unwin, 1971.

Greve, J., Page, D. and Greve, S., *Homelessness in London*, Edinburgh, London: Scottish Academic Press, 1971.

Greve, J., *Homelessness in Britain*, York: Joseph Rowntree Foundation, 1991.

Holmans, A., *Housing Demand and Need in England 1991–2011*, York: York Publishing Services for the Joseph Rowntree Foundation, 1995.

Hughes, D. and Lowe, S., *Social Housing Law and Policy*, London: Butterworths, 1995.

Longmate, N., *The Workhouse*, London: Temple Smith, 1974.

Loveland, I., 'The Status of Children as Applicants under the Homlessness Legislation — Judicial Subversion of Legislative Intent', *Child and Family Law Quarterly*, 1996, vol. 8, pp. 89–104.

Malpass, P. and Murie, A., *Housing Policy and Practice*, Basingstoke: Macmillan, 1994.

May, T., *An Economic and Social History of Britain 1760–1970*, Harlow: Longman, 1987.

Merrett, S., *State Housing in Britain*, London: Routledge & Kegan Paul, 1979.

Morgan, J., 'No Children or Pets — Child Exclusion in Privately Rented Housing', *Child and Family Law Quarterly*, 1996, vol. 8, pp. 1–11.

Newton, J., *All in One Place: The British Housing Story 1973–1993*, London: CHAS, 1994.

Pascall, G. and Morley, R., 'Women and Homelessness: Proposals from the Department of the Environment. I. Lone Mothers; II. Domestic Violence', *Journal of Social Welfare and Family Law*, 1996, vol. 18, pp. 189–202, 327–340.

Power, S., Whitty, G. and Youdell, D., *No Place to Learn: Homelessness and Education*, London: Shelter, 1995.

Prescott-Clarke, P., Clemens, S. and Park, A., *Routes into Local Authority Housing: A Study of Local Authority Waiting Lists and New Tenancies*, London: HMSO, 1994.

Raynsford, N., 'The Housing (Homeless Persons) Act 1977', in Deakin, N. (ed.), *Policy Change in Government*, London: RIPA, 1986.

Richards, J., 'A Sense of Duty', in Grant, C. (ed.) *Built to Last?*, London: *Roof*, 1992.

Rose, M.E., *The Relief of Poverty 1834–1914*, Basingstoke: Macmillan, 1972.

Watchman, P. and Robson, P., 'The Homeless Persons Obstacle Race', *Journal of Social Welfare Law*, 1981.

Watchman, P. and Paustie, M., *Homeless People and the Law*, London: Butterworths, 3rd ed., 1996.

Watson, S. and Austerberry, H., *Housing and Homelessness: a Feminist Perspective*, London: Routledge & Kegan Paul, 1986.

Wohl, A., *The Eternal Slum: Housing and Social Policy in Victorian London*, London: Edward Arnold, 1977.

Wood, P., *Poverty and the Workhouse in Victorian Britain*, Stroud: Alan Sutton, 1991.

# EIGHTEEN

## The implementation of the homelessness legislation
## I: Eligibility, homelessness, priority need and intentionality

### 18.1  INTRODUCTION

Part VII, Housing Act 1996 sets out the conditions which must be satisfied before a local authority owes the full duty under s. 193 to rehouse an applicant for a minimum period of two years. The local authority must be satisfied that the applicant:

(a)  is eligible for assistance;
(b)  is homeless;
(c)  is in priority need of accommodation; and
(d)  did not become homeless intentionally.

Even if the applicant fulfils the above requirements, only limited duties arise if there is other suitable accommodation available in the area (s. 197). The authority to which application is made may also consider whether the applicant has a local connection with the district of another authority to which it may refer the application (see **19.2.5**). Lesser duties may be owed to, e.g. an applicant who is eligible, unintentionally homeless but not in priority need, or one who is eligible, intentionally homeless and in priority need (see **19.2.3**).

### 18.2  INITIAL INQUIRIES

If the local housing authority has reason to believe that an applicant is homeless or threatened with homelessness, s. 184, Housing Act 1996 obliges it to make such inquiries as are necessary to establish:

(a)  whether the applicant is eligible for assistance; and
(b)  if so, whether any duty, and if so what duty, is owed to the applicant.

The authority may also make inquiries as to whether the applicant has a local connection with the district of another local housing authority in England, Wales or Scotland (s. 184(3)). On completion of the inquiries, the authority must notify the applicant of its decision and, if any issue is decided against the applicant's interests, the reasons for the decision. Notification and reasons must also be given to the applicant if the authority have referred, or intend to refer, the case to another authority under s. 198. The applicant must be informed of the right to request a review of the decision and the time within which such a request must be made (see s. 202). A local housing authority is under a duty to secure accommodation while the inquiries under s. 184 are being carried out (s. 188, see **19.2.2**).

## 18.3  ELIGIBILITY

In the parliamentary debates on the Housing (Homeless Persons) Bill, homelessness appears to have been viewed as a fundamentally domestic issue. Concern was voiced about British passport holders from troubled countries overseas (Malawi and Uganda were cited as examples) who sought refuge in Great Britain (*Hansard*, 1977, vol. 926, col. 984) and it was also recognised that a duty to accommodate might arise in relation to a couple, one of whom was Italian and the other French, who had become homeless in this country (ibid., col. 930). Otherwise, attention seemed to focus on 'rascally Irishmen' who 'popped up again and again throughout the proceedings in Committee' (ibid., col. 1673). The UK's membership of the EEC seems to have been overlooked, specifically Council Regulation 1612/68, Article 9(1) of which provides that 'a worker who is a national of a member state and who is employed in the territory of another member state shall enjoy all the rights and benefits accorded to national workers in matters of housing, including ownership of the house he [or she] needs'.

The Housing (Homeless Persons) Act 1977 contained no express restrictions on the kinds or categories of persons who could apply for accommodation. It was soon established, however, that no duty was owed to illegal immigrants to the UK or those who had overstayed the period for which they were granted leave to enter or were in breach of a deportation order. Such persons had committed a criminal offence or were at least in breach of the immigration laws and, as such, were not lawfully here (*R v Hillingdon LBC, ex parte Streeting* [1980] 1 WLR 1425; *R v Secretary of State for the Environment, ex parte Tower Hamlets LBC* [1993] QB 632).

The Housing Act 1996 has introduced important restrictions and provides that the homelessness provisions contained in Part VII are available only to those who are 'eligible for assistance' (s. 185(1)). Applicants are not eligible for assistance if they are subject to immigration control under the Asylum and Immigration Act 1996 unless they come within a class prescribed by regulations. The current exceptions are:

(a)   refugees;
(b)   people granted exceptional leave to enter and remain; and
(c)   asylum seekers and their dependants whose asylum claim has not been rejected and who either applied for asylum at the port on arrival, or applied for asylum within three months of a declaration by the Home Secretary that their country of origin has undergone an upheaval (Housing Accommodation and Homelessness (Persons subject to Immigration Control) Order 1996 SI 1996/1982 as amended by the Homelessness (Persons Subject to Immigration Control) (Amendment) Order 1997 (SI 1997/628)).

Even if asylum seekers are not ineligible under s. 185, they are not eligible for assistance if they have 'any accommodation in the UK, however temporary, available for . . . occupation' (s. 186).

Those who are ineligible include:

(a)   illegal entrants;
(b)   people overstaying their visa requirements or given only temporary admission to the UK;
(c)   EU nationals in breach of residence directives;
(d)   people whose visas allow them no recourse to public funds;
(e)   people who are not habitually resident in the Common Travel Area (i.e. the UK, the Republic of Ireland, the Channel Islands and the Isle of Man). The habitual residence test does not apply to, *inter alia*:

(i)   a person who is a 'worker' for the purpose of EEC regulations;
(ii)   a person who has a right to reside in the UK under an EEC Council Directive.

In *R* v *Westminster City Council, ex parte Castelli and Tristan-Garcia* (1996) 28 HLR 616 the applicants, who were homeless and in priority need, were both nationals of EU member states and had entered the UK lawfully without leave because they were seeking employment or self-employment. However, by the time the council reached its decisions on their applications, they were no longer seeking employment or self-employment and neither of them had applied for or been granted leave to remain in the UK. The Home Office was aware of their situation but, because nothing had been done to secure their removal, it was held that they were entitled to accommodation under what is now s. 188 while the initial inquiries were carried out. Westminster Council's lawyer was reported as saying that the *Castelli* decision gave 'rights of housing to all EU nationals, even if they do not have a right of residence' (*Guardian*, 22 February 1996). It should be noted, however, that those 'rights of housing' were confined to the relatively minimal rights contained in what is now ss. 184 and 188. As indicated above, the most extensive duty of local authorities under the homelessness legislation is owed to those who are not only homeless and in priority need but also homeless unintentionally. The inquiries carried out under s. 184 might well have revealed intentionality on the part of Castelli and

Tristan-Garcia. Since the Housing Act 1996 came into force, there is also the extended definition of homelessness to be taken into account.

## 18.4  HOMELESS

### 18.4.1  General principles

By s. 175(1), Housing Act 1996:

a person is homeless if he [or she] has no accommodation available for his [or her] occupation, in the UK or elsewhere, which he [or she]—

(a)   is entitled to occupy by virtue of an interest in it or by virtue of an order of the court,
(b)   has an express or implied licence to occupy, or
(c)   occupies as a residence by virtue of any enactment or rule of law giving him [or her] the right to remain in occupation or restricting the right of another person to recover possession.

Until the Housing Act 1996 came into force, the local authority could not take into account the existence of any housing abroad which the applicant was entitled to occupy in determining whether or not the applicant was homeless in this country. However, it *was* relevant in deciding whether or not he or she was intentionally homeless (see **18.7**). Now, as a result of the extended definition of homelessness, only the general duty under s. 179 (see **19.2.1**) of providing advice and information will be owed to people who have left their parental or family homes in Spain and have found work but no accommodation in the UK, as there is still accommodation available for their occupation elsewhere, i.e. in Spain. Such people may, of course, apply to have their names put on the housing register (see **Chapter 9**) but, unless they have medical problems or dependent children live with them, they are unlikely to attract sufficient points to move to the top of the register. If they are to stay in the UK, they will have to secure accommodation for themselves in the private sector, or stay with friends or relatives.

Section 175(1)(a) includes legal and equitable interests in property and, therefore, covers owners and tenants. The Code of Guidance states that homeless applicants may include those who are no longer entitled to occupy accommodation because their landlord has defaulted on the mortgage of the property (para. 13.6). A person will have an express or implied licence to occupy (under s. 175(1)(b)) if, e.g. he or she is a lodger, or lives with relatives or is an employee with a service occupancy. Protection given by law (s. 175(1)(c)) will include, e.g., statutory tenants under the Rent Act 1977 who have no proprietary interest in the property but merely 'a status of irremoveability' (see **4.2.3**).

Section 175(1) makes no mention of:

(a)    those who have been trespassers from the outset and remain so, and
(b)    those who have excluded tenancies and licences (and to whom, therefore, the notice to quit and court order provisions of the Protection from Eviction Act 1977 do not apply) which have been brought to an end.

Both will be statutorily homeless even though no possession order has been made against them: they are not 'roofless', but neither do they have accommodation within any of the specified classes (see, e.g. *R* v *Portsmouth CC, ex parte Knight* (1983) 10 HLR 115 and *R* v *Surrey Heath Borough Council ex parte Li* (1984) 16 HLR 79).

While s. 175(1)(a) is expressed in terms of an 'entitlement' to occupy, the Code of Guidance speaks, rather confusingly, of a 'legal right' to occupy. It goes on to state that someone who has been occupying accommodation (or is an assured shorthold tenant) and whose licence (or tenancy) has been terminated is homeless because he or she no longer has a legal right to continue to occupy. This statement should be approached with caution as regards assured shorthold tenancies (see below).

A person is also homeless (s. 175(2)(a)):

if he [or she] has accommodation but—

(a)    ... cannot secure entry to it, or
(b)    it consists of a moveable structure, vehicle or vessel designed or adapted for human habitation and there is no place where he [or she] is entitled or permitted both to place it and to reside in it.

This provision aimed principally at residential occupiers who have been illegally evicted. On a practical level, it has proved to be of little value, however, because local authorities have tended to regard as intentionally homeless applicants who have not used the legal remedies open to them to achieve reinstatement. According to the Code of Guidance, s. 175(2)(a) could also apply to those whose accommodation is being occupied illegally by squatters. The effect of s. 175(2)(b) is that a mobile home, caravan, houseboat, etc. will qualify where there is nowhere both to place it and to live in it. In *R* v *Chiltern DC ex parte Roberts et al* (1990) 23 HLR 387, travelling showmen were considered to be neither homeless nor threatened with homelessness whilst moving from fair to fair during the fairground season and residing at each fairground in caravans on a temporary basis. Gypsies and other travellers are increasingly likely to fall within s. 175(2)(b) following the repeal by s. 80(1), Criminal Justice and Public Order Act 1994 of the Caravan Sites Act 1968, Part II, which imposed upon local authorities a duty to provide sites for them.

### 18.4.2  Reasonableness

Section 175(3) provides that 'a person shall not be treated as having accommodation unless it is accommodation which it would be reasonable for him to continue to occupy'. The requirement of reasonableness was added to definition of homelessness by s. 14(1), Housing and Planning Act 1986 in response to the House of Lords ruling in *R* v *Hillingdon LBC, ex parte Pulhofer* [1986] AC 484 in which a couple and their two children occupied a single bedroom in a guest house. The room contained a single and a double bed, and neither cooking nor washing facilities. The House of Lords upheld the local authority's decision that the family were not homeless. The words 'appropriate' or 'reasonable' were not to be imported for the purpose of describing 'accommodation' nor was it relevant that the accommodation might be statutorily unfit or overcrowded. Their Lordships made it clear, however, that not all places in which a person might choose or be constrained to live could properly be regarded as accommodation; it would be 'a misuse of language to describe Diogenes [who lived in a barrel] as having occupied accommodation within the meaning of the Act'.

The Code of Guidance (para. 13.8) acknowledges that there is no simple rule of reasonableness and it lists various factors which authorities may consider in reaching their decision.

**18.4.2.1  Physical conditions**  As regards physical conditions, it must be asked whether the condition of the property is so bad compared with other accommodation in the area that it would not be reasonable to expect someone to continue to live there. Alternatively, it may be that the physical characteristics of the accommodation make it unsuitable for the applicant (e.g. a wheelchair user).

The cases demonstrate, however, that conditions must be fairly bad if an authority's decision on reasonableness is to be successfully challenged. In *R* v *Westminster CC, ex parte Ali* (1983) 11 HLR 83, the court quashed the council's decision that it was reasonable for a couple and their five children to continue to occupy a room measuring 10 feet by 12 feet, and in *R* v *Preseli DC, ex parte Fisher* (1984) 17 HLR 147 the court held that a one-roomed boat with no bath, shower, WC, electricity, hot water, or kitchen sink, occupied by the applicant, her children and two friends was not accommodation of which it was reasonable to remain in occupation. However, in *R* v *South Herefordshire DC, ex parte Miles* (1983) 17 HLR 82, a couple and their children occupied a rat-infested hut which measured approximately 10 feet by 20 feet. It had no mains services, although services were available in a nearby caravan occupied by relatives. The hut was held to constitute accommodation of which continued occuption could be considered reasonable (albeit on the borderline of what was reasonable) while there were only two children. On the birth of the third child, it crossed the borderline into unreasonableness.

In *R* v *Medina BC, ex parte Dee* (1992) 24 HLR 562, the accommodation consisted of an elderly prefabricated beach bungalow which was in a poor state of repair, and suffered from persistent dampness. In deciding that it would be reasonable for the applicant and her newborn baby to live there, the authority had failed to take into account:

(a)  the fact that the property was on the borderline of unfitness; and
(b)  medical advice given to the applicant that it was inappropriate accommodation for a baby.

The significance of medical evidence which was available, or could easily have been made so, was also apparent in *R* v *Wycombe DC, ex parte Holmes* (1990) 22 HLR 150, a case which demonstrates that the location of the accommodation may be significant as well as its condition. Here, the accommodation was satisfactory in itself but was situated just off a very steep hill. The applicant suffered from severe back problems which were exacerbated when she became pregnant and meant that during her pregnancy she was effectively housebound.

**18.4.2.2 Overcrowding** The Code of Guidance also recognises that overcrowding may make continued occupation of the accommodation unreasonable and that authorities may wish to refer to Part X of the Housing Act 1985 on overcrowding (see **16.6**). However, statutory overcrowding is not, by itself, sufficient to determine whether it is unreasonable for the applicant to continue to live there but it can be a key factor if there are other factors which suggest unreasonableness. Overcrowding must also be considered in relation to general housing circumstances in the area.

**18.4.2.3 Domestic violence** Section 177(1) provides that it is not reasonable for a person to continue to occupy accommodation if it is probable that this will lead to domestic violence against him or her, or against:

(a)    a person who normally resides with him or her as a member of his or her family; or
(b)    any other person who might reasonably be expected to reside with him or her.

For this purpose 'domestic violence' means violence or threats of violence which are likely to be carried out from someone with whom a person is associated. Section 178(1) provides that a person is 'associated with another person' if:

(a)    they are or have been married to each other;
(b)    they are cohabitants or former cohabitants;
(c)    they live or have lived in the same household;
(d)    they are relatives;
(e)    they have agreed to marry one another (whether or not that agreement has been terminated);
(f)    in relation to a child, each of them is a parent of the child or has, or has had, parental responsibility for the child.

The Code of Guidance (para. 13.9) defines a 'relative' as father, mother, stepfather, stepmother, son, daughter, stepson, stepdaughter, grandmother, grandfather, grandson or grandaughter, brother, sister, uncle, aunt, niece or nephew (whether of the full blood, half-blood or by affinity) of a person or a spouse or former spouse, or cohabitee or former cohabitee.

The violence or threat of violence is not confined to instances within the home (as in *R* v *Kensington & Chelsea RLBC, ex parte Hammell* [1989] QB 518 where the applicant had suffered alleged violence and harassment by her former husband, who lived nearby). The fact that violence has not yet occurred does not, on its own, suggest that it is not likely to occur. Authorities should not base their assessment of a likely threat of violence solely on whether there has been actual violence in the past. An injunction ordering a person not to molest the applicant or enter the applicant's home will not necessarily prevent such behaviour. Authorities may inform applicants of the option to take out an injunction, but should make it clear that there is no obligation to do so if they feel it would be ineffective (Code of Guidance, para. 13.10). Figures from the Department of the Environment suggest that women escaping domestic violence constitute a significant proportion of the statutorily homeless: about 15% of people accepted as homeless are categorised as having lost their last settled address owing to relationship breakdown with violence (Hague et al, 1993: 134). Despite the sympathetic tone of the Code of Guidance, it appears that some local authorities have taken a much harsher approach (see Pascall et al, 1996).

**18.4.2.4   Violence or threats of violence from someone not associated with the applicant**   The Code of Guidance also refers to 'violence or threats of violence from someone *not* associated with the applicant' and suggests that the authority will need to consider the seriousness of the violence, or threats of violence, the frequency of occurrence and the likelihood of reoccurence. It states that violence or threats of violence could include racial harassment or attacks, violence against a person, sexual abuse or harassment, and harassment on grounds of religious creed. Again, the authority may advise an applicant to pursue any available legal remedies but urges that this should not be done as a matter of policy. It will depend on the merits of an individual case and the need to ensure the applicant's proper safety. In *R v London Borough of Hillingdon, ex parte H* (1988) *The Times*, 17 May (a case on intentionality), it was held that the local authority should have regard to harassment, whether or not it was domestic in nature. The case involved a soldier who left his accommodation because of harassment by the IRA.

**18.4.2.5   Temporary accommodation**   According to the Code of Guidance, it should not be regarded as reasonable for someone to continue to occupy on a long-term basis some types of 'crisis' accommodation (e.g., women's refuges, direct access hostels, and night shelters). This is an interesting point given the immediate judicial history to the 1996 Act. Section 175(1) obviously covers a person who is sleeping rough (i.e. one who is 'roofless'), but has also been held to extend to someone occupying temporary accommodation (i.e. one who is 'houseless'). In *R v Ealing LBC, ex parte Sidhu* (1983) 2 HLR 45 the applicant was living in a women's refuge and in *R v Waveney DC, ex parte Bowers* [1983] QB 238, an alcoholic who had suffered serious brain damage as a result of a road accident was staying at a night shelter, on a night-by-night basis, and could be turned away if the shelter was full. Each of the occupiers was a licensee which, strictly speaking, brought them within what is now s. 175(1)(b), Housing Act 1996. In both cases, however, the applicants were held to be homeless. In *Sidhu*, Hodgson, J (reiterating the comments of the judge in the county court) said it was important that 'refuges be seen as temporary crisis accommodation, and that women living in refuges were still homeless under the terms of the Act'. To suggest otherwise would make it necessary for voluntary organisations to issue 28-day notices as soon as women came in, thereby bringing them under the threat of homelessness. That, he said, would be 'totally undesirable and would simply add stress to stress'. If living in crisis accommodation took women out of the homeless category, 'the protection afforded by the Act would be removed from a whole class of persons that it was set uparte to helparte and for whom it was extremely important' (at p. 53).

In *R v Brent LBC, ex parte Awua* [1995] 2 WLR 315, the local authority had housed the applicant in private sector leasing accommodation (see **17.4**) as a stage in performing its duty to secure her with long-term housing. The House of Lords approved the decision in *Bowers* but held that there was no wording in the Act from which it could be implied that 'accommodation' in what is now s. 175 (nor indeed s. 60) was to be construed as a 'settled home', nor anything to suggest that a local authority could not reasonably expect a person to continue to occupy temporary accommodation under s. 175. 'Accommodation' meant a place it would be reasonable to occupy with regard to general local authority housing conditions (s. 58(2A) and (2B)) and this was not qualified by any requirement of permanence. Lord Hoffmann, giving the leading speech in *Awua*, referred to *R v Hillingdon LBC, ex parte Pulhofer* [1986] AC 484. Given their Lordships' rejection in that case of any implication as to physical suitablity, it was highly improbable that they would have accepted an implication that the accommodation must in some sense be 'settled'. The concept of being 'threatened with homelessness' deals with precariousness of tenure and does not fit easily, he said, with an implication that a person whose tenure is more secure can be regarded as not merely threatened with homelessness but actually homeless. In *Awua*, the accommodation was temporary but it was, none the less, reasonable for Ms Awua to continue to occupy. By refusing the authority's offer of more permanent accommodation, she had made herself intentionally homeless from the PSL accommodation and was owed no further duty.

The temporary accommodation enjoyed by Ms Awua certainly lasted for longer than the stay of those accommodated in refuges and night shelters but *Awua* does not appear to preclude the acceptance as homeless of some applicants other than the literally roofless. *Bowers* and *Sidhu* are still good law to the effect that short-term occupants in emergency-type accommodation are homeless.

**18.4.2.6 Security of tenure** 'Security of tenure' (or lack thereof) is another factor relevant to the issue of reasonableness. An applicant may have no security of tenure and be required to leave his or her accommodation, or it may be clear that there is no defence against possession proceedings. In these circumstances the Code of Guidance suggests that the authority may wish to start to process the application and make arrangments (if appropriate) to secure accommodation immediately. It warns authorities to be alert to the possibility of collusion between landlords and the applicant. It should be noted, however, that it may or may not be unreasonable for an applicant who has an assured shorthold tenancy which has been properly terminated by notice to continue to occupy the accommodation pending a court order for possession. There are conflicting authorities: *R* v *London Borough of Croydon, ex parte Jarvis* (1993) 26 HLR 194; cf. *R* v *London Borough of Newham, ex parte Ugbo* (1993) 26 HLR 263.

### 18.4.3    General housing conditions

In determining whether it would be, or would have been, reasonable for a person to continue to occupy accommodation, regard may be had to the general housing circumstances in the district of the authority to which application has been made (s. 177(2), Housing Act 1996). This involves consideration of a range of questions, not confined to the condition of the housing formerly occupied but extending to issues of employment and the availability of welfare benefits. The authority is 'fully entitled to take into account the difficulties of accommodation and the difficulties of employment in their area, and in the context of someone coming from abroad, the difficulties in this country in general' (*R* v *Hammersmith and Fulham London Borough, ex parte Duro-Rama* (1983) 9 HLR 71). It calls for a 'balancing exercise' between housing conditions in the authority's area and the accommodation which has been left and involves other questions such as the 'pattern of life' followed by the applicant (*R* v *London Borough of Tower Hamlets, ex parte Monaf* (1988) 20 HLR 329).

However, where the accommodation seriously infringes the statutory standards relating to unfitness or overcrowding, the general housing circumstances in the area are likely to be less influential in the assessment of reasonableness. The applicant may therefore be 'homeless' while living in unsatisfactory accommodation even though general conditions in the locality are undoubtedly poor. Thus, in *R* v *Westminster CC, ex parte Ali* (1983) 11 HLR 83, McCullough J found it astonishing that anyone should regard it as reasonable that a family of seven should live in one room measuring10 feet by 12 feet. As to the general housing circumstances in the area, he commented that '[n]o evidence has been placed before me that accommodation in the area of the Westminster City Council is so desperately short that it is reasonable to accept overcrowding of this degree' (at p. 93).

However, at a time of serious housing shortage in some areas, the consideration of general housing circumstances may mean that people end up living in potentially life-threatening conditions. In *R* v *Kensington & Chelsea Royal London Borough Council, ex parte Ben-el-Mabrouk* (1995) 27 HLR 564, the applicant, his wife and very young child lived on the top floor of a house in multiple occupation in Kensington. The house was one in which there was a real risk of fire and no adequate means of escape. The local authority decided that the applicant was not homeless as it was accommodation which it was reasonable to continue to occupy, given that the owner had been served with a notice under s. 352, Housing Act 1985 (see **16.7**) requiring him to instal an adequate means of fire escape. In the High Court, it was held that it was not reasonable for the applicant to continue living in the flat and that accordingly he was homeless. Effective action was needed either to provide a means of escape or to ensure that the toparte flat was vacated. Any delay was unacceptable because it left a period during which the applicant and his family unprotected. On appeal, the authority expressed its concern that, if the judge's decision was upheld, anyone who could demonstrate a lack of adequate fire escape in a house of multiple occupation could in effect demand to be rehoused by the authority at once. The Court of Appeal allowed the council's appeal, acknowledging the difficulties encountered by local authorities in discharging their duties under the homelessness legislation, and the fact that there were 4,500 households in houses in multiple occupation in the council's area alone.

## 18.4.4   Availability

By s. 176, Housing Act 1996,

> accommodation shall be regarded as available for a person's occupation only if it is available for occupation by him together with—
>
> (a)   any other person who normally resides with him as a member of his family, or
> (b)   any other person who might reasonably be expected to reside with him.

This requires consideration of two issues:

(a)   are there persons with whom it is reasonable for the applicant to reside?
(b)   was the accommodation available for the occupation of the applicant and those persons?

In addressing the first question, the Code of Guidance states that the phrase 'a member of his [her] family' in s. 176(a) will clearly cover established households where there is a close blood or marital relationshiparte 'Any other person' for the purposes of s. 176(b) might cover, e.g., cohabiting couples such as a man and a woman living together as husband and wife (see *R* v *Peterborough City Council, ex parte Carr* (1990) 22 HLR 206, adults with foster children, or housekeepers, companions or carers who live with elderly people or people with a disability. People who normally live with the applicant but who are unable to do so for no other reason than that there is no accommodation in which they can live together will normally be included in the assessment (Code of Guidance, para. 13.2).

In *Re Islam* [1983] 1 AC 688 (a case on intentionality), the applicant had spent 16 years living and working in Uxbridge. He returned to Bangladesh to marry and went back to visit his wife on five subsequent occasions, resulting in the birth of four children. While they waited for clearance to join him in the

UK, his wife and children lived with his parents in Bangladesh. He lived in a rented room which he shared with another man. He had never lived with his family. In the Court of Appeal, Lord Denning MR held that Mr Islam had been in notional occupation, through his wife and children, of the family home in Bangladesh. When they left the family home to join him in the UK, he, albeit notionally, had also left and rendered himself (and them) intentionally homeless. Sir Denys Buckley took the view that either:

(a)   the accommodation in Uxbridge and Bangladesh could together constitute the available accommodation, or

(b)   by bringing his family over, Mr Islam had become intentionally homeless from his rented room.

The House of Lords disagreed and allowed Mr Islam's appeal. Mr Islam had never occupied accommodation which was 'available' within the meaning of what is now s. 191(1). The shared room in this country was clearly not 'available', and there was no evidence that the accommodation in Bangladesh was ever available to the applicant himself, nor that he was ever in occupation of it. Further, rooms in two separate continents could not be combined to make uparte 'available accommodation'.

## 18.5   THREATENED WITH HOMELESSNESS

Section 175(4) provides that 'a person is threatened with homelessness if it is likely that he will become homeless within 28 days'. Where an applicant is eligible for assistance, threatened with homelesness unintentionally and in priority need, the local authority must take reasonable steps to secure that accommodation does not cease to be available (s. 195(2), Housing Act 1996). The Code of Guidance states that 'timely advice' and assistance' can sometimes prevent the loss of existing accommodation. If the authority believes that other suitable accommodation is available in its district, it has a duty to offer such advice and assistance as it considers is reasonably required to enable the applicant to secure that accommodation (s. 197(2)). Otherwise, it must secure that accommodation is available for the applicant for the minimum two-year period under s. 193. Where there is intentionality, the local authority must simply provide such advice and assistance as it considers appropriate to prevent the loss of the applicant's existing occupation (s. 195(5)).

The Code of Guidance emphasises that local authorities should normally expect family members who are living at home to continue to do so provided that the accommodation is adequate. In a telling phrase, it states that 'it is obviously proper for individuals to look first to their families for accommodation before turning to a wider community' (para. 9.22).

## 18.6   PRIORITY NEED

### 18.6.1   General principles

By s. 189(1), Housing Act 1996, the following have a priority need for accommodation:

(a)    a pregnant woman or a person with who she resides or might reasonably be expected to reside;

(b)    a person with whom dependent children reside, or might reasonably be expected to reside;

(c)    a person who is vulnerable as a result of old age, mental illness or handicaparte or physical disability, or other special reason, or such persons with whom such persons reside or might reasonably be expected to reside;

(d)    a person who is homeless or threatened with homelessness as a result of an emergency such as flood, fire or other disaster.

When he introduced the Housing (Homeless Persons) Bill, Stephen Ross acknowledged that the 'first call on available resources in areas of housing difficulty should go to those most in need'. The Bill therefore included the notion of priority groups introduced by the 1974 circular. Ross recognised that 'if one is homeless the need for accommodation as just as great as if one is single and healthy as it is if one has children or if one is disabled' but that those who are single and healthy are in a better position to help themselves (*Hansard*, 1977, vol. 926, col. 903).

Authorities are generally either reluctant and/or unable to accept responsibility for applicants falling outside the priority need categories. An authority cannot fetter its discretion, however, by adopting a policy that people within specified groups, e.g. the single or childless homeless, should never be considered 'vulnerable' within s. 189(1)(c) above.

### 18.6.2  Pregnancy

The priority given to dependent children and pregnant women is, it has been said, an indication of 'the centrality of the family to housing' (Watson, 1986: 12) which is 'particularly important to the new right's ideology of the family' (Clapham et al, 1990: 121). Pregnancy, however, proved the most controversial of the priority need groups when the Housing (Homeless Persons) Bill was being debated in the House of Commons. It was claimed that teenage girls would deliberately become pregnant to improve their chances of obtaining council housing and that, having been allocated housing, some women would then proceed to have an abortion. Some Conservative MPs predicted that giving housing rights to pregnant women would lead to a large increase in lone parent families.

Pregnancy qualifies as a priority irrespective of its length. The relevant time is when the authority makes its decision. 'A person with whom she resides or might reasonably be expected to reside' would obviously include the father of the unborn child even if he has never previously lived with the mother 'unless, presumably, she is under 16, in which case he might not "reasonably be expected" to reside with her' given that sexual intercourse with a girl under 16 is a criminal offence under s. 6, Sexual Offences Act 1956 (Hoath, 1989: 82).

### 18.6.3  Dependent children

This is the most common category of priority need. The Act does not define
'dependent' but, according to the Code of Guidance, it means all children
under 16 and those between 16 and 18 who are in, or are about to begin,
full-time education or training or are otherwise unable to support themselves
and who live at home (para. 14.2). A person aged 16 or 17 may not be
financially dependent on his or her parents, but may be sufficiently dependent
in other ways to come within the subsection. The children need not be the
applicant's own children but may be, e.g., grandchildren, adopted children or
foster children.

Dependent children are not classified as in priority need in their own right;
nor will they qualify as vulnerable merely because of their youth or because of
any disability. They depend on their parents or those looking after them to
decide where they are to live and the offer of accommodation can only sensibly
be made to those in charge of them. While a child is entitled to apply under the
Act, the duty to make an offer of accommodation is owed only to those who are
capable of understanding and responding to such an offer. Whether a person
has sufficient mental capacity to be an 'applicant' is a matter for the authority's
discretion, which can be challenged by judicial review on grounds of *Wednesbury* unreasonableness (*R v Oldham MBC, ex parte Garlick*; *R v Bexley LBC, ex
parte Bentum*; *R v Tower Hamlets LBC, ex parte Begum (Ferdous)* [1993] 2 WLR
609). A child of 16 or under may leave home and cease to be dependent on his
or her parents or those with whom he or she was living and may be in priority
need because of some 'other special reason' as in *Kelly v Monklands DC* 1986
SLT 165 in which a homeless girl of 16 with no assets or income had left home
because of violence.

Where the child's parents are living apart, court orders are a starting point
from which to determine residence and dependancy but where children are in
fact residing with a parent, the grant of a custody order is irrelevant (*R v Ealing
LBC, ex parte Sidhu* (1983) 2 HLR 45). Section 189(1)(b) does not require that
the child be 'wholly and exclusively' dependant on the applicant, nor does it
refer to 'whole and exclusive' residence, but only in exceptional cases will a
child have two residences enabling both parents to fall within the definition of
priority need (*R v Port Talbot Borough Council, ex parte McCarthy* (1991) 23
HLR 207).

### 18.6.4  Vulnerability

Those who are vulnerable 'have, for the most part, no direct relationship with
the labour market' and, therefore, 'can be defined as deserving of assistance, in
that the provision of state help would not be expected to inhibit the qualities of
initiative and self-reliance which the undeserving homeless (those who could,
theoretically compete in the labour market and provide for themselves) are
deemed to lack' (Clapham et al, 1990: 121).

'Vulnerability' means 'less able to fend for oneself so that injury or detriment
will result where a less vulnerable man will be able to cope without harmful

effects' (*R* v *Waveney DC, ex parte Bowers* [1983] QB 238) or 'vulnerability in housing terms or in the context of housing' (*R* v *Bath City Council, ex parte Sangermano* (1984) 17 HLR 94). The correct approach is to ask:

(a)   whether there is vulnerability at all; and
(b)   whether the vulnerability is attributable to to any of the factors (singly or in combination) set out in s. 189(1)(c).

In *Ortiz* v *City of Westminster* (1995) 27 HLR 364 it was held that to establish vulnerability, an applicant must be able to show both:

(a)   that to some material extent he or she is less able to obtain suitable accommodation than the ordinary person; and
(b)   that if he or she fails to obtain it, he or she will suffer more than most.

In that case, the applicant, who was an alcoholic and drug addict, was held to have failed at the first hurdle, having been notified by the council that on her discharge from a hospital detoxification unit, suitable accommodation would be available to her, including private lettings, bed and breakfast and supervised hostel accommodation.

**18.6.4.1   Old age**   Customarily, people at or past retirement age are considered vulnerable on account of old age. The Code of Guidance suggests that authorities should look at whether age has made it hard for the applicant to fend for himself or herself, and that all applications from people over 60 should be considered carefully, especially where the applicant is leaving tied accommodation (para. 14.6). A lesser age may be one factor in a number which make up vulnerability as a result of special reason (*R* v *Waveney DC, ex parte Bowers* [1983] QB 238).

**18.6.4.2   Mental illness or handicap or physical disability**   A distinction may be drawn between psychotic illness and mental handicap. The latter will not necessarily amount to vulnerability (*R* v *Bath City Council, ex parte Sangermano* (1984) 17 HLR 94). Whether epilepsy renders a person vulnerable is a question of fact and degree and the position of any particular sufferer may need to be reassessed from time to time (*R* v *Sheffield City Council, ex parte Leek* (1994) 26 HLR 669). Vulnerability will be established if grand mal attacks take place with intense regularity (*R* v *Wandsworth LBC, ex parte Banbury* (1986) 19 HLR 76). See also *R* v *Reigate and Banstead BC, ex parte Di Domenico* (1987) 20 HLR 153; *R* v *Lambeth LBC, ex parte Carroll* (1988) 20 HLR 142.

The Code of Guidance states that chronically sick people, including those with AIDS and HIV related illnesses, may be vulnerable not only because their illness has progressed to the point of physical or mental disability but because the manifestations or effects of their illness, or common attitudes to it, make it very difficult for them the find stable or suitable accommodation (see Cowan, 1995).

**18.6.4.3  Other special reason**  The phrase 'other special reason' should not be construed using the *eiusdem generis* rule. The word 'vulnerable' relates to a need for housing and is not limited to physical or mental conditions suggested by the other categories. The word 'special' points to the fact that the circumstances of the applicant are particularly serious and different from those of other homeless persons (*R* v *Kensington & Chelsea RLBC, ex parte Kihara*, (1996) 29 HLR 147). In *Kihara,* decided after in-country asylum seekers had been stripped of their entitlement to welfare benefits but before the eligibility provisions of the Housing Act 1996 came into force, it was held that the applicants were in priority need for some 'other special reason'. Their financial impecuniosity did not amount to a special reason on its own but should be considered in the light of other circumstances, i.e. the lack of access to income or capital, the absence of friends and family in the UK and an inability to speak English, which stood them apart from most homeless persons.

The Code of Guidance focuses on homeless young people in the context of 'other special reason' and recognises that they may be at risk in a variety of ways, e.g. violence or sexual abuse from a person with whom they are associated, or the likelihood of drug or alcohol abuse or prostitution. It suggests that certain groups of young people will be less able to fend for themselves: those leaving or who have been in local authority care, juvenile offenders (including those discharged from young offender institutions), those who have been physically or sexually abused, those with learning disabilities, those who have been the subject of statements of special educational need, those who lack family contact and support. It highlights the responsibilities of social services departments under ss. 20 and 27, Children Act 1989 in providing accommodation for certain children.

The Code of Guidance also recognises that childless adults may be vulnerable if they have suffered or threatened with harassment or violence on account of their gender, race, colour, ethnic or national origin, or religion (para. 7.17).

### 18.6.5  Emergency

The 'emergency' cases fall into the 'unforeseen homelessness' situation, reminiscent of the National Assistance Act 1948. If not actually flood or fire, the emergency must be of a similar nature and does not include unlawful eviction. Emergencies which can give rise to priority need are not confined to those amounting to *'force majeure'* but embrace all emergencies consisting of physical damage, even fires or floods deliberately or accidentally caused by human beings (*R* v *Bristol CC, ex parte Bradic* (1995) 27 HLR 584).

### 18.7  INTENTIONALITY

#### 18.7.1  General principles

The Housing (Homeless Persons) Bill 1977, as originally drafted, contained no provision for intentionality but the local authority lobby forced through amendments, fearing that people would jump the waiting list queue for council housing by making themselves deliberately homeless. The Bill was attacked as 'a charter for scroungers and scrimshankers' (*Hansard*, 1977, vol. 926, col. 929), a 'charter for queue jumpers' (ibid.) and 'a charter for the rent-dodger, for the scrounger and for the encouragement of the homeleaver' (ibid., col. 972). There was concern that authorities in seaside areas would have to accommodate those who 'come off the beach' and apply for housing (ibid., col. 973). Most homelessness cases have involved the issue of intentionality.

The Housing Act 1996 sets out three ways in which a person can become homeless or treatened with homelessness intentionally:

(a)   deliberate acts or failures to act (s. 191(1));
(b)   collusion (s. 191(3));
(c)   failure to secure accommodation (s. 191(4)).

Section 196 deals with the issue of intentionality when a person is 'threatened with homelessness'.

## 18.7.2   Deliberate act or failures to act

A person becomes homeless intentionally 'if he deliberately does or fails to do anything in consequence of which he ceases to occupy accommodation which is available for his occupation and which it would have been reasonable for him to continue to occupy' (s. 191(1)). The elements of the subsection are:

(a)   the applicant must deliberately have done something or failed to do something;

(b)   the loss of accommodation must be in consequence of the act or omission;

(c)   there must be a cessation of occupation as distinct from a failure to take up accommodation;

(d)   the accommodation must have been available for the occupation of the homeless person; and

(e)   it must have been reasonable for the homeless person to continue to occupy the accommodation.

The onus is on the local authority to satisfy itself of intentionality. It is not for applicants to prove that they are unintentionally homeless (*R* v *Woodspring, ex parte Walters* (1984) 16 HLR 73). The enquiries which the authority makes need not be detailed 'CID type' enquiries (*Lally* v *Royal Borough of Kensington & Chelsea* (1980) *The Times*, 27 March) and the court should intervene 'only if no reasonable authority could have been satisfied on the basis of the enquiries made' (*R* v *Royal Borough of Kensington & Chelsea, ex parte Bayani* (1990) 22 HLR 406).

### 18.7.3    Whose act or omission results in intentional homelessness?

The 'person' referred to in s. 191(1) is the applicant. This means that a person who is found to be intentionally homeless does not lose all chance of being rehoused under the Act because the application can then be made by someone who resides or might reasonably be expected to reside with the applicant and who is unintentionally homeless. The issue first arose in *R v North Devon District Council, ex parte Lewis* [1981] 1 WLR 328 in which a man had become intentionally homeless by leaving his job and thereby losing his tied accommodation. The woman with whom the man was living then applied in her own name. The court held that her case was not governed by the decision on his application and that she was entitled to separate consideration. However, her acquiescence in his decision to leave his job mean that she, by association, had committed an act of intentionality. *Lewis* (and the concept of 'infectious intentionality' to which it gave rise) has been applied in a number of cases, among them *R v West Dorset DC, ex parte Phillips* (1984) 17 HLR 336 in which the applicant's husband had spent the rent money on drink, resulting in the family's eviction. It was held that the applicant was entitled to be found unintentionally homeless. She had not acquiesced in her husband's behaviour, but had lost her temper and attacked him when she learned of the debt. Further, where the debt is so great by the time the applicant finds out about it that it is too late to do anything, mere knowledge of the debt cannot be said to amount to acquiescence (*R v East Northamptonshire DC, ex parte Spruce* (1988) 20 HLR 508) unless the applicant is aware of the commitments and has a sound grasp of the financial situation (*R v London Borough of Barnet, ex parte O'Connor* (1990) 22 HLR 486). In *R v Cardiff City Council, ex parte John* (1982) 9 HLR 56 nuisance and annoyance by a man with whom the tenant had lived for some time resulted in the tenant's eviction, even though it occurred only when she was out of the flat, and he was both younger and considerably larger than her, and she was unable to control his behavior. She was held to have acquiesced in his conduct by failing to evict him.

'Infectious intentionality' is not confined to cohabitants but may extend to conduct by lodgers or children whom the tenant has failed to control (*Smith v Bristol CC* [1981] LAG Bull 287; *Devonport v Salford City Council* (1983) 8 HLR 54; *R v Rochester upon Medway CC, ex parte Williams* [1994] EGCS 35).

An application cannot be made by minors where there is intentionality on the part of their parents (*R v Oldham MBC, ex parte Garlick*; *R v Bexley LBC, ex parte Bentum*; *R v Tower Hamlets LBC, ex parte Begum (Ferdous)* [1993] 2 WLR 609).

### 18.7.4    What is a 'deliberate' act or omission?

#### 18.7.4.1    The Code of Guidance    The Code of Guidance (paras. 15.6 and 15.7) states that, in general, the following should not be considered as a deliberate act or omission:

(a)   where the authority has reason to believe that the applicant is incapable of managing his or her own affairs on account of age, mental illness or handicap;

(b)   where an applicant has lost his or her home or was obliged to sell it because he or she got into rent or mortgage arrears owing to real financial difficulties (for example because he or she became unemployed or ill or suffered greatly reduced earnings or family breakdown) and genuinely could not keep up rent payments or loan repayments even after claiming benefits, and for whom no further financial help is available. In the case of mortgagors, authorities must look at the applicant's ability to pay the mortgage when it was taken on, given his or her financial circumstances at the time.

(c)   where an owner-occupier, who is faced with foreclosure or possession proceedings to which there is no defence, sells before the mortgagee recovers possession through the courts or surrenders the property to the lender; or

(d)   where a tenant, faced with possession proceedings to which there is no defence and where the granting of a possession order is mandatory, surrenders the property to the landlord.

Acts or omissions which may be regarded as deliberate could include:

(a)   where someone chooses to sell his or her home in circumstances where he or she is under no risk of losing it, or has lost it because of wilful and persistent refusal to pay rent or mortgage instalments, when he had the money to do so;

(b)   where someone could be said to have neglected his or her affairs having disregarded advice from qualified persons;

(c)   voluntary surrender of adequate accommodation in this country or abroad which it would have been reasonable for the applicant to continue to occupy (see *R* v *London Borough of Ealing, ex parte Sukhija* (1994) 26 HLR 726);

(d)   where someone is evicted because of anti-social behaviour such as nuisance to neighbours, harassment, etc; or

(e)   where someone leaves a job with tied accommodation and the circumstances indicate that it would have been reasonable for him or her to continue in the employment.

Some of these 'grounds' of intentionality are considered further below.

**18.7.4.2   Rent and mortgage arrears**   When approaching the question of arrears, the authority must enquire into why the arrears have arisen and whether or not there has been 'wilful default' (*R* v *Wyre BC, ex parte Joyce* (1983) 11 HLR 73). If the applicant has taken on financial commitments knowing full well that there is little prospect of keeping up the necessary payments, it will go beyond the stage of honest incompetence and amount to intentionality (*R* v *Wandsworth LBC, ex parte Onwudiwe* (1993) 26 HLR 302).

It cannot be reasonable to continue to occupy accommodation if the applicants can no longer pay the rent or make the mortgage payments without depriving themselves of the ordinary necessities of life, such as food, clothing, heat and transport (*R* v *London Borough of Hillingdon, ex parte Tinn* (1988) 20 HLR 305). A conscious decision to devote what resources the applicant has to his or her children, rather than the payment of rent, is not to be treated automatically as a 'deliberate' act, and inability to pay is a relevant matter in deciding whether a failure to pay is 'deliberate' (*R* v *Wandsworth LBC, ex parte Hawthorne* [1994] 1 WLR 1442). What amounts to a necessity is a matter for the authority. In *R* v *Brent LBC, ex parte Baruwa* (1997) 29 HLR 915, the Court of Appeal upheld the local authority's decision that expenditure on university fees and child care costs were not necessities.

In *R* v *Leeds CC, ex parte Adamiec* (1991) 24 HLR 138 a sale before repossession was sought by the building society was upheld as intentional, even though in the long run the applicant could probably not have afforded to continue living in the house, having been unable to work following an industrial accident.

**18.7.4.3  Omission to pursue other remedies**  Two common examples of omission which are alleged to amount to intentional homelessness are:

(a)  failure of an illegally evicted private tenant to take action against the landlord to gain entry; and

(b)  failure by a spouse or cohabitee to use remedies offered by family law in order to secure peaceful occupation of the home. In *R* v *Wandsworth LBC ex parte Nimako-Boateng* (1984) 11 HLR 95, it was suggested that there might be circumstances where it would be reasonable for a woman to seek to remain in occupation by obtaining a court order to restrain her partner. However, failure to take such proceedings should not be regarded as 'deliberate' if they are unlikely to protect the applicant sufficiently to enable her to return to the former matrimonial home (*Charles* v *Charles* [1984] LAG Bull 81).

**18.7.4.4  Loss of tied accommodation**  Departure from a person's job may result in the loss of tied accommodation. There will be intentional homelessness only if there is a sufficient link, or proximity, between the act which caused the loss of the job, and the loss of the accommodation (*R* v *Thanet District Council, ex parte Reeve* (1981) *The Times*, 25 November. Thus, a direct act, e.g. theft from an employer, which could reasonably be foreseen to lead to loss of job and accommodation, may amount to intentional homelessness. Someone who loses his or her job for incompetence, which will usually be a course of conduct spread over a period of time, cannot be said to be carrying out a deliberate act. The necessary intention or state of mind is absent unless proof exists that a course of incompetent conduct had been adopted in order to provoke dismissal. The fact that someone appears to have resigned from his or her job voluntarily does not necessarily indicate intentional homelessness; it may be a case of constructive dismissal.

**18.7.5  Was an act or omission in good faith?**

An act or omission in good faith on the part of the person unaware of any relevant fact is not to be treated as deliberate (s. 191(2), Housing Act 1996).

Ignorance of a relevant fact (e.g. that full entitlement to housing benefit had not been claimed or that the prospects of the success of a business venture were very small) do not amount to deliberate acts. In *R v Exeter City Council, ex parte Tranckle* (1994) 26 HLR 244, the applicant and her husband found a pub to run. The landlord had recently died, the pub was in poor condition and no accounts were available but the brewery assured the couple that it could be turned into a profitable venture. The applicant's husband became the tenant and they obtained a business loan secured on their house. The business failed and the couple fell into arrears with their loans. They separated and the brewery obtained a possession order in respect of the pub. At the same time the house was also being repossessed. The local authority decided that the applicant was intentionally homeless because of her decision to secure a loan on her house without properly assessing the business's profitability. The Court of Appeal held that the applicant had not become homeless intentionally. Although she had entered into imprudent financial arrangements, she had done so in good faith, unaware of a relevant fact, i.e. that the pub's prospects of success were very slender indeed.

If it is established that the applicant was ignorant of a relevant fact, the authority must not ask whether that ignorance was unreasonable but whether it was in good faith. There is a distinction here between honest blundering and dishonesty, and a fraudulent act can never be in good faith. In *R v London Borough of Barnet, ex parte Rughooputh* (1993) 25 HLR 607, the applicant, who owned a flat, was persuaded to buy a grocery store. She obtained a mortgage for £46,000, having convinced the building society that she was working although she was actually unemployed. When the business failed, the building society repossessed her flat and she applied to local authority for housing. The court upheld the authority's decision that she was intentionally homeless, having obtained the mortgage by giving false information.

### 18.7.6 Causation and the chain of intentionality

In *R v Hammersmith & Fulham LBC, ex parte P* (1989) 22 HLR 21, at p. 26, Schiemann J described causation as 'a notorious minefield in jurisprudence and philosophy'. The fundamental principle is that there must be a 'continuing causal connection between the deliberate act [or omission] in consequence of which homelessness resulted ..'. (Lord Fraser in *Din v Wandsworth LBC* [1981] 3 All ER 881, at p. 890). The present homelessness must be a consequence of a past act or omission. Earlier versions of the Code of Guidance pointed out that, in assessing whether someone has become intentionally homeless, 'it is open to the authority to look beyond the most immediate cause of that homelessness' and a particularly controversial matter has been just how far back an authority can look for the original cause of the homelessness. If there is a *novus actus* which breaks the chain of causation, the original act or omission which gave rise to intentional homelessness from previous accommodation cannot be regarded as the effective cause of the applicant's present homelessness or being threatened with homelessness. The *novus actus* is most likely to consist of a period, between the act of intentionality and the application, spent in other accommodation.

In *De Falco, Silvestri* v *Crawley BC* [1980] QB 460, the De Falcos had left Naples to come to England to work. They stayed with two sets of relatives while they looked for (and found) jobs. When the second relative eventually asked them to leave, they approached Crawley BC for assistance. The housing authority decided they were intentionally homeless because they had come to England without having ensured that they had permanent accommodation to come to.

In *Dyson* v *Kerrier DC* [1980] 1 WLR 1205, Ms Dyson shared a council flat with her sister in Huntingdon. Soon after the birth of Ms Dysons's baby, her sister moved to Cornwall. It was not long before Ms Dyson followed her, surrendering the tenancy of her council flat in order to take on what she knew to be an insecure 'winter let' of private sector accommodation next door to her sister. Before her landlord recovered possession, she applied to Kerrier DC for assistance. After her eviction, the council decided that she was homeless intentionally as she had voluntarily terminated the tenancy of her council flat in Huntingdon. The Court of Appeal dismissed her argument that the housing authority was only entitled to have regard to acts or omissions immediately preceding her homelessness and was not entitled, therefore, to have regard to what had happened in Huntingdon. *Lambert* v *Ealing LBC* [1982] 2 All ER 394 concerned M. Lambert ('a real Frenchman', in the words of Lord Denning MR, with 'three charming daughters'). Having sold his business in Grenoble because of financial problems, he and his daughters came to England in a motor caravan. He arranged their education and put his name on the council waiting list. He then entered into a series of 'holiday' letting agreements. During this period he obtained a job as a van driver for a patisserie. When his rental agreements expired he tried, unsuccessfully, to obtain alternative accommodation. He then applied to Ealing BC who decided that he had become intentionally homeless. Following *De Falco* and *Dyson*, the Court of Appeal upheld the authority's decision, on the ground that:

> When M. Lambert sold up and left France, he became homeless. He was intentionally homeless because he had given up his home in France. That intentional homelessness was the effective cause of his becoming homeless in England. The intervening 18 months do not alter the fact that he was intentionally homeless.

In *Din* v *Wandsworth LBC* [1981] 3 All ER 881 the applicants left secure accommodation in Wandsworth despite advice from the local housing aid centre that they should stay where they were as they had a possible defence to a claim by their landlord for possession. They moved in with a relative in Uxbridge but, after a short time, he asked them to leave and Mr Din approached Wandsworth LBC for assistance. The court upheld the authority's decision that he was intentionally homeless because he had voluntarily terminated his tenancy. It made no difference that by the time of the application the family would have been homeless in any event.

It was asserted in a number of cases that the chain of causation could be broken only by a period spent in 'settled' accommodation. In *R* v *London*

*Borough of Brent ex parte Awua* [1995] 3 WLR 215, however, the House of Lords held that the term 'accommodation' is not so limited. It said that the only relevant question was whether the accommodation which had been lost, could fairly be described as accommodation which it would have been reasonable for the applicant to continue to occupy. It would appear, therefore, that in most cases there will be no need for authorities to work back through the applicant's history of housing; only if the accommodation most recently left by the applicant is that which it would not have been reasonable for him or her to continue to occupy will such a process be necessary. It is submitted that the only accommodation likely to fall within this category will be the emergency type accommodation referred to in **16.4.1** such as refuges or night shelters.

### 18.7.7 Availability

The accommodation which has been lost must have been 'available for the applicant's occupation' (s. 191(1)). Availability has already been considered in **18.4.4**.

### 18.7.8 Was it reasonable to continue to occupy the accommodation?

Reasonableness has already been considered in relation to 'homelessness' in **18.4.2**.

### 18.7.9 Collusion

Where a person enters into an arrangement which requires him or her leave accommodation which it would have been reasonable to continue to occupy, and the purpose of the arrangement is to enable that person to become entitled to assistance under Part VII, he or she will be treated as becoming homeless intentionally unless another 'good reason' for the homelessness exists (s. 191(3)). Collusion is not confined to arrangements between friends and relatives but can also occur between landlords and tenants. The Code of Guidance advises authorities that they should not rely merely on hearsay or unfounded suspicions in satisfying themselves that it exists. Examples of other 'good reasons' for the applicant's homlessness would include overcrowding and relationship breakdown (para. **15.10**).

### 18.7.10 Failure to secure accommodation

Where the applicant was given advice and assistance under s. 197 (duty where other suitable accommodation is available) but failed to secure suitable accommodation when he or she might reasonably have been expected to do so, the applicant will be treated as having become homeless intentionally on any further application under Part VII (s. 191(4)).

## References

Clapham, D., Kemp P. and Smith, S., *Housing and Social Policy*, Basingstoke: Macmillan, 1990.

Cowan, D., 'HIV and Homelessness: Lobbying, Law, Policy and Practice', *Journal of Social Welfare and Family Law*, 1995, vol. 17, pp. 43–66.

Hague, G. and Malos, E., *Domestic Violence: Action for Change*, Cheltenham: New Clarion Press, 1993.

Hoath, D., *Public Housing Law*, London: Sweet & Maxwell, 1989.

Pascall, G. and Morley, R., 'Women and Homelessness: Proposals from the Department of the Environment. I. Lone Mothers; II. Domestic Violence', *Journal of Social Welfare and Family Law*, 1996, vol. 18, pp. 189–202, 327–340.

Watson, S. and Austerberry, H., *Housing and Homelessness: a Feminist Perspective*, London: Routledge & Kegan Paul, 1986.

# NINETEEN

## The implementation of the homelessness legislation
## II: Duties of local authorities, local connection and the right to a review

### 19.1  INTRODUCTION

As stated in the last chapter, s. 21(1)(b), National Assistance Act 1948 required local authority welfare departments to provide 'temporary accommodation' to those whose urgent need for such accommodation could not reasonably have been foreseen. By 1977, however, there was strong support for the view that, instead of a short stay in temporary accommodation to tide them over their difficulties, what most homeless people really needed was 'a permanent solution to their problem which they had been unable to arrange for themselves' (Stephen Ross MP, *Hansard*, 1977, vol. 926, cols. , 898–899).

The Housing (Homeless Persons) Act 1977 provided that where a local housing authority was satisfied that an applicant for accommodation had a priority need and was not satisfied that he or she became homeless intentionally, it had a duty to 'secure that accommodation becomes available for his [or her] occupation'. That duty, subsequently incorporated into s. 65(2), Housing Act 1985, was commonly referred to as the 'full' duty. Lesser duties (of securing that accommodation was made available for the applicant's occupation for such period as would give him or her a reasonable opportunity of securing accommodation for himself or herself, and/or of furnishing the applicant with advice and assistance to enable him or her to do so) were owed to those who had a priority need but were intentionally homeless, or those who were unintentionally homeless but had no priority need.

The Department of the Environment's then Code of Guidance stated that the accommodation secured in order to discharge the full duty must be 'long-term settled accommodation, commonly referred to as permanent' but the duty was diluted as the depletion of council stock and the increase in the number of people applying to local authorities for housing made its execution more difficult to achieve. The accepted construction following *Dyson* v *Kerrier District Council* [1980] 1 WLR 1205 was that the full duty required the provision of indefinite accommodation, while in *R* v *Slough Borough Council, ex parte Ealing London Borough Council* [1981] QB 801 Lord Denning MR said that the local authority was 'to secure that accommodation is available for [the applicant] indefinitely and not merely for a short time' (at p. 811). Lord Lowry's statement in *Din* v *Wandsworth LBC* (1983) AC 657 that 'there is no temporal adverbial qualification of the word "occupation"' (at p. 677E) was relied upon in, for example, *R* v *London Borough of Camden, ex parte Wait* (1986) 18 HLR 434 in which it was held that the accommodation to be provided must be 'indefinite in length'. In more recent cases the courts inclined to use the phrase 'settled' accommodation (see, e.g. *R* v *Rushcliffe Borough Council ex parte Summerson* (1992) 25 HLR 577), and in *R* v *Wandsworth London Borough Council ex parte Crooks* (1995) *The Independent*, 30 March) it was held that the obligation to provide 'settled' accommodation had been fulfilled by placing a homeless person in private rented accommodation under an assured shorthold tenancy. In *R* v *London Borough of Brent, ex parte Awua* [1995] 2 WLR 315 the House of Lords held that there was, in fact, no duty to provide 'settled' accommodation at all. What there did appear to be was an indefinite duty to secure accommodation but in discharging that duty, no account need be taken of the security of tenure of the accommodation provided so long as it lasted for at least 28 days (otherwise the applicant would be regarded as 'threatened with homelessness').

Taking the view that homelessness is a consequence of an emergency or crisis, the 1995 White Paper stated the government's intention that, in future, local authorities would have a duty merely to secure suitable accommodation for not less than 12 months for 'families and vulnerable people who have nowhere to go' and who are found to be unintentionally homeless. This 12-month period was intended to tide people over 'the immediate crisis of homelessness, and to give them time to find longer term accommodation'. It was felt that in many parts of the country, 12 months would be long enough for a household with real housing need to be offered a long-term tenancy by means of the housing register with a local authority, housing association or other social landlord.

Much of the responsibility for the current housing malaise was placed with the courts, their interpretation of the legislation having enabled anyone who was accepted by the local housing authority as statutorily homeless to be given priority in the allocation of 'a life-long tenancy' (Department of the Environment, 1995: 36). This disingenuous statement was misleading on two counts. First, as indicated above, there has never been any legal entitlement to a 'life-long' tenancy. Indeed, despite the exhortation of the then Code of Guidance, the courts have gone to great lengths to avoid using the words 'permanent' or 'life-long' to denote the type of accommodation to be secured in discharging the full duty. In fact they have recognised that, in the light of new forms of housing provision (such as PSL) which have emerged since the Code of Guidance was drafted, the notion of 'permanence' is outdated (*R* v *London Borough of Brent, ex parte Macwan* (1994) 26 HLR 528), and that to interpret 'accommodation' in s. 65(2) as 'permanent' would result in the imposition on local authorities of duties which, given their depleted housing stocks, they would not be able to fulfil — hence the liberal interpretation of the word 'settled' in *Crooks* (ibid.).

Secondly, even if the courts had interpreted s. 65(2) as imposing a duty to provide permanent accommodation, there is no evidence to be found from the parliamentary debates during the passage of the Housing (Homeless Persons) Bill that Parliament ever intended anything different. Such was the concern among MPs who opposed the Bill as to what they perceived as the likely outcomes of the legislation — that those who were not genuinely homeless, or who did not belong to the area in which they were applying for accommodation, would be given council house tenancies in preference to local applicants whose names had been on the waiting list for some time — that attention was centred on the issues of intentionality and local connection. The type of accommodation to be secured by the local authority in what was to become s. 65(2) was virtually ignored but the very presence of the lesser duty owèd to the intentionally homeless in priority need (of securing that accommodation is made available for the applicant's occupation 'for such period as the local authority considers will give him a reasonable opportunity of securing accommodation for himself') makes it quite clear that Parliament intended something different (and, presumably, longer term) to be provided via s. 65(2) for the unintentionally homeless in priority need.

While the Housing Act 1996 was being debated in the House of Commons, the minimum period was extended from 12 months to two years, and is now contained in s. 193, Housing Act 1996. Soon after coming to power in 1997, however, the Labour government began to dismantle the changes made by the previous Conservative government to the homelessness legislation. The effect of the Housing (Reasonable and Additional Preference) Regulations 1997 (SI 1997/1902) is that local authorities should not require applicants who are accepted as eligible for assistance, unintentionally homeless and in priority need to spend time in temporary accommodation provided under Part VII of the 1996 Act if there is accommodation available which could be offered to them immediately through the housing register. The two-year duty under s. 193 does not prevent immediate allocation of accommodation through the register where the applicant has sufficient priority. The s. 193 duty ceases if the applicant accepts an offer of suitable accommodation through the allocation scheme of Part VI (see Department of the Environment's Code of Guidance on Parts VII and VII of the Housing Act 1996, para. 20.14A).

## 19.2  DUTIES UNDER THE HOUSING ACT 1996

### 19.2.1 Duty of local housing authority to provide advisory services

According to the Code of Guidance, the 1996 Act makes information and advice a key component of the strategy for dealing with homelessness, both for people in general who need advice and for homeless applicants specifically. 'Timely advice, ' it says 'can prevent the loss of a home, and give all the parties concerned a chance to assess the most suitable course of action' (para. 9.1).

For the first time, therefore, local authorities have a duty to secure that advice and information about homelessness and its prevention is provided free of charge to any person in their district. They may provide the advice and information themselves or arrange for it to be provided by, or in conjunction with, another organisation (s. 179, Housing Act 1996). It is up to each authority to determine what precisely an advisory service covers but information and advice is likely to be sought on local housing opportunities (including private sector options), housing registers and allocations policy, landlords and letting agents, housing status, security and rights of occupation, harassment and illegal eviction, possession proceedings, connsequences of relationship breakdown and implications for tenancies, income maximisation (including welfare benefits, housing benefit), rent levels, rent and mortgage arrears, and other money or debt issues which could lead to homelessness, local authority duties towards homeless households, housing conditions, grants and repairs (Code of Guidance, para. 9.11).

### 19.2.2   Interim duty to accommodate

Where an authority considers that an applicant may be eligible for assistance, homeless and in priority need, it comes under a duty under s. 188, Housing Act 1996 to secure accommodation while it carries out enquiries under s. 184 to establish what further duty under Part VII may be owed. This duty arises regardless of whether or not the applicant has a local connection with another authority. It ends once the authority have notified the applicant of their decision on his or her application. Any further duty towards a homeless applicant is determined by the outcome of the local authority's enquiries. If the authority decides that no further duty is owed, it will wish to give the applicant reasonable notice to quit (Code of Guidance, para. 20.1) but it can, if it wishes, continue to secure that the accommodation is available pending the outcome of a review (see **19.3.1.2**). The Code of Guidance states that while circumstances may sometimes dictate the use of bed and breakfast accommodation to provide emergency accommodation, it should only generally be used as a last resort and should not be regarded as suitable accommodation for families with children (para. 20.2). It should be noted however, that it is standard practice for some Inner London authorities to use bed and breakfast for virtually all applicants while enquiries are being carried out under s. 184.

### 19.2.3   Duties to specific categories of applicant

**19.2.3.1   Applicant not eligible for assistance**   No duty is owed to a person who is not eligible for assistance, apart from the general duty contained in s. 179 of securing that advice is available (see **19.2.1**).

**19.2.3.2 Applicant eligible for assistance but not homeless or threatened with homelessness**  No duty is owed to a person who is not eligible for assistance, apart from securing that advice is available under s. 179 (see **19.2.1**).

**19.2.3.3 Applicant eligible for assistance, intentionally homeless but not in priority need**  The local authority must provide the applicant with advice and such assistance as it considers appropriate in any attempt by the applicant to find accommodation for himself or herself (s. 190(3), Housing Act 1996). The local authority owes no duty of care that any premises to which it directs the applicant are reasonably safe, especially as regards fire (*Ephraim* v *London Borough of Newham, ex parte Mirza* (1993) 25 HLR 207).

**19.2.3.4 Applicant eligible for assistance, intentionally homeless and in priority need**  The authority must secure that accommodation is available for the applicant's occupation for such period as it considers will give the applicant a reasonable opportunity of securing accommodation (s. 190(2)(a)). The Code of Guidance suggests that in most areas 28 days might be expected to be long enough for the applicant but that local circumstances, including how readily other accommodation is available and the applicant's particular circumstances, will need to be taken into account (para. 20.3). Advice and assistance as in **19.2.3.3** must also be provided (s. 190(2)(b)).

**19.2.3.5 Applicant eligible for assistance but threatened with homelessness intentionally, whether or not in priority need**  The local authority must provide advice and such assistance as it considers appropriate to prevent the loss of the applicant's existing accommodation (s. 195(5)).

**19.2.3.6 Applicant eligible for assistance, unintentionally homeless but not in priority need**  The local authority must provide advice and assistance as at **19.2.3.3** (s. 192(2)).

**19.2.3.7 Applicant eligible for assistance, threatened with homelessness unintentionally, and in priority need**  The local authority must take reasonable steps to secure that the applicant's existing accommodation does not cease to be available for his or her occupation (s. 195(2)). This duty is subject to s. 197 (duty where other suitable accommodation available).

**19.2.3.8 Applicant eligible for assistance, unintentionally homeless and in priority need**  This is the most extensive duty owed by a local authority to homeless households. The local authority has a duty to provide suitable accommodation for a minimum period of two years (s. 193(3)) which may be extended in certain circumstances (s. 194). However, the duty under s. 193 is subject to:

(a)  s. 197, where suitable alternative accommodation is available in the local authority's district; and

(b)   the local authority's right to make further enquiry as to whether it can refer the applicant to another authority under s. 198.

The s. 193 duty is a far cry, therefore, from the full duty under s. 65(2), Housing Act 1985 which the earlier Code of Guidance construed as a duty to provide permanent accommodation.

### 19.2.4   Suitable alternative accommodation in the district

If the local authority is satisfied that suitable alternative accommodation is available in its district, it has a duty merely to provide the applicant with such advice and assistance as it considers is reasonably required to enable him or her to secure such accommodation (s. 197(2)). This duty applies in cases where the authority would otherwise be under a duty:

(a)   to secure accommodation for persons who are eligible for assistance, in priority need and not homeless intentionally (s. 193); or

(b)   to prevent accommodation ceasing to be available for persons who are eligible for assistance, threatened with homelessness unintentionally and in priority need (s. 195(2)).

The Code of Guidance describes the duty under s. 197 as 'an intermediate stage between the advisory role of the local authority and their full housing duty' which requires the applicant to take responsibility for securing his or her own accommodation with the authority's help' (para. 20.5). It 'is intended to provide a practical way in which applicants can help themselves without having to place themselves entirely in the hands of the local authority'. It ceases if the applicant fails to take reasonable steps to secure the accommodation (s. 197(3)). Further, if the applicant then makes a further application under Part VII, he or she will be treated as having become intentionally homeless (ss. 191(4) and 196(4)).

In deciding what advice and assistance to provide under s. 197, and whether the applicant has taken reasonable steps, the authority shall have regard to all the circumstances including:

(a)   the characteristics and personal circumstances of the applicant, and

(b)   the state of the local housing market and the type of accommodation available (s. 197(4)).

As the Code of Guidance explains, 'an applicant may have a disability which limits the type of accommodation which may be suitable and/or available to him or her or there may be a limited range of private accommodation available to families with children. The level of help will need to reflect the level of ability, disability or vulnerability for the applicant and anyone who might reasonably be expected to reside with him or her' (para. 20.9).

Active involvement on the part of the local authority is required in assisting the applicant in his or her efforts to secure accommodation. It is not enough, therefore, for the authority merely to hand the applicant a list of letting agents in the area or copies of advertisements from the local newspaper. Active involvement may include offering rent guarantees or helping with deposits. Authorities should seek to assist the applicant to find suitable accommodation which is available for as long a period as possible and avoid the possibility of homelessness recurring in the future (Code of Guidance, para. 20.10).

The 1996 Act gives no indication as to the duration of the suitable accommodation but, as from 1 September 1997, accommodation is not suitable under s. 197 unless the authority is reasonably satisfied that it will continue to be available for at least two years. This means that an authority can only comply with the s. 197 duty by identifying a specific landlord and address, the terms of the tenancy and details of the rent. It is not enough that the authority simply hands out a leaflet of local letting agents, for example, even where there is a 'ready supply of vacancies' in the area (Campbell, R., 1997).

### 19.2.5 Local connection

**19.2.5.1 Introduction**  One of the principal objectives of the Housing (Homeless Persons) Act 1977 was to end 'shuttling' homeless people between different local authorities, each alleging that the applicant had a stronger connection with the other. If, however, the authority to which application is made is satisifed that the applicant is eligible for assistance, unintentionally homeless and in priority need (i.e. is someone to whom the full duty under s. 193 is owed), it may also consider whether the applicant has a local connection with the district of another authority to which the application may then be referred (s. 198, Housing Act 1996). In *R v Slough BC, ex parte Ealing LBC* [1981] QB 801, the applicants were former council tenants who had been evicted by Slough BC. When they applied to be rehoused, Slough decided that they were intentionally homeless. They then approached Ealing LBC which decided they were unintentionally homeless but, because they had no local connection with Ealing, referred them back to Slough. Lord Denning MR likened the situation to the disputes under the Poor Law 200 years ago, when each parish was reponsible for the relief of those who were poor and unable to work.

> When a poor man moved from one parish to another, the question arose: which parish was responsible? The disputes, Blackstone tells us, 'created an infinity of expensive law-suits between contending neighbourhoods, concerning those settlements and removals' . . . History tends to repeat itself. If our present cases are anything to go by, we are in for another dose of the same medicine (at pp. 807, 808).

Where there is a dispute between two or more authorities as to which of them is to bear the responsibility for securing accommodation, it may be resolved by reference to the Local Authority Association Joint Local Connection Agreement (the 'Local Authority Agreement'). If the housing authorities fail to reach agreement, the matter must be referred to arbitration (s. 198(5)). Until the dispute is resolved, it is the authority to which application was initially made which must accommodate the applicant.

The local connection provisions only allow the transfer of the most extensive housing duty (such as it is) which arises under s. 193. They are irrelevant to all other duties, including the duty under s. 184 to make enquiries into homelessness, priority need and intentionality. However, this need not prevent arrangements being made with another authority for that other authority to assist in securing accommodation under s. 213 of the 1996 Act (co-operation between authorities).

**19.2.5.2  Meaning of 'local connection'**  By s. 199(1), Housing Act 1996 a person has a local connection with the district of a local housing authority:

(a)  because he or she is, or in the past was, normally resident in that district, and that residence is or was of his or her own choice;
(b)  because he or she is employed there;
(c)  because of family associations; or
(d)  because of special circumstances.

The conditions for referral are also met where a household is placed in accommodation which is out-of-area in discharge of a homelessness duty under s. 193(2) or s. 195(4). The authority retains 'responsibility' for that household in the event of a further two-year duty being owed within a period of five years of the date when accommodation was first made available.

It is the date of application which is relevant for determining whether any of the 'grounds' of local connection apply.

(a)  *Residence*  Residence must be 'of choice'. It is not of choice if the applicant, nor any person who might reasonably be expected to reside with the applicant, is serving in the regular armed forces, or is imprisoned or is detained under the Mental Health Act 1959. The Local Authority Agreement suggests a working definition of 'normal residence' as being established by six months in the area during the previous 12 months, or not less than three years during the previous five-year period.

(b)  *Employment*  A person who is serving in the regular armed forces is not regarded as being employed in an area. There is no indication that 'employment' for the purposes of s. 199 excludes self-employment or that employment need be full-time.

(c)  *Family associations*  The Local Authority Agreement limits family associations to parents, adult children, or brothers and sisters who have been in the area for five years. A first cousin once removed is not sufficient (*R v Hammersmith & Fulham LBC, ex parte Advic* (1996) 28 HLR 897).

(d)  *Special circumstances*  This phrase is not defined in the Act nor does the Code of Guidance give any assistance. The Local Authority Agreement mentions families returning from abroad, those leaving the armed forces or those who wish to return to an area where they were brought up or lived for a considerable length of time in the past. In *R v Vale of White Horse DC, ex parte*

*South and Hay* (1984) 17 HLR 160, an unsuccessful attempt was made to establish a local connection by the applicants' involvement with an evangelical church which was the most importance influence on their lives.

**19.2.5.3  Restrictions on referral**  Before a referral under s. 198 can be made, it must be determined that:

(a)  neither the applicant, nor any person who might reasonably be expected to reside with the applicant has a local connection with the district applied to;

(b)  the applicant, etc. does have such a connection with the area of another authority;

(c)  none of them will be at risk of domestic violence in the area of that authority.

**19.2.5.4  No local connection**  If a person accepted as eligible for assistance, unintentionally homeless and in priority need has no local connection with the area of any housing authority in Great Britain, then the duty to secure accommodation rests with the authority to which application has been made for assistance, as in *R v Hillingdon London Borough Council, ex parte Streeting* [1980] 3 All ER 413 which concerned a refugee from Ethiopia. However, s. 206(1)(b) provides that a local housing authority may discharge its housing functions by securing that the applicant obtains suitable accommodation from 'some other person'. That 'other person' does not have to be within the authority's area and means that the authority to which the application is made may even be able to arrange accommodation with an agency in the country from which the applicant comes. In *R v Bristol City Council, ex parte Browne* [1979] 3 All ER 344, the duty to secure accommodation lay with Bristol but the 'other person' from which the council sought to secure accommodation was the authority in the Republic of Ireland from whose district Mrs Browne had fled to escape her violent husband. It was not, therefore, a referral under what is now s. 198 as it was outside the legislation's jurisdiction. The Divisional Court ruled that Bristol had acted neither unlawfully nor unreasonably despite the fact that the decision to return Mrs Browne to the Republic of Ireland was based on an assurance made over the telephone by a welfare officer in Tralee that Mrs Browne could be safely accommodated there.

**19.2.6  Cessation of the duty under s. 193**

The duty under s. 193 comes to an end if at any time the applicant:

(a)  refuses an offer of suitable accommodation, having been informed by the local housing authority of the possible consequence of refusal. The authority must notify him or her that they regard themselves as having discharged their duty under this section (s. 193(5)); or

(b)  ceases to be eligible for assistance under Part VII, as defined in ss. 185 and 186 (s. 193(6)(a)); or

(c)   becomes homeless intentionally from the accommodation made available for his or her occupation (s. 193(6)(b)); or

(d)   accepts an offer of accommodation under Part VI (allocation of housing), (s. 193(6)(d)); or

(e)   voluntarily ceases to occupy as his or her only or principal home the accommodation made available under s. 193 (s. 196(3)(c)); or

(f)   having been informed of the possible consequence of refusal, refuses an offer of suitable accommodation under Part VI which it was reasonable for the applicant to accept, and the authority notify him or her accordingly within 21 days of the refusal (s. 196(7)). An applicant may reasonably be expected to accept an offer of accommodation under Part VI even though he or she is under contractual or other obligations in respect of existing accommodation, provided that those obligations can be brought to an end before the applicant is required to take up the offer.

A person who ceases to be owed the duty under this section may make a fresh application to the authority for accommodation or assistance in obtaining accommodation (s. 193(9)).

### 19.2.7   Power to continue providing accommodation

Where a local authority has secured accommodation under s. 193 for two years, it may continue to do so for further periods of up to two years although most applicants in long-term housing are likely to have been allocated accommodation through the housing register before the end of the minimum period. The power to continue the provision of accommodation exists if the local housing authority is satisfied, on a review carried out towards the end of the two-year period, that the likely situation at the end of the period will be that:

(a)   the applicant continues to have a priority need;

(b)   there is no other suitable accommodation available for the applicant's occupation in its district; and

(c)   the applicant wishes the authority to continue securing that accommodation is available for his or her occupation; and

(d)   the applicant is still an eligible person (s. 194(2)).

The authority must also satisfy itself that none of the events which leads to a cessation of its duty by virtue of s. 193(6) and (7) has occurred (see **19.2.6**). On completing the review the authority must notify the applicant of its determination and of whether it proposes to exercise, or continue to exercise, its power under this section.

A range of factors will have to be taken into account in determining whether or not to continue to secure accommodation after the minimum period has ended. Of key importance is whether the household would be homeless again if the accommodation did not continue to be provided but account may also be taken of the efforts which the members of the household have made themselves to find accommodation (Code of Guidance, para. 20.28).

The authority may at any time, whether in consequence of a review or otherwise, give notice to the person concerned that it proposes to cease exercising its power under this section in his or her case (s. 194(5)). The notice must specify:

(a)   the day on which it will cease exercising its power under this section; and
(b)   any action which it intends to take as a result (such as deciding to evict from accommodation provided from its own stock, or withdrawing any support such as rent guarantees in the case of other accommodation).

The notification must be given not less than 28 days in advance of the date on which the authority proposes to cease exercising its power (s. 194(6)).

### 19.2.8   Sources of accommodation

By s. 206 a local authority may discharge its housing functions under Part VII of the 1996 Act by:

(a)   providing accommodation from its own stock;
(b)   securing that the applicant obtains accommodation from 'some other person'; and
(c)   giving the applicant such advice and assistance as will enable him or her to secure accommodation from some other person.

In each case, the accommodation must be 'suitable' (see **19.2.10**). The Act also gives authorities power to make reasonable charges for the accommodation (s. 206(2)). Authorities are required by the Act to secure accommodation in their own areas, so far as reasonably practicable (s. 208(1)). If they provide accommodation in another area, they must notify the local authority in that other area within 14 days of the provision of the accommodation, of the applicant's name, address, number and description of other people who normally reside with the applicant or might be expected to do so, the date on which the accommodation was made available and the duty which the authority was discharging (s. 208(2)–(4)).

**19.2.8.1   Provision from the authority's own stock**   The Code of Guidance states that authorities must balance the limited, short-term requirements of homeless people with the greater, longer-term requirements from other, general needs applicants for housing, giving priority to the latter. An authority may set aside part of its stock to accommodate people accepted as homeless but should avoid concentrating homeless people in a particular area or estate (para. 21.20).
Section 207 provides that authorities shall not provide accommodation in their own stock for more than two years continuously or for two years in any three, regardless of the number of applications made by the applicant during this period. The aim of this provision 'is to preserve the principle of a single

route into long-term social housing' (HL Debs, vol. 574, col. 133). There are two exceptions to this rule:

(a)   hostel accommodation; and
(b)   accommodation leased to the authority (s. 207(1)(a), (b)).

**19.2.8.2  Securing accommodation from another person**   Where an authority secures accommodation from another landlord, it must ensure that the accommodation is 'available' and 'suitable'. The Code of Guidance (para. 21.23) identifies the main options as follows:

(a)   *Registered social landlords*   If asked, registered social landlords are obliged under s. 213 to assist local authorities in carrying out their duties under the homelessness legislation by co-operating as far as is reasonable in the circumstances. In cases where whole stock transfers have taken place, other registered social landlords in the area may need to be approached for assistance. Where accommodation is provided to assist a housing authority in discharging an interim duty (i.e. under s. 188, s. 190, s. 200 or s. 204(4)), a tenancy granted cannot be an assured tenancy unless the landlord notifies the applicant that it is, or unless 12 months have elapsed since the applicant was notified of the decision which brought the interim duty to an end. Where a registered social landlord assists a housing authority to discharge any other homelessness duty, the tenancy granted will be an assured shorthold tenancy. Such a tenancy cannot be converted to an assured tenancy unless it is allocated through the housing register under Part VI (s. 209(3)).

(b)   *Private renting*   Local authorities are permitted to incur expenditure on rent deposits and guarantees to help homeless people to secure accommodation in the private sector.

The Code of Guidance states that where tenancies secured in the private rented sector are assured shorthold tenancies, authorities should, where practicable, ensure that accommodation is available either for an initial term of two years or, if less, that there is a reasonable prospect of the tenancy continuing beyond the initial shorthold term. If a tenancy for less than two years is not renewed within the minimum period of duty, the local authority's duty to secure accommodation until the end of the minimum period continues, unless the applicant has become intentionally homeless, or there are other reasons why the duty to secure accommodation has ceased.

(c)   *Private sector leasing*   Since 1 April 1997 local authorities have been able to take out leases for up to 10 years on property owned by private landlords without being required to provide captial cover for the cost of the lease.

(d)   *Lodgings*   The Code of Guidance regards lodgings as suitable for some young and/or single people.

(e)   *Hostels*   The Code of Guidance points out that some people may benefit from the supportive environment provided by hostels. They can offer short-term support to those at crisis point to enable them to move on to independent living. Because some hostels are designed to meet short-term needs only, they are unlikely to be appropriate in fulfilling an authority's two-year duty.

(f)  *Other housing authorities*  Another housing authority which is under less housing pressure may be able to assist in the provision of interim accommodation, especially where victims of violence and/or harassment do not wish to return to the area where the perpetrator of the violence/harassment lives, or for assisting those with special housing needs.

(g)  *Other social landlords*  Section 213 obliges other social landlords, i.e. new town corporations and housing action trusts, to co-operate, as far as is reasonable in the circumstances, with a local authority in carrying out is homeless function under the Housing Act 1996 if asked to do so.

(h)  *Occupiers of caravans, houseboats, etc., including gypsies*  If a duty to secure accommodation arises where a person has become homeless because there is nowhere he or she is entitled or permitted to put and live in a caravan, houseboat, or other moveable structure (s. 175(2)), the authority is not required to make equivalent accommodation available, although of course it may do so if resources permit.

(i)  *Mobile homes*  Although mobile homes may sometimes provide emergency accommodation, e.g. to discharge the interim duty, they may not be satisfactory for households with children, or for the elderly or disabled people. The Code of Guidance urges authorities to satisfy themselves that the accommodation is suitable, paying particular regard to conditions and facilities on the site. It states that caravans designed primarily for holiday use should not be regarded as suitable for homeless people.

(j)  *Women's refuges*  Securing accommodation in a refuge may not count as a discharge of an authority's duty. Refuges should be used for the minimum time necessary before securing suitable accommodation elsewhere. Authorities should not delay securing other accommodation for an applicant placed in a womens' refuge in the hope that she might return to her partner. It is also important to ensure that places in refuges continue to be available for others in need. If the refuge terminates a licence because the household no longer needs to be in the refuge, the authority have a duty to secure alternative accommodation straightaway.

(k)  *Bed and breakfast*  The Code of Guidance exhorts authorities to explore all alternatives before resorting to bed and breakfast hotels or other specialised bed and breakfast establishments. If, as a last resort, authorities have to use such accommodation as a short-term measure until more suitable accommodation is available they should to ensure that homeless people are allowed to use their rooms during the day and have adequate access to cooking facilities especially if there are young children and that the accommodation meets the statutory requirements on standards for houses in multiple occupation.

**19.2.9   Availability**

The Housing Act 1996 requires that the accommodation must be 'available'. It must be capable, therefore, of accommodating the whole household, that is, the applicant and any other person who normally resides with the applicant as a member of his or her family, and any other person who might reasonably be expected to reside with the applicant, e.g., a carer (see **18.4.4**).

**19.2.10   Suitability**

The accommodation provided by, or found for, the applicant for the purposes of Part VII of the Housing Act 1996 must be suitable (s. 210). In assessing suitability, the local housing authority must have regard to Parts IX, X and XI of the 1985 Act (slum clearance, overcrowding, houses in multiple occupation). The accommodation must be suitable not only for the applicant but also for anyone who normally resides with the applicant, or might reasonably be expected to do so. It has been suggested that:

> suitability imports questions of fact and degree, and is dependent upon all the circumstances of the case, including the size, composition and health of the applicant's household, and the applicant's preferences as to area and type of accommodation, as well as the availability of housing and the pressures upon the local housing authority from competing applicants (per Leggat LJ in *R* v *Brent LBC, ex parte Macwan* (1994) 26 HLR 528 at p. 534).

The Homelessness (Suitability of Accommodation) Order 1996 (SI 1996/3204) specifies, *inter alia*, that in determining whether accommodation is suitable for a person an authority must take into account the affordability of the accommodation for the applicant and, in particular, must take account of:

(a)   the applicant's financial rescources, including:

(i)     salary, fees and other remuneration;
(ii)    social security benefits;
(iii)   payments due under a court order for the making of periodical payments to a spouse or to, or for the benefit of, a child;
(iv)    payments of child support maintenance under the Child Support Act 1991;
(v)     pensions;
(vi)    contributions to accommodation costs made by other members of the household;
(vii)   benefits derived from a policy of insurance;
(viii)  savings and other capital sums; and

(b)   the costs of the accommodation, including

(i)     rent;
(ii)    service charges, council tax, deposits; and

(c)   payments which the applicant is required to make under a court order for the making of periodical payments to a spouse or former spouse, or to or for the benefit of a child, and payments of child support maintenance under the Child Support Act 1991; and

(d)   the applicant's other reasonable living expenses.

The Homelessness (Suitability of Accommodation)(Amendment) Order 1997 (SI 1997/1741) specifies that for the purposes of s. 197(1) of the 1996 Act (duty where other suitable accommodation is available) accommodation is not to be regarded as suitable unless the authority is satisfied that it will be available for occupation by the applicant for at least two years, starting on the date when the applicant secures the accommodation. The Code of Guidance suggests that if the accommodation is provided by a private landlord under a fixed-term lease of two years or more, the authority may wish to encourage the applicant to negotiate a break clause so that the applicant can quit before the end of the tenancy in case an opportunity arises to move into a permanent tenancy in the social sector (para. 21.14B). In all cases where a homeless household is assisted under s. 197(1), the authority should check whether it is within the landlord's gift to make an offer of availability for two-years, whether the landlord intends to occupy the property as his or her home before the two-year period comes to an end, and whether the landlord has acted previously in a manner which might suggest that an assurance as to the duration of the letting might not be kept (para. 21.14D).

The Code of Guidance points out that local authority stock which is awaiting demolition, improvement or repair may, in some circumstances, offer suitable accommodation while at the same time avoiding stock needlessly standing empty. It should be in a reasonable state of repair and with adequate heating. The length of time for which it is available is also relevant, bearing in mind the need to provide stability for the household during the minimum period of duty (para. 21.21).

### 19.3   CHALLENGING THE DECISION OF A LOCAL AUTHORITY

#### 19.3.1   Internal review

For the first time, the homelessness legislation provides an aggrieved applicant with a right to have the decision reviewed by the authority:

(a)   on the applicant's eligibility for assistance under ss. 185 and 186;

(b)   on what duty (if any) is owed under ss. 190 to 193 and 195 to 197 (duties to persons found to be homeless or threatened with homelessness);

(c)   on any decision to notify another authority that the conditions for a referral of the applicant under s. 198(1) are met;

(d)   on whether the local connection referral conditions are met under s. 198(5);

(e)   as to the duties owed to an applicant whose case is considered for referral or referred under the local connection provisions in s. 200(3) or (4);
(f)   on the suitability of accommodation offered under (b) or (e) above.

The applicant is only entitled to one internal review, after which alternative means of redress must be sought (s. 202(4)).

### 19.3.1.1   Right of appeal   If the applicant is

(a)   dissatisfied with the decision on the review; or
(b)   not notified of the decision on the review within the time prescribed in the regulations;

he or she has a right of appeal to the county court on a point of law (s. 204(1)).

### 19.3.1.2   Provision of accommodation pending review or appeal   The authority may continue to secure that accommodation is available for the applicant's occupation until the determination of an appeal (s. 204(4)). In *R v London Borough of Camden, ex parte Mohammed* (1997) *The Times,* 20 June, the High Court reviewed Camden's policy of providing accommodation pending a review in exceptional circumstances only. At the time of the hearing, the council had carried 51 reviews of decisions, but only four had been successful. The judge agreed that the authority's restrictive policy was justified in view of the low success rate. He stated that the relevant matters which local authorities must take into account include the merits of the case, new material or information provided by the applicant which could have a real effect upon the decision under review, and the impact on the applicant of an adverse decision.

### 19.3.2   Local Government Ombudsman

An applicant who is aggrieved about the decision on review may complain to a Local Government Ombudsman if he or she considers that unfair treatment has resulted from maladministration, e.g. the authority has delayed taking action without good reason, taken into account irrelevant considerations or ignored relevant ones, not followed their own rules or complied with the law, not fulfilled undertakings given to the applicant, given the applicant the wrong information, or not reached a decision in the correct way (Code of Guidance, para. 17.21).

### References

Campbell, R., 'Mending the Safety Net', *Roof,* November/December 1997, p. 19.
Department of the Environment, *Our Future Homes: Opportunity, Choice, Responsibility,* Cmnd. 2901, London; HMSO, 1995.

# Index

Abandonment  138
Absentee tenants
  *animus revertendi*  38–9
  *corpus possessionis*  38
  intention to return  38–9
  physical presence  38
Addison Act  103–4
Agricultural property  53
  assured agricultural occupancies  44
  repossession  77
  secure tenancy exclusion  137
Almshouses  138
*Animus revertendi*  38–9
Anti-social behaviour
  conduct  142–6
  domestic violence  146
  illegal or immoral user  144
  injunctions against  144–5
  introductory tenancies  131
  power of arrest  145–6
  repossession ground  79
Appeals
  accommodation pending review  302
  local authority decisions  302
  rent assessment committee decisions
    190
Armed forces, landlord member of  77–8
Assignment
  premium paid in connection with
    146–7
  secure tenancies  152–4
    exchange  152–3
    relationship breakdown  153–4

Assignment — *continued*
  to successor  154–5
  statutory tenancy  37
  without permission  77
Assured agricultural occupancies  44
Assured shorthold tenancy
  assured agricultural occupancies  44
  containing provision  44
  creation  43
  exceptions  43–4
  excluded by notice  43–4
  former secure tenancies  44
  long, at low rent  44
  meaning  42–3
  rents  189
    fixed-term  200
    periodic  199
  replacing non-shortholds  44
  second successions  44
  termination
    by landlord  80
    by tenant  80
  written statement of terms  44
Assured tenancy  14
  rents
    determination
      rent assessment committee
        198, 200
      statutory disregards  198–9
    periodic  197–8
    statutory  196–7
  succession
    fixed-term  211–12

Assured tenancy — *continued*
    periodic   212
Asylum seekers   265

Bed and breakfast accommodation
    290, 299
Board or attendance   47–8
Breach of contract   91
Breach of tenancy obligations,
    repossession ground   70–1
Building societies
    approved landlords   14
    Business Expansion Scheme   20
Business Expansion Scheme   19–20
Business tenancies   31–2, 56
    licensed premises   53
    secure tenancy exclusion   138
    statutory tenancy   37–8, 42

Campaign for Homeless and Rootless
    256
Catholic Housing Aid Society   256
'Cathy Come Home'   255
Charities
    as landlord   149
    right to buy exclusion   166
    *see also individual charities eg* Shelter
Child Poverty Action Group   256
Children
    homelessness   260
    housing priority   275, 276
Church of England parsonage houses
    56
    repossession   76
Civil liability
    breach of contract   91
    defences   93
    harassment and eviction   90–4
    measure of damages   93–4
Cohabitees
    joint tenancy   29
    same-sex partners   210
    succession   207–8, 210
Company lets *see* Business tenancies
Competitive tendering *see* Compulsory
    competitive tendering
Compulsory competitive tendering
    full introduction   185–6
    functions   184–5
    housing management   176, 183–6
Compulsory purchase   177, 178

Conduct   142–6
    repossession ground   79
    *see also* Anti-social behaviour
Continued residence
    absentee tenants   38–9
    company lets   37–8
    through other people   39–40
    two homes   40–1
*Corpus possessionis*   38
Council housing   48–9
    abandonment   138
    allocation
        additional preference   126–7
        cohabitees   126
        dependent children   275, 276
        discrimination   126
        emergency cases   278
        homelessness and   119–21
        Housing Act (1996)   124–9,
            263–302
        judicial review   125, 128
        mental illness or disability   277
        old age   277
        physical disability   277
        pregnancy   275
        priority needs   126, 248, 274–8
        problem families   126
        reasonable preference   119, 123,
            126–7
            giving reasons   128–9
        scheme   124–5
            points   125
            quota   126
            types of   125–6
        vulnerability   276–7
        young people   278
        *see also* Homelessness; Local
            authorities, duty to homeless
    delegation of management function
        158, 174–5
    Housing Register   119
        information on   121–2
        joint   121
        qualifying persons   122–3
        refusal of application   123–4
        removal from   123–4
        *see also* allocations
    inferior to market housing   3
    inter-war years   102–7
    investment 1919–1954   10–11
    legal framework   118–19

Council housing — *continued*
  privatisation    3, 174–87
    delegation of management function
      158, 174–5
    *see also* Large scale voluntary stock
      transfers; Management
  residualisation    164
  right to buy *see* Right to buy
  services other than housing    119
  tenure    4
  waiting list *see* Housing Register
  *see also* Secure tenancies; Social housing
Criminal liability
  enforcement    88–90
  harassment    84–8
  unlawful eviction    83–4
Cross' Act    101
Crown lettings    55, 167
Cullingworth Committee    126
Cullingworth Report (1969)    255

Damages
  aggravated    92
  defences    93
  disrepair remedy    230–1
  exemplary    92
  general    92
  harassment and eviction    92–3
  landlord's repair remedy    233
  measure    93–4
  special    92
Death of tenant    79
Defective Premises Act (1972)    228
Demolition
  order    237
  repossession    78–9, 149
Deterioration
  dwelling house    72
  furniture    73, 146
  premises or common parts    146
Development Board for Rural Wales
  134
Development land    136
Disabled persons
  accommodation required for    150
  council house allocation    277
  right to buy exclusion    166–7
Disrepair *see* Deterioration; Repairs
Domestic violence    146
  homelessness and    269–70
  repossession ground    79

Dwelling-house
  deterioration    72
  'let as separate dwelling'    30–2
  one unit    32–3
  protection requirement    30–4
  purpose of letting    31–2
  rent    30–1
  'separate' dwelling    33–4
  shared accommodation
    with landlord    33–4
    with other tenants    34

Elderly persons
  dwellings, right to buy exclusion    167
  priority housing    277
Employees
  dwelling-house required for    150
    employee of landlord    76
  right to buy exclusion    166
  secure status exclusion    135–6
Enforcement
  harassment    88–90
  local authority prosecutions    89–90
  unlawful eviction    88–90
Environmental Protection Act (1990)
  234–6
Eviction *see* Harassment; Protection from
  Eviction Act (1977); Unlawful
  eviction

*Fair deal for Housing* (White Paper)    109
Fair rents    3, 109–10, 189
  capital value/fair yield method    195–6
  defects or improvements to property
    193
  determination methods    193–6
  disregards    192–3
  market rent less scarcity factor    194
  matters taken into account    191–2
  outgoings plus profit    196
  personal circumstances    192
  registered comparables    194–5
  registration    190–1
  rent assessment committee    190
  rent officer    190
  scarcity    192–3
  state of repair    191
Family arrangements    27
Finer Report (1974)    255
Fitness for habitation    12, 217, 236–8
  condition and homelessness    272–3

Fitness for habitation — *continued*
  number of occupants   241
  private rented sector   22
Fixed-term tenancies
  rents   196, 200
  succession   211–12, 214
  termination by landlord   61, 138
'Flitting'   8
Forfeiture
  landlord's repair remedy   234
  possession and   94–5
Furnished lettings   12–13, 46–7
Furniture   73, 146

General Improvement areas   113
Glastonbury Report (1971)   255
Greve Report (1971)   255
Grounds for possession *see* Repossession
Gypsies   299

Harassment   15
  causes   84–5
  civil liability   90–4
  criminal liability   84–8
  damages   92
    measure   93–4
  defences   93
  enforcement   88–90
  legislation   82–3
  meaning   84
  multiple occupation   90
  nuisance   91–2
  offences   86–8
  persons affected   85–6
  quiet enjoyment covenant   91
  statutory tort   93
  tort   91–2
  trespass   91–2
  using violence to secure entry   90
  *see also* Protection from Eviction Act
    (1977)
Holiday lettings   47, 51–3
  Housing Act (1988) protection   97
  out of season   75–6
Home, meaning   1
Homelessness
  advisory services   274, 289–90
  allocation of council housing   119–21
    *see also* Council housing
  asylum seekers   265
  availability   273–4, 285, 300

Homelessness — *continued*
  affordability   300–1
  suitability   300–1
  British passport holders   264
  casual wards   251, 252
  causation   245–8, 283–5
    social factors   247–8
  Children Act (1989)   260
  definitions   243–5
  domestic violence   269–70
  EC nationals   264, 265–6
  eligibility   264–6
  emergency cases   278
  general housing conditions   272–3
  general principles   266–7
  help organisations   256
  history   250–9
  homeless persons   248–9
  hostels   133, 253, 270, 298–9
  Housing Act (1996)   258–9, 263–302
  Housing (Homeless Persons) Act
    (1977)   257–8, 286
  illegal immigrants   264–5
  inquiries   263–4, 290
  insecure accommodation   245
  intentional   120
    acts or omissions
      deliberate   279, 280–2
      in good faith   282–3
    causation   283–5
    chain of intentionality   283–5
    Code of Guidance   280–1
    collusion   285
    failure to secure accommodation
      285
    general principles   278–9
    infection intentionality   280
    loss of tied accommodation   282
    mortgage arrears   281–2
    omission to pursue other remedies
      282
    person acting   280
    rent arrears   281–2
  intolerable housing conditions   245
  local authorities *see* Council housing;
      Local authorities, duty to homeless
  local connection   264, 293–5
  lone parents   248
  meaning   266–7
  National Assistance Act (1948)
      252–7, 259, 286

Homelessness — *continued*
  National Health Service and
      Community Care Act (1990)
      259
  numbers of homeless people   249–50
  outdoor relief   250, 251
  overcrowding   269, 272
  physical condition of property
      268–9, 272
  Poor Law   250–2
  priority needs   274–8
    dependent children   275, 276
    mental illness or disability   277
    old age   277
    physical disability   277
    pregnancy   275
    vulnerability   276–7
  reasonableness   267–72, 285
  refugees   265
  reports   255–6
  roofless   267
  rooflessness   243, 244
  security of tenure   271–2
  temporary accommodation   250, 255,
      270–1, 287
  threatened with   274
  timely advice and assistance
      274, 289–90
  vagrants   250, 251
  violence
    domestic   269–70
    non-domestic   270
  workhouses   250–1, 253
Hostels   133, 253, 270, 298–9
  Housing Act (1988) protection   97
Households, statistics   6
Houselessness   244
Housing Act (1923)   104–5
Housing Act (1930)   105–7
Housing Act (1985)
  introductory tenancies *see* Introductory
      tenancies
  remedies
    fitness standard   236–8
    overcrowding   238–40
  secure tenancies *see* Secure tenancies
Housing Act (1988)
  agricultural holdings   53
  assured tenancies *see* Assured shorthold
      tenancy; Assured tenancy
  board or attendance   48

Housing Act (1988) — *continued*
  business tenancies   56
  Crown lettings   55
  dwelling house let with other land
      50–1
  'dwelling-house' requirement   30–4
  excluded tenancies and licences
      48–56, 95–7
  expensive housing   49
  holiday lettings   51–3
  landlord's repair obligations   225–6
  licensed premises   53
  mortgagor grants, without permission
      56
  no/low rent tenancy   50
  overcrowded dwellings   56
  parsonage houses   56
  public bodies   55
  rent requirement   30–1
  repossession
    adjournment   64
    breach of tenancy obligation   70–1
    by mortgagee   75
    conduct   79
    contracting out   60
    death of tenant   79
    demolition   78–9
    deterioration of furniture   73
    deterioration and tenant neglect   72
    domestic violence   79
    fixed-term tenancies   61
    grant induced by false statement   80
    grounds   69–80
    immoral or illegal use   71–2
    ministers of religion   76
    non-payment of rent   70
    notice of proceedings   62–3
    nuisance   71
    occupation wanted
      employee of landlord   76
      landlord or his family   74–5
    out of season holiday lets   75–6
    periodic tenancies   62
    postponement   64
    principles   60
    reasonableness   64
    reconstruction   78–9
    statutory periodic tenancies   61–2
    student accommodation   76
    suitable alternative accommodation
        65–8

Housing Act (1988) — *continued*
    suspension   64–5
    termination
        by landlord   61–3
        by tenant   60
    requirements   25
    resident landlords   53–5
    shared ownership   48
    student letting   51
    succession
        fixed-term   211–12
        periodic   212
    tenancy   25–30
    trespassers   96–7
Housing Act (1996)
    council housing allocations   124–9
    homelessness   258–9
    *see also* Homelessness; Local
        authorities, duty to homeless
Housing action areas   113
Housing action trusts   110, 175, 180
    accommodation required by   150
    composition   181
    disposals by   182–3
    functions   181–2
    landlord condition   134
Housing Association Grant (HAG)
    113
Housing associations   48, 174–5
    accommodation required by   150
    accountability   114–15
    approved landlords   14
    funding   113–14
    landlord condition   134
    letting by   55
    meaning   112–13
    nature   114
    registered social landlords   115–16
    registration   112
    rents   200
        housing benefit and   201–2
    right to buy exclusion   166
    tenants' guarantee   114
    tenure   4
Housing benefit   21
    local reference rent   202
    rents and   201–2
        maximum rent   202
Housing co-operatives
    landlord condition   134
    letting by   55

Housing Corporation   112, 113, 115
    large scale voluntary stock
        transfers   176
    secure tenancies   134–5
Housing (Financial Provisions) Act
    (1924)   104–5
Housing (Homeless Persons) Act
    (1977)   257–8, 286
Housing Investment Programmes   111
Housing Investment Trusts   15–16
Housing management *see* Management
Housing and Planning Act (1919), social
    housing   103–4
Housing policy
    determinants   2–11
    functions   1–2
    market-place   2–3
    social democratic model   3–4
    state intervention   3
    translating into action   2
*Housing Programme 1965–1970* (White
    Paper)   109
Housing Register   119, 121–4
    information on   121–2
    joint   121
    qualifying persons   122–3
    refusal of application   123–4
    removal from   123–4
Housing Rents and Repairs Act
    (1954)   11
Housing Revenue Account   106–7, 179,
    203
Housing for Wales   112

Illegal immigrants   264–5
Illegal or immoral user   71–2, 144
Improvements   155–6, 218–19
    *see also* Repairs
Increase of Rent and Mortgage Interest
    (War Restrictions) Act (1915)   9–10
Insurance companies   20
Intentionally homeless *see* Homelessness,
    intentional
Introductory tenancies   130–2
    ceasing to be   131
    right to repair scheme   233
    secure status exclusion   135
    succession   214–15

Joint Charities Group   256
Joint tenancy   28–9

Key money *see* Premiums
Keys, retention by owner   29

Landlord condition   134–5
Landlord and Tenant Act (1985)   223–4
Landlords
  accommodation for employee   76
  accommodation required for   73–5
  approved   14
  charity   149
  member of armed forces   77–8
  private rented sector   18–20
  property companies   19
  repair obligations *see* Repairs
  resident   12–13, 34–5, 47, 53–5
  termination of tenancy by
    Housing Act (1988)   61–3
    Rent Act (1977)   61
  *see also* Management
Large scale voluntary stock
    transfers   110, 111, 115, 176–80
  compulsory purchase   177, 178
  consultation   177–9
  housing corporations   176
  restrictions   179–80
  tenants' guarantee   176
Lawful visitors   227–8
Licences   28
  secure tenancies and   132–3
  temporary accommodation   133
Licensed premises   53
  secure tenancy exclusion   137
Licensees   27, 28
Local authorities
  challenging decisions   301–2
  delegation of housing management
    function   158, 174–5
  as developers   5
  disposals by housing action trust
    to   182–3
  duty to homeless
    accommodation from another
      landlord   298
    accommodation pending review
      302
    advisory services   274, 289–90
    appeal rights   302
    applicants, duties to   290–2
    availability   300
    bed and breakfasts   290, 299
    caravans   299

Local authorities — *continued*
  cessation of duty   295–6
  full duty   287
  gypsies   299
  hostels   298–9
  Housing Act (1996) duties
    289–301
  immediate crisis help   288, 289
  inquiries   263–4, 290
  interim duty   290
  internal review   301–2
  local connect   264, 293–5
  lodgings   298
  mobile homes   299
  Ombudsman   302
  permanent accommodation
    287, 288–9
  power to continue provision
    296–7
  private renting   298
  provision from own stock
    297–8
  refusal of offer   295, 296
  registered social landlords   298
  settled accommodation   288
  source of accommodation   297–9
  suitability   300–1
  suitable alternative accommodation
    292–3
  temporary accommodation   287
  women's refuges   299
  execution of repairs by   236, 241
  internal review   301–2
  landlord condition   134
  prosecutions for unlawful eviction
    89–90
  remedy of defects by   236, 241
  rents *see* Rents, public sector
  *see also* Council housing
Local Authority Agreement   293
Local Authority Association Joint Local
    Connection Agreement   293–4
Local connection   264, 293–5
  meaning   294–5
  no local connection   295
  restrictions on referral   295
Local Government Ombudsman
    124, 302
Local housing 'companies'   115
Lodgings   26–7, 47–8
Long leases   44, 135

Management   157–8
  best value   186
  compulsory competitive tendering
    176, 183–6
    full introduction   185–6
    functions   184–5
  consultation   177–9
  delegation of functions   158, 174–5
  housing action trusts   175, 176, 180–3
  'inertia vote'   175
  inertia voting   179
  multiple occupation   241
  'pick a landlord'   175
  registered housing associations   175
  secure tenants and   157–8
  tenant management organisations
    158
  Tenants' Choice   175, 179, 180
  voluntary stock transfers see Large scale
    voluntary stock transfers
Market model   2–3
Market rents   189–90
Mental disability see Disabled persons
Ministers of religion, housing   56, 76
Mobile homes   299
Morris Committee Report (1975)   255
Mortgage arrears   281–2
Mortgage interest relief   5
Mortgagee repossessions   75
Mortgagors, tenancies granted by   56
Multiple occupation
  execution of works by local authority
    241
  fit for number of occupants   241
  general works notices   240–1
  management   241
  meaning   240
  overcrowding   238–40, 241–2
  registration   240

National Assistance Act (1948)   252–7,
  259, 289
National Assistance Board   252
National Health Service and Community
  Care Act (1990)   259
Night shelters   270
Non-payment of rent
  Housing Act (1988) repossession
    70
  Rent Act (1977) repossession   69
Notice of seeking possession   139

Notice to quit
  by tenant   76–7
  Protection from Eviction Act
    (1977)   97–8
Nuisance
  harassment and eviction   91–2
  repossession ground   71

Old age
  housing priority   277
  right to buy exclusions   167
'Only or principal home'   41–2
Over-occupation   150–1
Overcrowding   56, 241–2
  causing or permitting   239–40
  homelessness and   269, 272
  Housing Act (1985)   238–40
  permitted numbers   239
  room standard   239
Owner-occupation   4, 5
  encouragement   14–15
  expansion   5–6

Parsonage houses   56, 76
Pension fund landlords   14
Periodic tenancies
  repossession   61–2
  termination by landlord   62, 139
Physically disabled persons
  accommodation required for   150
  council house allocation   277
  right to buy exclusion   166–7
'Pick a landlord'   175
Poor Law   250–2
Poplar Housing and Regeneration
    Community Association   115
Possession, see also Repossession
Prefabricated dwellings   107
Pregnancy, housing priority   275
Premiums   50
  assignment and   146–7
  Rent Act (1977)   13
Private rented sector   4
  approved landlords   14
  before 1915   8–9
  controlled tenancies   12
  decline   16–18
  furnished lettings   12–13
  Housing Investment Trusts   15–16
  Housing Rents and Repairs Act (1954)
    11

Private rented sector — *continued*
  Increase of Rent and Mortgage Interest
    (War Restrictions) Act (1915)
    9–10
  landlords  18–20
  premiums  13
  regulated tenancies  11–12
  Rent Act (1957)  11
  Rent Act (1965)  11–12
  Rent Act (1977)  13–14
  rent control *see* Rent control
  resident landlords  12–13
  revival attempts (present)  14–16
  standards  22
  tenants  20–1
  type of housing  21–2
Privatisation of council housing *see*
    Management
Protected shorthold tenancies  14
  repossession  77
Protected tenancy  25
  change of use  31–2
  purpose of letting  31–2
Protection from Eviction Act (1977)
  eviction without due process of law
    95–7
  excluded tenancies and licences
    95–7
  forfeiture  94–5
  notice to quit  97–8
  *see also* Unlawful eviction
Public bodies, letting by  55
Public housing *see* Council housing; Local
    authorities, duty to homeless; Social
    housing

Quality Street  22
Quiet enjoyment  91

Rachmanism  11, 15, 17, 81–2
Reasonable preference  119, 123,
    126–7
  giving reasons  128–9
Reconstructions  78–9
Refugees  265
Registered social landlords  298
  disposals by housing action trust to
    182–3
  domestic violence repossessions  79
  registration  115
  right to acquire  115–16

Regulated tenancies  11–12, 25
  *see also* Protected tenancy; Rent Act
    (1977); Statutory tenancy
Relationship breakdown  153–4
Rent Act (1957)  11
Rent Act (1965)  11–12
Rent Act (1977)
  agricultural holdings  53
  board  47–8
  business tenancies  56
  Crown lettings  55
  dwelling house let with other
    land  50–1
  'dwelling-house' requirement  30–4
  exclusions  46–8, 49–56
  expensive housing  49
  fair rents *see* Fair rents
  holiday lets  47, 51–3
  licensed premises  53
  low rent  50
  mortgagor grants, without permission
    56
  no/low rent  50
  overcrowded dwellings  56
  parsonage houses  56
  private rented sector  13–14
  public bodies  55
  rent control  30–1
  rent requirement  30–1
  repossession
    adjournment  64
    agricultural property  77
    assignment without permission  77
    breach of tenancy obligation  70–1
    by mortgagee  75
    contracting out  59
    deterioration
      furniture  73
      tenant neglect  72
    grounds  68, 69–80
    immoral or illegal use  71–2
    landlord member of armed forces
      77–8
    ministers of religion  76
    non-payment of rent  69
    notice to quit by tenant  76–7
    nuisance  71
    occupation required
      employee of landlord  76
      landlord or his family  73–4
    order for possession  58

Rent Act (1977) — *continued*
  out of season holiday lets   75–6
  postponement   64
  principles   59–60
  protected shorthold tenancies   77
  reasonableness   64
  student accommodation   76
  subletting
    at excessive rent   77
    without permission   77
  suitable alternative accommodation
      58, 65–8
  suspension   64–5
  termination
    by landlord   61
    by tenant   59–60
  requirements   24–5
  resident landlords   47, 53–5
  statutory tenancy *see* Statutory tenancy
  student lettings   47, 51
  succession *see* Succession
  tenancy   25–30
Rent arrears   281–2
  possession ground   140, 141–2
  usual reasons   141–2
Rent Assessment Committees   12
  appeals against decisions   190
  assured tenancies   198, 200
Rent control
  decline in private rental sector   17–18
  fair *see* Fair rents
  first world war and   9–1
  Increase of Rent and Mortgage Interest
      (War Restrictions) Act (1915)
      9–1
  means-tested allowances   12
  pendulum 1991–1954   10–11
  phasing out of controlled tenancies   12
  Rent Act (1957)   11
  Rent Act (1977)   30–1
Rent officers   12
Rent a room relief   53
Rent to mortgage terms   169–70
Rent-free occupation   97
Renting
  social trends   5–7
  *see also* Council housing; Housing
      associations; Private rented sector
Rents
  fair *see* Fair rents
  non-payment   69–70

Rents — *continued*
  premiums   50
  'realistic'   108
  rebates for poorer tenants   107, 110
Rents, housing associations   200, 201–2
Rents, private sector   188–200
  assured shorthold tenancies   189
    fixed-term   200
    periodic   199
  assured tenancies
    fixed-term   196
    periodic   197–8
    statutory   196–7
    rent assessment committee
      198, 200
    statutory disregards   198–9
  compulsory national control
      (1915–1965)   188
  fair *see* Fair rents
  Housing Act (1988) *see* assured
      tenancies
  housing benefit and   201–2
  individual regulation (Rent Act
      1965)   188
  legislative background   188–90
  market   189–90
  Rent Act (1977) *see* Fair rents
Rents, public sector   202–3
  housing benefit and   201–2
Repairs
  *caveat emptor*   217
  costs   219
  express obligations   218
  fit for habitation   236–8
  general works notice   240–1
  inherent defects   219–20
  landlord's obligations
    common or essential parts   221–2
    common law   220–2
    correlative obligations   222
    in course of construction   222
    damage consequential to decorations
      224
    Defective Premises Act (1972)   228
    exterior   225
    furnished accommodations   220–1
    Housing Act 91988)   225–6
    installations   225
    'keep in repair'   224–5
    Landlord and Tenant Act (1985)
      223–4

Repairs — *continued*
 lawful visitors 227–8
 low rent premises 222–3
 negligence 227
 nuisance 226
 Occupiers Liability Act (1957)
 227–8
 standard of repair 226
 statutory 223–6
 structure 225
landlord's remedies
 damages 233
 forfeiture 234
 self-help 234
multiple occupation
 execution of works by local authority
 241
 fit for number of occupants 241
 general works notices 240–1
physical condition of property
 268–9
public law remedies
 abatement notice 235–6
 action by tenants and other occupiers
 236
 enforcement 235–6
 Environmental Protection Act
 (1990) 234–6
 remedy of defects by local authority
 236
 statutory nuisances 235
public remedies
 closing order 237
 demolition order 237
 fitness standard 236–8
 Housing Act (1985) 236–8
 repair notice 237, 238
responsibility for 217–29
standard 220, 226
tenant's obligations
 tenant-like user 228–9
 waste 229
tenant's remedies
 damages 230–1
 receiver appointment 231–2
 repudiatory breach 232–3
 right to repair scheme 233
 self-help 231
 set-off against rent 231
 specific performance 231
Repossessed property 20

Repossession
 accommodation required
 employee 150
 employee of landlord 76
 housing association or trust 150
 landlord or his family 73–5
 person with special needs 150
 physical disabled person 150
 adjournment 64
 agricultural property 77
 anti-social behaviour 142–6
 assignment without permission 77
 breach of tenancy obligation
 70–1, 140, 142
 conduct 79
 contracting out 59, 60
 court considers reasonable 140–8
 death of tenant 79
 demolition 78–9, 149
 deterioration 146
 furniture 73, 146
 tenant neglect 72
 domestic violence 79, 146
 employment use 147
 fixed-term tenancies 61
 grant induced by false statement 80
 grounds 68, 69–80, 140–51
 Housing Act (1988)
 adjournment 64
 breach of tenancy obligation 70–1
 by mortgagee 75
 conduct 79
 contracting out 60
 death of tenant 79
 demolition 78–9
 deterioration
 furniture 73
 tenant neglect 72
 domestic violence 79
 fixed-term tenancies 61
 grant induced by false statement 80
 grounds 69–80
 immoral or illegal use 71–2
 ministers of religion 76
 non-payment of rent 70
 notice of proceedings 62–3
 nuisance 71
 occupation required
 employee of landlord 76
 landlord or his family 74–5
 out of season holiday lets 75–6

Repossession — *continued*
  periodic tenancies   62
  postponement   64
  principles   60
  reasonableness   64
  reconstruction   78–9
  statutory periodic tenancies   61–2
  student accommodation   76
  suitable alternative accommodation
      65–8
  suspension   64–5
  termination
      by landlord   61–3
      by tenant   60
  immoral or illegal use   71–2
  landlord is a charity   149
  landlord member of armed forces
      77–8
  ministers of religion   76
  mortgagee   75
  non-payment of rent   69, 70
  notice of proceedings   62–3
  notice of seeking   139
  notice to quit by tenant   76–7
  nuisance   71, 142–6
  order for possession   58
  out of season holiday lets   75–6
  over-occupation   150–1
  overcrowding   149
  periodic tenancies   62
  postponement   64
  principles   59–60
  protected shorthold tenancies   77
  reasonableness   64
  reconstruction   78–9, 149
  redevelopment   149
  Rent Act (1977)
      adjournment   64
      agricultural property   77
      assignment without permission   77
      breach of tenancy obligation   70–1
      by mortgagee   75
      contracting out   59
      deterioration
          furniture   73
          tenant neglect   72
      grounds   68, 69–80
      immoral or illegal use   71–2
      landlord member of armed forces
          77–8
      ministers of religion   76

Repossession — *continued*
  non-payment of rent   69
  notice to quit by tenant   76–7
  nuisance   71
  occupation required
      employee of landlord   76
      landlord or his family   73–4
  order for possession   58
  out of season holiday lets   75–6
  postponement   64
  principles   59–60
  protected shorthold tenancies   77
  reasonableness   64
  student accommodation   76
  subletting
      at excessive rent   77
      without permission   77
  suitable alternative accommodation
      58, 65–8
  suspension   64–5
  termination
      by landlord   61
      by tenant   59–60
  rent arrears   140, 141–2
secure tenancies
  anti-social behaviour   142–6
  breach of tenancy obligation
      140, 142
  demolition   149
  deterioration   146
      furniture   146
  domestic violence   146
  employee   150
  employment use   147
  grounds   140–51
  housing association or trust   150
  if court considers reasonable   140–8
  if suitable alternative
      accommodation   148–51
  landlord is a charity   149
  notice of seeking   139
  nuisance   142–6
  over-occupation   150–1
  overcrowding   149
  person with special needs   150
  physical disabled person   150
  reconstruction   149
  redevelopment   149
  rent arrears   140, 141–2
  suitable alternative accommodation
      available   148–9

Repossession — *continued*
   reasonableness 149–51
   temporary accommodation 147–8
   tenant's false statements 146
  statutory periodic tenancies 61–2
  student accommodation 76
  subletting
   at excessive rent 77
   without permission 77
  suitable alternative accommodation
   58, 65–8, 148–51
  suspension 64–5
  temporary accommodation 147–8
  tenant's false statements 146
  termination
   by landlord 61–3
   by tenant 59–60
Resident landlord 12–13, 47, 53–5
  fit for habitation 217
  improvement 218–19
  meaning 218–20
  renewal 218–19
  rules 34–5
'Residing with' 205, 206, 215–16
Retention of keys 29
Right to buy 110, 120
  discount 162, 168–9
   repayment 169
  enforcement 171–2
  excluded properties 166–7
  expansion of home-ownership 163–4
  general consent 159, 160–1
  procedure 170–1
  purchase price 167–8
  qualifying period 158, 164–6
  qualifying tenant 164–6
  registered social landlords 115–16
  rent to mortgage terms 169–70
  residualisation 164
  sales before 1980 159–62
  secure tenancies 158–72
  statistics 161, 162, 163–4
  subject matter of 164
Rooflessness 243, 244, 267

Same-sex partners, succession 210, 213
Secure tenancies
  assignment 152–4
   exchange 152–3
   relationship breakdown 153–4
   to successor 154–5

Secure tenancies — *continued*
  consultation 157–8
  exchange 152–3
  exclusions
   agricultural holdings 137
   almshouses 138
   business tenancies 138
   development land 136
   employment occupancies 135–6
   homeless accommodation 136
   introductory tenancies 135
   licensed premises 137
   long leases 135
   short-term arrangements 137
   student lets 137–8
   temporary accommodation
    during improvements etc. 137
    for moving jobs 136–7
  grounds for possession
   anti-social behaviour 142–6
   breach of tenancy obligation
    140, 142
   court considers reasonable 140–8
   demolition 149
   deterioration 146
    furniture 146
   domestic violence 146
   employee 150
   employment use 147
   housing association or trust 150
   landlord is a charity 149
   nuisance 142–6
   over-occupation 150–1
   overcrowding 149
   person with special needs 150
   physical disabled person 150
   reconstruction 149
   redevelopment 149
   rent arrears 140, 141–2
   suitable alternative accommodation
    148–51
    available 148–9
    reasonableness 149–51
   temporary accommodation 147–8
   tenant's false statements 146
  housing management *see* Management
  improvements
   added value 156
   conditions 156
   written consent 155
  information requirement 157

Secure tenancies — *continued*
  right to buy *see* Right to buy
  right to repair scheme   233
  shared accommodation   133–4
  sub-letting   155
  succession
    fixed-term   214
    general principles   212–13
    periodic   214
    residence with tenant   215
    same-sex partners   213
    successor conditions   213
  tenancy agreement   157
  termination by landlord   138–51
    fixed tenancies   138
    grounds *see* grounds for possession
    notice of seeking possession
      139
    periodic tenancies   139
    possession grounds   140–51
    procedural requirements   138–9
    requirements   140
  termination by tenant   138
    abandonment   138
  variation   156
Security of tenure
  decline in private rental sector and
    17–18
  lack, homelessness and   271–2
  rent control and   11
  *see also* Termination of tenancy
Seebohm Committee   255–6
Seebohm Report (1968)   255
Service occupiers   27
SHAC   256
Shared accommodation   27–30
  Housing Act (1988) protection   96
  with landlord   34–5
  landlord condition   134–5
  with other tenants   34
  secure tenancies and   133–4
  tenant condition   134, 135
Shelter   245, 256
Shorthold tenancies, assured *see* Assured
    shorthold tenancies
Slum clearance   17, 101, 107, 108, 255
Social democratic model   3–4
Social housing
  anti-social behaviour *see* Anti-social
    behaviour
  conduct of tenant   142

Social housing — *continued*
  *Fair deal for Housing* (White Paper)
    109
  grant   113–14
  history
    1964–1979   109–10
    1979 to date   110–12
    Housing Act (1923)   104–5
    Housing Act (1930)   105–7
    Housing (Financial Provisions) Act
      (1924)   104–5
    Housing and Planning Act (1919)
      103–4
    inter-war years   102–7
    post-war to 1964   107–9
    pre-first world war   100–2
  housing action trusts *see* Housing action
    trusts
  housing associations *see* Housing
    associations
  *Housing Programme 1965–1970* (White
    Paper)   109
  Housing Revenue Account   106–7,
    179, 203
  prefabricated dwellings   107
  realistic rents   108
  rebates   107, 110
  right to buy   110
  slum clearance   101, 107, 108
  tenants' choice provisions   110
  voluntary stock transfers   110, 111
  *see also* Council housing; Secure
    tenancies
Spouses
  occupation by   41
  succession   207–8
State benefits   21
State intervention   3
  *see also* Council housing; Homelessness
Statutory tenancy   25, 35–41
  assignment   37
  company lets   37–8, 42
  continued residence
    absentee tenants   38–9
    company lets   37–8
    through other people   39–40
    two homes   40–1
  nature of   36–7
  occupation
    by spouse   41
    'only or principal home'   41–2

Statutory tenancy — *continued*
  *see also* continued residence
  requirements   36
  termination
    court order   36
    disclaimer by trustee in bankruptcy
      35
    notice to quit   35
    surrender   35
  value of   37
Student lettings   47, 51
  repossession   76
  secure tenancy exclusion   137–8
Subletting
  at excessive rent   77
  secure tenancies   155
  without permission   77
Succession
  assignment to successor   154–5
  assured tenancies
    fixed-term   211–12
    periodic   212
  claimant with home elsewhere   216
  introductory tenancies   214–15
    residence with tenant   215
  Rent Act (1977)   13, 205–11
    death of first successor
      on or after 15 January   211
      before 15 January 1989   210–11
    death of original tenant
      on or after 15 January 1989
        208–10
      before 15 January 1989   206–8
    family residing with him   205
    member of family   208–10
    residence requirement   206
    same-sex partners   210
    spouses and cohabitees   207–8
  residence with tenant   215–16
  same-sex partners   210, 213
  secure tenancies
    fixed-term   214
    general principles   212–13
    periodic   214
    residence with tenant   215
    same-sex partners   213
    successor conditions   213
Suitable alternative accommodation
  'alternative'   66
  character   67–8
  environmental factors   67–8, 149

Suitable alternative accommodation
  — *continued*
  extent   67–8
  Housing Act (1988) repossession
    65–8
  local authority and   292–3
  meaning   148
  place of work   67
  removal expenses   68
  Rent Act (1977) repossession
    58, 65–8
  secure tenancy possession   148–51
  security of tenure   66
Surrender of tenancy   59

Temporary accommodation
  133, 136–7
  bed and breakfasts   290, 299
  homelessness and   250, 255, 270–1,
    287
  secure tenancy possession   147–8
Tenancy   25–30
  cohabitees   29
  definition   132
  exclusive possession   26, 27
  joint   28–9
  licences   132–3
  non-exclusive possession   27–30
  period of time certain   26
  regulated   11–12
  requirements   26–7
  retention of keys   29
  separate agreements   28
  *see also individual types e.g.* Assured
    tenancy; Introductory tenancies
Tenant
  absentee
    *animus revertendi*   38–9
    *corpus possessionis*   38
    intention to return   38–9
    physical presence   38
    statutory tenancy   38–9
  condition   134, 135
  conduct *see* Anti-social behaviour
  death   79
  management organisations   158
  notice to quit   76–7
  private rented sector   20–1
  repair obligations *see* Repairs
Tenants' Choice   175, 179, 180
Tenants' guarantee   176

Tenure
  council renting  4
  housing association renting  4
  owner-occupation  4, 5
  private renting  4
  social trends  5–7
  statistics  4
Termination of tenancy
  by landlord
    assured shorthold  80
    fixed-term tenancies  61, 138
    Housing Act (1988)  61–3
    notice of proceedings  62–3
    periodic tenancies  62, 139
    Rent Act (1977)  61
    secure tenancies see Secure tenancies
    statutory periodic tenancies  61–2
  by tenant
    assured shorthold  80
    Housing Act (1988)  60
    Rent Act (1977)  59–60, 76–7
    secure tenancies  138
  surrender  59
Tied accommodation  282
Torrens' Act  101
Tort
  harassment and eviction  91–2
  statutory  93
Trespassers
  harassment and eviction  91–2
  Housing Act (1988) protection  96–7
Trustee in bankruptcy  35
Two houses  40–1

Unfit for human habitation see Fitness for
  habitation

Unlawful eviction  15
  civil liability  90–4
    damages  92–3
    defences  93
    measure of damages  93–4
  criminal liability  83–4
  enforcement  88–90
  legislative history  81–3
  nuisance  91–2
  quiet enjoyment covenant  91
  Rachmanism  11, 15, 17, 81–2
  statutory tort  93
  tort  91–2
  trespass  91–2
  using violence to secure entry  90
  see also Protection from Eviction Act
    (1977)
Urban development corporations
    180
  landlord condition  134

Vagrants  250, 251
Violence
  domestic  79, 146, 269–70
  non-domestic  270
  to secure entry  90
Visitors, lawful  227–8
Voluntary stock transfer, large scale see
    Large scale voluntary stock transfers

Waiting lists see Housing Register
Waste doctrine  229
Women's refuges  270, 299
Workhouses  250–1, 253

'Yield gap'  19